RETHINKING OUR CLASSROOMS, VOLUME 1

SUSAN LINA RUGGLES

RETHINKING OUR CLASSROOMS, VOLUME 1
Teaching for Equity and Justice

New Edition

A RETHINKING SCHOOLS PUBLICATION

Editors of *Rethinking Our Classrooms, Volume 1,* New Edition:
Wayne Au, Bill Bigelow, Stan Karp

Editors of *Rethinking Our Classrooms, Volume 1,* First Edition:
Bill Bigelow, Linda Christensen, Stan Karp, Barbara Miner, Bob Peterson

Business Manager: Mike Trokan
Design: Joanna Dupuis
Production Editor: Jacqueline Lalley

The editors of *Rethinking Our Classrooms, Volume 1,* New Edition, would like to give special thanks to Rethinking Schools editors Terry Burant, Kelley Dawson Salas, David Levine, Larry Miller, Kathy Williams, Rita Tenorio, and Stephanie Walters and former Rethinking Schools editors Catherine Capellaro, Beverly Cross, Cynthia Ellwood, Brenda Harvey, and Robert Lowe. The editors would also like to thank Janet Mays, Susan Bates, Becky Leichtling and Jennifer Morales for editorial, administrative, and production assistance.

Rethinking Our Classrooms, Volume 1, New Edition, is published by Rethinking Schools, Ltd., a nonprofit publisher advocating the reform of public schools. We stress a commitment to social justice, with a particular focus on issues of race and urban schools. We seek to promote a grassroots, activist perspective that combines theory and practice and links classroom issues to broader social concerns. Rethinking Schools, Ltd., consists of our flagship publication, *Rethinking Schools,* a quarterly magazine that provides classroom articles and policy analyses; Rethinking Schools Press, a publisher of classroom material and policy books; and Rethinking Schools Online at www.rethinkingschools.org.

Subscription rates for *Rethinking Schools* magazine are $17.95 a year or $29.95 for two years. Bulk order subscriptions available upon request. Ordering information for *Rethinking Our Classrooms,* New Edition, is included at the end of this book.

For more information:
Rethinking Schools
1001 E. Keefe Ave., Milwaukee, WI 53212
414-964-9646, fax 414-964-7220
Email editorial: bbpdx@aol.com
Email business: RSBusiness@aol.com

To order:
Call toll-free: 800-669-4192
Order online: www.rethinkingschools.org

To contact the editors:
Bill Bigelow: bbpdx@aol.com
Stan Karp: stan.karp@gmail.com
Wayne Au: wayne.au@sbcglobal.net

The cover graphic is "Aim High," a portrait of Anthony Fishoe Lacy. It was painted by FISHOE, an artist in Montgomery, Alabama.

Library of Congress Cataloging-in-Publication Data
Rethinking our classrooms : teaching for equity and justice / editors Wayne Au ... [et al.]. -- 2nd ed.
     p. cm.
Includes index.
ISBN 978-0-942961-33-1 (v. 1)
1. Critical pedagogy--United States. 2. Multicultural education--United States. 3. Social justice--Study and teaching--United States. I. Au, Wayne, 1972-
    LC196.5.U6R48 2007
    370.11'5--dc22
        2006101223

Preface

Publishing the first edition of *Rethinking Our Classrooms* in 1994 was a landmark accomplishment for Rethinking Schools. Until then, the organization had published only a quarterly journal and occasional pamphlets. This first book marked the beginning of Rethinking Schools' growth from a Milwaukee-based quarterly to a publisher that provides social justice resources for teachers and prospective teachers around the country. It set the tone, style, and standard for many more books to come, including a second volume of *Rethinking Our Classrooms* in 2001.

Thirteen years and 160,000 copies later, profound changes in the social, political, and educational landscape have intensified the need to work for social justice in public education. No Child Left Behind (NCLB) has fueled the trend toward increased testing and standardization. We suffer from top-down and outside-in education reform that does not respect teachers, students, or their communities. More and more, elementary teachers must teach scripted reading curricula, and teachers in all grade levels are increasingly pressured to teach to tests. The marginalizing of multicultural, anti-racist education is making it more difficult for the histories and voices of our children's communities to enter the classroom. Beyond our schools, war and militarism, environmental degradation, and heightened class and racial inequality threaten all of us, but especially children.

This new edition of *Rethinking Our Classrooms, Volume 1,* has been expanded to speak to these challenges. We've added essays on science and environmental education, immigration and language, military recruitment, teaching about the world through mathematics, and gay and lesbian issues. Updated essays on NCLB, standards, and testing address the intensified assaults on public education.

This revised edition, enriched by new writers addressing new topics, continues to uphold the values and aspirations of Rethinking Schools. We still see the classroom as a primary site for school reform, celebrate the work and perspectives of teachers, and maintain that anti-racist, social justice education must be at the fore of any analysis of public schooling and at the center of classroom practice.

Over the past 13 years, we have heard from K–12 teachers, university educators, and others across the country that *Rethinking Our Classrooms* has helped them in their efforts to ensure a quality education for every child. We hope this new edition proves even more useful than its predecessor.

—the editors

Contents

Rethinking Our Classrooms: Teaching for Equity and Justice

Volume 1, New Edition

Part Four: Rethinking Our Assumptions

Part Five: Beyond the Classroom

Part Six: Resources

Introduction: Creating Classrooms for Equity and Social Justice

Rethinking Our Classrooms begins from the premise that schools and classrooms should be laboratories for a more just society than the one we now live in. Unfortunately, too many schools are training grounds for boredom, alienation, and pessimism. Too many schools fail to confront the racial, class, and gender inequities woven into our social fabric. Teachers are often simultaneously perpetrators and victims, with little control over planning time, class size, or broader school policies—and much less over the unemployment, hopelessness, and other "savage inequalities" that help shape our children's lives.

But *Rethinking Our Classrooms* is not about what we cannot do; it's about what we can do. Brazilian educator Paulo Freire writes that teachers should attempt to "live part of their dreams within their educational space." Classrooms can be places of hope, where students and teachers gain glimpses of the kind of society we could live in and where students learn the academic and critical skills needed to make it a reality. We intend the articles in *Rethinking Our Classrooms* to be both visionary and practical; visionary because we need to be inspired by each other's vision of schooling; practical because for too long teachers have been preached at by theoreticians, well removed from classrooms, who are long on jargon and short on specific examples.

We've drawn the articles, stories, poems, and lessons in *Rethinking Our Classrooms* from different academic disciplines and grade levels. Despite variations in emphasis, a common social and pedagogical vision unites this collection. This vision is characterized by several interlocking components that together comprise what we call a social justice classroom. In *Rethinking Our Classrooms* we argue that curriculum and classroom practice must be:

- **Grounded in the lives of our students.** All good teaching begins with a respect for children, their innate curiosity and their capacity to learn. Curriculum should be rooted in children's needs and experiences. Whether we're teaching science, mathematics, English, or social studies, ultimately the class has to be about our students' lives as well as about a particular subject. Students should probe the ways their lives connect to the broader society, and are often limited by that society.

- **Critical.** The curriculum should equip students to "talk back" to the world. Students must learn to pose essential critical questions: Who makes decisions and who is left out? Who benefits and who suffers? Why is a given practice fair or unfair? What are its origins? What alternatives can we imagine? What is required to create change? Through critiques of advertising, cartoons, literature, legislative decisions, military interventions, job structures, newspapers, movies, agricultural practices, or school life, students should have opportunities to question social reality. Finally, student work must move outside the classroom walls, so that scholastic learning is linked to real world problems.

- **Multicultural, anti-racist, pro-justice.** In our earlier publication *Rethinking Columbus,* we used the Discovery myth to demonstrate how children's literature and textbooks tend to value the lives of Great White Men over all others. Traditional materials invite children into Columbus's thoughts and dreams; he gets to speak, claim land, and rename the ancient homelands of Native Americans, who appear to have no rights. Implicit in many traditional accounts of history is the notion that children should disregard the lives of women, working people, and especially people of color—they're led to view history and current events from the standpoint of the dominant groups. By contrast, a social justice curriculum must strive to include the lives of all those in our society, especially the marginalized and dominated. As anti-racist educator Enid Lee points out (see interview, p. 15), a rigorous multiculturalism should engage children in a critique of the roots of inequality in curriculum, school structure, and the larger society—always asking: How are we involved? What can we do?

- **Participatory, experiential.** Traditional classrooms often leave little room for student involvement and initiative. In a "rethought" classroom, concepts need to be experienced firsthand, not just read about or heard about. Whether through projects, role plays, simulations, mock trials, or experiments, students need to be mentally, and often physically, active. Our classrooms also must provoke students to develop their democratic capacities: to question, to challenge, to make real decisions, to collectively solve problems.

- **Hopeful, joyful, kind, visionary.** The ways we organize classroom life should seek to make children feel significant and cared about—by the teacher and by each other. Unless students feel emotionally and physically safe, they won't share real thoughts and feelings. Discussions will be tinny and dishonest. We need to design activities where students learn to trust and care for each other. Classroom life should, to the greatest extent possible, prefigure the kind of democratic and just society we envision and thus contribute to building that society. Together students and teachers can create a "community of conscience," as educators Asa Hilliard and Gerald Pine call it.

■ **Activist.** We want students to come to see themselves as truth-tellers and change-makers. If we ask children to critique the world but then fail to encourage them to act, our classrooms can degenerate into factories for cynicism. While it's not a teacher's role to direct students to particular organizations, it is a teacher's role to suggest that ideas should be acted upon and to offer students opportunities to do just that. Children can also draw inspiration from historical and contemporary efforts of people who struggled for justice. A critical curriculum should be a rainbow of resistance, reflecting the diversity of people from all cultures who acted to make a difference, many of whom did so at great sacrifice. Students should be allowed to learn about and feel connected to this legacy of defiance.

■ **Academically rigorous.** A social justice classroom equips children not only to change the world but also to maneuver in the one that exists. Far from devaluing the vital academic skills young people need, a critical and activist curriculum speaks directly to the deeply rooted alienation that currently discourages millions of students from acquiring those skills.

A social justice classroom offers more to students than do traditional classrooms and expects more from students. Critical teaching aims to inspire levels of academic performance far greater than those motivated or measured by grades and test scores. When

children write for real audiences, read books and articles about issues that really matter, and discuss big ideas with compassion and intensity, "academics" starts to breathe. Yes, we must help students "pass the tests," (even as we help them analyze and critique the harmful impact of test-driven education). But only by systematically reconstructing classroom life do we have any hope of cracking the cynicism that lies so close to the heart of massive school failure, and of raising academic expectations and performance for all our children.

■ **Culturally sensitive.** Critical teaching requires that we admit we don't know it all. Each class presents new challenges to learn from our students and demands that we be good researchers, and good listeners. These days, the demographic reality of schooling makes it likely that white teachers will enter classrooms filled with children of color. As African-American educator Lisa Delpit writes in her review of the book *White Teacher* (see p. 158), "When teachers are teaching children who are different from themselves, they must call upon parents in a collaborative fashion if they are to learn who their students really are." They must also call upon culturally diverse colleagues and community resources for insights into the communities they seek to serve. What can be said about racial and cultural differences between teachers and students also holds true for class differences.

* * *

We're skeptical of the "inspirational speakers" administrators bring to faculty meetings, who exhort us to become super-teachers and classroom magicians. Critical teaching requires vision, support, and resources, not magic. We hope the stories, critiques, and lesson ideas here will offer useful examples which can be adapted in classrooms of all levels and disciplines and in diverse social milieus. Our goal is to provide a clear framework to guide classroom transformation.

But as vital as it is to reimagine and reorganize classroom practice, ultimately it's insufficient. Teachers who want to construct more equitable, more meaningful, and more lively educational experiences for children must also concern themselves with issues beyond the classroom walls. For example, if a school uses so-called ability grouping to sort students, then no matter how successful we are in our efforts to remake classroom life, many students will still absorb negative messages about their capacity to achieve. We need to confront tracking and standardized testing, the funding inequalities within and between school districts, and the frequent reluctance of teacher unions to address issues of quality education. Rethinking our classrooms requires inventing strategies so that teachers can make alliances with parents and community organizations who have an interest in equity. Toward this end we've offered a chapter, "Beyond the Classroom."

As we go to press with *Rethinking Our Classrooms,* there are many reasons to be discouraged about the future: Districts across the country continue to slash budgets; violence continues to plague schools; attempts to privatize the schools have not slowed; and the country's productive resources are still used to make more technological goodies, fancier athletic shoes, and more sophisticated weaponry, rather than used in less profitable arenas like education and affordable housing.

There is a Zulu expression: "If the future doesn't come toward you, you have to go fetch it." We hope *Rethinking Our Classrooms* will be a useful tool in the movement to go fetch a better future: in our classrooms, in our schools, and in the larger society. There are lots of us out there. Critical and activist teachers work all across the country. Let's make our voices heard.■

—the editors

PART ONE

POINTS OF DEPARTURE

Although the one-room schoolhouse is a relic of the past, certain patterns within American education have proven stubbornly durable: the dominance of the teacher's voice, reluctance to accept cultural diversity, and uncritical acceptance of the social and political order.

The articles in this introductory chapter show how teachers can challenge these patterns through classroom alternatives which deepen learning and enrich interactions between students and teachers.

Lions

By Langston Hughes

A lion in a zoo,
Shut up in a cage,
Lives a life
Of smothered rage.

A lion in the plain,
Roaming free,
Is happy as ever
A lion can be.

Langston Hughes is probably the most famous poet of the Harlem Renaissance. He chose to write about ordinary people—as he said, "workers, roustabouts, and singers, and job hunters ... people up today and down tomorrow ... beaten and baffled, but determined not to be wholly beaten." (See p. 212 for lesson ideas.)

Unlearning the Myths That Bind Us
Critiquing cartoons and society

By Linda Christensen

I was nourished on the milk of American culture: I cleaned the dwarves' house and waited for Prince Charming to bring me life; I played Minnie Mouse to Mickey's flower-bearing adoration, and, later, I swooned in Rhett Butler's arms—my waist as narrow and my bosom every bit as heaving as Scarlett's. But my daddy didn't own a plantation; he owned a rough and tumble bar frequented by loggers and fishermen. My waist didn't dip into an hourglass; in fact, according to the novels I read my thick ankles doomed me to be cast as the peasant woman reaping hay while the heroine swept by with her handsome man in hot pursuit.

Our students suckle the same pap. Our society's culture industry colonizes their minds and teaches them how to act, live, and dream. This indoctrination hits young children especially hard. The "secret education," as Chilean writer Ariel Dorfman (1983) dubs it, delivered by children's books and movies, instructs young people to accept the world as it is portrayed in these social blueprints. And often that world depicts the domination of one sex, one race, one class, or one country over a weaker counterpart. After studying cartoons and children's literature, my student Omar wrote, "When we read children's books, we aren't just reading cute little stories, we are discovering the tools with which a young society is manipulated."

Beverly Tatum, who wrote the book *Why Are All the Black Kids Sitting*

The jealous stepmother in Disney's *Snow White*.

WALT DISNEY CO.

Together in the Cafeteria? (1997), helps explain how children develop distorted views of people outside of their racial/cultural group:

The impact of racism begins early. Even in our preschool years, we are exposed to misinformation about people different from ourselves. Many of us grow up in neighborhoods where we had limited opportunities to interact with people different from our own families. … Consequently, most of the early information we receive about "others"—people racially, religiously, or socioeconomically different from ourselves—does not come as a result of firsthand experience. The secondhand information we receive has often been distorted, shaped by cultural stereotypes, and left incomplete.

Cartoon images, in particular the Disney movie *Peter Pan*, were cited by the children in a research study as their number one source of information. At the age of three, these children had a set of stereotypes in place.

Children's cartoons, movies, and literature are perhaps the most influential genre "read." Young people, unprotected by any intellectual armor, hear or watch these stories again and again, often from the warmth of their mother's or father's lap. The messages, or "secret education," linked with the security of their homes, underscore the power these texts deliver. As Tatum's research suggests, the stereotypes and world view embedded in the stories become accepted knowledge.

I want my students to question this accepted knowledge and the secret education delivered by cartoons as well as by the canon. Because children's movies and literature are short and visual we can critique them together. We can view many in a brief period of time, so students can begin to see patterns in media portrayals of particular groups and learn to decode the underlying assumptions these movies make. Brazilian educator Paulo Freire (in Shor and Freire, 1987) wrote that instead of wrestling with words and ideas, too often students "walk on the words." If I want my students to wrestle with the social text of novels, news, or history books, they need the tools to critique media that encourage or legitimate social inequality.

To help students uncover those old values planted by Disney, Mattel, and Nike, and construct more just ones, I begin this "unlearning the myths" unit with two objectives. First I want students to critique portrayals of hierarchy and inequality in children's mov-

ies and cartoons. Then I want to enlist them to imagine a better world, characterized by relationships of respect and equality.

Exposing the Myths: How to Read Cartoons

Prior to watching any cartoons, I ask students to read the preface and first chapter of Ariel Dorfman's book *The Empire's Old Clothes: What the Lone Ranger, Babar, and Other Innocent Heroes Do to Our Minds* (1983).

Students keep track of their responses in a dialogue journal. I pose the question: Do you agree with Dorfman's position that children receive a "secret education" in the media? Do you remember any incidents from your own childhood that support his allegations?

This is difficult for some students. The dialogue journal spurs them to argue, to talk back, and create a conversation with the writer. Dorfman is controversial. He gets under their skin. He wrote:

Industrially produced fiction has become one of the primary shapers of our emotions and our intellect in the twentieth century. Although these stories are supposed to merely entertain us, they constantly give us a secret education. We are not only taught certain styles of violence, the latest fashions, and sex roles by TV, movies, magazines, and comic strips; we are also taught how to succeed, how to love, how to buy, how to conquer, how to forget the past and suppress the future. We are taught more than anything else, how not to rebel.

Many students don't want to believe that they have been manipulated by children's media or advertising. No one wants to admit that they've been "handled" by the media. They assure me that they make their own choices and the

media has no power over them—as they sit in their Fubu, Nike, Timberlands or whatever the latest fashion rage might be. And Dorfman analyzes that pose:

There has also been a tendency to avoid scrutinizing these mass media products too closely, to avoid asking the sort of hard questions that can yield disquieting answers. It is not strange that this should be so. The industry itself has declared time and again with great forcefulness that it is innocent, that no hidden motives or implications are lurking behind the cheerful faces it generates.

Justine, a senior in my Contemporary Literature and Society class, was bothered by Dorfman's quest "to dissect those dreams, the ones that had nourished my childhood and adolescence, that continued to infect so many of my adult habits." In her dialogue journal she responded:

Personally, handling the dissection of dreams has been a major cause of depression for me. Not so much dissecting—but how I react to what is found as a result of the operation. It can be overwhelming and discouraging to find out my whole self-image has been formed mostly by others or underneath my worries about what I look like are years (17 of them) of being exposed to TV images of girls and their set roles given to them by TV and the media. It's painful to deal with. The idea of not being completely responsible for how I feel about things today is scary. So why dissect the dreams? Why not stay ignorant about them and happy? The reason for me is that those dreams are not unrelated to my everyday life. They influence how I behave, think, react to things. … My dreams keep me from dealing with an unpleasant reality.

In looking back through this passage and others in her dialogue with Dorfman, Justine displayed discomfort with prying apart her identity and discovering where she received her ideas; yet, she also grudgingly admitted how necessary this process was if she wanted to move beyond where she was at the time. Her discomfort might also have arisen from feeling incapable of changing herself or changing the standards by which she was judged in the larger society. But she knew such questioning was important.

In a later section of her journal, she wrote, "True death equals a generation living by rules and attitudes they never questioned and producing more children who do the same." Justine's reaction may be more articulate than some, but her sentiments were typical of many students. She was beginning to peel back the veneer covering some of the injustice in our society, and she was dismayed by what she discovered.

Charting Stereotypes

I start by showing students old cartoons because the stereotypes are so blatant. We look at the roles women, men, people of color, and poor people play in the cartoons. I ask students to watch for who plays the lead. Who plays the buffoon? Who plays the servant? I encourage them to look at the race, station in life, and body type of each character. What are the characters' motivation? What do they want out of life? What's their mission? If there are people of color in the film, what do they look like? How are they portrayed? What would children learn about this particular group from this film?

How does the film portray overweight people? What about women other than the main character? What jobs do you see them doing? What do they talk about? What are their main concerns? What would young children learn about women's roles in society if they watched this film and believed

it? What roles do money, possessions, and power play in the film? Who has it? Who wants it? How important is it to the story? What would children learn about what's important in this society?

As they view each episode, they fill in

Young people, unprotected by any intellectual armor, hear or watch these stories again and again, often from the warmth of their mother's or father's lap.

a chart answering these questions. Students immediately start yelling out the stereotypes because they are so obvious. Early in the unit, I show a Popeye cartoon, "Ali Baba and the 40 Thieves," that depicts all Arabs with the same face, same turban, same body—and they are all thieves swinging enormous swords. At one point in the cartoon, Popeye clips a dog collar on helpless Olive Oyl and drags her through the desert. Later, the 40 thieves come riding through town stealing everything—food, an old man's teeth, numbers off a clock—even the stripe off a barber pole. The newer cartoons—like *Mulan*, *Aladdin*, and *Pocahontas*—are subtler and take more sophistication to see through, but if students warm up on the old ones, they can pierce the surface of the new ones as well.

On first viewing, students sometimes resist critical analysis. After watching a Daffy Duck cartoon, for example, Kamaui said, "This is just a dumb little cartoon with some ducks running around in clothes." Then students start to notice patterns—like the absence of female characters in many of the older cartoons. When women do appear, they look like Jessica Rabbit or *Playboy* centerfolds—even in many of the new and improved children's movies.

After filling in a few charts, col-

lectively and on their own, students write about the generalizations children might take away from these tales. From experience, I've discovered that I need to keep my mouth shut for a while. If I'm the one pointing out the

stereotypes, it's the kiss of death to the exercise. Besides, students are quick to find the usual stereotypes on their own: "Look, Ursula the sea witch is ugly and smart. Hey, she's kind of dark looking. The young, pretty ones only want to hook their man; the old, pretty ones are mean because they are losing their looks." Kenneth noticed that people of color and poor people are either absent or servants to the rich, white, pretty people. Tyler pointed out that the roles of men are limited as well. Men must be virile and wield power or be old and the object of "good-natured" humor. Students began seeing beyond the charts I'd rigged up for them. They looked at how overweight people were portrayed as buffoons in episode after episode. They noted the absence of mothers, the wickedness of stepparents.

Later in the unit, Mira, a senior, attacked the racism in these Saturday morning rituals. She brought her familiarity with Native American cultures into her analysis:

Indians in Looney Tunes are also depicted as inferior human beings. These characters are stereotypical to the greatest degree, carrying tomahawks, painting their faces, and sending smoke signals as their only means of communication. They live in tipis and their language reminds the viewer of Neanderthals. We begin to imagine Indians as savages with bows and arrows and long black braids. There's no room in our minds for knowledge of the differences between tribes, like the Cherokee alphabet or Celilo salmon fishing.

> I don't want students to believe that change can be bought at the mall, or that the pinnacle of a woman's life is an 'I do' that leads to a 'happily ever after.'

A Black Cinderella?

After viewing a number of cartoons, Kenya scolded parents in an essay, "A Black Cinderella? Give Me a Break." She wrote: "Have you ever seen a black person, an Asian, a Hispanic in a cartoon? Did they have a leading role or were they a servant? What do you think this is doing to your child's mind?" She ended her piece, "Women who aren't white begin to feel left out and ugly because they never get to play the princess." Kenya's piece bristled with anger at a society that rarely acknowledges the wit or beauty of women of her race. And she wasn't alone in her feelings. Sabrina wrote, "I'm not taking my kids to see any Walt Disney movies until they have a black woman playing the leading role."

Both young women wanted the race of the actors changed, but they didn't challenge the class or underlying gender inequities that also characterize the lives of Cinderella, Ariel, and Snow White.

Kenya's and Sabrina's anger is justified. There should be more women of color who play the leads in these white-on-white wedding cake tales. Of course, there should also be more women of color on the Supreme Court, in Congress, as well as scrubbing up for

surgeries. But I want students to understand that if the race of the character is the only thing changing, injustices may still remain.

So I have students read Mary Carter Smith's delightful retelling of Cinderella, "Cindy Ellie, A Modern Fairy Tale" (1989), which reads like laughter—bubbly, warm, spilling over with infectious good humor and playful language. In Smith's version, Cindy Ellie, who lived in East Baltimore, was "one purty young black sister, her skin like black velvet." Her father, "like so many good men, was weak for a pretty face and big legs and big hips." Her stepmother "had a heart as hard as a rock. The milk of human kindness had curdled in her breast. But she did have a pretty face, big legs, and great big hips. … Well, that fool man fell right into that woman's trap."

Cindy Ellie's stepsisters were "two big-footed, ugly gals" who made Cindy Ellie wait on them hand and foot. When the "good white folks, the good Asian folks, and the good black folks all turned out and voted for a good black brother, running for mayor" there was cause for celebration, and a chance for Cindy Ellie to meet her Prince Charming, the mayor's son. With the help of her Godma's High John the Conqueror Root, Cindy Ellie looked like an "African Princess." "Her rags turned into a dazzling dress of pink African laces! Her hair was braided into a hundred shining braids, and on the end of each braid were beads of pure gold! … Golden bracelets covered her arms clean up to her elbows! On each ear

hung five small diamond earrings. On her tiny feet were dainty golden sandals encrusted with dazzling jewels! Cindy Ellie was laid back!"

The students and I love the story. It is well told and incorporates rich details that do exactly what Sabrina, Kenya, and their classmates wanted: It celebrates the beauty, culture, and language of African A racism mericans. It also puts forth the possibility of cross-race alliances for social change.

But, like the original tale, Cindy Ellie's main goal in life is not working to end the plight of the homeless or teaching kids to read. Her goal, like Cinderella's, is to get her man. Both young women are transformed and made beautiful through new clothes, new jewels, new hairstyles. Both have chauffeurs who deliver them to their men. Cindy Ellie and Cinderella are nicer and kinder than their stepsisters, but the Prince and Toussant, the mayor's son, don't know that. Both of the Cinderellas compete for their men against their sisters and the rest of the single women in their cities. They "win" because of their beauty and their fashionable attire. Both of these tales leave young women with two myths: Happiness means getting a man, and transformation from wretched conditions can be achieved through consumption—in their case, through new clothes and a new hairstyle.

I am uncomfortable with those messages. I don't want students to believe that change can be bought at the mall, nor do I want them thinking that the pinnacle of a woman's life is an "I do" that supposedly leads them to a "happily ever after." I don't want my female students to see their "sisters" as competition for that scarce and wonderful commodity—men. As Justine wrote earlier in her dialogue journal, it can be overwhelming and discouraging to find that our self-images have been formed by others, but if we don't dissect them, we will continue to be influenced by them.

Writing as a Vehicle for Change

Toward the end of the unit, students write essays critiquing cartoons. I hope that these will encourage students to look deeper into the issues—to challenge the servant/master relationships or the materialism that makes women appealing to their men. For some students the cartoon unit exposes the wizardry that enters our dreams and desires, but others shrug their shoulders at this. It's OK for some people to be rich and others poor; they just want to see more rich people of color or more rich women. Or better yet, be rich themselves. They accept the inequalities in power and exploitative economic relationships. Their acceptance teaches me how deep the roots of these myths are planted and how much some students, in the absence of visions for a different and better world, need to believe in the fairy tale magic that will transform their lives—whether it's a rich man or winning the lottery.

Many students write strong critiques following the viewing. But venting their frustrations with cartoons—and even sharing it with the class—can seem an important but limited task. Yes, they can write articulate pieces. Yes, they hone their arguments and seek the just-right examples from their viewing. Through critiques and the discussions that follow, they are helping to transform each other—each comment or observation helps expose the engine of our society, and they're both excited and dismayed by their discoveries.

But what am I teaching them if the lesson ends there? That it's enough to be critical without taking action? That we can quietly rebel in the privacy of the classroom while we practice our writing skills, but we don't really have to do anything about the problems we uncover, nor do we need to create any-

Jessica in Disney's *Roger Rabbit*.

WALT DISNEY CO.

thing to take the place of what we've expelled? Those are not the lessons I intend to teach. I want to develop their critical consciousness, but I also hope to move them to action.

For some the lesson doesn't end in the classroom. Many who watched cartoons before we start our study say they can no longer enjoy them. Now instead of seeing a bunch of ducks in clothes, they see the racism, sexism, and violence that swim under the surface of the stories.

Pam and Nicole swore they would not let their children watch cartoons. David told the class of coming home one day and finding his nephews absorbed in Looney Tunes. "I turned that TV off and took them down to the park to play. They aren't going to watch that mess while I'm around." Radiance described how she went to buy Christmas presents for her niece and nephew. "Before, I would have just walked into the toy store and bought them what I knew they wanted—Nintendo or Barbie. But this time, I went up the clerk

and said, 'I want a toy that isn't sexist or racist.'"

Students have also said that what they now see in cartoons, they also see in advertising, on prime time TV, on the news, in school. Turning off the cartoons doesn't stop the sexism and racism. They can't escape, and now that they've started analyzing cartoons, they can't stop analyzing the rest of the world. And sometimes they want to stop. Once a student asked me, "Don't you ever get tired of analyzing everything?"

During a class discussion Sabrina said, "I realized these problems weren't just in cartoons. They were in everything—every magazine I picked up, every television show I watched, every billboard I passed by on the street." My goal of honing their ability to read literature and the world through the lens of justice had been accomplished at least in part. But as Justine wrote earlier, at times my students would like to remain "ignorant and happy." Without giving students an outlet for their despair, I was indeed creating "factories of cynicism" (Bigelow, et al., 1994) in my classroom—and it wasn't pretty.

Taking Action

I look for opportunities for students to act on their knowledge. In Literature and U.S. History class, these occasions have presented themselves in the form of unfair tests and outrageous newspaper articles about Jefferson that provoked spontaneous student activism. But in my Contemporary Literature and Society class, I discovered that I had to create the possibility for action.

Instead of writing the same classroom essays students had written in years before, I asked students to create projects that would move beyond the classroom walls. Who could they teach about what they learned? I wanted their

projects to be real. Who could their analysis touch enough to bring about real change? Students filled the board with potential readers of their work: Parents, peers, teachers, children's book authors, librarians, Disney, video store owners, advertisers.

My only rule was that they had to write a piece using evidence from cartoons or other media. Don't just rant in general, I told them. Use evidence to support your thesis. The examples might come from cartoons, advertisements, novels, your mother or father's advice. You might use lines from TV or movies. You don't have to stick to cartoons—use the world.

We discussed possible options:

■ Focus on one cartoon—critique it, talk about it in depth. Write about *Mulan* or *Peter Pan*. Using the chart,

analyze the representation of men, women, people of color, and poor people in that movie.

■ Focus on the portrayal of one group. Write about how women, men, African Americans, Latinos, Arabs, overweight people or the poor are depicted and give examples from several cartoons or across time.

■ Take an issue—like the representation of women—and relate it to your life and/or society at large.

One group of playful students wanted to create a pamphlet that could be distributed at PTA meetings throughout the city. That night they went home with assignments they'd given each other—Sarah would watch Saturday morning cartoons; Sandy, Brooke, and Carmel would watch after-school cartoons; and Kristin and Toby

---

Rethinking 'The Three Little Pigs'

By Ellen Wolpert

There's scarcely a parent or young child who isn't familiar with "The Three Little Pigs." It has a simple plot line, is easily remembered, and it's so much fun imitating the big bad wolf as he huffs and puffs and "blo-o-ws" the house down.

I find the story is also useful to talk about the stereotypes in so many of our favorite tales.

I first became aware of the story's hidden messages when we were doing a unit on housing several years ago at my daycare center. As part of the unit, we talked about different homes and the many approaches to solving a basic human need: a place to live.

During the discussion I suddenly thought to myself, "Why are brick homes better than straw homes?"

To this day, I'm not completely sure why that question popped into my mind. I do know, however, that I

had been sensitized by the movement for a multicultural curriculum, which had taught me to take a questioning approach to even the most seemingly innocuous materials and to look beneath the surface for hidden assumptions.

After thinking about it, I realized that one of the most fundamental messages of "The Three Little Pigs" is that it belittles straw and stick homes and the "lazy types" who build them. On the other hand, the story extols the virtues of brick homes, suggesting that they are built by serious, hard-working people and strong enough to withstand adversity.

Is there any coincidence that brick homes tend to be built by people in Western countries, often by those with more money? That straw homes are more common in non-European cultures, particularly Africa and Asia?

Once I realized some of these hidden messages, the question became what to do about it. In my experience, the best approach is not to put down such beloved tales and refuse to read them, but to use them to pose questions for children. One might explain, for example, that in many tropical areas straw homes are built to take best advantage of cooling breezes. In some areas, straw homes are on stilts as protection from insects and animals or to withstand flooding.

Such a perspective then becomes part of a broader process of helping children to understand why homes are different in different parts of the world—and that just because something is different doesn't mean it's inferior.

Ellen Wolpert is the coordinator of the Cambridge Community Partnerships for Children, in Cambridge, Mass.

were assigned before-school cartoons. They ended up writing a report card for the various programs. They graded each show A through F and wrote a brief summary of their findings:

Duck Tales: At first glance the precocious ducks are cute, but look closer and see that the whole show is based on money. All their adventures revolve around finding money. Uncle Scrooge and the gang teach children that money is the only important thing in life. Grade: C-

Teenage Muntant Ninja Turtles: Pizza-eating Ninja Turtles. What's the point? There isn't any. The show is based on fighting the 'bad guy,' Shredder. Demonstrating no concern for the townspeople, they battle and fight, but never get hurt. This cartoon teaches a false sense of violence to kids: fight and you don't get hurt, or solve problems through fists and swords instead of words. Grade: D

Popeye: This show oozes with horrible messages from passive Olive Oyl to the hero 'man' Popeye. This cartoon portrays ethnic groups as stupid. It is political also—teaching children that Americans are the best and conquer all others. Grade: F

On the back of the pamphlet, they listed some tips for parents to guide them in wise cartoon selection.

Catkin wrote about the sexual stereotyping and adoration of beauty in children's movies. Her article described how she and other teenage women carry these messages with them still:

Women's roles in fairy tales distort reality—from Jessica Rabbit's six-mile strut in *Who Framed Roger Rabbit?* to Tinker Bell's obsessive vanity in *Peter Pan*. These seemingly innocent stories teach us to look for our faults. As Tinker Bell inspects her tiny body in a mirror only to find that her minute hips are simply too huge, she shows us how to turn the mirror into an enemy. … And this scenario is repeated in girls' locker rooms all over the world.

Because we can never look like Cinderella, we begin to hate ourselves. The Barbie syndrome starts as we begin a lifelong search for the perfect body. Crash diets, fat phobias, and an obsession with the materialistic become commonplace. The belief that a product will make us rise above our competition, our friends, turns us into addicts. Our fix is that Calvin Klein push-up bra, Guess jeans, Chanel lipstick, and the latest in suede flats. We don't call it deception; we call it good taste. And soon it feels awkward going to the mailbox without makeup.

Catkin wanted to publish her piece in a magazine for young women so they would begin to question the origin of the standards by which they judge themselves.

Most students wrote articles for local and national newspapers or magazines. Some published in neighborhood papers, some in church newsletters. Some have had their work published nationally.

The writing in these articles was tighter and cleaner than for-the-teacher essays because it had the potential for a real audience beyond the classroom walls. The possibility of publishing their pieces changed the level of students' intensity for the project. Anne, who turned in hastily written drafts last year, said, "Five drafts and I'm not finished yet!"

But more importantly, students saw themselves as actors in the world; they were fueled by the opportunity to convince some parents of the long-lasting effects cartoons impose on their children, or to enlighten their peers about the roots of some of their insecurities.

Instead of leaving students full of bile, standing around with their hands on their hips, shaking their heads about how bad the world is, I provided them the opportunity to make a difference.■

Linda Christensen (LChrist@aol.com) is director of the Oregon Writing Project at Lewis and Clark College and is an editor of Rethinking Schools *magazine.*

References

Bigelow, Bill, et al. *Rethinking Our Classrooms: Teaching for Equity and Justice.* Milwaukee: Rethinking Schools, 1994, p. 4.

Dorfman, Ariel. *The Empire's Old Clothes: What the Lone Ranger, Babar, and Other Innocent Heroes Do to Our Minds.* New York: Pantheon, 1983, p. ix.

Smith, Mary Carter. "Cindy Ellie, A Modern Fairy Tale," in Goss, Linda (Ed.). *Talk That Talk: An Anthology Of African-American Storytelling.* New York: Touchstone, 1989, pp. 396-402.

Shor, Ira and Freire, Paulo. *A Pedagogy for Liberation.* South Hadley, MA: Bergin & Garvey, 1987, p. 10.

Tatum, Beverly. *'Why Are All the Black Kids Sitting Together in the Cafeteria?' and Other Conversations About Race.* New York: Basic Books, 1997, pp. 4-5.

10 Quick Ways to Analyze Children's Books for Racism and Sexism

By the Council on Interracial Books for Children

Both in school and out, young children are exposed to racist and sexist attitudes. These attitudes—expressed over and over in books and in other media—gradually distort their perceptions until stereotypes and myths about minorities and women are accepted as reality. It is difficult for a librarian or teacher to convince children to question society's attitudes. But if a child can be shown how to detect racism and sexism in a book, the child can proceed to transfer the perception to wider areas. The following ten guidelines are offered as a starting point in evaluating children's books from this perspective.

1. Check the Illustrations

Look for Stereotypes. A stereotype is an oversimplified generalization about a particular group, race, or sex, which usually carries derogatory implications. In addition to blatant stereotypes, look for variations which in any way demean or ridicule characters because of their race or sex.

Look for Tokenism. If there are non-white characters in the illustrations, do they look just like whites except for being tinted or colored in? Do all minority faces look stereotypically alike, or are they depicted as genuine individuals with distinctive features?

Who's Doing What? Do the illustrations depict minorities in subservient and passive roles or in leadership and action roles? Are males the active "doers" and females the inactive observers?

2. Check the Story Line

The Civil Rights Movement led publishers to weed out many insulting passages, particularly from stories with black themes, but the attitudes still find expression in less obvious ways. The following checklist suggests some of the subtle (covert) forms of bias to watch for.

Standard for Success. Does it take "white" behavior standards for a person of color to "get ahead"? Is "making it" in the dominant white society projected as the only ideal? To gain acceptance and approval, do people of color have to exhibit extraordinary qualities—excel in sports, get A's, etc.? In friendships between white children and children of color, is it the child of color who does most of the understanding and forgiving?

Resolution of Problems. How are problems presented, conceived, and resolved in the story? Are people of color considered to be "the problem"?

Are the oppressions faced by people of color and women represented as causally related to an unjust society? Are the reasons for poverty and oppression explained, or are they just accepted as inevitable? Does the story line encourage passive acceptance or active resistance? Is a particular problem that is faced by a person of color resolved through the benevolent intervention of a white person?

Role of Women. Are the achievements of girls and women based on their own initiative and intelligence, or are they due to their good looks or to their relationship with boys? Are sex roles incidental or critical to characterization and plot? Could the same story be told if the sex roles were reversed?

3. Look at the Lifestyles

Are people of color and their setting depicted in such a way that they contrast unfavorably with the unstated norm of white middle-class suburbia? If the non-white group is depicted as "different," are negative value judgments implied? Are people of color depicted exclusively in ghettos, barrios, or migrant camps? If the illustrations and text attempt to depict another culture, do they go beyond oversimplifications and offer genuine insights into another lifestyle? Look for inaccuracy and inappropriateness in the depiction of other cultures. Watch for instances of the "quaint-natives-in-costume" syndrome (most noticeable in areas like costume and custom, but extending to behavior and personality traits as well).

4. Weigh the Relationships Between People

■ Do the whites in the story possess the power, take the leadership, and make the important decisions? Do people of color and females function in essentially supporting roles?

■ How are family relationships depicted? In African-American families, is the mother always dominant? In Latino families, are there always lots of children? If the family is separated, are societal conditions—unemployment, poverty—cited among the reasons for the separation?

5. Note the Heroes

For many years, books showed only "safe" non-white heroes—those who avoided serious conflict with the white establishment of their time. People of color are insisting on the right to define their own heroes (of both sexes) based on their own concepts and struggles for justice.

■ When minority heroes do appear, are they admired for the same qualities that have made white heroes famous or because what they have done has benefited white people? Ask this question: "Whose interest is a particular figure really serving?"

6. Consider the Effects on a Child's Self-Image

■ Are norms established which limit the child's aspirations and self-concepts? What effect can it have on African-American children to be continuously bombarded with images of the color white as the ultimate in beauty, cleanliness, virtue, etc., and the color black as evil, dirty, menacing, etc.? Does the book counteract or reinforce this positive association with the color white and negative association with black?

■ What happens to a girl's self-esteem when she reads that boys perform all of the brave and important deeds? What about a girl's self-esteem if she is not "fair" of skin and slim of body?

■ In a particular story, is there one or more person with whom a child of color can readily identify to a positive and constructive end?

7. Consider the Author or Illustrator's Background

Analyze the biographical material on the jacket flap or the back of the book. If a story deals with a multicultural theme, what qualifies the author or illustrator to deal with the subject? If the author and illustrator are not members of the group being written about, is there anything in their background that would specifically recommend them as the creators of this book? The same criteria apply to a book that deals with the feelings and insights of women or girls.

8. Check Out the Author's Perspective

No author can be wholly objective. All authors write out of a cultural as well as personal context. Children's books in the past have traditionally come from white, middle-class authors, with one result being that a single ethnocentric perspective has dominated American children's literature. With the book in question, look carefully to determine whether the direction of the author's perspective substantially weakens or strengthens the value of

his/her written work. Are omissions and distortions central to the overall character or "message" of the book?

9. Watch for Loaded Words

A word is loaded when it has insulting overtones. Examples of loaded adjectives (usually racist) are "savage," "primitive," "conniving," "lazy," "superstitious," "treacherous," "wily," "crafty," "inscrutable," "docile," and "backward."

■ Look for sexist language and adjectives that exclude or ridicule women. Look for use of the male pronoun to refer to both males and females. The following examples show how sexist language can be avoided: "ancestors" instead of "forefathers;" "firefighters" instead of "firemen;" "manufactured" instead of "manmade;" the "human family" instead of the "family of man."

10. Look at the Copyright Date

Books on "minority" themes—usually hastily conceived—suddenly began appearing in the mid-1960s. There followed a growing number of "minority experience" books to meet the new market demand, but most of these were still written by white authors, edited by white editors, and published by white publishers. They therefore reflected a white point of view.

The copyright dates, therefore, can be a clue as to how likely the book is to be overtly racist or sexist, although a recent copyright date is no guarantee of a book's relevance or sensitivity. The copyright date only means the year the book was published. It usually takes a minimum of a year—and often much more than that—from the time a manuscript is submitted to the publisher to the time it is actually printed and put on the market. This time-lag meant very little in the past, but in a time of rapid change and changing consciousness, when children's book publishing is attempting to be "relevant," it is increasingly significant.■

Celebrating the Joy in Daily Events

By Linda Christensen

In a classroom where students and I critique everything from Donald Duck to U.S. foreign policy, I also need to prompt kids to celebrate the ordinary, the common daily events they take pleasure in. I want to find ways to coax joy back into the room, especially when students feel down about the ways of the world. Students are bombarded with messages that their route to happiness is a Diet Pepsi, a new deodorant, or a shampoo that will make them irresistible. At times, students and I explicitly examine ads and their messages, but I also use odes, a traditional poetic form, to help students re-see the beauty in the world outside the mall.

I stumbled across odes many years ago when I fell in love with Pablo Neruda's poetry. Students read Neruda's "Ode to My Socks," in which he praises a pair of socks given him by a friend. The odes allow students to find the positive in their daily lives. Neruda's odes also push students to use concrete details and imagery in their pieces. I use *Selected Odes of Pablo Neruda*, which has the original Spanish as well as the English translation.

1. Students read the poem (see p. 13) in both languages. (This validates students who speak Spanish as well as locating writing in the broader linguistic world. I encourage students who speak more than one language to write in either or both languages.)

2. We discuss how Neruda describes the socks: "two woolen /fish, /two long sharks/of lapis blue/shot/with a golden thread,/two mammoth blackbirds." The more time we examine the imagery in Neruda's poem, the more students attempt daring, outrageous imagery. We also note how he talks about both the gift and the giver.

3. Then I ask students to make a list of objects they might praise—a gift, an everyday object, something that has meaning for them even though it might not seem important to anyone else. A few students share their ideas, helping to dislodge memories for their classmates.

4. I turn off the lights and ask students to take a few deep breaths and close their eyes. (They hate this at first. They're afraid other people might look at them. It takes patience to get this to work in my classes.) Then I ask students to think about what they are going to praise. I do this part slowly—30 to 60 seconds for each question. There's a tendency to rush because the class is silent, but it takes a while to get a visual image. I ask students to remember what the object looks like, smells like, sounds like, what else it reminds them of, how they came to get it. I find the guided visualization helps students remember more detail. When I turn the lights back on, I ask students to write in silence.

5. With classes of younger students, I sometimes begin by asking them to write a paragraph describing the object and a paragraph about how they came to have the object. They can use these details in their poems.

Students have written odes to the Spanish language, their skin, their weight, lesbians, a mother's hands, animal cookies, ham, a grandfather's hat, tap dance, coffee, Jefferson High School, chocolate chip cookies, the color red, writing, and more. The ode became a form they returned to frequently in their writing.

Sarah Scofield, whose beautiful reading of Neruda's poetry in Spanish allowed her to share her linguistic talent with classmates, wrote this poem:

Ode to Spanish

A language
As beautiful as music:
Melodious verbs
Harmonious adjectives
Rhythmic nouns
Intertwine as I speak.
An orchestra of words
Conducted by my tongue.
I compose
A new song
As those around me listen.
Musical sentences
Rich with the notes
Of culture.
A romance language
stirring the hearts
of its listeners.
The music plays on
As I watch with wonder how
My untrained yet experienced tongue
conducts the orchestra,
and the music pleases me.

I don't want to exaggerate the importance of this lesson. It is a small weapon in my fight against cynicism and despair. But I do believe that if I want my students to imagine a more just society, I must spend time teaching them how to find what's good as well as to find what's bad. My classroom provides a small space to help students not only construct a critique, but also to build a community that can laugh and share joy. (See p. 213 for suggestions on organizing read-arounds.)■

Ode to My Socks • Oda a los calcetines

By Pablo Neruda

Maru Mori brought me	Me trajo Maru Mori
a pair	un par
of socks	de calcetines
knitted with her own	que tejió con sus manos
shepherd's hands,	de pastora,
two socks soft	dos calcetines suaves
as rabbits.	como liebres.
I slipped	En ellos
my feet into them	metí los pies
as if	como en
into	dos
jewel cases	estuches
woven	tejidos
with threads of	con hebras del
dusk	crepúsculo
and sheep's wool.	y pellejo de ovejas.
Audacious socks,	Violentos calcetines,
my feet became	mis pies fueron
two woolen	dos pescados
fish,	de lana,
two long sharks	dos largos tiburones
of lapis blue	de azul ultramarino
shot	atravesados
with a golden thread,	por una trenza de oro,
two mammoth blackbirds,	dos gigantescos mirlos,
two cannons,	dos cañones:
thus honored	mis pies
were	fueron honrados
my feet	de este modo
by	por
these	estos
celestial	celestiales
socks.	calcetines.
They were	Eran
so beautiful	tan hermosos
that for the first time	que por primera vez
my feet seemed	mis pies me parecieron
unacceptable to me,	inaceptables
two tired old	como dos decrépitos
fire fighters	bomberos, bomberos,
not worthy	indignos
of the woven	de aquel fuego
fire	bordado,

of those luminous	de aquellos luminosos
socks.	calcetines.
Nonetheless,	Sin embargo
I resisted	resistí
the strong temptation	la tentación aguda
to save them	de guardarlos
the way schoolboys	como los colegiales
bottle	preservan
fireflies,	las luciérnagas,
the way scholars	como los eruditos
hoard	coleccionan
sacred documents.	documentos sagrados,
I resisted	resistí
the wild impulse	el impulso furioso
to place them	de ponerlos
in a cage	en una jaula
of gold	de oro
and daily feed them	y darles cada día
birdseed	alpiste
and rosy melon flesh.	y pulpa de melón rosado.
Like explorers	Como descubridores
who in the forest	que en la selva
surrender a rare	entregan el rarísimo
and tender deer	venado verde
to the spit	al asador
and eat it	y se lo comen
with remorse,	con remordimiento,
I stuck out	estiré
my feet	los pies
and pulled on	y me enfundé
the	los
handsome	bellos
socks,	calcetines
and	y
then my shoes.	luego los zapatos.
So this is	Y es ésta
the moral of my ode:	la moral de mi oda:
twice beautiful	dos veces es belleza
is beauty	la belleza
and what is good is doubly	y lo que es bueno es doblemente
good	bueno
when it is a case of two	cuando se trata de dos calcetines
woolen socks	de lana
in wintertime.	en el invierno.

translated by Margaret Sayers Peden

Pablo Neruda was born on July 12, 1904, in a small frontier town of southern Chile, the son of a railroad worker and a teacher. He was active in the struggle for social justice for his entire adult life. He received the Nobel Prize for Literature in 1971 and died in 1973.

Taking Multicultural, Anti-Racist Education Seriously

An interview with Enid Lee

Enid Lee conducts online and on-site professional development with school communities working to ensure academic excellence for all students through anti-racist education. She presents institutes, gives talks, and writes about language, culture, race, and racism in education. Her publications include Beyond Heroes and Holidays: A Practical Guide to K–12, Anti-Racist, Multicultural Education and Staff Development, *which she co-edited. She is a Virtual Scholar at Teaching for Change. She was interviewed by Barbara Miner.*

What do you mean by a multicultural education?

The term "multicultural education" has a lot of different meanings. The term I use most often is "anti-racist education."

Multicultural or anti-racist education is fundamentally a perspective. It's a point of view that cuts across all subject areas, and addresses the histories and experiences of people who have been left out of the curriculum. Its purpose is to help us deal equitably with all the cultural and racial differences that you find in the human family. It's also a perspective that allows us to get at explanations for why things are the way they are in terms of power relationships, in terms of equality issues.

So when I say multicultural or anti-racist education, I am talking about equipping students, parents, and teachers with the tools needed to combat racism and ethnic discrimination, and to find ways to build a society that includes all people on an equal footing.

It also has to do with how the school is run in terms of who gets to be involved with decisions. It has to do with parents and how their voices are heard or not heard. It has to do with who gets hired in the school.

If you don't take multicultural education or anti-racist education seriously, you are actually promoting a monocultural or racist education. There is no neutral ground on this issue.

Why do you use the term "anti-racist education" instead of "multicultural education?"

Partly because, in Canada, multicultural education often has come to mean something that is quite superficial: the dances, the dress, the dialect, the dinners. And it does so without focusing on what those expressions of culture mean: the values, the power relationships that shape the culture.

I also use the term anti-racist education because a lot of multicultural education hasn't looked at discrimination. It has the view, "People are different

and isn't that nice," as opposed to looking at how some people's differences are looked upon as deficits and disadvantages. In anti-racist education, we attempt to look at—and change—those things in school and society that prevent some differences from being valued.

Oftentimes, whatever is white is treated as normal. So when teachers choose literature that they say will deal with a universal theme or story, like childhood, all the people in the stories are of European origin; it's basically white culture and civilization. That culture is different from others, but it doesn't get named as different. It gets named as normal.

Anti-racist education helps us move that European perspective over to the side to make room for other cultural perspectives that must be included.

What are some ways your perspective might manifest itself in a kindergarten classroom, for example?

It might manifest itself in something as basic as the kinds of toys and games that you select. If all the toys and games reflect the dominant culture and race and language, then that's what I call a monocultural classroom even if you have kids of different backgrounds in the class.

I have met some teachers who think that just because they have kids from different races and backgrounds, they have a multicultural classroom. Bodies of kids are not enough.

It also gets into issues such as what kind of pictures are up on the wall? What kinds of festivals are celebrated?

What are the rules and expectations in the classroom in terms of what kinds of language are acceptable? What kinds of interactions are encouraged? How` are the kids grouped? These are just some of the concrete ways in which a multicultural perspective affects a classroom.

How does one implement a multicultural or anti-racist education?

It usually happens in stages. Because there's a lot of resistance to change in schools, I don't think it's reasonable to expect to move straight from a monocultural school to a multiracial school.

First there is this surface stage in which people change a few expressions of culture in the school. They make welcome signs in several languages, and have a variety of foods and festivals. My problem is not that they start there. My concern is that they often stop there. Instead, what they have to do is move very quickly and steadily to transform the entire curriculum. For example, when we say classical music, whose classical music are we talking about? European? Japanese? And what items are on the tests? Whose culture do they reflect? Who is getting equal access to knowledge in the school? Whose perspective is heard, whose is ignored?

The second stage is transitional and involves creating units of study. Teachers might develop a unit on Native Americans, or Native Canadians, or people of African background. And they have a whole unit that they study from one period to the next. But it's a separate unit and what remains intact is the main curriculum, the main menu. One of the ways to assess multicultural education in your school is to look at the school organization. Look at how much time you spend on which subjects. When you are in the second stage you usually have a two- or three-week unit on a group of people or an area that's been omitted in the main curriculum.

You're moving into the next stage of structural change when you have elements of that unit integrated into existing units. Ultimately, what is at the center of the curriculum gets changed in its prominence. For example, civilizations. Instead of just talking about Western civilization, you begin to draw on what we need to know about India, Africa, China. We also begin to ask different questions about why and what we are doing. Whose interest is it in that we study what we study? Why is it that certain kinds of knowledge get hidden? In mathematics, instead of studying statistics with sports and weather numbers, why not look at employment in light of ethnicity?

Then there is the social change stage, when the curriculum helps lead to changes outside of the school. We actually go out and change the nature of the community we live in. For example, kids might become involved in how the media portray people, and start a letter-writing campaign about news that is negatively biased. Kids begin to see this as a responsibility that they have to change the world.

I think about a group of elementary school kids who wrote to the manager of the store about the kinds of games and dolls that they had. That's a long way from having some dinner and dances that represent an "exotic" form of life.

In essence, in anti-racist education we use knowledge to empower people and to change their lives.

Teachers have limited money to buy new materials. How can they begin to incorporate a multicultural education even if they don't have a lot of money?

We do need money and it is a pattern to underfund anti-racist initiatives so that they fail. We must push for funding for new resources because some of the information we have is downright inaccurate. But if you have a perspective, which is really a set of questions that you ask about your life, and you have the kids ask, then you can begin to fill in the gaps.

Columbus is a good example. It turns the whole story on its head when you have the children try to find out what the people who were on this continent might have been thinking and doing and feeling when they were being "discovered," tricked, robbed and murdered. You might not have that information on hand, because that kind of knowledge is deliberately suppressed. But if nothing else happens, at least you shift your teaching, to recognize the native peoples as human beings, to look at things from their view.

There are other things you can do without new resources. You can include, in a sensitive way, children's backgrounds and life experiences. One way is through interviews with parents and with community people, in which they can recount their own stories, especially their interactions with institutions like schools, hospitals and employment agencies. These are things that often don't get heard.

I've seen schools inviting grandparents who can tell stories about their own lives, and these stories get to be part of the curriculum later in the year. It allows excluded people, it allows humanity, back into the schools. One of the ways that discrimination works is that it treats some people's experiences, lives, and points of view as though they don't count, as though they are less valuable than other people's.

I know we need to look at materials. But we can also take some of the existing curriculum and ask kids questions about what is missing, and whose interest is being served when things are written in the way they are. Both teachers and students must alter that material.

How can a teacher who knows little about multiculturalism be expected to teach multiculturally?

I think the teachers need to have the time and encouragement to do some reading, and to see the necessity to do so. A lot has been written about multiculturalism. It's not like there's no information. If you want to get specific, a good place to start is back issues of the *Bulletin of the Council on Interracial Books for Children.*

You also have to look around at what people of color are saying about their lives, and draw from those sources. You can't truly teach this until you reeducate yourself from a multicultural perspective. But you can begin. It's an ongoing process.

Most of all, you have to get in touch with the fact that your current education has a cultural bias, that it is an exclusionary, racist bias, and that it needs to be purged. A lot of times people say, "I just need to learn more about those other groups." And I say, "No, you need to look at how the dominant culture and biases affect your view of non-dominant groups in society." You don't have to fill your head with little details about what other cultural groups eat and dance. You need to take a look at your culture, what your idea of normal is, and realize it is quite limited and is in fact just reflecting a particular experience. You have to realize that what you recognize as universal is, quite often, exclusionary. To be really universal, you must begin to learn what Africans, Asians, Latin Americans, the aboriginal peoples and all silenced groups of Americans have had to say about the topic.

How can one teach multiculturally without making white children feel guilty or threatened?

Perhaps a sense of being threatened or feeling guilty will occur. But I think it is possible to have kids move beyond that.

First of all, recognize that there have always been white people who have fought against racism and social injustice. White children can proudly identify with these people and join in that tradition of fighting for social justice.

Second, it is in their interest to be opening their minds and finding out how things really are. Otherwise, they will constantly have an incomplete picture of the human family.

The other thing is, if we don't make it clear that some people benefit from racism, then we are being dishonest. What we have to do is talk about how young people can use that from which they benefit to change the order of things so that more people will benefit.

If we say that we are all equally discriminated against on the basis of racism or sexism, that's not accurate. We don't need to be caught up in the guilt of our benefit, but should use our privilege to help change things.

I remember a teacher telling me last summer that after she listened to me on the issue of racism, she felt ashamed of who she was. And I remember wondering if her sense of self was founded on a sense of superiority. Because if that's true, then she is going to feel shaken. But if her sense of self is founded on working with people of different colors to change things, then there is no need to feel guilt or shame.

What are some things to look for in choosing good literature and resources?

I encourage people to look for the voice of people who are frequently silenced, people we haven't heard from: people of color, women, poor people, working-class people, people with disabilities, and gays and lesbians.

I also think that you look for materials that invite kids to seek explanations beyond the information that is before them, materials that give back to people the ideas they have developed, the music they have composed, and all those things which have been stolen from them and attributed to other folks. Jazz and rap music are two examples that come to mind.

I encourage teachers to select materials that reflect people who are try-ing and have tried to change things to bring dignity to their lives, for example Africans helping other Africans in the face of famine and war. This gives students a sense of empowerment and some strategies for making a difference in their lives. I encourage them to select materials that visually give a sense of the variety in the world.

Teachers also need to avoid materials that blame the victims of racism and other "isms."

In particular, I encourage them to look for materials that are relevant. And relevance has two points: not only where you are, but also where you want to go. In all of this we need to ask what's the purpose, what are we trying to teach, what are we trying to develop?

What can school districts do to further multicultural education?

Many teachers will not change curriculum if they have no administrative support. Sometimes, making these changes can be scary. You can have parents on your back and kids who can be resentful. You can be told you are making the curriculum too political.

What we are talking about here is pretty radical; multicultural education is about challenging the status quo and the basis of power. You need administrative support to do that.

In the final analysis, multicultural or anti-racist education is about allowing educators to do the things they have wanted to do in the name of their profession: to broaden the horizons of the young people they teach, to give them skills to change a world in which the color of a person's skin defines their opportunities, where some human beings are treated as if they are just junior children.

Maybe teachers don't have this big vision all the time. But I think those are the things that a democratic society is supposed to be about. ∎

My Hair Is Long

By Loyen Redhawk Gali

My hair is as long as a pony's tail
and as shiny as a river.
My skin is as brown as a bear
getting up in the sunlight.
My eyes are as big as berries
but as dark as buffalo hide.
My ears are like pears cut in half
ready to eat.
My heart is like the drum beat as
I dance in the arbor.
My hands are soft as a rabbit's fur
in the forest.
My legs are as long as a baby deer's legs
as they run along the edge of the river.
My stomach is as big as a buffalo's
as it grazes through the land.
My voice is like the scream of an eagle
but can be as quiet as a mouse.
When I laugh, it sounds like
a woodpecker getting some food.
And my smile is as big as a lake.

Loyen Redhawk Gali was 11 years old when she wrote this poem as a student in Oakland, California. (See p. 212 for lesson ideas.)

PART TWO

RETHINKING MY CLASSROOM

Theoretical recipes for changing the classroom are many; practical examples are few.

In this chapter, classroom teachers at various grade levels share their personal struggles to transform their teaching. They explain how they work with young people to confront and transcend key dilemmas such as tracking, student passivity, and social injustice.

Race and Respect Among Young Children

By Rita Tenorio

When Angela came to talk to me, she was close to tears. With a sympathetic "witness" on each side, she said, "Matt called me a name. I don't like it."

Matt was summoned for a quiet conference. "What did he call you?" I asked Angela. "Brownski," she said, "He's making fun of me."

Matt came to his own defense. "Well, I was just teasing," he said. "I mean, I wasn't talking about her color or anything."

Unfortunately, blond, blue-eyed Matt *was* talking about Angela's skin color. When he didn't get his way with the puzzle they were sharing, he used this seemingly innocent word as a put-down. He knew he'd get a reaction from Angela and counted on the power of his light skin to win the argument. He hadn't counted on Angela speaking out.

In more than 30 years of teaching I have learned that, contrary to what adults often believe, young children are not "colorblind." Instead, they have an unstated but nonetheless sophisticated understanding of issues of race and power. One of our most important roles as teachers, I believe, is to recognize racism's effect on children, address the issue directly, and give students the beginning skills and strategies they will need to combat racism in their lives.

In this instance I encouraged Angela to tell Matt why she was angry. I also reminded Matt of our classroom rules and our prohibition against name-calling and put-downs. Matt apologized,

Kindergartners at La Escuela Fratney.

both seemed satisfied, and they went back to their puzzle.

The issue was resolved—for the moment. Questions remained, however. Would Matt react differently the next time he wanted his way? Had Angela become more assertive in responding to insults? While I felt that Matt's put-down reflected a deeper problem, I had handled it the same way I would have handled any squabble. Most importantly, I hadn't resolved more fundamental questions: What

was my role in exploring these issues with young children? What should be my next step?

Dealing with issues of race is perhaps the most complicated problem I have encountered as a kindergarten teacher. For many years, the problem didn't seem to "exist," and was glossed over as part of the view that "all children are the same, black, white or brown." As I developed as a teacher and explored issues such as "whole language" and heterogeneous grouping, I've struggled to develop a better understanding of anti-racist teaching. Some of the factors that have been crucial in my development have been the support of my colleagues, a districtwide curriculum reform, and my involvement in a two-way bilingual school that embraces an anti-racist teaching philosophy.

As Janet Brown McCracken states in her book *Valuing Diversity*, "curriculum is what happens" in the classroom every day. What may seem innocent "pretend" play among young children is actually a rehearsal for later activities in life. Thus, I've learned to observe children's play and intervene when necessary to counteract discriminatory behaviors. Interactions where children put each other down or where children reflect the discrimination that is so prevalent in our world provide opportunities for strong lessons in counteracting stereotypes and racism. They are as much a part of the curriculum as teaching a science lesson or reading a story.

In the first year of my teaching I came across a quote that asked, "How much must a child trust himself, others, and the world in order to learn?" Throughout the years I've worked with children and their families, I've always felt that trust was a key component to success. The changes I've made in designing the curriculum in my class have deepened my respect for the notion of trust. I've come to understand that feeling "safe" in school includes the students knowing that the teacher understands and respects their experience and background.

The 'Best' Environment

As a kindergarten teacher I had been trained to provide a nurturing environment in my classroom. I wanted to provide a safe place where children could believe in themselves, become more independent and organized, plan and think through a task, and acquire the social skills needed for success in school.

As I began my career, I gathered ideas and activities; attended workshops on art, music, games, and stories; and planned a variety of lessons. I thought I was giving students the

> Dealing with issues of race is perhaps the most complicated problem I have encountered as a kindergarten teacher.

best curriculum possible. Even in those early years, multicultural education was part of this curriculum. Moving from holiday to holiday, we learned about cultures all over the world. I changed bulletin boards and literacy activities to correspond to the holidays, and proudly integrated the activities into our daily lessons. We learned about our "differences" and celebrated our "similarities." I insisted that "we can all live together" and forbade words or actions that would "hurt" anyone.

My message was that everyone would be treated fairly and equally in our classroom. I made sure we were all going to be the same.

It worked. At least I thought it worked.

My classroom was filled with active, playful, well-disciplined children. I held high expectations for all the children and by all obvious measures they were growing and learning in ways that pleased both me and their parents. Yet over the years I became uncomfortable with my approach.

Seeing the Flaws

In the late 1980s I, like many teachers, was influenced by the whole language philosophy and research on the benefits of heterogeneous groupings.

Whole language helped me understand that my curriculum, while framed in a multisensory approach that included both academics and play, lacked choices. My plan was just that, mine. The day's activities were only minimally influenced by my students' interests and talents. Further, writing was not an integral part of the literacy process. And while we had many fine children's books in the classroom, I was still locked into the district's basal reading program.

As I learned about heterogeneous grouping, I saw other flaws. I still had students "tracked" for math and reading instruction, with children grouped according to their skills. While all children improved, the "top" group got furthest ahead while the "low" group struggled.

Most importantly, even in my fair and "equal" classroom environment, I still had frustrating conflicts such as the one between Matt and Angela. Sometimes it centered around a verbal put-down, other times it involved body language; white or lighter-skinned children would get up and move if a brown Latino or African-American child sat next to them. Life on the playground could be even rougher, and certain students would be isolated or ridiculed if they were different.

Even the children's "make-believe" stories were at times defined by race. Comments like, "You can't be the queen; there are no black queens," caught me off guard. Equally disturbing, more often than not the children accepted these hierarchies without complaint.

While I knew that kindergarten children were too young to intellectually understand the complexities of issues such as racism or prejudice, their behaviors showed the influence of societal stereotypes and biases. Throughout my career, I have had children who vehemently believed that Indians all live in "teepees" or, even worse, that there were no more Indians "cause the cowboys killed them all."

I had wanted to believe that children arrived in kindergarten with an open mind on all subjects. But the reality is different. Children mirror the attitudes of society and of their families.

Researchers have found that between the ages of 2 and 5, children not only become aware of racial differences but begin to make judgments based on that awareness. Having watched on average over 5,000 hours of TV by age 5, it is no wonder that some children believe all Indians are dead. Television's influence is further compounded by the segregated lives many children lead prior to coming to school.

Taking the First Steps

I began to reshape my kindergarten to be less teacher-centered and more heterogeneously grouped. It felt good to get rid of the workbooks and replace them with quality literature and the children's own stories. I was particularly amazed at how much the children liked to write in their journals and how quickly they learned to read the familiar stories they helped to choose.

Issues of bias, the children's personal interactions, and multicultural education were more complicated. When it came to changing the curriculum and countering tracking, the key to success was reinforcing and building upon the knowledge students brought with them to school. Yet on issues of race, if I merely supported the children's natural "instincts" and knowledge, I would end up reinforcing stereotypes and prejudice. I wasn't sure how to resolve this contradiction. I only knew that the

transition in this area would not be so easy.

In the early childhood area where "color blindness" was the prevailing attitude, there were few resources for dealing with racism and bias. I did not have broad personal experience in dealing with these issues, especially in deciding what was appropriate for young children.

Many colleagues shared my concern as we, like others in urban districts in the late 1980s, struggled with system-wide curriculum reform. I found necessary support and ideas from networking with other teachers. Further, my individual transition was supported by systemwide changes as the Milwaukee Public Schools initiated a curriculum and adopted as their first of 10 goals

that "students will project anti-racist, anti-biased attitudes through their participation in a multilingual, multi-ethnic, culturally diverse curriculum."

Other developments helped spur my thinking. In a unique opportunity, I was part of the founding staff of a new two-way, English/Spanish bilingual school called La Escuela Fratney. The language component, while important in its own right, was part of a broader framework that had at its core a multicultural, "anti-racist" curriculum. We wanted our students to not only learn about the history and culture of the major ethnic groups, but to also understand racism's influence on all of us. Here was my chance to forge an entirely new kindergarten curriculum.

I found several important resources

Dealing with Prejudice

Do deal with the situation immediately.

Do confirm that the particular type of abuse is hurtful and harmful and will not be tolerated.

Do value the feelings of others by active, sensitive listening.

Do take steps to support the victim and enable him or her to develop a stronger sense of self.

Do take those involved aside to discuss the incident.

Do explain to students why such incidents occur and undertake ongoing, long-term (proactive) strategies with the class for combating stereotyping, prejudice, and negative attitudes to differences.

Do apply consequences to the attacker in accordance with the school rules, code of behavior, and race/ethnocultural relations policy.

Don't ignore it, let it pass unchallenged, or let intangible fears block your ability to act.

Don't overreact with another put-down of the offender.

Don't impose consequences before finding out exactly what happened from those involved.

Don't focus entirely on applying consequences to the offender while ignoring the feelings of the victim.

Don't embarrass either party publicly.

Don't assume that the incident is an isolated occurrence divorced from the overall context in which it occurred.

Don't humiliate the attacker when imposing consequences. Remember that the attacker may feel like a victim, too.

Reprinted from Unity in Diversity: A Curriculum Resource Guide for Ethnocultural Equity and Anti-racist Education, *Ontario Ministry of Education, April 1991.*

to help in this transition. One was the opportunity to work with Enid Lee, an African-Canadian educator who specializes in anti-racist education. Her insights helped me redefine multicultural education and try to incorporate an anti-racist perspective into every subject. Another valuable resource was *The Anti-Bias Curriculum* by Louise Derman-Sparks and the ABC Task Force, which includes not only curriculum ideas but also concrete examples of ways to deal with interactions among students.

Both Lee and *The Anti-Bias Curriculum* taught me an important lesson: It is not the awareness of racial and cultural differences that leads to prejudice and racism, but how people respond to those differences. I realized I needed to do two things. First, I had to immediately respond to unacceptable behavior by the children, such as racist put-downs or slurs. Second, I had to develop a curriculum that included anti-bias lessons that help students recognize and respond to stereotypes and prejudice.

Taking a Stance

My goal of an anti-bias curriculum was helped by our vision at Fratney, where we have adopted schoolwide themes that give teachers a chance to proactively address issues of race. For example, during the first theme ("We Respect Ourselves and Others") we strive to build the kindergarten community by learning about each other's lives and families. Our reading lessons include literature that reflects the culture and experience of the students. A favorite activity is making a big puzzle on which each piece has the name of a student and describes "something that I'm very good at." Because the makeup of our kindergarten population includes Latino, African-American and white children, the value of various cultures is underscored.

Together we define our classroom rules and discuss what "fairness" means to each of us. Playground problems become the topics for class discussions or role plays during which students hear from each other how they might more peacefully resolve their disputes. We learn about people who have worked for fairness and equality. We practice the use of I-messages to respond to name calling. A student might say, "I feel bad when you call me names so please stop," rather than responding with another put-down.

The other themes, "We Send Messages When We Communicate," "We Make a Difference on Planet Earth," and "We Share the Stories of the World," offer the same potential for development.

I find such an approach helps to increase children's awareness of themselves and of their peers. Much more difficult has been the process of immediately intervening when children are mean to each other or say stereotypical or inappropriate things. It's much easier to let a remark slide, rationalizing that the children don't really understand what they've said or that it might lead to a discussion with which we as teachers are not entirely comfortable. During the Gulf War, for instance, many students used very negative terms when referring to the Iraqis. Another year, certain children used the word "fag" as a deliberate put-down.

For me, some of the most "teachable moments" in multicultural/anti-racist teaching have come in responding to children's negative remarks. First, I put a stop to the behavior and make clear that it is inappropriate. Then I try to explain why it is inappropriate and acknowledge the "victim's" feelings.

Often the remark is unrelated to the conflict at hand, and I try to help the parties focus on the real problem. The child who told her classmate that "there are no black queens," for instance, needs to understand not only that her remark is incorrect, but also that she has insulted her friend. Next, she had to see the real issue was that she wanted to wear the rhinestone crown and sequin dress which were part of the playhouse scenario. Beyond that moment, it's good to have discussions of the queens throughout African history, perhaps using a piece of literature like *Mufaro's Beautiful Daughters*, by John Steptoe, or *Ashanti to Zulu*, by Margaret Musgrove.

Some of the stereotypes at Fratney are related to our two-way bilingual program and the fact that some students are hearing Spanish for the first time. For example, I remember when an English-speaking student named Sean referring to Miguel, a Spanish-speaking student, said, "I don't want to sit next to him. He talks funny."

One response might have been, "Miguel is very nice, Sean. In our room we take turns sitting next to all the kids." But such a response would not have addressed Sean's nervousness or curiosity about a different language. It may have merely caused Sean to be less verbal about his feelings while still avoiding Latino classmates. In my view, Sean's remark was really a question to the adults as he tried to understand and get used to an unfamiliar situation.

A more appropriate response might be, "Miguel doesn't talk funny, Sean. He's speaking Spanish like the other people in his family. You and I are speaking English. In our classroom, we'll be learning a lot about both languages. It's fine for you to ask questions about what Miguel is saying, or say that you don't understand. But it's not OK to say that he talks funny. That's a put-down to all of us who speak Spanish."

Another constant source of comments is skin color. A child may say, for instance, "Jonathan is too brown. I'm glad I'm lighter than him." One response from the teacher might be, "We're all the same. It doesn't matter what color you are." While meant to promote equality, it doesn't address the child's view that "being lighter is bet-

ter." In addition, it might send Jonathan a very negative message. Such a comment from a child indicates that they are quite aware that we are *not* all the same.

I've found it difficult to respond to these types of insults, particularly because a historical explanation of slavery and why society views light skin

> We must provide each of our children a world where they are truly valued.

more positively is inappropriate for this age. Yet it's important that the teacher intervene immediately to contradict the notion of "brown as bad." It's also appropriate to give Jonathan a chance to share his feelings. The teacher might use this incident as the basis for a unit of study about skin color and people's perceptions related to this issue.

Most important, dismissing or ignoring negative remarks confuses students and sends them the message that the teacher doesn't really believe their stated view that "everyone is equal."

The Journey Continues

My role as teacher continues to be one of providing that safe, nurturing environment and preparing students for their experiences ahead. I strive to move children from the extremes of, on one hand, being afraid to do much of anything, or, on the other, being completely impulsive in their behavior. I want them to view kindergarten as a place where they can take risks and feel success. All of this remains a challenge. And at times I'm discour-

aged by the enormous influence that the larger society has on their awareness and biases.

I know that I must also be willing to take risks and make mistakes. I must be open to the experiences of our children and their families. I must recognize and respond to the students' negative behaviors. It's a struggle, but I believe it's a worthwhile one. We must provide each of our children a world where they are truly valued.

Early childhood educators hold an incredible amount of influence over the minds of the children they teach. As the cliché goes, "All I really need to know I learned in kindergarten." For today's students, "all they need to know" goes beyond the traditional formula of playing fair and putting things back in their place. It includes developing the skills and strategies to counteract the racism in their lives. ∎

Rita Tenorio is an early childhood educator and a founding editor of Rethinking Schools *magazine. She is the administrator of La Escuela Fratney in Milwaukee.*

Holding Nyla

Lessons from an inclusion classroom

By Katie Kissinger

JAQUAN FLEMING, MENDOTA GRADE SCHOOL, MADISON, WIS.

Nyla came into our Head Start classroom wheeled by her special assistant and surrounded by three early intervention (EI) specialists. I could barely see her for the equipment, adults, and silence that encapsulated her.

Nyla had "severely involved" cerebral palsy. In addition to muscle dysfunction, she had orthopedic impairment, vision impairment, and was medically fragile. Her "feeding regimen" and "handling regimen" both involved technical training.

I was completely overwhelmed.

My Head Start class had just merged with the early intervention program. It was 1992, and we were embarking on our first experience with inclusion classrooms, and although Nyla's special assistant and her three EI specialists had all been through the necessary training, I was one of her classroom teachers and I was intimidated.

Realities of Inclusion

The model we developed for our newly formed Head Start service was to merge the traditional "handicapped preschool," which had been serving all

of the children ages 3 to 5 with disabilities, with typically developing low-income Head Start children, also ages 3 to 5.

The special education teachers and the early childhood teachers merged into a classroom team of four to plan for and address the needs of all the children.

I mostly loved the idea of inclusion. I had been struggling to teach about diversity and social justice in a northeastern corner of Oregon where there was almost no racial, linguistic, or economic status diversity. I thought including kids with disabilities in our classroom would help the preschoolers make meaningful connections with people who are different from them. I had no clue what we were getting into.

Facing Fears

After the second week of school, I have a tradition of spending the weekend thinking of each child in my class. I review what I learned about them, what I want to learn more about, and the ways I am beginning to feel connected to them. When I thought of Nyla, I drew a blank: a blank instead of a child with an emerging story, instead of a smile or a funny anecdote. I was surprised at myself, mad at myself, disappointed in myself. How could I have a child in my classroom for two weeks and not have one story or even an irritation to reflect on? What was this really about?

Then I had a memory. The summer I turned five, my family went on our annual family vacation to visit relatives in Colorado. We went to the nursing home to see my Great-Granddaddy Greenwell. We had on our church clothes. It was hot, and my brothers and I were grouchy about having to dress up.

Almost 50 years later, I can still remember the odor when we walked through the doors of the nursing home. We hovered in the hallway and eventually saw a nurse wheeling Great-Grandpa toward us. He was a tall man, more than six feet, but in the wheelchair, he looked old, very wrinkled, and very scary to me. And he smelled even worse than the hallway. As the only girl child in our family, I suddenly became the designated representative. "Go hug Great-Granddaddy Greenwell," someone said. I took one trembling step forward and then whirled around and ran toward the door.

Recalling that memory, it struck me: That was the only close encounter I had ever had with a person using a wheelchair in my entire life up to that point. I was avoiding Nyla because I was afraid. It may sound odd, but once I realized this, I knew what to do. I had faced fears before.

On Monday morning, I went into the classroom and told the early intervention team that I wanted to take both

> By facing my own fears and connecting with Nyla, I became a better role model for my students.

the handling and feeding trainings for Nyla's caregiving. I completed both of those, but I had serious doubts when they introduced the feeding topic by telling us how many children had died in feeding incidents the prior year. When I was approved for safe caregiving, I asked the specialists if I could get Nyla out of her wheelchair and hold her for circle time. They were hesitant because this was not standard practice but decided we could try it.

As soon as I had Nyla in my arms, my relationship with her began. From that day on, for circle time, Nyla was either in my arms or in her "corner chair," which put her on the same level as the other seated children.

As soon as I changed my behavior and began a relationship with Nyla, the other children began to see her as a classmate. I have never had a clearer lesson about the power of the teacher as a role model.

Our class talked often about all of Nyla's equipment. The kids were really interested in her wheelchair and all of the equipment she used. We all talked

together each time she used a different piece of equipment or if we were going to try to make her safe and comfortable on any of the traditional "toys" like the wagon and the wheelbarrow. And because holding her involved keeping her muscles supported, we looked at the ways her wheelchair and other pieces supported her muscles, including her footrest.

We began to address the ways her equipment got in the way of her connection to the other children. I started asking questions like, "Can't she be at the table with everyone else?" "Can't she stay in the room for this exercise and invite other kids to join her?" "Can't she ride in the wagon or wheelbarrow instead of the wheelchair when we play outside?"

Sometimes those questions led to my education about her fragile muscle system. Other times they led to the EI/special ed team's education about the value of Nyla's relationship to the other children or to play. These conversations and experiences transformed us all.

Questioning Injustice

After learning how to integrate Nyla and other special-needs children into the classroom community, we found that our inclusive classroom provided opportunities for students to question and address things that are unfair in the world.

For example, we ordered a set of rubber people dolls for children to play with in the dollhouse. We were all excited when we found the Lakeshore Learning Materials Company sold dolls that represented people with disabilities. When the toys arrived, we brought the boxes to circle time and opened them up together. Joshua unwrapped a man in a wheelchair. He exclaimed, "Here he is, the guy with the wheelchair just like Nyla's." Josh passed the doll around the circle and when Mikey got it, he said, "Wait a minute. There's a problem. This guy's feet don't reach the footrest on his wheelchair."

Sure enough, there was about a half-inch gap between the guy's feet and the footrests.

Another student said, "That would make his legs really tired, if they couldn't rest."

"What could we do about this problem? How could we make this work?" I asked.

"Let's look at Nyla's chair and see how it works first," said Mikey.

Then another child shouted, "What if we make a wood block to put in the hole between his feet and the foot rest?"

Several kids went scurrying over to the woodworking table and grabbed small scraps of wood. We were eventually able to craft a little wooden filler for the gap. The children were delighted with their invention and very pleased that the "guy" now could sit comfortably in his wheelchair.

I wanted to take things one step further, so the next day I asked the children, "Do you think we should tell the company about the problem we found with the guy's wheelchair?" They all agreed that we should. I set up our flip chart so I could write down their ideas. "What should we tell them?" I asked.

"Tell them it's stupid to make a chair that doesn't work," said Josh.

"Dear Mr. Lakeshore, that's a bad wheelchair you made," added another child.

"How about making better wheelchairs for kids to play with?" someone asked.

"We're not paying for this wheelchair because it's broke," Marisa declared.

Nyla was there in the circle, and although she did not have any formal expressive language at that point, she showed her excitement by squealing.

Eventually we wrote a letter to Lakeshore, saying we thought they made a mistake. We sent them a picture of our redesigned wheelchair and asked them if they knew how uncomfortable their wheelchair would be. We also said that we would not be buying more Lakeshore toys until they fixed this problem. We all went together to the post office to mail the letter, Nyla leading the way in her wheelchair with Mikey, the proud young engineer, helping to push her.

By the way, we never got a response from Lakeshore, but they have now fixed the gap problem with the wheelchairs.

Another day, our class started out on a field trip to the local feed store. It was a trip we had made the year before and loved. When we arrived, I had the horrifying realization that Nyla would not be able to visit the second floor, which had all the great farm tools. (This was part of our machines study.) I gathered up the children and said, "I just realized that I made a really big mistake. I forgot that this store does not have wheelchair access to the second floor."

I was going to ask the children what they thought we should do when one of the children interrupted me and said, "No, Katie. The store guy made a big mistake. He didn't think we would be friends with Nyla, but we are. And we're mad, because if she can't go, we're not going." Needless to say, we wrote another letter.

Nyla's Best Friend

In the process of developing the inclusion model, there was a great deal of questioning and, in some cases, trepidation on the part of parents. Nyla's mother, in particular, had expressed concerns about Nyla leaving the "handicapped preschool." She was used to working with the EI team and reluctant to have her daughter in a Head Start classroom. She wondered how Nyla's needs and safety could be ensured with so many other children in the classroom. And she wondered how Nyla's classmates would respond to her.

We were not always able to answer these questions to Nyla's mom's satisfaction. After about five months of indecision, she decided to pull Nyla out of the program. When we could not talk her out of her decision, I asked that we at least have a few days of closure and time for the children to say their good-byes. It was a very hard few days.

On the last afternoon, Nyla's mother came to pick her up and we were finishing our "good-bye circle," where the child who is leaving sits in the middle of the circle and we go around with each person taking a turn saying what they like about the person and what they will miss when they're gone. It is always both a heartwarming and heart-wrenching ceremony. This one was particularly wrenching.

Andy, a student who had overcome initial fear of Nyla's differences, got up from his seated space, knelt by Nyla and said, "Nyla, you are my best friend. I love you and I don't want you to go." I heard the classroom door close and when I looked up through my tears, I saw that Nyla's mom was gone. One of the other teachers came over to me and whispered, "She has changed her mind."

Later, Nyla's mom told me that in her wildest dreams, she had never believed that Nyla would have a best friend. And she was moved to see a whole classroom of children welcoming her daughter into their community.

I made important discoveries in those first years of working in an inclusion classroom. By facing my own fears and connecting with Nyla, I became a better role model for my students, who quickly grew to love and accept her. I realized that solidarity is something we can nurture from the youngest ages. ∎

Katie Kissinger is an early childhood education consultant and part-time college instructor. She lives in Boring, Ore.

Teaching for Social Justice
One teacher's journey

By Bob Peterson

It's November and a student brings in a flier about a canned food drive during the upcoming holiday season. The traditional teacher affirms the student's interest—"That's nice and I'm glad you care about other people"—but doesn't view the food drive as a potential classroom activity.

The progressive teacher sees the food drive as an opportunity to build on students' seemingly innate sympathy for the downtrodden, and, after a class discussion, has children bring in cans of food. They count them, categorize them, and write about how they feel.

The critical teacher does the same as the progressive teacher—but more. The teacher also uses the food drive as the basis for a discussion about poverty and hunger. How much poverty and hunger is there in our neighborhood? Our country? Our world? Why is there poverty and hunger? What is the role of the government in making sure people have enough to eat? Why isn't it doing more? What can we do in addition to giving some food?

Participating in a food drive isn't the litmus test of whether one is a critical teacher. But engaging children in reflective dialogue is.

Unfortunately, a lack of reflective dialogue is all too common in American schools. Less than 1 percent of instructional time in high school is devoted to discussion that requires reasoning or an opinion from students, according to researcher John Goodlad in his study of American schooling. A similar

Students in Bob Peterson's class at La Escuela Fratney.

SUSAN LINA RUGGLES

atmosphere dominates many elementary classrooms, where worksheets and mindless tasks fill up children's time.

Divisions between traditional, progressive, and critical teaching are often artificial and many teachers use techniques common to all three. As I attempt to improve my teaching and build what I call a "social justice classroom," however, I have found it essential to draw less on traditional methods and more on the other two.

What follows is an outline of lessons that I have learned as I have tried, sometimes more successfully than others, to incorporate my goal of critical/social justice teaching into my classroom practice over the past 25 years.

There are five characteristics that I think are essential to a critical/social justice classroom:

■ A curriculum grounded in the lives of our students.

■ Dialogue.

■ A questioning / problem-posing approach.

■ An emphasis on critiquing bias and attitudes.

■ The teaching of activism for social justice.

A well organized class based on collaboration and student participation is a prerequisite for such a program. I'd also like to add that such "characteristics" are actually goals—never quite reached by even the best teachers, but always sought by all good teachers.

Curriculum Grounded in the Lives of Our Students

A teacher cannot build a community of learners unless the lives of the students are an integral part of the curriculum. Children, of course, talk about their lives constantly. The challenge is for teachers to make connections between what the students talk about and the curriculum and broader society.

I start the year with a six-week unit on the children's families and backgrounds. To begin the unit I have students place their birthdates on the class timeline—which covers nearly 600 years (an inch representing a year), and which runs above the blackboard and stretches around two walls. Students write their names and birthdates on 3x5 cards and tie the cards with yarn to the hole in the timeline that corresponds to their year of birth. On the second day we place their parents' birthdates on the timeline, on the third day those of their grandparents or great-grandparents. Throughout the year, students add dates that come up in our study of history, literature, science, and current events. The timeline provides students with a visual representation of time, history, and sequence, while fostering the understanding that everything is interrelated.

The weekly writing homework assignment during this family background unit consists of children collecting information about their families—how they were named, stories of family trips, favorite jokes, an incident when they were young, a description of their neighborhood. Students share these writings with each other and at times with the whole class. They use these assignments as rough drafts for autobiographies which are eventually bound and published. The assignments also inspire classroom discussion and further study. For example, one of my students, Faviola Perez, wrote a poem about her neighborhood, which led to discussions about violence and what we might do about it. The poem goes:

My Street at Night

My mom says, "Time to go to bed."

The streets at night
are horrible
I can't sleep!
Cars are passing
making noise
sirens screaming
people fighting
suffering!
Suddenly the noise goes away
I go to sleep
I start dreaming
I dream about people
shaking hands
caring
caring about our planet
I wake up
and say
Will the world be
like this some day?

In the discussion that followed, many students shared similar fears and gave examples of how family members or friends had been victims of violence. Others offered ways to prevent violence.

"We shouldn't buy team jackets," said one student.

"The police should keep all the criminals in jail forever," was another suggestion. Needless to say, the students don't have a uniform response, and I use such comments to foster discussion. When necessary or appropriate, I also interject questions that might help the students deepen or reconsider their views. I also try to draw connections between such problems and conflicts that I witness daily in the class. When a student talks about a killing over a mundane argument or a piece of clothing, for instance, I ask how these differ from the conflicts in our school and on our playground, and how we might solve them.

Focusing on problems in writing and discussion acknowledges the seriousness of a child's problem; it also fosters community because the students recognize that we share common concerns. Ultimately, it can help students to re-examine some of their own attitudes that may in fact be a part, albeit small, of the problem.

Throughout the rest of the year I integrate an examination of children's lives and their community into all sections of the curriculum. In reading groups, children relate contemporary and classic children's books to their own lives. For example, I have students divide their paper vertically: On one side they copy an interesting sentence from a book they are reading; on the other side they write how that reminds them of something in their own lives. The students then share and discuss such reflections.

In math we learn percentages, fractions, graphing, and basic math through examining their own lives. For example, my 5th-grade class keeps logs of the time that they spend watching television, graph it, and analyze it in terms of fractions and percentages. As part of our school's nine-week theme called "We Send Messages When We Communicate," they surveyed all the classes in the school to see how many households had various communication equipment, from telephones to computers to VCRs.

Such activities are interesting and worthwhile but not necessarily critical. I thus tried to take the activity a step further—to help them question if watching television is always in their best interests. For instance, we found that some of our students could save over 1,000 hours a year by moderating their TV watching.

"I can't believe I waste so much time watching TV," one girl stated during a discussion.

"You're not wasting it," replied one boy. "You're learning what they want you to buy!" he said sarcastically.

Similar discussions helped children become more conscious of the impact of television and even led a few to reduce the hours they watched.

One problem, however, that I have encountered in "giving voice" to students is that the voices that dominate are sometimes those of the more aggressive boys or those students who are more academically skilled. I try to overcome this problem by using structures that encourage broader participation. During writing workshop, for example, I give timed "free writes" where children write about anything they want. Afterward they share their writing with another student of their choice. Students then nominate classmates to share with the entire class, which often has the effect of positive peer pressure on those who don't normally participate in class. By hearing their own voices, by having other students listen to what they have to say, children become more self-confident in expressing their own ideas, and feel more a part of the classroom community.

Dialogue

The basic premise of traditional teaching is that children come to school as empty vessels needing to be filled with information. "Knowledge" is something produced elsewhere, whether by the teacher or the textbook company, and then transferred to the student.

This approach dominates most schools. "Reform" usually means finding more effective ways for children to remember more "stuff" or more efficient ways to measure what "stuff" the students have memorized.

I agree that children need to know bunches of stuff. I cringe any time one of my 5th graders confuses a basic fact like the name of our city or country. But I also know that the vast bulk of stuff memorized by children in school is quickly forgotten, and that the empty vessel premise is largely responsible for the boring, lecture-based instruction that dominates too many classrooms.

The curricular stuff that I want the children to learn will be best remembered if it relates to what they already know, if they have some input into what stuff is actually studied, and if it is studied through activities rather than just listening.

To initiate dialogue I may use a song, poem, story, news article, photo, or cartoon. These dialogue triggers are useful for both classroom and small-group discussion. I often use them as starting points in social studies, writing, or math lessons. I have a song, word, poster, and quotation of the week which, whenever possible, are related to our curriculum topics.

For example, during the study of the American Underground Railroad, I used the song "New Underground Railroad," written by Gerry Tenney and sung by Holly Near and Ronnie Gilbert. The song compares the Underground Railroad in the United States to the movement to save Jews during World War II and to the sanctuary movement to help "illegal" Salvadoran refugees in the 1980s. My student from El Salvador connected immediately to the song. She explained to the class the problems of violence and poverty that her family had faced in El Salvador. This one song raised many more questions, for example: Why did the Nazis kill people? What is anti-Semitism? Who runs El Salvador? Why does the United States send guns to El Salvador? Why are people from El Salvador forced to come to the United States secretly?

Another trigger that I use is overhead transparencies made from provocative newspaper or magazine photographs. For example, for a poetry lesson during writing workshop, I used a *New York Times* photograph taken during a winter cold spell that showed piles of snow-covered blankets and cardboard on park benches near the White House. (See photo, p. 32.) Many students initially thought the piles were trash.

When I told them that they were homeless people who had been snowed upon while asleep, my students were angry. The discussion ranged from their own experiences seeing homeless people in the community to suggestions of what should be done by the president.

"That's not fair," one student responded.

"Clinton said he'd take care of the homeless people if he got elected and look what he's done," said a second student. "Nothing."

"I didn't vote for him," said a third. "Us kids never get to do anything, but I know that if we were in charge of the world we'd do a better job."

"Like what?" I asked.

"Well, on a day that cold he should have opened up the White House and let them in," responded one student. "If I were president, that's what I'd do."

One of my students, Jade Williams, later wrote a poem:

Homeless

I walk to the park
I see homeless people lying
on a bench I feel sad
to see people sleeping outside
nowhere to go I felt
to help them let them stay
in a hotel
give them things
until they get
a job and
a house to stay
and let them
pay me back
with their love

A Questioning/Problem-Posing Approach

Lucy Calkins, director of the Teachers College Reading and Writing Project, argues that teachers must allow student viewpoints to be part of the curriculum. "We can't give children rich lives, but we can give them the lens to appreciate the richness that is already there in their lives," she writes in her book, *Living Between the Lines*.

But even that approach is not enough. We should also help students to probe the ways their lives are both connected to and limited by society. This is best done if students and teachers jointly pose substantive, challenging questions for the class to try to answer.

Any time a student poses a particularly thoughtful or curious question in my class, we write it down in the spiral notebook labeled "Questions We Have" that hangs on the board in front of the room. Not every question is investigated and thoroughly discussed, but even the posing of the question helps students to consider alternative ways of looking at an issue.

In a reading-group discussion, for example, the question arose of how it must have felt for fugitive slaves and free African Americans to fear walking down the street in the North during the time of slavery. One student said, "I sort of know how they must have felt." Others immediately doubted her statement, but then she explained.

"The slaves, especially fugitive slaves, weren't free because they couldn't walk the streets without fear of the slave masters, but today are we free?" she asked. "Because we can't walk the streets without fear of gangs, violence, crazy people, drunks, and drive-bys."

In reading groups a common assignment is to pose questions from the literature that we read. For example, while reading *Sidewalk Story* by Sharon Bell Mathis, a children's novel in which the main protagonist, a young girl, struggles to keep her best friend from being evicted, my students posed questions about the ethics of eviction, failure to pay rent, homelessness, discrimination, and the value of material possessions over friendship.

"Is it better to have friends or money?" a student asked, which formed the basis of a lengthy discussion.

Other questions that students have raised in our "Questions We Have" book include: Who tells the television what to put on? Why do geese fly together in an angle? Did ministers or priests have slaves? How many presidents owned slaves? Why haven't we had a woman president? How do horses sweat? If we are free, why do we have to come to school? When did photography start? Who invented slavery? Why are people homeless? What runs faster, a cheetah or an ostrich? Did any adults die in the 1913 massacre of 73 children in Calumet County, Michigan? (in reference to the Woody Guthrie song about a tragedy that grew out of a labor struggle).

Some questions are answered by students working together using reference materials in the classroom or school library. (Cheetahs can run up to 65 miles an hour while ostriches run only 40 mph.) Other questions are subjects of group discussion; still others we work on in small groups. For example, the question "What is the difference between the master/slave relationship and parent/child relationship?" developed one afternoon when a child complained that his parent wouldn't allow him out in the evening for school story hour. A girl responded that we might as well all be slaves, and a third student posed the question. After a brief group discussion, I had children work in groups of three or four and they continued the debate. They made two lists, one of similarities and one of differences, between the master/slave relationship and the parent/child relationship. They discussed the question in the small groups, then a spokesperson from each group reported to the class.

The fascinating thing was not only the information that I found about their lives, but also how it forced children to reflect on what we had been studying in our unit on slavery and the Underground Railroad. When one student said, "Yeah, it's different because masters whipped slaves and my mom doesn't whip me," another student responded by saying, "All masters didn't whip their slaves."

When another student said that their mothers love them and masters didn't love their slaves, another girl gave the example of the slave character Izzie in the movie *Half Free, Half Slave* that we watched, in which Izzie got special privileges because she was the master's girlfriend. Another girl responded that that wasn't an example of love; she was just being used.

In this discussion, students pooled their information and generated their own understanding of history, challenging crude generalizations typical of children this age. It was clear to all that the treatment of slaves was unjust. Not so clear was to what extent and how children should be disciplined by their parents. "That's abuse!" one student remarked after hearing about how one child was punished.

"No, it's not. That's how my mom treats me whenever I do something bad," responded another.

While no "answers" were found, the posing of this question by a student, and my facilitating its discussion, added both to kids' understanding of history and to their sense of the complexity of evaluating what is fair and just in contemporary society.

It's important that children see themselves as actors in the world, not just things acted upon.

Homeless people sleep under blanket-covered park benches across the street from the White House. Teachers can use news photos such as this to spark discussion about contemporary social issues.

Emphasis on Critiquing Bias

Raising questions about bias in ideas and materials—from children's books to school texts, fairy tales, news reports, song lyrics, and cartoons—is another key component of a social justice classroom. I tell my 5th graders it's important to examine "the messages that are trying to take over your brain" and that it's up to them to sort out which ones they should believe and which ones promote fairness and justice.

To recognize that different perspectives exist in society is the first step toward critiquing materials and evaluating what perspectives they represent or leave out. Ultimately it helps children see that they, too, can have their own values and perspectives independent of what they last read or heard.

"Whose point of view are we hearing?" I ask.

One poem that is good to initiate such a discussion is Paul Fleischman's dialogue poem, "Honeybees," from *Joyful Noise: Poems for Two Voices*. (See p. 55.) The poem is read by two people, one describing the life of a bee from the perspective of a worker, and one from the perspective of a queen. Children love to perform the poem and often want to write their own. They begin to understand how to look at things from different perspectives. They also start to identify with certain perspectives.

After hearing the song of the week, "My Country 'Tis of Thy People You're Dying," by Buffy Sainte-Marie, one of my students wrote a dialogue poem between a Native American and a U.S. soldier about smallpox-infected blankets the U.S. government traded for land. In another instance, as part of a class activity when pairs of students were writing dialogue poems between a master and a slave, two girls wrote one between a field slave and a house slave, further deepening the class's understanding about the complexity of slavery. During writing workshop six weeks later, three boys decided to write a "Triple Dialogue Poem" that included the slave, a slave master, and an abolitionist.

Students also need to know that children's books and school textbooks contain biases and important omissions. I find the concept of "stereotypes" and "omission" important to enhance children's understanding of such biases.

For example, around Thanksgiving time I show my students an excellent filmstrip called "Unlearning Native American Stereotypes" produced by the Council on Interracial Books for Children. It's narrated by Native American children who visit a public library and become outraged at the various stereotypes of Indians in the books. One year after I showed this, my kids seemed particularly angry at what they had learned. They came the next day talking about how their siblings in first grade had come home with construction paper headdresses with feathers. "That's a stereotype," my kids proudly proclaimed. "What did you do about it?" I asked. "I ripped it up," "I slugged him," came the chorus of responses.

After further discussion, they decided there were more productive things they could do than to hit their siblings. They scoured the school library for books with Indian stereotypes and found few. So they decided to investigate the 1st-grade room. They found a picture of an Indian next to the letter I in the alphabet strip on the wall. They came back excited, declaring that they had "found a stereotype that everybody sees every day!" They decided they wanted to teach the 1st graders about stereotypes. I was skeptical, but agreed, and after much rehearsal they entered the 1st-grade classroom to give their lesson. Returning to my classroom, they expressed frustration that the 1st graders didn't listen as well as they had hoped, but nonetheless thought it had gone well. Later the two students, Paco Resendez and Faviola Alvarez, wrote in our school newspaper:

> We have been studying stereotypes of Native Americans. What is a stereotype? It's when somebody says something that's not true about another group of people. For example, it is a stereotype if you think all Indians wear feathers or say "How!" Or if you think that all girls are delicate. Why? Because some girls are strong.

The emphasis on critique is an excellent way to integrate math into social studies. Students, for example, can tally numbers of instances certain people, viewpoints, or groups are presented in a text or in mass media. One year my students compared the times famous women and famous men were mentioned in the 5th-grade history text. One reaction by a number of boys was that men were mentioned far more frequently because women must not have done much throughout history. To help facilitate the discussion, I provided background resources for the students, including biographies of famous women. This not only helped students better understand the nature of "omission," but also generated interest in reading biographies of women.

In another activity I had students tally the number of men and women by occupation as depicted in magazine and/or TV advertisements. By comparing their findings to the population as a whole, various forms of bias were uncovered. Another interesting activity is having students tally the number of biographies in the school library and analyze them by race, gender, and occupation.

One of my favorite activities involves comparing books. I stumbled on this activity one year when my class read a story about inventions in a reading textbook published by Scott Foresman. The story stated that the traffic light was invented by an anonymous policeman. Actually it was invented by the African-American scientist Garrett A. Morgan. I gave my students a short piece from an African-American history book and we compared it with the Scott Foresman book. We talked about which story we should believe and how one might verify which was accurate. After checking out another book about inventions, the students realized that the school text was wrong.

The Teaching of Activism for Social Justice

The underlying theme in my classroom is that the quest for social justice is a never-ending struggle in our nation and world; that the vast majority of people have benefited from this struggle; that we must understand this struggle; and that we must make decisions about whether to be involved in it.

I weave the various disciplines around this theme. When I read poetry and literature to the children, I often use books that raise issues about social justice and, when possible, in which the protagonists are young people working for social justice. In math, we will look at everything from the distribution of

Songs That Promote Justice

Following are a few of the songs that I use in my classroom.

"Bread and Roses," written by James Oppenheim, sung by Judy Collins.

"Dear Mr. President," Pink and the Indigo Girls.

"Deportee," Woody Guthrie.

"Don't Laugh at Me," Peter, Paul and Mary.

"Family Tree," Tom Chapin.

"1492," Nancy Schimmel.

"Garbage!" written by Bill Steele, sung by Pete Seeger.

"Have You Been to Jail for Justice," Peter, Paul and Mary.

"If It Were Up to Me," Cheryl Wheeler.

"The Letter," Ruben Blades.

"Lives in the Balance," Jackson Browne.

"Masters of War," Bob Dylan.

"Mr. Wendal," Arrested Development.

"My Country 'Tis of Thy People You're Dying," Buffy Sainte-Marie.

"New Underground Railroad," written by Gerry Tenney, sung by Holly Near and Ronnie Gilbert.

"1913 Massacre," written by Woody Guthrie, sung by Jack Elliott.

"Not in My Name," John McCutcheon.

"Sister Rosa," The Neville Brothers.

"There But for Fortune," Phil Ochs.

"Unite Children," The Children of Selma.

"Wearing of the Green," traditional Irish.

"Why?" Tracy Chapman.

"You Can Get It If You Really Want," Jimmy Cliff.

"Young and Positive," Sweet Honey in the Rock.

wealth in the world to the percentage of women in different occupations. The class songs and posters of the week also emphasize social struggles from around the world. I also have each student make what I call a "people's textbook"—a three-ring binder in which they put handouts and some of their own work, particularly interviews that they conducted. There are sections for geography, history, current events, songs, poetry, and mass media. I also have a gallery of freedom fighters on the wall—posters of people we have studied.

In addition to studying movements for social justice of the past, students discuss current problems and possible solutions. One way I do this is by having students role-play examples of discrimination and how they might respond.

I start with kids dramatizing historical incidents such as Sojourner Truth's successful attempt to integrate street cars in Washington, D.C., after the Civil War, and Rosa Parks' role in the Montgomery, Ala., bus boycott. We brainstorm contemporary problems where people might face discrimination, drawing on our current events studies and interviews children have done with family members and friends.

One day in the spring of 1993, my class was dramatizing contemporary examples. Working in small groups, the students were to choose a type of discrimination—such as not being allowed to rent a house because one receives welfare, or not getting a job because one is a woman—and develop a short dramatization. Afterward, the kids would lead a discussion about the type of discrimination they were acting out.

After a few dramatizations, it was Gilberto, Juan, and Carlos' turn. It was a housing discrimination example—but with a twist. Gilberto and Juan were acting the part of two gay men attempting to rent an apartment, and Carlos was the landlord who refused to rent to them. I was surprised, in part

because in previous brainstorming sessions on discrimination none of my students had mentioned discrimination against gay people. Further, as is often the case with 5th graders, in the past my students had shown they were prone to uncritically accept anti-gay slurs and stereotypes. But here were Gilberto, Juan, and Carlos transferring our class discussion of housing discrimination based on race to that of sexual orientation.

The dramatization caused an initial chorus of laughs and jeers. But the students also listened attentively. Afterward, I asked the class what type of discrimination had been modeled.

"Gayism," one student, Elvis, yelled.

It was a new word to me, but it got the point across. The class then went on to discuss "gayism." Most of the kids agreed that it was a form of discrimination. During the discussion, one student mentioned a gay rights march on Washington a week earlier. (Interestingly, Gilberto, Juan, and Carlos said they were unaware of the march.)

Elvis, who coined the term "gayism," then said: "Yeah, my cousin is one of those lesi… les…"

"Lesbians," I said.

"Yeah, lesbian," he said. He then added enthusiastically: "And she went to Washington to march for her rights."

"That's just like when Dr. King made his dream speech at the march in Washington," another student added.

Before long the class moved on to a new role play. But the "gayism" dramatization lingered in my memory.

One reason is that I was pleased that the class had been able to move beyond the typical discussions around gay issues—which had in the past seemed to center on my explaining why students shouldn't call each other "faggot." More fundamentally, however, the incident reminded me of the link between the classroom and society, not

only in terms of how society influences the children who are in our classrooms, but also in terms of how reform movements affect daily classroom life.

It's important not only to study these progressive social movements and to dramatize current social problems, but to encourage students to take thoughtful action. By doing this they see themselves as actors in the world, not just things to be acted upon.

One of the best ways to help students in this area is by example—to expose them to people in the community who are fighting for social justice. I regularly have social activists visit and talk with children in my classes. I also explain the activities that I'm personally involved in as an example of what might be done.

I tell students they can write letters, circulate petitions, and talk to other classes and children about their concerns. My students have gone with me to marches that demanded immigrant rights. Two of my students testified before the City Council, asking that a Jobs With Peace referendum be placed on the ballot. Another time students testified with parents in front of the City Council that special monies should be allocated to rebuild our school playground.

If we neglect to include an activist component in our curricula, we cut students off from the possibility of social change. We model apathy as a response to the world's problems.

Such apathy is not OK. At a time when cynicism and hopelessness increasingly dominate our youth, helping students understand the world and their relationship to it by encouraging social action may be one of the few antidotes. Schools are a prime place where this can take place. Teachers are a key element in it happening.■

Bob Peterson (REPMilw@aol.com) teaches 5th grade at La Escuela Fratney in Milwaukee and is an editor of Rethinking Schools *magazine.*

Forgiving My Father

By Justin Morris

I'd like to forgive you father,
but I don't know your heart.
Your face,
is it a mirror image of mine?

I'd like to forgive you father,
but I find your absence a fire
that your face might be able to extinguish.
I'd like to forgive you father, but my last name
isn't the same as yours
like it's supposed to be.
You rejected me, Dad,
but can I sympathize for your ignorance?
For all the birthdays
you didn't send me a card,
for the Christmases
when I'd wake up,
and you weren't sitting by the tree waiting for me.
What about the summer nights
where prospects of you began to fade?
Fade like you did seventeen years go.
Out of my life.

I'd like to forgive you father,
but I don't know you.
And for that
I hate you.

Justin Morris was a student at Jefferson High School in Portland, Ore., when he wrote this poem. (See p. 212 for teaching ideas.)

Playing with Gender
Lessons from an Early Childhood Center

By Ann Pelo

Three 4-year-old boys sat in a circle, each with a doll tucked under his shirt.

"It's time to have our babies!" Nicholas declared. One by one, the boys pulled their babies from their shirts and cradled them tenderly for a moment before they leaped into action, cutting the babies' umbilical cords, wrapping them snuggly in small cotton blankets, and holding their babies to their chests to nurse.

"You gotta feed your baby some milk," Jeremy instructed. "When your baby cries, that means he wants some milk."

"Or he might have a poopy diaper," Sam added. "Then you gotta change the diaper or the baby gets a rash."

"We're the dads of these babies," Nicholas said.

"But dads can't have babies," Sam objected. After a brief pause, he found a way to resolve the conundrum: "We're human sea horses!"

The boys tended to their babies gently and deliberately, alternating between nursing and diapering their newborns. Their game stretched until lunchtime, when they carefully tucked their babies into little improvised bassinets—dress-up clothes bundled into soft nests.

At the beginning of the school year, teachers at Hilltop Children's Center, the full-day childcare program where I work in Seattle, took up a research question: How are the children exploring and expressing their identities through their dramatic play?

This was the second year we had explored a year-long research question as a way to make our teaching more intellectually engaging for ourselves as well as for the children. Working with a research question helps us with detailed observation of children's play, and our observations are the foundation for our curriculum planning.

We chose the research question because we wanted to bring an intentional focus to our learning about anti-bias principles and practices. We'd said for a long time that anti-bias, culturally relevant practices were integral to our program. But we hadn't invested institutional energy to explore what this means or to reshape our pedagogy. The research question helped us do that.

Hilltop is located in an affluent Seattle neighborhood, and, with only a few exceptions, the staff and families are mainly white. They are also, for the most part, politically and socially liberal and highly educated. While many of the teachers live paycheck to paycheck, as most childcare workers do, the families at Hilltop are from upper-income brackets. With our research question, we began to look directly at the issues of culture and class that shape our program. We wanted to deepen our understanding of what it means to do anti-bias work in a privileged community.

When we began our work with the research question, our goal was to learn about how the children understand gender, race, class, and other core elements of cultural identity, so that we could either reinforce their

understandings or challenge them. We wanted to get better at responding to the subtle "teachable moments" that children create. And we wanted to plan curriculum that counters racist, sexist, and classist understandings. We didn't anticipate the ways our study would lead us right to the heart of anti-bias teaching and learning.

Our Research Begins

There are 55 preschool-aged children at Hilltop, in four classroom groupings of various sizes, each with two, three, or four teachers (we have 12 teachers in our preschool classrooms). Each team comes together for collaborative curriculum planning for an hour and a half once a week. As the mentor teacher at Hilltop, I facilitate each team's meetings. Teachers bring detailed notes about children's play and conversations to the team meetings. We study teachers' observations and ask ourselves the following questions: What questions are the children expressing in their play? What understandings or experiences are they drawing on? What theories are they testing? How does this present an opportunity for us to strengthen the values we want to pass on to the children?

From our study and reflection, we plan one or two concrete next steps the teachers will take in the classroom and in communications with the children's families. These steps are intended to extend, deepen, or challenge children's thinking about identity, difference, and issues of culture. These next steps, in turn, launch us into another round of observation and study.

Early in the year, Sandra brought to her team meeting the notes she'd made as Nicholas, Jeremy, and Sam played about birthing and caring for babies. As we looked beneath the surface details of the game, teachers began to tease out elements of identity and culture.

"Sam clearly understands that men don't birth babies, but he wanted to be in that 'maternal' role and found a way to do that by being a sea horse," Megan said.

"I was curious about why they wanted to play this game at all," Sandra added. The teachers shared hypotheses. One teacher pointed out that Sam's mom had recently had a baby: "Maybe this game is a way for Sam to stay connected to his mom." Another teacher called attention to the boys' knowledge of the tasks of caring for babies, and the mastery they demonstrated with diapers and nursing; clearly, they'd been watching adults take care of babies. A third teacher commented on Sam's leadership role in the game: "That's new for Sam, to give direction to a game. I see this game as a way for him to try on this new role, now that there are younger kids in the group and some of the older kids have gone on to

---

Trying to Be a Boy

Makely: "I'm trying hard to be a boy."

Megan: "Why?"

Makely: "They have cooler bikes."

Jamice: "They're stronger than us girls."

Makely: "No, actually girls can do more sooner than boys."

Jamice: "Well, they can pee standing up."

Makely: "But that's not why I want to be one. They get treated better! They get to watch more violent things like Pokemon and Yu-Gi-Oh. Plus their clothes are really cool—like I have old clothes from my brothers and they're so cool."

---

kindergarten."

I nudged the teachers to turn their attention back to the elements of gender identity in this game: "The boys acknowledged that men don't give birth or nurse babies, but they weren't willing to let go of the maternal role. Instead, they let go of being human and became sea horses, which allowed them to stay male and keep doing the maternal work that's associated with being female. They seem to be wrestling with how to be both male and maternal. What can we learn about their understandings of masculinity? Of moms and dads?"

I wanted to move us away from individualistic explanations. While these factors are important, they don't give us the full picture of children's identities. In our discussion about the three boys' play, I hoped to focus us on gender identity, through their internalized understandings of masculinity, caregiving work, and the distinctions between motherhood and fatherhood.

It took a lot of effort continually to refocus the discussion on the social and political contexts shaping this play—and my efforts weren't particularly successful. At the time, I attributed the struggle to the newness of our work with the research question; we were still training ourselves to look through the lens offered by the question. I expected

that this would soon become a regular, familiar practice. I underestimated the work we had in front of us.

Unexpected Challenges

Week by week, our teams' collections of observations expanded.

■ Three-year-old Claudia emphatically refused the role of princess in a game with three other girls. "I hate princesses, and that's why I'm a boy!" she exclaimed fiercely.

■ Two-year-old Juliet chose a mask to wear. It was a mask with long braids and with freckles. "This is a girl mask," she explained, "because it has freckles." She noticed the mask that Molly was wearing, a mask with short hair: "You look like a boy in that mask, Molly."

■ Matthew and Joshua, 4-year-old buddies, slipped capes over their shoulders. "We're rescue heroes and our job is to save babies who are in danger!" Joshua called out, as he and Matthew raced across the room.

■ Three-year-old Kathryn initiated a game with John. She draped a piece of silky fabric over his shoulders, shawl-like, exclaiming delightedly, "You're Cinderella!" Then she shifted the fabric onto his shoulders to be more like a cape: "Now you're the prince." Back and forth, from shawl to cape, Cinderella to prince, Kathryn transformed John again and again.

As fall slipped into winter, a couple things became increasingly apparent to me. Within the context of our research question, children's exploration of gender identity had become teachers' primary focus. When we launched our research question in the fall, we'd started out with a bigger frame. We naively expected that we'd be looking at race, class, and gender, all lumped together under the vague heading of "culture." As the fall progressed, our focus narrowed as gender became the lens through which we explored the idea of cultural identity.

Certainly, the children's play provided us with many opportunities to pay attention to gender. But, more significantly, gender was comfortable terrain for our staff of predominantly white women. We were familiar with considering the impact of sexism on our lives. We assumed that we shared values and goals about what we want children to learn about gender identity. Gender seemed a safe starting place for our staff as we stepped into more conscious and intentional anti-bias work.

The other striking aspect of our work with the research question was that, even within the fairly comfortable arena of gender identity exploration, teachers continued to struggle to stay focused on the social and political aspects of children's play. In their discussions about their observations, teachers emphasized children's individual developmental and family stories. For example, reflecting on Claudia's assertion that she hates princesses and that's why she's a boy, teachers made the following observations: "Claudia's mom is athletic and strong, and not very 'princessy.' Maybe she's trying to figure out how to be like her mom and she doesn't have words for that." "Claudia doesn't really like to play princess games. She's more interested in building and construction sorts of games."

I asked, "What if Claudia's comment isn't really about princesses at all? What if she's trying to find words for questions about what it means to be a girl or a boy? What if she's asking, 'To be a girl, do I have to wear dresses and play games about being rescued and feasting and dancing? If I don't do that stuff, does that make me a boy? What is possible for me as a girl?'"

With our research question we wanted to develop the habit of paying attention to the ways children's play reflects their understandings of their political and social contexts. We wanted to strengthen this practice in ourselves until it became as easy and instinctive for us as paying attention to children's individual circumstances like their family relationships, their play and learning styles, their skills with literacy or math. But this effort was much more difficult than we'd imagined.

Why was this so challenging?

Claiming Our Cultural Perspectives

Four months into our work with the research question, I experienced a dramatic moment of understanding. During one week's team meeting, Lisa brought an observation of 5-year-old Jamie's play with his younger friend, 3-year-old Laura:

Jamie ran to greet Laura at the door as soon as she arrived. He swept her into his arms, exclaiming, "Let's play baby and dad!" Laura grinned her agreement, and Jamie picked her up, carrying her to the drama area. As their game unfolded, Jamie told Laura what to do: "Now cry, baby." "Now go to sleep." "Now eat, baby." Laura cheerfully followed Jamie's directions. Jamie picked her up, set her down, rolled her over, changed her diaper, put her to bed, woke her up; Laura didn't move her body on her own, but

> We'd been paying attention to children's gender identities but we'd failed to acknowledge our own experiences, values, and tensions related to gender.

waited for Jamie to instruct her or physically to move her.

Lisa's co-teacher, Kirstin, had an immediate and strong reaction: "I see Jamie and Laura play this game just about every morning that they're both here, and I've been putting a stop to it. I tell Laura that she's a powerful girl, that she can move her own body. And I tell Jamie to let Laura walk, that he's not to carry her anymore."

Lisa quickly echoed Kirstin's passionate words: "I absolutely agree with your decision. This game really bugs me, and I'm not sure why—but I don't like it."

Jamie and Laura's baby game was in itself fairly innocuous in the context of our program; we tend to be quite comfortable with kids' physicality and with affectionate, informal touch between children. However, Lisa and Kirstin had stepped away from the usual perspectives that shape discussions at Hilltop about this sort of game. They began their conversation by focusing on aspects of Jamie's and Laura's personal circumstances: Jamie's much older than Laura, he's an only child and just beginning to develop the flexibility in his play that makes room for other children's contributions; Laura is young and is just beginning to move into collaborative play. But Kirstin and Lisa quickly left this terrain of individual psychology and circumstances and

stepped emphatically into the terrain of gender identity.

"As a woman, I hate seeing a girl being so passive," said Kirstin, startling me with the force behind her words.

"I see Jamie telling Laura what to do and even moving her body for her and all my protectiveness for Laura as a 16-year-old girl on a date comes out," Lisa continued. "I want Laura to tell Jamie, 'No!' and I want Jamie to hear it!"

Lisa and Kirstin were responding to the children's play as women, reflecting on Jamie and Laura's play through their own experiences. They responded to their students' play with their hearts as well as from a more considered, measured place of intellectual reflection.

As I listened to Kirstin and Lisa talk, I experienced a sudden clarifying of what we'd been working with (and against) all fall. We'd been paying attention to children's gender identities but not paying attention to our own understandings and identities. We'd failed genuinely to acknowledge our own lenses, our own experiences, values, questions, and tensions related to gender. In order to see children as cultural beings, we must see ourselves as cultural beings, and we hadn't tended to that work.

We weren't asking central questions of ourselves: What does each of us know about gender? How have we each experienced the meaning and impact of gender in our lives? What values and goals do we each hold for children's learning about gender identity? With the research question, we'd challenged ourselves to pay attention to gender identity as the children experience and understand it. Now, we needed to investigate the ways in which we adults express and explore our gender identities.

I brought this new awareness to Claudia's teachers, eager to examine her comments about hating princesses and being a boy through the lens of the teachers' experiences of gender. "We've been trying to understand what's going on for Claudia," I said. "But we haven't talked about what each of us has experienced about gender. I think that could help us understand Claudia's experience. When you think about Claudia rejecting princesses and claiming to be a boy, do you see any connection to what you've experienced in your life?"

Sandra started talking before I finished my question: "Yes! When I was a little girl, growing up with two sisters, I knew early on that I wasn't like them. It wasn't about being lesbian or straight or anything like that, but I knew I didn't like to play dolls and dress up like they did. I wanted to be outside riding my bike or playing tag."

Sonja nodded in eager understanding. "I remember really clearly my feeling of relief when I learned the word 'tomboy.' There was a word to describe how I was in the world! There were other people like me!"

Megan listened intently, adding, "I think of 'tomboy' as a little insulting. Why do girls who are athletic have to be called anything other than girls? Why some cute word that refers to boys?"

We talked for a while about how our early experiences shaped who we

are now, as teachers and as women. We considered the ways these early experiences could help us understand Claudia's comment.

"It helps me think about Claudia being like I was as a kid," said Sandra. "She's not necessarily trying to figure out if she's a girl or a boy, but what it means to be someone who's not a girlie girl. Maybe the only language she has for 'not a girlie girl' is 'boy.'"

"When I remember my own girlhood, trying to reconcile what I felt excited by and what I knew I was supposed to be excited by as a girl, it helps me think about Claudia," said Sonja.

"I wonder if Claudia knows the word 'tomboy'?" I asked. "I wonder what it would mean to her to hear your stories about growing up as girls."

The teachers made plans to share their stories with Claudia and the rest of the group, as well as to bring in photos of themselves from childhood soccer games and tree-climbing adventures. Their planning was anchored by an explicit awareness of their political and social experiences and perspectives, and by their goals for children. These teachers, all of whom are female, knew how it feels to be a girl growing up in a sexist culture, and they wanted to support Claudia as she claimed her identity as a girl who rejects princess play and embraces full-bodied adventure.

Our Journey Continues

All four preschool teaching teams come together for a two-hour meeting once a month for reflection and study. At the full-staff meeting after my conversations with Kirstin and Lisa, and Sonja, Sandra, and Megan, I shared my new awareness and questions.

"I've noticed that, in our team meeting discussions about our research question, we've struggled to stay connected to the political and social contexts of children's play," I said. "We're really good at seeing kids as individuals with individual life stories, but we're not as good at seeing them as political, cultural beings. When we fail to recognize children's social identities, we erase fundamental aspects of who they are and who their families are. And when we fail to give voice to our cultural identities or to acknowledge our co-teachers' cultural perspectives, we erase fundamental aspects of ourselves," I added.

I posed several questions for discussion during our full-staff meeting:

■ Why is it an effort for us at Hilltop to address the political and social context that shapes children's identities?

■ What are the societal values and belief systems that focus us on individual circumstances rather than broader cultural identities?

■ What do we gain when we emphasize political and social identity—both the children's and our own?

The discussion that unfolded was rich with insight and with contradiction.

Lisa described her sense of not wanting to emphasize what could divide people: "I want to bring us closer together, not make us feel different and separated."

Susan said, "Our society's storyline is that we achieve or fail as individuals. When we emphasize being women, or people of color, or white, we either are held back or we get unfair advantages—according to society's storyline."

"We haven't had to look at these issues as teachers at Hilltop because of our cultural privilege on many fronts," I added. "It's an aspect of white privilege not to think about race, for example. We need to keep asking ourselves: How have we each experienced the meaning and impact of gender—or race, or class—in our lives? What values and goals do we each hold for children's learning?"

During the rest of that staff meeting, we took the first steps toward explicitly naming the cultural lenses that shape how each of us experiences our teaching and learning. First, Lisa and Kirstin recapped our discussion about Jamie and Laura's game. And Sonja, Sandra, and Megan told the story of their conversation about Claudia and tomboys. Then, we practiced doing what these teachers had done, acknowledging our cultural perspectives as we studied children's play. Teachers worked in small groups with one of several observations of children's play that I provided. A typical example focused on a conversation I'd overheard among several children as they tried to figure out why their buddy (a girl) had commented that "she's trying hard to be a boy."

I asked teachers to read and talk about each observation "not as teachers trying to understand the children's points of view, but as who you are: a lesbian, or a person from a working-class background, or a Filipina, or a European American, or a woman." I posed several questions to guide their discussion of the observation:

■ What caught your attention right away? What was your first reaction or judgment?

■ What experiences in your life are you tapping into?

■ What values come to the surface for you? Can you trace those values back to their roots in the political and social context of your life?

With this activity, I introduced what I hoped would become a regular element in our team meetings: I wanted us to make explicit the social and political contexts and assumptions that shape our thinking and planning as teachers, so that we bring clarity and awareness to our planning for the children's learning. I wanted us to acknowledge and claim our work as political work—seeing teaching as not only about supporting children's individual development and learning, but also about cultivating particular values and practices that counter oppression and enhance justice.

This staff meeting launched us into a new stage of our journey. Our practice with the research question unearthed our collective discomfort with talking about culture—and talking about culture is essential if we are to take up the work of anti-bias, culturally relevant teaching and learning. Probably at the beginning of the year we could have said that we needed to examine our own political and social identities at the same time as we pay attention to children's political and social identities. But without our observations of the children's interactions and our deeply felt reactions, our inquiry would have remained abstract.

For too long, our anti-bias efforts at Hilltop were standard-issue: brown play dough, books with characters from a range of families, dolls with different skin colors. The new work we're aiming to do is much less comfortable and easy; it makes us squirm and stammer and get angry and defensive to look at the ways in which our cultural privileges have been knit together to form the fabric of our program.

As we continue to do this work, we expect to look more closely at race, building on our work last year around gender. And we've added a step to our curriculum planning process. This year, in addition to reflecting on the possible meanings of the children's play, we've committed to considering the personal social-political experiences and identities that we bring to our observations before we begin planning next steps and curriculum investigations to take up with the children. Our encounter with the research question is slowly, surely transforming our practice. ■

Ann Pelo teaches at Hilltop Children's Center in Seattle. With Fran Davidson, she authored That's Not Fair: A Teacher's Guide to Activism with Young Children *(Redleaf Press, 2000).*

The Challenge of Classroom Discipline

By Bob Peterson

One of the most challenging tasks in any elementary classroom is to build a community where students respect one another and value learning. Too often, children use put-downs to communicate, resolve conflicts violently, and have negative attitudes toward school and learning. These problems often are based in society. How can one tell students not to use put-downs, for example, when that is the predominant style of comedy on prime-time television?

But schools often contribute to such problems. Approaches based on lecturing by teachers, passive reading of textbooks, and "fill-in-the-blank" worksheets keep students from making decisions, from becoming actively involved in their learning, and from learning how to think and communicate effectively.

Involving Students in Decision-Making

If a teacher wants to build a community of learners, a number of things have to happen. Students need to be involved in making decisions. They need to work regularly in groups. They need a challenging curriculum that involves not only listening but actually doing. They need to understand that it is OK to make mistakes, that learning involves more than getting the "right" answer.

At the same time, teachers need to make sure that students are not set up for failure. Teachers need to model

Student involvement is key to a successful class.

what it means to work independently and in groups so that those who have not learned that outside of school will not be disadvantaged. Teachers need to be clear about what is and what is not within the purview of student decision-making. And teachers need to learn to build schoolwide support for this kind of learning and teaching.

The parameters of students' decision-making range from choosing what they write, read, and study, to deciding the nature of their collaborative projects, to helping establish the classroom's rules and curriculum.

Each year I have students discuss their vision of an ideal classroom and the rules necessary in such a classroom. I explain how certain rules are made by the state government, by the school board, by the school itself, and by the classroom teacher. I let kids know that

I will be willing to negotiate certain rules, but that my willingness to agree to their proposals (because ultimately I hold authority in the classroom) is dependent on two things: the soundness of their ideas and their ability as a group to show that they are responsible enough to assume decision-making power. I also tell kids that if they disagree with rules made outside of the classroom, they should voice their concerns.

Things don't always go smoothly. One year while discussing school rules the kids were adamant that anybody who broke a rule should sit in a corner with a dunce cap on his or her head. I refused on the grounds that it was humiliating. Eventually we worked out other consequences including time-outs and loss of the privilege to come to the classroom during lunch recess.

The cooperative learning technique of the "T-Chart" is helpful in getting kids to understand what a community of learners looks like during different activities. The teacher draws a big "T" on the board and titles the left side "looks like" and the right side "sounds like." Kids brainstorm what an outside visitor would see and hear during certain activities. For example, when we make a "T-chart" about how to conduct a class discussion, students list things like "one person talking" under "sounds like" and "kids looking at the speaker" and "children with their hands raised" under "looks like." We hang the T-chart on the wall; this helps most children remember what is appropriate behavior for different activities.

Classroom organization is another essential ingredient in building a community of learners. The desks in my class are in five groups of six each, which serve as "base groups." I divide the students into these base groups every nine weeks, taking into account language dominance, race, gender, and special needs, creating heteroge-

neous groups to guard against those subtle forms of elementary school "tracking."

Dividing Students into Base Groups

Throughout the day children might work in a variety of cooperative learning groups, but their base group remains the same. Each group has its own bookshelf where materials are kept and homework turned in. Each group elects its own captain who makes sure that materials are in order and that his or her group members are "with the program." For example, before writing workshop, captains distribute writing folders to all students and make sure that everyone is prepared with a sharpened pencil.

Sometimes the group that is the best prepared to start a new activity, for example, will be allowed to help in dramatization or be the class helpers for that lesson. This provides incentive for team captains to get even the most recalcitrant students to join in with classroom activities.

By organizing the students this way, many of the management tasks are taken on by the students, creating a sense of collective responsibility. Arranging the students in these base groups has the added advantage of freeing up classroom space for dramatizations or classroom meetings where kids sit on the floor.

When students use their decision-making power unwisely, I quickly restrict that power. During reading time, for example, students are often allowed to choose their own groups and books. Most work earnestly, reading cooperatively, and writing regularly in their reading response journals. If a reading group has trouble settling down, I intervene rapidly and give increasingly restrictive options to the students. Other students who work successfully in reading groups model

how a reading group should be run: The students not only conduct a discussion in front of the class, but plan in advance for a student to be inattentive and show how a student discussion leader might respond.

A well-organized class that is respectful and involves the students in some decision-making is a prerequisite for successful learning. Cooperative organization and student involvement alone won't make a class critical or even build a community of learners, but they are essential building blocks in its foundation.■

Bob Peterson (REPMilw@aol.com) teaches 5th grade at La Escuela Fratney in Milwaukee and is an editor of Rethinking Schools *magazine.*

Helping Students Deal with Anger

By Kelley Dawson Salas

"Let me go! LET ME GO!!!" Michael's screams fill the entire second floor hallway. I imagine the noise bolting like lightning down the stairway, forcing its way through the double doors at the bottom, and arriving abruptly in the principal's office.

Arms flail and a fist connects with my teaching partner's ribs. I speak in what I hope is a soothing voice, although I know it is tinged with tension: "Michael, it's gonna be OK. As soon as you settle down we can let you go."

By the time Michael is allowed to bring his hoarse voice and his 3rd-grade body back into our classroom the next morning, I have decided that I need to teach my young students some strategies for dealing with anger.

Earlier in the year, after Michael's first few outbursts, I had sought help for Michael from people outside of our classroom. I was in my first year of teaching, learning what kids were all about for the very first time. I was going to school twice a week to meet the requirements of my alternative certification program. I simply didn't feel I had the time or the experience to help Michael respond to his emotions more appropriately.

"What can we do to find out what is behind Michael's angry behaviors? Can he receive counseling from the social worker or psychologist?" I asked our Collaborative Support Team. Michael did see the psychologist a few times after that. Both the social worker and I made calls to the family. But the flare-ups continued, and I was not the only person to notice. More than once, the students saw Michael fly into a tantrum. They saw how he put his head down on his desk and covered it up with his coat from time to time. They took a step backwards as he pushed a chair out of the way or hit another student on the playground and called it an accident. They had seen me give him a choice of "cooling down" and getting back to work or leaving the classroom.

Other staff also were aware of Michael. One day, I heard a specialist who had stepped in to supervise my students say, "We have to be real careful of Michael when he comes back to the classroom. We don't know what he'll do, do we?"

I didn't like the sound of that. I, the teacher, was Anglo, almost all of the students were Latino, and Michael was one of three African-American boys. I did not want our classroom to be a place where students or staff were allowed to reinforce stereotypes that link anger with boys and men, especially African-American boys and men.

In fact, Michael was normally an outgoing, upbeat kid who was well-liked by his classmates and teachers. But the emotionally charged interactions that took place fairly regularly in our classroom indicated that something needed to change. As I tried to help Michael through a long process of learning how to identify his feelings and emotions and respond constructively, I also went through an important learning process.

I taught about anger during these moments, I would only be singling Michael out and escalating the problem. The rest of the students would pick up on my cue and would probably label him as an angry person. I might send an incorrect message that the only people who feel angry are those who act out the way Michael did.

Instead, I tried to plan a few simple lessons that would help all students consider what anger is, what other emotions or experiences it is linked to, and how we can respond. Over the course of the next four weeks, I developed and taught four short lessons. I drew upon my own personal experiences with anger and tantrums to put the lessons together. The resources I used were minimal. I am sure there are much more extensive curricula on this topic. The important thing for me and my students was that these lessons helped us create a common framework for thinking about anger. Later I would refer to this framework in crisis moments or in interventions with Michael.

I wanted my students to be able to identify the experiences and emotions that lead to what might be described as angry behaviors. I wanted them to recognize different responses to anger that they and others use. Most important, I wanted students to consider the choices we have for responding to strong emotions such as anger. I wanted them to recognize that when we are upset, we can either choose a course of action that is unsafe or

unhealthy for ourselves and others, or we can choose a course of action that is safe and healthy. I hoped this discussion would lead students not only to see that it is unacceptable to allow anger and strong emotions to explode in outbursts, but also to identify and practice safe responses when they feel angry.

I led three discussions with my students. First, we made a list of "things that make us angry." Students cited a great many sources of anger, from the trivial to the unjust. Some of their responses: "I get mad when I can't find the remote;" "when people treat me like I'm stupid;" "when we lose part of our recess;" and "when my mom hits me."

Second, we made a list of "things people do when they're mad." I encouraged the students to share examples of things they personally do when they're mad, and allowed them to share things they'd seen other people do. Many student responses were negative, hurtful or unsafe, such as: "I punch the nearest person;" "hurt myself;" "bang my own head against the wall;" "kick or slam a door as hard as I can;" and "yell at the person who's making me mad."

A couple of students offered what I would categorize as "safe" responses to anger: "I go for a bike ride to blow off steam;" "I go in my room and read until I'm not mad anymore;" "I talk to my mom about what's making me mad." I asked the students, "Can you think of any other things like that, things that would help you to cool down or solve the problem?"

They suggested a few more: "You could talk to an adult you trust;" "go for a walk or go outside and play;" "tell the person who's making you mad how you feel."

Finally, we made a large poster to hang in the classroom that showed different responses to anger. The students each made their own copy of the poster

I wanted my students to be able to identify the experiences and emotions that lead to what might be described as angry behaviors.

Classroom Dynamics

I had to consider all the factors that contributed to our classroom dynamic. I had to examine my own beliefs, attitudes, and responses to Michael's behaviors. I had to consider how my actions as a white teacher of students of color affected Michael's emotions and responses. I had to try different approaches. These responsibilities weighed on me as I planned my course of action, and I continue to consider them as I reflect on what I did and what I might do differently next time. For example, at the time I characterized Michael's outbursts as anger. Whether that is the appropriate emotional term, I am not sure; perhaps he was expressing frustration, or loneliness, or pain. I realize, in retrospect, that I used the term "anger" to describe strong emotional outbursts that may have had their origin in any number of emotions.

Teaching about anger immediately after a conflict with Michael didn't make sense. All eyes were on him. If

for their own use. In the center, the question "What can you do when you feel angry?" prompted kids to remember the responses we had brainstormed in the previous activity. The top half of the poster was reserved for writing in safe or healthy responses to anger, while the bottom half was labeled "unsafe/scary." While completing this activity, we had a chance to discuss the idea that each person must make a choice when she is angry about what course of action she's going to take. I again reminded students that some responses to anger are safe and some are not.

Several complexities surfaced in our discussions. Michael, who in addition to his tantrums had also been known to crumple his papers in frustration or to put his head down and "drop out" during class time, asked about how to classify these kinds of actions. "Is it safe to crumple up your paper? You're not hurting anyone if you do that."

"Well, let's think about that one," I responded. "It might not be physically dangerous to anyone, but is it hurting you in any way? Does it hurt you when you put your head down for hours and decide not to learn or do your work?" My hope was that Michael would slowly come to realize that he was hurting himself with some of his behaviors.

Michael participated during these sessions just as any other student. I did not single him out or use him as an example; in fact, I tried hard not to allow myself or other students to refer to his behavior in our discussions. I did keep a close eye on him, and noticed that he participated actively. His brainstorming worksheets also gave me an idea of some things that made him angry, and some of his usual responses to anger at school and at home. This was important to my work with Michael because it allowed me to think about possible causes of his behaviors

without having to do it in a moment of crisis, and without making him feel like he was being singled out.

Looking back on these discussions, it seems necessary to discuss with students some of the complexities of responding to feelings of anger. Rather than just telling students to respond "safely" to a situation that makes them mad, they need to be taught to consider

for social justice, I use my anger at injustice to guide my own actions on a daily basis. Students can and should be aware that emotions often described as anger are not categorically "bad." Just as anger on an individual level can compel us to address a problem or make a change, the anger we feel when we witness injustice on a societal level should guide us toward changing unjust and

> I allowed my teaching to take a brief detour in pursuit of an answer to the students' important question: How and when can we hold adults responsible for their angry behaviors?

the source of their anger and to develop a response that is not only safe but also effective. Routine bickering with a sibling might be effectively solved by some time apart, while a series of name-calling incidents or physical bullying by a classmate will not be resolved just by walking away one more time. Students should be encouraged to see the difference between a response which simply helps them blow off steam, and one that actively seeks to address the cause of their anger and solve the problem.

Our discussions around anger focused mostly on interpersonal relationships, and sought to understand what an individual can do when he or she feels angry. Looking back at this focus on individual interactions, I see that I missed an opportunity to guide students in an inquiry into other types of anger. I think it is important to help students understand that anger exists not only on an individual level, but can be related to societal issues of oppression and injustice.

This in turn could lead to a discussion of the role anger can play in the fight for social justice. As an activist

oppressive systems. Rosa Parks comes quickly to mind as an example any 3rd grader can understand.

Adult Behavior

It was during our talks about anger that students' questions provided a springboard to an additional discussion that could have turned into a whole unit of its own. As we looked together at the abundance of unsafe or violent responses to anger, a few students began to ask, "If we're not supposed to throw tantrums, why do so many adults do it?"

They're right, I thought. How can I tell them that they should choose safe responses to anger when so many adults choose verbal outbursts or even physical violence? I allowed my teaching to take a brief detour in pursuit of an answer to the students' important question: How and when can we hold adults responsible for their angry behaviors?

I designed a lesson in which I talked about my own experiences with adults and anger, and shared a poem about a parent's angry outbursts. Together we discussed a few key concepts about adult anger and tantrums. We discussed the fact that adults, just like kids, must make choices about how to act when they are angry. Some adults make poor choices, I said. I also wanted to make sure that my students didn't internalize feelings of guilt over an adult's anger, as if they were somehow to blame for the outburst. I pointed out that it is not a child's fault if an adult they know responds to anger in a way that hurts others. I referred back to a previous unit we had done on human rights and asserted that as human beings, we have a right to live free from the threat of angry outbursts and violence. We agreed that it is important for us to talk with someone we trust if someone is threatening that right. Adults can change their behaviors, and may need help to do so.

These affirmations provided a very basic introduction which could have easily turned into a much more profound examination of anger and violence in families—our discussion only scratched the surface.

I did not assume or suspect that Michael was dealing with anger or violence in his own family. Rather, I planned this lesson in order to address the students' concerns and to give students a clear message that adults are responsible for making safe choices when faced with anger. By helping students see the connection between their responses to anger and adults' responses, I tried to encourage them to understand that each of us has a lifelong responsibility to resolve anger appropriately and safely. It is not appropriate to use our feelings as an excuse to lash out at others.

The school year went on. Michael did not miraculously change overnight, but he did make some changes, and so did I. In situations where he resorted to angry behaviors, we had a language in which to talk about his feelings and

his choices for responding to them. I also had developed more sensible and effective strategies for helping Michael through tough times.

Later in the year when Michael was angry, he was no longer as likely to say to me: "Look what you made me do." He knew I would respond by saying, "You choose what you do." Many times, I said to him, "It's clear to me that you're feeling frustrated or angry. Are you choosing to deal with your feelings in a safe way?" Things got easier. The cooling down periods got shorter. He seemed to be taking more responsibility for his actions and developing some strategies for what to do when he felt frustrated or angry.

For my part, I tried to become more flexible and to stop trying to force Michael to respond exactly as I wanted him to when he felt angry. I gave him more time to cool down. I always tried to get to what triggered his discontent and to acknowledge his feelings. Perhaps most important, I learned not to touch Michael while he was angry, or to try to move him physically. I had seen that that simply did not work.

Workable Solution

I was relieved that we had found a somewhat workable solution to Michael's behavior in our classroom. Part of me continued to wonder whether there were circumstances in Michael's life that were causing anger and frustration to build up. I kept working with his family and advocating with school support staff for additional help for him. I talked with Michael often about his feelings and tried to be alert to signs of a more serious problem without making unfounded assumptions.

Michael and I worked together for a year and I think each one of us made some progress. As I struggled to become an effective teacher in my first year on the job, I was willing to learn from anyone who wanted to teach.

Michael proved to have a lot of lessons in store for me. How little I would have learned had I simply written him off. For his part, Michael could have just as easily have turned his back on me. I am thankful to him for giving me a chance to be his teacher and to learn from him. ∎

Kelley Dawson Salas is a teacher at La Escuela Fratney in Milwaukee and an editor of Rethinking Schools *magazine.*

Building Community from Chaos

By Linda Christensen

Recently, I read a book on teaching that left me feeling desolate because the writer's vision of a joyful, productive classroom did not match the chaos I faced daily. My students straggled in, still munching on Popeye's chicken, wearing Walkmen, and generally acting surly because of some incident in the hall during break, a fight with their parents, a teacher, a boyfriend or girlfriend. This year, more than any previous year, they failed to finish the writing started in class or read the novel or story I assigned as homework. Many suffered from pains much bigger than I could deal with: homelessness, pregnancy, the death of a brother, sister, friend, cousin due to street violence, the nightly spatter of guns in their neighborhoods, the decay of a society.

For too many days during the first quarter, I felt like a prison guard trying to bring order and kindness to a classroom where students laughed over the beating of a man, made fun of a classmate who was going blind, and mimicked the way a Vietnamese girl spoke until they pushed her into silence.

Each September I have this optimistic misconception that I'm going to create a compassionate, warm, safe place for students in the first days of class because my recollection is based on the final quarter of the previous year. In the past, that atmosphere did emerge in a shorter time span. But the students were more homogeneous, and we were living in somewhat more secure and less violent times. While students shared the tragedies of divorce and loss of friendships, their class talk

DAVID MCLIMANS

was less often disrupted by the pressure cooker of society—and I was more naive and rarely explored those areas. We were polite to each other as we kept uncomfortable truths at bay.

Now, I realize that classroom community isn't always synonymous with warmth and harmony. Politeness is often a veneer mistaken for understanding, when in reality it masks uncovered territory, the unspeakable pit that we turn from because we know the anger and pain that dwells there. At Jefferson High School in Portland, Oregon, where the interplay of race, class and gender creates a constant background static, it's important to remind myself that real community is forged out of struggle. Students won't always agree on issues, and the fights, arguments,

tears, and anger are the crucible from which a real community grows.

Still, I hate discord. When I was growing up, I typically gave up the fight and agreed with my sister or mother so that a reconciliation could be reached. I can remember running to my "safe" spot under my father's overturned rowboat whenever anger ran loose in our house.

Too often these days I'm in the middle of that anger, and there's no safe spot. My first impulse is to make everyone sit down, be polite, and listen to each other, a great goal that I've come to realize doesn't happen easily. Topics like racism and homophobia are avoided in most classrooms, but they seethe like open wounds. When there is an opening for discussion, years of anger and pain surface. But students haven't been taught how to talk with each other about these painful matters.

I can't say that I've found definitive answers, but as the year ended, I knew some of the mistakes I made. I also found a few constants: To become a community, students must learn to live in someone else's skin, understand the parallels of hurt, struggle, and joy across class and culture lines, and work for change. For that to happen, students need more than an upbeat, supportive teacher; they need a curriculum that teaches them how to empathize with others.

Sharing Power and Passion

Before I could operate on that level, I had to find a way to connect with my students. Ironically, violence was the answer. This year none of the get-acquainted activities that I count on to build a sense of community worked in my fourth-block class. Students didn't want to get up and interview each other. They didn't want to write about their names. They didn't want to be in the class, and they didn't want any jive-ass let's-get-to-know-each-other games or activities. Mostly, our 90-minute blocks were painfully long as I failed daily to elicit much response other than groans, sleep, or anger. It's hard to build community when you feel like you're "hoisting elephants through mud" as my friend Carolyn says. I knew it was necessary to break through their apathy and uncover something that made these students care enough to talk, to read, to write, to share—even to get angry.

My fourth-block class first semester was Senior English, a tracked class where most of the students were short on credits to graduate—as TJ said, "We're not even on the five year plan"—but long on humor and potential. They came in with their fists up and their chins cocked. They had attitudes. Many of them already had histories with each other.

To complicate matters, our year opened with a storm of violence in the city. The brother of a Jefferson student

Building community begins when students get inside the lives of others.

was shot and killed. Two girls were injured when random bullets were fired on a bus. A birthday party at a local restaurant was broken up when gunfire sprayed the side of the restaurant. So violence was on the students' minds. I learned that I couldn't ignore the toll the outside world was taking on my students. Rather than pretending that I could close my door in the face of their mounting fears, I needed to use that information to reach them.

In the first days, the only activity that aroused interest was when they wrote about their history as English students—what they liked, what they hated, and what they wanted to learn this year. Many of these students skulked in the low track classes and they were angry—not at tracking, because they weren't aware that another kind of education might be possible, but at the way their time had been wasted on meaningless activity. "The teacher would put a word on the board and then make us see how many words we could make out of the letters. Now what does that prepare me for?" Larry asked. But they also hated reading novels and talking about them because novels "don't have anything to do with our lives." The other constant

in many of their written responses was that they felt stupid.

For the first time, they got excited. I knew what they didn't want: worksheets, sentence combining, reading novels and discussing them, writing about "stuff we don't care about." But I didn't know what to teach them. I needed to engage them because they were loud, unruly, and out of control otherwise. But how? I decided to try the "raise the expectations" approach and use a curriculum I designed for my Contemporary Literature and Society class which receives college credit.

During those initial days of listening to these seniors and trying to read the novel *Thousand Pieces of Gold*, by Ruthann Lum McCunn, I discovered that violence aroused my students. Students weren't thrilled with the book; in fact, they weren't reading it. I'd plan a 90-minute lesson around the reading and dialogue journal they were supposed to be keeping, but only a few students were prepared. Most didn't even attempt to lie about the fact that they weren't reading and clearly weren't planning on it.

In an attempt to get them involved in the novel, I read aloud an evocative passage about the unemployed peasants sweeping through the Chinese countryside pillaging, raping, and grabbing what was denied them through legal employment. Suddenly students saw their own lives reflected back at them through Chen, whose anger at losing his job and ultimately his family led him to become an outlaw. Chen created a new family with this group of bandits. Students could relate: Chen was a gang member. I had stumbled on a way to interest my class. The violence created a contact point between the literature and the students' lives.

This connection, this reverberation across cultures, time, and gender challenged the students' previous notion that reading and talking about novels didn't have relevance for them. They could empathize with the Chinese but also explore those issues in their own lives.

This connection also created space to unpack the assumption that all gangs are bad. Chen wasn't born violent. He didn't start out robbing and killing. Lalu, the novel's main character, remembered him as a kind man who bought her candy. He changed after he lost his job and his family starved.

Similarly, kids in gangs don't start out violent or necessarily join gangs to "pack gats" and shoot it out in drive-bys. Because the tendency in most schools is to simultaneously deny and outlaw the existence of gangs, kids rarely talk critically about them.

A few years ago, scholar Mike Davis wrote an article analyzing the upsurge of gang activity in L.A. He found it linked to the loss of union wage jobs. I hadn't explored Portland's history to know whether our situation is similar to L.A.'s, but I suspected economic parallels. When I raised Davis's research, kids were skeptical. They saw other factors: the twin needs of safety and belonging.

Our discussion of gangs broke the barrier. Students began writing about violence in their own lives and their neighborhoods. TJ explained his own brushes with violence:

[T]he summer between my sophomore and junior years, some of my friends were getting involved in a new gang called the Irish Mob. ... My friends were becoming somebody, someone who was known wherever they went. The somebody who I wanted to be. ... During the next couple of weeks we were involved in six fights, two stabbings, and one drive-by shooting. We got away on all nine cases. The next Saturday night my brother was shot in a drive-by. The shooters were caught the same night.

Kari wrote that she joined a gang when she was searching for family. Her father lost his job; her mother was forced to work two jobs to pay the rent. Kari assumed more responsibility at home: cooking dinner, putting younger brothers and sisters to bed, and cleaning. While at middle school,

> For too many
> days during the
> first quarter,
> I felt like a
> prison guard.

Kari joined the Crips. She said at first it was because she liked the "family" feel. They wore matching clothes. They shared a language and nicknames. In a neighborhood that had become increasingly violent, they offered her protection. She left the gang after middle school because she was uncomfortable with the violence.

Students were surprised to learn that Hua, a recent immigrant from Vietnam, was also worried about her brother who had joined a gang. Her classmates were forced to reevaluate their initial assessments of her. While she had seemed like an outsider, a foreigner, her story made a bond between them.

At first, I worried that inviting students to write about violence might glorify it. It didn't turn out that way. Students were generally adamant that they'd made poor choices when they were involved in violent activities. As TJ states in his essay, "I wanted to be known wherever I went. ... But I went about it all wrong and got mixed in. ... It was nothing I had hoped for. Sure I was known and all that, but for all the wrong reasons."

More often students shared their

fears. Violence was erupting around them and they felt out of control. They needed to share that fear.

Through the topic of violence I captured their interest, but I wanted them to critique the violence rather than just describe it. I had hoped to build a community of inquiry where we identified a common problem and worked to understand it by examining history and our lives. That didn't happen. It was still early in the year, and students were so absorbed in telling their stories and listening to others it was difficult to pull them far enough away to analyze the situation. I didn't have enough materials that went beyond accusations or sensationalism, but the topic itself also presented practical and ethical problems, especially around issues of safety and confidentiality.

I want to be clear: Bringing student issues into the room does not mean giving up teaching the core ideas and skills of the class; it means I need to use the energy of their connections to drive us through the content.

For example, students still had to write a literary essay. But they could use their lives as well as Lalu's to illustrate their points. Students scrutinized their issues through the lens of a larger vision as James did when he compared the violence in his life to the violence in Lalu's:

Lalu isn't a gang member, but some of the folks, or should I say, some of the enemies she came in contact with reminded me of my enemies. Bandits in the story represented the worst foes of my life. In some ways bandits and gangs are quite similar. One would be the reason for them turning to gang life. Neither of them had a choice. It was something forced upon them by either educational problems or financial difficulties. It could have been the fact that their families were corrupt or no love was shown. Whatever the reasons, it was a way of survival.

Finding the heartbeat of a class isn't always easy. I must know what's happening in the community and the lives of my students. If they're consumed by the violence in the neighborhood or the lack of money in their house, I'm more likely to succeed in teaching them if I intersect their preoccupation.

Building community means taking into account the needs of the members of that community. I can sit students in a circle, play getting-to-know-each-other games until the cows come home, but if what I am teaching in the class holds no interest for the students, I'm just holding them hostage until the bell rings.

A Curriculum of Empathy

As a critical teacher I encourage students to question everyday acts or ideas that they take for granted (see "Unlearning the Myths That Bind Us," p. 3 and "Teaching Standard English: Whose Standard?" p. 154). But I also teach them to enter the lives of characters in literature, history, or real life whom they might dismiss or misunderstand. I don't want their first reaction to difference to be laughter or withdrawal. I try to teach them how to empathize with people whose circumstances might differ from theirs. Empathy is key in community building.

I choose literature that intentionally makes students look beyond their own world. In the class I teach with Bill Bigelow, we used an excerpt from Ronald Takaki's *A Different Mirror* about Filipino writer Carlos Bulosan. Bulosan wrote, "I am an exile in America." He described the treatment he received, good and bad. He wrote of being cheated out of wages at a fish cannery in Alaska, being refused housing because he was Filipino, being tarred and feathered and driven from town.

We asked students to respond to the reading by keeping a dialogue journal. Dirk, who is African-American, wrote, "He's not the only one who feels like an exile in America. Some of us who were born here feel that way too." As he continued reading, he was surprised that some of the acts of violence Bulosan encountered were similar to those endured by African Americans. In his essay on immigration, he chose to write about the parallels between Bulosan's life and the experiences he's encountered:

> When I was growing up I thought African Americans were the only ones who went through oppression. In the reading, "In the Heart of Filipino America," I found that Filipinos had to go through a lot when coming to America. I can relate with the stuff they went through because my ancestors went through sort of the same thing.

Dirk went on to describe the parallels in housing discrimination, lynching, name calling, being cheated out of wages that both Filipinos and African Americans lived through.

Besides reading and studying about "others," we wanted students to come face to face with people they usually don't meet as a way of breaking down their preconceived ideas about people from other countries. For example, during this unit, we continued to hear students classify all Asians as "Chinese." In the halls, we heard students mimic the way Vietnamese students spoke. When writing about discrimination, another student confessed that she discriminated against the Mexican students at our school. Our students were paired with English-as-Second-Language students who had emigrated from another country—Vietnam, Laos, Cambodia, Eritrea, Mexico, Guatemala, Ghana. They interviewed their partner and wrote a profile of the stu-

dent to share in class. Students were moved by their partners' stories. One student whose brother had been killed at the beginning of the year was paired with a student whose sister was killed fighting in Eritrea. He connected to her loss and was amazed at her strength. Others were appalled at how these students had been mistreated at their school. Many students later used the lives of their partners in their essays on immigration.

Besides making immigration a contemporary rather than a historical topic, students heard the sorrow their fellow students felt at leaving "home." In our "curriculum of empathy," we forced our class to see these students as individuals rather than the ESL students or "Chinese" students, or an undifferentiated mass of Mexicans.

A curriculum of empathy puts students inside the lives of others. By writing, interior monologues (see "Promoting Social Imagination," p. 126), acting out improvisations, taking part in role plays (see "Role Plays: Show Don't Tell," p. 130), and creating fiction stories about historical events, students learn to develop understanding about people whose culture, race, gender, or sexual orientation differs from theirs.

"Things changed for me this year," Wesley wrote in his end-of-the-year evaluation. "I started respecting my peers. My attitude has changed against homosexuals and whites." Similarly, Tyrelle wrote, "I learned a lot about my own culture as an African American but also about other people's cultures. I never knew Asians suffered. When we wrote from different characters in movies and stories I learned how it felt to be like them."

Sharing Personal Stories

Building community begins when students get inside the lives of others in history, in literature, or down the hallway, but they also learn by exploring their own lives and coming to terms with the people they are "doing time" with in the classroom. Micere Mugo, a Kenyan poet, recently said, "Writing can be a lifeline, especially when your existence has been denied, especially when you have been left on the margins, especially when your life and process of growth have been subjected to attempts at strangulation." For many of our students their stories have been silenced in school. Their histories have been marginalized to make room for "important" people, their interests and worries passed over so I can teach Oregon history or *The Scarlet Letter*.

To develop empathy, students need to learn about each others' lives as well as reflect on their own. When they hear personal stories, classmates become real instead of cardboard stereotypes: rich white girl, basketball-addicted black boy, brainy Asian. Once they've seen how people can hurt, once they've shared pain and laughter, they can't so easily treat people as objects to be kicked or beaten or called names. When students' lives are taken off the margins, they don't feel the same need to put someone else down.

Any reading or history lesson offers myriad opportunities for this kind of activity. I find points of conflict, struggle, change, or joy and create an assignment to write about a parallel time in their lives. We've had students write about times they've been forced to move, been discriminated against or discriminated against someone else, changed an attitude or action, worked for change, lost a valuable possession. Obviously, losing a treasured item does not compare to the Native Americans' loss of their land, but telling the story does give students a chance to empathize with the loss as well as share a piece of themselves with the class.

When I was a child, my mother took me to the pond in Sequoia Park on Sundays to feed the ducks. They'd come in a great wash of wings and waves while I broke the bread into pieces to throw to them. I loved to watch them gobble up the soggy loaf, but I began noticing how some ducks took more than others. In fact, some ducks were pushed

> Given a chance, students will share amazing stories.

to the side and pecked at. I've noticed the same thing happens in classrooms. Students find someone who they think is weak and attack them. In my fourth-block class, the victim was Jim. He'd been in my class the year before. I'd watched him progress as a writer and thinker. In his end of the year evaluation, he drew a picture of himself as a chef; his writing was the dough. In an essay, he explained how writing was like making bread. He was proud of his achievements as a writer.

In both classes, Jim was a victim. He was going blind because of a hereditary disease. It didn't happen overnight, but he struggled with terror at his oncoming blindness. Because he was steadily losing his eyesight, he was clumsy in the classroom. He couldn't see where he was going. He knocked into people and desks. He accidently overturned piles of books. Students would respond with laughter or anger. Some days he cried silently into the fold of his arms. He told me, "I know the darkness is coming." Several male students in the class made fun of him for crying as well. One day, Amber was in a typically bad mood, hunched inside her too-big coat and snarling at anyone who came near. When Jim bumped her desk on the way to the pencil sharpener and her books and papers tumbled on the floor, she blew up at him for bumbling around the room. Jim apologized profusely and retreated into his shell after her attack.

A few days later I gave an assignment for students to write about their ancestors, their people. First, they read Margaret Walker's poems, "For My People" and "Lineage" and others. I told them they could imagine their people as their immediate ancestors, their race, their nationality or gender. Jim wrote:

To My People with Retinitis Pigmentosa

Sometimes I hate you
like the disease
I have been plagued with.
I despise the "sight" of you
seeing myself in your eyes.
I see you as if it were you
who intentionally
damned me to darkness.
I sometimes wish
I was not your brother;
that I could stop
the setting of the sun
and wash my hands of you forever
and never look back
except with pity,
but I cannot.
So I embrace you,
the sun continues to set
as I walk into darkness
holding your hand.

Students were silenced. Tears rolled. Kevin said, "Damn, man. That's hard." Amber apologized to Jim in front of the class. At the end of the year she told me that her encounter with Jim was one of the events that changed her. She learned to stop and think about why someone else might be doing what they're doing instead of immediately jumping to the conclusion that they were trying to annoy her.

My experience is that, given a chance, students will share amazing stories. Students have told me that my willingness to share stories about my life—my father's alcoholism, my family's lack of education, my poor test scores, and many others, opened the way for them to tell their stories. Students have written about rape, sexual abuse, divorce, drug and alcohol abuse. And through their sharing, they make openings to each other. Sometimes a small break. A crack. A passage from one world to the other. And these openings allow the class to become a community.

Students as Activists

Community is also created when students struggle together to achieve a common goal. Sometimes the opportunity spontaneously arises out of the conditions or content of the class, school, or community. During Bill's and my first year teaching together, we exchanged the large student desks in our room with another teacher's smaller desks without consulting our students. We had forty students in the class, and not all of the big desks fit in the circle. They staged a "stand in" until we returned the original desks. One year our students responded to a negative article in a local newspaper by organizing a march and rally to "tell the truth about Jefferson to the press." During the Columbus quincentenary, my students organized a teach-in about Columbus for classes at Jefferson. Of course, these "spontaneous" uprisings only work if teachers are willing to give over class time for the students to organize, and if they've highlighted times when people in history resisted injustice, making it clear that solidarity and courage are values to be prized in daily life, not just praised in the abstract and put on the shelf.

But most often I have to create situations for students to work outside of the classroom. I want them to connect ideas and action in tangible ways. Sometimes I do this by asking students to take what they have learned and create a project to teach at nearby elementary or middle schools. Students in Literature and U.S. History write children's books about Abolitionists, the Nez Perce, Chief Joseph, and others. After students critique the media (see "Unlearning the Myths That Bind Us," p. 3), they are usually upset by the negative messages children receive, so I have them write and illustrate books for elementary students. They brainstorm positive values they want children to receive, read traditional and contemporary children's books, critique the stories, and write their own. They develop lesson plans to go with their books. For example, before Bev read her book about John Brown she asked, "Has anyone here ever tried to change something you thought was wrong?" After students shared their experiences, she read her book. Students also created writing assignments to go with their books so they could model the writing process.

Students were nervous before their school visits. As they practiced lesson plans and received feedback from their peers, there was much laughter and anticipation. They mimicked "bad" students and asked improper questions that have nothing to do with the children's book: Is she your girlfriend? Why are your pants so baggy? Why does your hair look like that?

When they returned, there were stories to share: children who hugged their knees and begged them to come back; kids who wouldn't settle down; kids who said they couldn't write. My students proudly read the writings that came out of "their" class. They responded thoughtfully to each student's paper.

James, a member of my English 12 class, was concerned by the number of young children who join gangs. He and several other young men wrote stories about gang violence and took them to our neighborhood elementary school.

He strode into the class, wrote "gangs" in big letters on the board and sat down. The 5th-grade class was riveted. He and his teaching mates read their stories and then talked with students about gangs. As James wrote after his visit:

> For a grown person to teach a kid is one thing. But for a teenager like myself to teach young ones is another. Kids are highly influenced by peers close to their age or a little older. I'm closer to their age, so they listen to me. ... Some of these kids that I chatted with had stories that they had been wanting to get off their chest for a long time. ... When I came to class with my adventures of being a gangster, that gave them an opportunity to open up. Spill guts. [No one] should object to me teaching these shorties about gang life, telling them that it's not all fun and games. It's straight do or die. Kill or be killed.

The seriousness with which the students understand their lives was in sharp contrast to the seeming apathy they displayed at the year's beginning. Through the year, I came to understand that the key to reaching my students and building community was helping students excavate and reflect on their personal experiences, connecting it to the world of language, literature, and society. We moved from ideas to action, perhaps the most elusive objective in any classroom.

Community and activism: These are the goals in every course I teach. The steps we take to reach them are not often in a straight path. We stagger, sidestep, stumble, and then rise to stride ahead again. ■

Linda Christensen (LChrist@aol.com) is director of the Oregon Writing Project at Lewis and Clark College and is an editor of Rethinking Schools magazine.

Discipline: No Quick Fix

By Linda Christensen

Creating a climate of respect is easy to talk about and hard to practice. Ideally, we want a space where students listen respectfully and learn to care about each other. A sign in our hallway reads: No Racist or Sexist Remarks. I've often said, "I just don't tolerate that kind of behavior." But this year, it was like saying, "I don't tolerate ants." I have ants in my kitchen. I can spray chemicals on them and saturate the air with poison and "not tolerate" them, or I can find another solution that doesn't harm my family or pets in the process. If I just kick kids out of class, I "don't tolerate" their actions, but neither do I educate them or their classmates. And it works about as well as stamping out a few ants. I prepare them for repressive solutions where misbehavior is temporarily contained by an outside authority, not really addressed. Sometimes, I am forced to that position, but I try not to be.

Dealing with Name-Calling

One year, students in the class Bill Bigelow and I co-teach were often rude to each other. Their favorite put-down was "faggot." (This in a class where a young woman came out as a lesbian.) During the first weeks, several young women complained that they had been called names by boys in class. They felt the hostility and wanted to transfer out. They didn't feel comfortable sharing their work or even sitting in the class because they were pinched, hit, or called names when our backs were turned. As one of the main, but certainly not the only, instigators, Wesley

wrote in his end of the year evaluation, "I started the year off as I finished the last year: bad, wicked and obnoxious. I was getting kicked out of class and having meetings with the deans about my behavior every other day."

For critical teachers trying to build community, this creates a serious problem. Do we eliminate this student? When, after trying time-outs, calling his home, talking with his coach, and keeping him after class, we finally kicked him out—his friends said, "They're picking on him." Which wasn't true. But it set us up as the bad guys and divided us from the students we wanted to win over.

Increased police presence in the area has created situations where students gain honor by taunting the cops in front of peers. This carries over to class, where we represent the same white authority as the police until students get to know us. While Wesley was not skilled academically, in other respects he was brilliant. He was an artist at toeing the line technically and creating total chaos in the process. He'd raise his hand and make perfectly nice comments about someone's paper in such a way that the entire class knew he was mocking the whole procedure. Even with two of us in the classroom, he defeated us at every turn. Clearly, we were playing on his terrain, and he knew the game better than we did even if we'd taught longer than he'd been alive.

Here we were teaching about justice, tolerance, equality, and respect, and yet when we had a problem with a talented student who didn't want to go along,

DAVID MCLIMANS

we turned him over to the deans. Ultimately, what lesson does that teach our students? That we talk a good game, but when pushed, we respond like other traditional teachers? It's a complex issue. I don't want to keep the class from progressing because of one or two students, but I don't want to "give up" on students either. On bad days, I threw him out. On good days, I tried to look behind his behavior and figure out what motivated it.

Looking Beyond the Words

In teaching critical literacy, I tell students to look behind the words to discover what the text is really saying; in working with "problem" students in class, I need to look behind the students' behavior. What is motivating this? How can I get to the root of the problem? In my experience, the more negative students feel about themselves and their intellectual ability, the more cruel or withdrawn they are in the classroom.

Tyrelle, Wesley's classmate, wrote early in the year that he felt stupid. "My problem is I don't like to read out loud because I don't think the class would like it. Every time I try to write or do something my teachers told me that's stupid, you did it wrong, or you can't spell. My friends [who were classmates] say it too. I don't say anything. I just act like I don't hear it, but I really do."

One day I overheard his friends teasing him about his spelling. After class I talked with him about it. I arranged for him to come in so we could work privately and I would teach him how to write. Because so many of his friends were in the class, he was afraid to ask for help. His way of dealing with the problem was to close down—put his head on his desk and sleep—or make fun of people who were trying to do their work. This did not totally stop, but once he found a way into his writing he would usually settle down and work.

During the second semester he wrote, "You guys have helped me become a better person because you were always after me, 'Tyrelle, be quiet. Tyrelle, pay attention.' After a while I learned how to control myself when it was time to." He'd also learned to separate himself from his friends so he could work.

Wesley, who admitted to being "bad, wicked and obnoxious," was also a victim of poor skills and low academic self-esteem. He'd sneak in after school for help with his writing, or I'd go over the homework readings and teach him how to "talk back" to the author. Sometimes he'd call me at home when he was stuck. At the end of the year his mother said, "He told me that he didn't think he could write. Now he says he knows how." With both of these students, recognizing the cause of the behavior—

embarrassment over poor skills—and helping them achieve success helped to change their behavior. Once the withdrawn or antisocial actions stopped, they contributed to the community rather than sabotaging it. This was not

> Helping students achieve success helps to change their behavior.

a miraculous, overnight change. On some days, the behavior backslid to day one, but most times there was steady improvement.

I have yet to discover a quick fix for out of control behavior. I try calling my students' homes in September to establish contact and expectations. I usually ask, "Is there anything you can tell me that will help me teach your child more effectively?" Parents know their child's history in schools and can give important insights. When my daughter didn't turn in a project, her teacher called me. I discovered that her class had long term work that students needed to complete at home. I appreciated the call because Anna insisted that she didn't have homework. Her teacher made me realize how much parents need to hear from teachers—not only for keeping track of homework, but so we can work in tandem.

Often working with a coach or activities advisor helps because they've established strong one-on-one relationships. They also have access to an area where the student feels successful. One coach, for example, told me that "Jeremy" just realized that he would play high school ball, maybe college ball, but he'd never be pro. He'd turned

from gangs to sports in the 7th grade, and the vision that fueled him was the NBA. Suddenly, that dream came against reality. He practiced hours every day, but he knew he wouldn't make it. His attitude had been sour and nasty for weeks. He needed a new vision. This information helped me to understand Jeremy and allowed me to get out the college guide and talk about choices. His final essay was "Life After Sports."

Mostly, I call students at night and talk with them after the day is over, their friends are no longer around, and both of us have had a chance to cool down. Students joke about how they can't get away with anything because Bill and I call their homes. I overheard one student say, "Man, I got to go to class today otherwise they'll call my uncle tonight." Perhaps it's just letting them know we care enough to take our time outside of school that turns them around.■

Linda Christensen (LChrist@aol.com) is director of the Oregon Writing Project at Lewis and Clark College and is an editor of Rethinking Schools *magazine.*

Honeybees

By Paul Fleischman

The following is a dialogue poem, to be read by two people. The first person reads down the left column, the second person, down the right. Capitalized phrases are to be read in unison.

BEING A BEE	BEING A BEE
	is a joy.
is a pain.	
	I'm a queen
I'm a worker	
I'LL GLADLY EXPLAIN.	I'LL GLADLY EXPLAIN.
	Upon rising, I'm fed
	by my royal attendants,
I'm up at dawn, guarding	
the hive's narrow entrance	
	I'm bathed
then I take out	
the hive's morning trash	
	then I'm groomed.
then I put in an hour	
making wax,	
without two minutes' time	
to sit and relax.	
	The rest of my day
	is quite simply set forth:
Then I might collect nectar	
from the field	
three miles north	
	I lay eggs,

or perhaps I'm on
larva detail

                 by the hundred.

feeding the grubs
in their cells,
wishing that I were still
helpless and pale.

                 I'm loved and I'm lauded,
                 I'm outranked by none.

Then I pack combs with
pollen—not my idea of fun

                 When I've done
                 enough laying

Then, weary, I strive

                 I retire

to patch up any cracks
in the hive.

                 for the rest of the day.

Then I build some new cells,
slaving away at
enlarging this Hell,
dreading the sight
of another sunrise,
wondering why we don't
all unionize.

TRULY, A BEE'S IS THE
WORST
OF ALL LIVES.

                 TRULY, A BEE'S IS THE
                 BEST
                 OF ALL LIVES.

Paul Fleischman writes books for young children—prose and poetry. (See p. 212 for lesson ideas.)

Teaching About Global Warming in Truck Country

By Jana Dean

MICHAEL DUFFY

M s. Dean, are you trying to tell me I can't drive a truck?"

Alex, an 8th grader, leaned back until he was perched on two chair legs, his arms crossed defiantly. It was the end of a class period, the second day of our class's study of climate change. I knew Alex expected he'd someday drive a big truck like his father.

"Not necessarily," I answered, "but together we are going learn enough science to understand global warming. Then we'll do something about it."

Global warming is a subject most of us don't like to think about. Worst-case scenario: Ocean currents come to a rolling stop, resulting in a domino effect of chain reactions and a climate unlike anything in the collective memory of humanity. In other words, the ecosystem as we know it is a goner, and it isn't going to be pretty. Among the predictions are wars over water and total economic and social collapse.

What's creating this change? Measurable increases in gases such as meth-

ane and carbon dioxide that absorb and hold heat radiating from the surface of the earth. What's worse, the global thermal balance that drives ocean currents reacts gradually. We've only begun to see the impact of changes that occurred in the atmosphere years ago. We may not feel the real global impact of atmospheric change until it's too late.

In the unit I taught, I wanted my students to understand the physics and chemistry that explain the anthropogenic (human-produced) causes of climate change. I also hoped my students would reflect on their own lives and consider how their own behavior could change to become more "climate friendly." I entertained the possibility of a broader political response, but accepted at the outset that I might not have time to build enough background in global economics and trade to expose the politics behind global inaction as the earth heats up. As a science teacher operating within the constraints of a bell schedule, I decided to prioritize the science.

And I had another motive, which was embedded in my answer to Alex's challenge two days into our study: Together we would do something about global warming. I wanted my students to join together to create change. For them, uniting across socioeconomic, racial, and political differences can be uncomfortable territory. Yet that's just what needs to happen as humanity faces a global environmental crisis.

I teach in a public middle school on the edge of Washington State's capital city. While mostly white, my students are socioeconomically diverse. To the north, Tumwater's middle- and working-class neighborhoods of houses and apartments merge with the city of Olympia. To the south, junkyards and machine shops set among small industry and warehouses gradually fade into a rural mix of wood lots, farms, subdivisions, and trailer parks. Many students spend an hour on the bus getting to school in the morning. The homes they leave behind range from upscale new houses to trailer parks in some of the most underserved neighborhoods in the county. Our community offers few private schools, and the district has only two middle schools, both of which serve a similar mix of suburban and rural areas: We get the wealthy students along with the poor.

When I first moved here in 1989, logging trucks still rumbled in from

It is hard to imagine change when it disrupts your sense of identity.

the surrounding forests to dump logs by the millions at our port. Many of those trees were hauled out of the woods by the relatives of my students. Even though the economy has changed, a rural cultural relationship to the land remains intact. Most families still have plenty of practical uses for a truck. They cut and haul firewood. They pull stumps. They keep livestock. Even many families that don't actively use a truck for work choose to drive one because on weekends they haul and hunt. I teach in truck country.

As the daughter of a gas station owner, I have many stories about trucks and a father who always smelled of grease and gasoline. I learned to drive my father's Ford when I was still too small to shift it without using both hands. Many of my students and I have truck culture in common.

Jimmy comes to school a few times a month hobbled after trying to lift "a tranny with guts in it." Kylie drives her quad ATV into ditches. Justin stays home some school days to help his dad with the fifth-wheel trailer. I figured our knowledge of fossil-fuel-powered internal combustion engines would support us in understanding the causes of global warming.

But when Alex first crossed his arms, I began to realize that indicting our beloved motors for global warming before building a ton of background would be like petting a cat in the wrong direction. At the same time, it was a sign that I was going in the right direction: Change doesn't happen without resistance. As auto-dependent rural people, we love the ease, convenience, and speed of the open road. My upfront commitment to action had activated in my students a fear of losing a way of life they'd been raised to inherit. Alex's statement, echoed by many of his classmates—yeah, what about my quad, my motorcycle?—worried me, and I had to talk myself into pushing past the resistance. But I would have to proceed carefully since fearful people have a hard time thinking critically.

Carbon Dioxide Would Have to Wait

I decided to carefully sidestep any mention of the causes of global warming until we thoroughly understood the effects.

To get a handle on the effects, we did two projects using a curriculum developed by the Union of Concerned Scientists. (See resources, p. 61.) The first involved following links on a world map to learn about scientifically proven signs of rising temperatures. The map is based on measurable data and climate models that predict increased flooding, drought, heat waves, and wildfires, along with more catastrophic weather events. The second had students studying the transmission cycle of tropical diseases and their vectors.

We learned that changes in climate are severely affecting the polar regions. In many parts of the arctic, sea ice has decreased by 50 percent or more. For the first time, scientists have observed open water at the North Pole. The population of penguins in the Antarctic has declined by one third. Large sinkholes have developed in Alaska as permafrost melts and the ground collapses. Glacial ice in Olympic National Park will be gone by 2070 if it continues to melt at the current rate. In tropical Africa, rising temperatures and rainfall have both increased the range, severity, and frequency of tropical diseases such as malaria and schistosomiasis.

I asked students to write about what concerned them most about global warming. As they shared aloud, I wrote down their worries on poster paper hung at the front of the class. The mood was somber. My students sat so still and silent we could hear each other swallow.

I learned that Ryan, who lives for hunting season, worried about elk that will suffer from diminishing alpine environments. Brandon loves penguins and lamented the loss of sea ice. Other students cited enormous wildfires attributable to warmer and drier trends in some parts of the world. Many of them felt deep concern about the spread of malaria and other tropical diseases.

Whenever I bring my students' awareness to big problems, I worry I will overwhelm them and short-circuit their potential for critical thinking. I knew that we'd be more likely to be able to push through to more learning if we took the time to talk about how we feel: Acknowledging feelings opens the way for clear thinking. Otherwise emotions and thoughts get muddled up in each other. But in my experience, asking 8th graders to name their feelings can be like trying to get a stone to talk.

I asked the class, "How many of you have ever had a time when things were going wrong and you felt there was nothing you could do about it?" Nearly every hand went up. "Turn to your partner and tell them the story you're thinking of. If you don't have one yet, go second." The room hummed with the noise of storytelling.

After five minutes of talking, I directed everyone to write down the incidents they had shared, and then we read to the class what we had writ-

ten. Jimmy wrote, "On Sunday night I was walking a friend home. Right as we walked in her driveway the cops had their spotlight on us. I got a ride back to my cousin's house in a cop car. It sucked." Kylie described being stuck in a ditch on her quad and not being able to get out. Julie read about being lost on a city bus. Warren read about moving: "I feel overwhelmed every time I have to move from house to house." Our stories helped us to see that when faced with an out of control situation—like global warming—we will feel angry, overwhelmed, stuck, confused, trapped, and scared.

I told my students, "As we continue to learn about global warming, expect to feel all of those feelings. We'll be learning and feeling together. In many of your stories you were alone. In the global warming story, we'll have each other."

Arctic Meltdown

I thought that by then we might have been ready to look again at the causes of climate change. *Arctic Meltdown, Rising Seas* (See resources, p. 61.) features stories and interviews of indigenous people in Alaska and in the Marshall Islands who are suffering as ice melts and sea levels rise.

Before showing the video, I asked students to listen carefully to the narrative for "Changes on the Ice" and "Changes on the Beach" and to take notes.

The video opens with footage of people in Alaska meeting with a scientist: "Polar bears are thin and hungry. Walruses are fewer and fewer every year, and we depend on them for our food."

The video continues with interviews of a family from the Marshall Islands who almost lost a baby in a rogue wave that swept in at high tide. With that story, feelings ran high. The class was silent. Interviews with Marshallese sci-

entists reveal that erosion due to higher sea levels is taking away their land and their way of life. The film then bombards us with a message about our cars, our trucks, our factories, our consumption.

As he put his notebook away, Ron slammed it shut and said: "I don't get it. What are we gonna do? Stop driving?" Consternation ran through the class. "What about my quad … my motorcycle … how will we get to school … too far to ride my bike." I had no answer.

Even though I had previewed the film, and knew it would challenge their assumptions, I wasn't ready for the strength of their opposition. Students' responses reminded me of how much harder it is to imagine change when it disrupts your sense of identity. My students have grown up with the expectation that they will have the privilege of driving. They weren't ready to give up their dreams of the open road.

How could I teach about the fossil fuel causes of global warming and at the same time respect local identity? I knew from the outset that in proposing change I'd meet with resistance. I would have to proceed very carefully to build science background in a non-politicized manner. I decided to wait to thoroughly teach the causes of global warming until I could figure out how to do it effectively. At this point in our learning, the film was too confrontational for these heirs of truck culture.

During the next class I acknowledged that the film had made some students feel uncomfortable, and that some of them felt angry. I explained that understanding the message of the film would take more science background, and that I was ready to teach them that background so they could form a powerful reasoned opinion about the film's message.

We spent the next two weeks building science background. I demonstrated the expansion of water as it heats by placing a flask with a stopper and a pipette over a candle. With a 5-degree rise in temperature, the water in the pipette rose more than 1 inch. The molecules in a warm fluid move more energetically and therefore occupy more space if they can. This is a factor in rising sea levels. Warm water takes up more space than cold water.

I created convection currents with smoke in a fish tank. Following the directions in the sourcebook *Physics Is Fun* (See resources, p. 61.) I cut holes at either end of a plywood lid, filled the tank with smoke and then started the current by placing a lit candle under one hole.

On a global scale, such rising and falling air and water currents are responsible for our climate as we know it. We then modeled the greenhouse effect with plastic bottles set on a sunny windowsill. One bottle had large holes cut in the side and the other had small ones. The second bottle simulated an atmosphere with more heat-trapping gases.

Charting Our Stuff

Finally, I felt we had enough background to learn about the anthropogenic sources of greenhouse gases. One of the problems with greenhouse gases is that they are invisible. Unlike the particles in the wood smoke that wafts through our neighborhoods all winter, the gases can't be seen. I wanted my students to connect these unseen gases to things they could see.

I told students they now had enough background to understand the science behind some of the causes of global warming that the film had quickly introduced. I told them we'd be starting with things they knew well: everyday items. They would find out what it took to make them. "For example," I said, "the materials to create one piece of paper weigh 98 times the paper itself, and 95 percent of the energy to make

---

The Science Behind Climate Change

The science behind climate change isn't hard: Burn carbon-based fuels (virtually all fossil fuels are carbon-based) and you add heat-trapping carbon to the atmosphere. Create oxygen-free conditions for decomposition, such as those in the still water behind a dam or in a landfill, and methane results.

Since pre-industrial times, the concentration of CO_2 in our atmosphere has risen by about a third, from 280 parts per million (ppm) to 378 ppm. Methane has doubled its concentration from 0.78 ppm to 1.76 ppm. CO_2 and methane levels haven't been this high since the age of the dinosaurs. Current methane levels are the highest they've been in 420,000 years. The current concentration of CO_2 is the highest it's been in 20 million years.

---

an aluminum can is expended before the metal reaches the plant that makes the container."

I explained the assignment: "Pick a product and place it on the end of your roll of adding machine tape [that I'd distributed]. Then work together to brainstorm everything everyone in your group knows about what it takes to make that product. For each thing you can think of, make a labeled drawing. Trace what it takes for as long as you can, drawing arrows between each step."

Justin, Sarah and Angel worked on a poster together. Angel was bursting with questions.

"Ms. Dean, what does it take to make cans?" she asked.

"Electricity."

"Ms. Dean, where does electricity come from?"

"A dam, or a steam plant powered by coal."

"OK. A dam," she simplified. "What does it take to make a dam?"

"Concrete."

"What does it take to make concrete?"

"It comes from rock, which is mined."

She rushed back to her group, eager to have them include what she'd just learned on their chart. As soon as she

got them going, she was back at me, ready to take it further.

"What does it take to make a mine?"

"An excavator."

"What does it take to make an excavator?"

I don't like to spoon-feed students, even when they are excited about pursuing a topic. I realized that with this one, Justin probably knew more about excavators than I did. Justin's got a lot of big equipment in his life. He's quiet and often lets other people do the talking. Until then he'd been relying on Angel for the answers, so I told Angel, "Ask Justin. He knows better than I do."

Before they had finished, their chart included three different kinds of metal, hydraulic fluid, oil, and diesel. As they ran out of time, they'd moved on to the road it would take to drive the excavator to the mine and Justin was working on describing a grader to his group so they could figure out what it took to make one of those.

By the end of the day, the charts stretched for up to 20 feet around the room. They demonstrated how much we knew about the world around us and made visible a lot of the process behind manufacturing products. I told my students, "I think you now have enough background to really understand the sources of greenhouse gases that the video introduced."

I was right. They were ready. Students listened and took notes attentively as I gave a half-hour lecture on the sources of the most common greenhouse gases. I provided for students 15 anthropogenic sources of these gases, including the extraction and production of fossil fuels, deforestation, hydropower, and livestock digestion. Also included on the chart were landfills, which account for 10 percent of anthropogenic methane, and fossil-fuel combustion, which accounts for 75 percent of anthropogenic CO_2.

Together students brainstormed a list of every fossil fuel they could think of. By the end of the period they saw greenhouse gases everywhere—in tailpipes of tractors, in stockyards, in the power behind the pump, in oil wells, in the manufacturing of hydraulic fluid, in the coal that powered the cement kiln.

I wanted to see if my students could apply what they finally seemed so eager to learn. The next day, I challenged them: "Show me how much you understand about the causes of global warming by making one more poster. Pick any product you want and show at least three ways CO_2 or methane results from its production." I can rarely claim universal success, but this time, every student in my class was able to make the connections I was looking for.

Taking Action

I polled my students on what action they wanted to take to combat global warming. I had them consider five levels of action by finishing sentence stems that read: "I can … . My family can … . Our school can … . Our country can … . The world can … ." At the individual level, most of them said something about walking or riding their bikes. They suggested their families could

turn off the lights. A few brought up the possibility of shorter showers. Many of them suggested reusing products and not buying anything they didn't need. A few mentioned looking for local producers to limit the transportation of goods to market. At the national level, they named efforts to support alternative fuels. Internationally, they wrote of treaties and a united global agenda to decrease dependence on fossil fuels. At the level of "our school" almost all of them named recycling as a way to make a difference.

This may have been the result of conventional and simplistic environmentalism that most students are exposed to. It's easy to believe that recycling is an easy way to solve environmental ills—sort paper, plastic, and aluminum and you feel like you've done something without changing the underlying patterns of consumption that create so much waste in the first place. But I had four reasons to pursue recycling as a collective action:

■ I teach 8th graders, many of whom are at their best when they are moving.

■ Our school didn't recycle at all.

■ A push to have the school recycle on the basis of global warming would give my students a chance to teach others about what they had learned, and teaching concepts goes a long way in strengthening them.

■ Landfills and the transportation of waste are a significant part of the problem.

I told the students they needed to find out exactly how recycling could reduce our contribution to global warming and how to set up a program in our school. They prepared questions and I invited the recycling coordinator from our local disposal company along with an educator from the county solid waste department to tell us what we needed to know.

Together, my students and I learned that our school currently produces two 10-yard dumpsters a week, most of which is paper. We learned that every resident of our county generates on average five pounds of waste per day, and that amount has increased by more than 15 percent over the past three years. The reasons? Increased packaging and consumption and reduced recycling. People are buying more stuff and throwing more of it away. We also learned that our waste goes from a local collection site into rail containers that make their way south to the Columbia River, then up the Gorge to Roosevelt Landfill. The trains depart daily and are

---

Resources on Global Warming

Arctic Meltdown/Rising Seas. Video produced by Greenpeace, 2001, 32 min. Distributor: www. videoproject.org. The Video Project, 200 Estates Dr., Ben Lomond, CA 95005. 800-4-PLANET.

Early Warning Signs: Global Warming Curriculum. Union of Concerned Scientists. www. climatehotmap.org/curriculum. The curriculum is downloadable as a PDF file and the map is an interactive student resource.

Physics Is Fun. Octavo Editions, 1995. Order at www.awsna.org/ catalog. This book is filled with easy-to-make and inexpensive demonstrations that show the beauty of the laws of physics.

Stormy Weather: 101 Solutions to Global Climate Change. Dauncey, Guy. New Society Publishers, 2001. This is an especially helpful teacher resource.

just about half a mile long. Almost all of western Washington's waste crosses the mountains for burial in the desert.

While my students asked their questions, I asked my own. "How does transporting waste create greenhouse gases?"

John asked, "What powers trains?"

"Diesel," I answered. "What gas will result?"

"Carbon dioxide."

Someone added, "Methane too when it's extracted."

We learned that the monstrous regional landfill is capped and lined with a thick rubber sheet that keeps the "garbage juice" from entering the ground water.

"Anaerobic decomposition," I said. "What gas comes from that?"

"Methane."

It turns out that over the course of 20 years methane is 62 times more powerful a greenhouse gas than CO_2 because it traps more heat radiated from the Earth's surface. Landfill operators have to do something with it, and usually, they burn it off. This environmental compromise results in more CO_2.

My students then took what they had learned and launched an incrementally growing schoolwide recycling effort. First they perfected a paper recycling system for our classroom and took responsibility for maintaining it. Students then set out to teach every 7th grader and the rest of the 8th graders in our building about the connection between waste and global warming. We visited 7th-grade science classes and the rest of the 8th-grade science classes and delivered recycling bins donated by the disposal company and posters depicting the connection between atmospheric gases and the catastrophes that so worried us when we first learned about the effects of global warming.

Students emphasized to others how important it was that everyone work together, and that we could only keep the support of our custodian if we stuck with it and emptied the bins every single day. Our effort is slowly expanding to recycle all the waste our school produces in the classrooms. The lunchroom is next.

Looking Back

Thinking over what my students learned, I wonder how it might have played out differently if I hadn't made the commitment to action so early. The student resistance that resulted may have cost us valuable learning and time. On the other hand, that activated resistance may have created in my students a powerful need to know that kept them engaged until we decided on action. But early on, I gave up on indicting auto emissions as a key greenhouse gas contributor—unfortunate, because the statistics are so impressive. According to Dauncey (see resources), an average SUV emits about 13 tons of CO_2 per year, while more efficient hybrid cars reduce that to 3 tons. If I had built more background before introducing fossil fuel emissions at all, there's a chance we could have gone further.

Also, we started our recycling effort too late in the year. As summer approached, I took on the tasks of identifying teacher captains and securing administrative and custodial support for our efforts. If the students had done this work, they might have learned more about how to create institutional change.

But the recycling project helped my middle school students see with their own eyes how the actions we take collectively speak much louder than words. And I want my students to see themselves as agents in our world, rather than subject to it. They made a change in their school that will last much longer than their short stay in 8th grade. And they've established a climate of concern in their school that I can take further next year.

The Future

A few weeks ago, Alex popped a piece of gum into his mouth. When he got to the garbage with his wrapper, he stopped. He looked at it. He looked at me.

"Ms. Dean, what am I supposed to do with this?"

"I don't know, Alex."

"I have aluminum and paper here right?"

"Yes."

He didn't say anything more. He stuck around after the bell to separate the foil from the paper so neither would end up in the landfill. Maybe when the time comes for Alex to buy his first truck, he'll stop and remember what he learned in 8th grade about global warming. ∎

Jana Dean teaches 8th-grade social studies and science at Bush Middle School in Tumwater, Wash. She belongs to Olympia's Educators for Social Justice.

Students Use Math to Confront Overcrowding

By Erin E. Turner and Beatriz T. Font Strawhun

DAVID MCLIMANS

In an overcrowded New York middle school, students discovered that math was a path to investigating and working to change conditions at their school.

After planning a unit with Erin, a university professor, Beatriz taught a six-week unit where students used mathematics to investigate issues of overcrowding at Francis Middle School, which is located in a predominantly working class African-American, Dominican, and Puerto Rican community in New York City. Erin was present in the classroom for all of the class discussions.

When the school opened in 1990, following a district call for the creation of more "small schools" for middle-grade students, the founding (and current) principal faced the near impossible task of finding available space for the school within the district. At that time, the elementary school that currently shares a building with Francis had vacated the top floor because of

continual problems with a leaking roof. Francis's principal claimed the space for the new school, repairs began, and the school opened shortly thereafter.

Although Francis began as a small school, districtwide changes in student enrollment caused the school's student population to grow dramatically, from approximately 145 students to 213 students, and it was projected to grow another 15 to 20 percent (an additional 30 to 40 students) the following year. So as students climbed the five flights of stairs to reach the once pigeon-infested fifth floor that now housed their school, they worried about how the narrow halls and lack of classroom space might accommodate their already cramped school community. Some students were concerned about the potential fire hazards created by the school's long, narrow hallways. A building across the street had recently been damaged in a fire, and in the aftermath of 9/11, students were all too aware of the dangers of being

trapped in a burning building. Others felt their classrooms, several of which had recently been subdivided to create multiple rooms, were too small and overcrowded. Floor-to-ceiling columns and smaller poles scattered throughout classrooms made simple tasks like seeing the chalkboard difficult.

It was students' concern about the lack of space at their school that guided the initial development of this project. One of our primary goals was to design a unit of study that drew upon students' interests and experiences, and provided students opportunities to learn and use mathematics in personally and socially meaningful ways. With this in mind, Beatriz asked students to make lists of issues about the school and local community that concerned them.

Several topics appeared repeatedly in students' lists, including violence in the neighborhood, health issues such as AIDS, racism and sexism in the media, and the "space crisis" at the school. While any one of these topics might have sparked a rich mathematical unit, we selected the issue of "Overcrowding at Our School" for several reasons, including (a) the rich mathematical content the unit would draw upon, (b) the opportunities it would provide for students to generate their own data, versus analyzing data from an external source, (c) the salience this issue had for students, and (d) the potential links to issues of equity and fairness.

Initially, students claimed they were more crowded than other schools and were eager to speak out in hopes of increasing their school space. Students were particularly bothered by the disparity they observed between their own school space and that of Longmore, another small middle school that had recently moved into the fourth floor of the same school building. (Note: When the fourth floor initially became available, Francis lobbied to move into it, but the request was not granted; the space was instead awarded to Longmore, a technology magnet school that attracted affluent, predominantly white families from across the district.)

Yet students were not sure how to talk about the crowding in terms that might convince others, and it was unclear to them how mathematics could support their argument. To help students connect their concerns about overcrowding with mathematical tools that would support their investigation, Beatriz posed questions such as, "How can we show them how much space we have? What kind of information would we need to collect? What kinds of measurements? How can we prove that we are more crowded than Longmore?" Students quickly realized that quantifying the school's space would be helpful.

One student, Jhana, raised a concern about the tight space in the hallways after second period, a time when all 213 students in the school were simultaneously released from their classrooms. In class, she repeatedly lobbied to investigate this. "What we need to know," she argued during a discussion, "is after second period, because that's when the most kids come out. How many kids get dismissed? . . . And

'With math it's like you have more defense.'

[we need] the area of all the hallways." Other students agreed that finding the area of classroom and hallway spaces would "give proof" to their claims of overcrowding, and so Beatriz prepared a series of mini-lessons that addressed concepts such as linear measurement, and how to find the area of spaces with mixed number dimensions, such as a hallway that measured 10 1/2 meters by 1 1/4 meters.

Jhana worked with several classmates to measure and calculate the area of the school's hallways, and used ratios to compare the hallway space per student at Francis to the hallway space per student at Longmore. She argued that ratios "make it easier to see the big difference," and noted:

> [Before] I wouldn't really use math. I would just say, LOOK how much space they have [in their school] instead of what we have [in our school]. . . . But I would really use math now. . . . Math made my argument make more sense, and have more of an idea, and actually tell what is happening, because it gave more detail to it.

As the class continued to analyze overcrowding at their school, they discovered disparities between their own space and that of other schools, and numerous instances where their school violated district building codes.

For example, during one lesson after students had worked in teams to measure and calculate the area of different classrooms and hallways, Beatriz asked each group to share their measurements. Students were shocked as they viewed the size of their own classrooms (e.g., 474, 497, and 567 square feet) compared to the classrooms at Longmore (e.g., 772, 864, and 918 square feet). One student commented, "It's not fair! They have a smaller amount of students and bigger classrooms. They have to keep cutting our classrooms in half because we have so many kids."

Ultimately, students decided to share this information with the district. They wrote letters to the superintendent, prepared fact sheets with the results of their analysis for administrators, and spoke at a school governing board meeting. As Jhana considered whether the students' analysis of the space crisis at their school made a difference, she commented: "Yes [we made a difference], because first of all, we found out something for ourselves, and we actually proved a point. Math made our argument make more sense. ... You couldn't do it without the math."

As mathematics educators, we would like all of our students to exhibit such passion about the power of mathematics. Jhana and her classmates invented novel problem-solving strategies, and used mathematics to analyze and act upon situations at their school. We believe that students' participation in this unit helped them develop a sense of themselves as people who make a difference.

Students Negotiate Curriculum

Throughout the "Overcrowding at Our School" project, the students had opportunities to insert their interests, goals, and purposes into the curriculum. For example, after several days of measuring classrooms and calculating areas, students formed small groups to pose their own problem about a particular aspect of the school space. Beatriz asked students to identify one issue dealing with overcrowding at the school and to discuss how they might use mathematics to find out more about the situation. As students posed problems that mattered to them, their desire to understand and affect the overcrowding increased their engagement in mathematics and enhanced the learning that occurred.

Angel, a tall and rather quiet African-American student, was not a frequent participant in problem-solving discussions before this unit. But when the class began to investigate overcrowding at their school, there was a notable shift in Angel's level of engagement. Angel was extremely concerned about the school's bathrooms.

She found it difficult to navigate among the other 10 or 12 people in the tight space. She noted that all females in the school, including 103 students and 15 teachers, had to share one rather small facility with only three working stalls, and a very small sink station. So when Beatriz asked Angel's group what aspect of the school space they wanted to investigate, the choice for Angel was obvious: "We want to know, why are the girls' bathrooms so small?"

Angel's group constructed a floor plan of the restroom, measured its dimensions, calculated the area, and then analyzed the bathroom space based on the number of stalls, the estimated wait time during peak use periods, and the space available for waiting. Angel spoke about how the opportunity to investigate an issue she cared about made her feel "mad curious" and drew her into the mathematics. She commented, "It was easier to do the math this way, instead of just learning it straight, like solving a problem, because we would actually really get into it, and that made it easier."

For other students, the opportunity to investigate real issues not only increased their engagement, but also pushed them to construct and apply important mathematical concepts.

Lianna, like Jhana, was concerned

Discussions began with matter-of-fact statements about the data, but shifted to an exploration of why particular discrepancies existed.

about the school's narrow and densely populated hallways. As she left Beatriz's classroom each day, she faced the challenge of navigating through one of the school's narrowest and most densely populated hallways. Not a student who was comfortable pushing her way through oncoming crowds of up to 80 children at a time, Lianna was often left standing just outside the door for four or five minutes while other students passed in and out of adjacent classrooms. Her group decided to compare the total hallway area at Francis with the area of the hallways of Longmore.

The mathematics that Lianna's group engaged in would qualify as rigorous in any sixth-grade classroom. They developed their own strategies for multiplying mixed numbers to find the area of hallways with dimensions like 18 3/4 by 1 1/4 meters, and subdivided irregular spaces into rectangular and triangular areas.

But Lianna was not content with simply stating the total hallway area of each school; she wanted to make her argument stronger, or to use her words, to "use more specifics so people will listen." When she overheard that a classmate, Thomas, had calculated hallway space per student, she was intrigued.

"How did you do that?" she asked. "We already found out the [hallway]

area of Longmore, and I want to see how much [space] they will each get. You found out how much each person will get in Francis, and I want to do the same thing in Longmore. But I don't know how to do it."

"You've got to know how many students there are," said Thomas.

"Sixty," said Lianna.

"Sixty students. And how much is the area?" asked Thomas.

"246 and 3/4 meters squared," she answered.

"So I am going to divide 60 into 246," said Thomas. "Because that way I can find out how much each person gets, cause it kind of divides it [the space] up."

Several days before this conversation, Beatriz had presented a mini-lesson designed to help students think about overcrowding in terms of "space to people" ratios. Many students found that comparing ratios helped support their claims about overcrowding, and some, like Thomas, had become adept at using this mathematical tool. It was not uncommon for students in the classroom to ask each other for help, or to question one another's strategies in order to understand them better, as Lianna did.

With Thomas's help, she figured out that if all students at Longmore entered the hallways at the same time, each student would have 4.1 square meters to herself or himself. She was shocked when she compared that figure to the less than 1 square meter of hallway space allotted to each student at her school.

Taking Action

We wanted to support students in sharing what they learned through their investigations with the school and neighborhood community. Beatriz helped students brainstorm ways to educate others about overcrowding at the school. Students generated lots of ideas, including distributing fliers, visiting the school board, going "on strike," making a large floor plan of the school to display, and compiling all their data to share with the district. Except for going on strike, the students implemented all of these ideas.

At the end of the unit, Naisha, a spirited and opinionated African-American student, spoke at a school advisory council meeting. This council represented the school at the district level, and helped make decisions on matters of spending, curriculum and assessment, staffing, and enrollment. Naisha embraced the opportunity and volunteered to prepare a speech. What follows is the text of the speech she presented to the board:

Good evening, my name is Naisha Watson. I am a 6th grader at Francis Middle School, and I am going to talk about overcrowding at our school. Our math class has been comparing our school to Longmore. We have noticed, as a class, that we have no space for kids to sit. … The board of education has a build-

ing code that the classrooms have to be at least 750 square feet for 30 children. As you can see on the graph, only three classrooms are big enough, the rest of the classrooms that are orange on the graph are smaller than 750 square feet. [Refers to a large diagram of the school created by several students.] … The board of education has another building code that says the hallways must be 5 feet and 8 inches wide. … There is only one hallway that is 5 feet and 8 inches. All the other hallways that are red on the graph do not meet the board of education building code. … In our school we have 213 kids. If there was a fire in our school, it would be a hazard to get through our narrow halls. So, as a school, we think we should have less students or more space.

Naisha felt that speaking out as a way of resisting the inequities her class discovered was not only necessary, but also potentially effective. "I think it's good [that we talked to the district], because if you keep talking to them then they will probably listen," she explained. "And you will get on their nerves and maybe then they will want to give us more space, or let us be in a different building with more space, [space] that is lawful."

Even though the students knew that the district lacked funds to build a new

school or add a floor to the building, they felt good about contributing to the public discussion of overcrowding at the school. As Lianna argued, "We have to say something because we are the students and we are the ones that have to live in the school everyday."

Not only did opportunities to engage in responsive action support students' sense of themselves as people who can and do make a difference, but using mathematics as a tool to support their actions challenged students' view of the discipline. For instance, when we initially asked Naisha what she thought of mathematics, she responded, "What do I think of math—you mean, numbers?" She described math as something she felt good about only when she got the answers right.

In contrast, as Naisha reflected on Beatriz's class at the end of the semester, she explained that unlike previous classes, where she studied material but never had the opportunity to "do anything" with what she learned, in this class, "we did something with it. … Without the math, then, we wouldn't have the area of the school, and we wouldn't really know. And the [district] meeting wouldn't have been as powerful as it was."

Naisha was not the only student to begin to recognize that math "made [her] arguments make more sense." Other students said math helped them to "prove how most stuff is not shared evenly" and "to prove to the district that our school was smaller," and that math "gave more details" and "specifics" to their arguments, and afforded them "more defense" in the problems they were fighting against. Students also spoke eloquently about how they drew upon mathematics to address "things in [the] community and school," and referred to this way of engaging with the discipline as "a lifelong thing," that is not only about mathematics but also about "things that you be in everyday, and it's a part of your life." Given that students often struggle to identify reasons why they should learn mathematics, these shifts in their understanding of the discipline are significant.

Further Reflections

As we reflected on the project, we found that creating spaces for students to pose their own problems and to inject their interests and concerns into the curriculum was a powerful way of supporting student activism. Occasionally, students posed problems about the school that did not lend themselves to rich mathematical investigations. We recognize that teachers have a responsibility to ensure that students learn certain content, and students' interests may not always lead them to a given mathematical idea. Beatriz had clear mathematical goals in mind for this unit (linear and area measurement, ratio, operations with fractions, and mixed numbers). But she thought it was equally important that students participated in mathematics projects that were personally and socially meaningful. We acknowledge that mathematics may not always be the best discipline to address the questions that students pose. Beatriz's challenge was to work with students to negotiate an intersection between their interests and the mathematical content they needed to study.

We also found that creating a class-room culture where critique was welcomed, and even expected, was essential. It was important for students to feel safe posing difficult questions, such as those that alluded to the connection between their particular situation at Francis (a poor school, with inadequate space and resources), and broader educational inequalities that exist along the lines of race and class. While classroom discussions began with matter-of-fact statements about the data students were collecting, through questions such as, "Why do you think it is like that?" the talk gradually shifted to an exploration of why particular discrepancies existed, namely those between Francis and Longmore. Students argued that the superior conditions at Longmore were not random, but directly related to the race and socioeconomic status of the students. "There are more white people than anyone else at that school," one student noted, and "the white people always get the good education, it's like an upper-class thing, for the white kids. … That's just how it is!" In further discussion, students suggested that the demographics (in particular, the socio-economic status) of Longmore students were unlike those of Francis, and that these differences in demographics might be linked to the discrepancies in the condition and size of school facilities, and to the "protection" of the school by those in power.

Beatriz opened a space in her classroom for students to approach their situation with a critical mind-set, and in doing so, she supported their sense that they can act and make a difference.

At the end of the study, it was still unclear whether the district would increase the school's allocated space or make any adjustment to the number of incoming students that Francis had to accept. So unfortunately, the students ended 6th grade not knowing whether their efforts had any direct impact. But over the summer, the district decided to reduce Francis' incoming class by approximately 30 students. This allowed the school to retain its current size of 213 students instead of increasing to 240 as initially planned. The district's action prevented an already overcrowded school from growing, which students welcomed as one small success.

Yet, what seems most important is not whether this particular "battle" was won or lost, but the shifts in understanding and increased critical awareness that students took from the experience. As Jhana put it: "We found out something for ourselves, and we actually proved a point. We made a difference. Math made our argument make more sense. You couldn't do it without the math." ∎

Erin E. Turner is an assistant professor of mathematics education at Santa Clara University. She is a former bilingual classroom teacher. She currently conducts collaborative research with math teachers at the elementary and middle school levels.

Beatriz T. Font Strawhun is a graduate of Pennsylvania State University and has taught in Austin and San Antonio, Texas; Pennsylvania; and New York City. She currently works with teachers at the University of Michigan in Ann Arbor.

Getting Off the Track
Stories from an untracked classroom

By Bill Bigelow

In school, I hated social studies. My U.S. history class was, in the words of critical educator Ira Shor, a memory Olympics, with students competing to see how many dates, battles, and presidents we could cram into our adolescent heads. My California history class was one long lecture, almost none of which I remember today, save for the names of a few famous men—mostly scoundrels. This marathon fact-packing was interrupted only once, as I recall, by a movie on raisins. Social studies—ostensibly a study of human beings—was nothing of the kind. "Poor History," writes Eduardo Galeano, "had stopped breathing: betrayed in academic texts, lied about in classrooms, drowned in dates, they had imprisoned her in museums and buried her, with floral wreaths, beneath statuary bronze and monumental marble."

Today, students who prove unresponsive to similar memory games are often labeled "slow learners,"—or worse—and find themselves dumped in a low-track class, called "basic" or "skills," understood by all as "the dumb class." This is classic victim-blaming, penalizing kids for their inability to turn human beings into abstractions, for their failure to recall disconnected factoids. And it's unnecessary. Tracking is usually advocated with good intentions; but its only educational justification derives from schools' persistence in teaching in ways that fail to reach so many children, thus necessitating some students' removal to less demanding academic pursuits.

Students in Bill Bigelow's classroom.

Untracking a school requires untracking instruction. Unfortunately, many of those who argue against tracking offer only the vaguest hints of what an effective untracked class could look like. Hence their critique that tracking delivers inferior instruction to many students, lowers self-esteem, reproduces social hierarchies, and reinforces negative stereotypes may have ironic consequences. Compelled by these and other arguments, schools that untrack without a thoroughgoing pedagogical transformation can end up simply with a system of tracking internal to each classroom. I've seen this in more than one "untracked" school: students who come to class able to absorb lectures, write traditional research papers, memorize discrete facts—and stay awake—succeed; those who can't, sit in the back of class

and sleep, doodle, or disrupt—and fail. Those of us critical of tracking need to offer a concrete and viable vision of an untracked classroom. Otherwise, the results of untracking will replicate the results of tracking, and many educators will lean back in their chairs and say, "I told you so."

Components of an Untracked Classroom

As a classroom teacher, I've found that an anti-tracking pedagogy has several essential and interlocking components. And while the examples I'll use are drawn from my high school social studies classes, these components remain as valid in other content areas or can be adapted.

- **Show, don't tell.** Through role plays, improvisations, and simulations students need to *experience*, not simply hear about, social dynamics.

■ **Assignments need to be flexible enough to adjust to students' interests or abilities.** Teachers can assign projects, poetry, personal writing, and critiques, which allow students to enter and succeed at their own levels of competence and creativity. This is not a suggestion to give easy assignments, but to adopt a flexible academic rigor. And in no way should this detract from students developing traditional scholastic skills they will need to pursue higher education.

■ **The curriculum needs to constantly draw on students' lives as a way of delving into broader social themes.** Knowledge needs to be both internal and external; history, government, sociology, literature is always simultaneously about "them" *and* us.

■ **The classroom environment needs to be encouraging, even loving.** All students need to know that their potential is respected, that they are included in a community of learners. A rhetoric of caring is insufficient. Both the form and content of the class must underscore every child's worth and potential.

■ **What we teach has to matter.** Students should understand how the information and analytic tools they're developing make a difference in their lives, that the aim of learning is not just a grade, simple curiosity, or "because you'll need to know it later."

■ **An anti-tracking pedagogy should explicitly critique the premises of tracking.** Students need to examine the history and practice of tracking in order to become aware of and expel doubts about their capacity to think and achieve. We cannot merely untrack our classrooms; we have to engage students in a dialogue about *why* we untrack our classrooms. More than this, the curriculum needs to critique the deeper social inequities and hierarchies that were the original stimulus for tracking and continue today to breed unjust educational practices.

■ **Finally, the method of evaluating students in an untracked class should embody the flexibility and caring described above.** We can't advocate creating flexible assignments that

> Role plays
> allow students
> to climb into
> history and
> explore it
> from the inside.

adjust to students' interests and abilities and then hold youngsters accountable to rigid performance criteria. Evaluation needs to be guided by principles of equity rather than efficiency.

The power of an anti-tracking approach lies in the interrelationship of these components, not in merely applying them checklist fashion. Lest my examples sound too self-congratulatory or facile, I should begin by confessing that all this is easier said than done, and my classroom is rarely as tidy as my written descriptions. My students, just like everyone else's, get off task, hold distracting side conversations, and often fail to complete their homework. The aim here is not to provide a cookbook of tried and true educational recipes but to contribute to a broader discussion about how we can teach for justice in an unjust society, and to explore how such a commitment can contribute to successful classroom practice.

Bringing the Curriculum to Life

Role plays, simulations, and improvisations allow students to climb into history and social concepts and to explore them from the inside. It's a first-person approach to society that gives each student an equal shot at grasping concepts and gaining knowledge. Students who are advanced in traditional academic terms are not held back with this more experiential approach, but neither are they privileged by their facility with, say, Standard English or their stamina in reading and memorizing textbook-speak. Just about every unit I teach includes at least one role play, simulation, or set of improvisations.

For example, in a unit on U.S. labor history, students role-play the 1934 West Coast longshore strike (see *The Power in Our Hands*, pp. 74-77 and 148-163). In five groups—longshoremen, waterfront employers, farmers, unemployed workers and representatives of the central labor council—students confront the choices that confronted the original strike participants. From each group's respective standpoint students propose solutions to the strike, decide whether they want the governor to call in the National Guard to protect strikebreakers, and determine how they will respond if the Guard is called upon. Not all groups have clear positions on the questions and so students have to use their creativity to design potential resolutions and their persuasive powers to build alliances with members of other groups.

The dynamics of the strike are lived in the classroom, experienced firsthand by students, instead of being buried in the textbook. Longshoremen negotiate with farmers to support the strike, waterfront employers seek to entice the unemployed with offers of work, and more than one group threatens violence if the governor calls in the Guard. Students must master lots of information in order to effectively represent their positions, but it's not just a memory Olympics—they have to *use* the information in the heat of deal-making and debate.

Most students have a great time,

running around the room negotiating and arguing with recalcitrant peers; often, students remain engaged after the bell rings. But the role play is not simply play. As Paulo Freire says, "Conflict is the midwife of consciousness," and the simulated conflict in role plays like this allows students to reflect on their own cynicism about people's capacity to unite for worthy goals.

After the role play I sometimes ask students to relate our discussion to their lives, and to write about a time when they were able to stick together with a group for a common objective. In our class read-around the next day and father, who are enslaved, that he's going to sell their children. He needs the money.

- An enslaved person encounters a poor white farmer on the road. The farmer accuses the slave of looking him directly in the eye, which is illegal.

- An enslaved person asks an owner if she or he can buy her or his freedom.

There's an obvious danger that students' performances of these and any role plays can drift toward caricature. Caricature may allow students to distance and insulate themselves from the enormity of the subject, but it can also allow them to trivialize one of the most horrendous periods in human history. However, the alternative of students remaining outside, removed from a subject like the enslavement of African people, seems to me a greater danger. So we talk about how we can't possibly know what people experienced, but through our performance, imagination, writing, and discussion we're going to do the best we can. And students have responded with passionate skits that have moved many in the class to tears— that have, in Toni Morrison's words, given "voice to the 'unspeakable.'"

As students perform the improvs I ask them to take notes on powerful lines or situations, as they'll be writing from the perspective of one or more of the characters. After each skit we discuss the problem posed, and how students handled it. As we progress, I draw on their improvs to teach about laws, different forms of resistance, how certain practices varied from region to region or in different time periods. It's a series of mini-lectures, but accessible to all students because they are linked to a shared experience.

Afterward I ask students to write an interior monologue—the inner thoughts—from the point of view of one of the characters in an improv. People have the freedom to write from the point of view of a character they repre-

Students have responded with passionate skits that have moved many in the class to tears.

on much larger issues: When are alliances between different social groups possible? What role does the government play, and should it play, in labor disputes? Is violence or the threat of violence justified in class conflict? Can people be out for themselves, but also support each other? These are big and tough questions, but because they draw on an experience every student watched and helped create, they are concrete rather than abstract. Regardless of past academic achievement, the activities and discussion challenge every student.

These and other questions can also lead us to explore the contemporary relevance of the strike. Often students-as-longshoremen cobble together an alliance including farmers, the unemployed, and the central labor council. What do you think happened in real life? I ask. "Sure we can get together," many a student has responded. "But we're just in a role play in a classroom. It's easy to get together in here. I don't think it could happen in real life." Most students are surprised to learn that it *did* happen in real life—working people in 1934 maintained a remarkable degree of solidarity. And from this knowledge we discuss when people can and cannot get together. Students also reflect

I encourage students to take notes on common themes they hear in each other's stories. Here, too, we can continue to pursue theoretical questions about unity, but it's a pursuit rooted in our experience, not one imposed on a class as an abstract academic inquiry. It is serious academic work, democratized through students' in-class experience and its connection to their lives.

Improvisation and Equal Access to the Curriculum

Improvisation is another kind of "leveling" role play that seeks to give all students equal access to information and theoretical insight. In a unit on U.S. slavery and resistance to slavery, I provide students with a set of first person roles for different social groups in the South, which supplements information already gleaned from films, a slide-lecture, poetry, a simulation, readings, and class discussions. They read these roles and in small groups select from a list of improvisation choices. They can also create their own improv topic or combine some of mine to form something new.

The topics are bare-bones descriptions requiring lots of student initiative to plan and perform. For example:

- A plantation owner tells a mother

sented or one they watched. I encourage students to "find your passion," as my teaching partner, Linda Christensen, likes to say—so they're free to rearrange and massage the assignment to fit their interest. Most students write the assigned interior monologue, but some prefer poems, dialogue poems, or letters. This, too, is a vital part of an anti-tracking pedagogy: Students need sufficient freedom to enter an assignment at a point of their choosing; they must be able to reconstruct the task according to their interests and abilities.

For example, after one set of improvisations, "Diane," a young woman with a low-track academic history, wrote a dialogue poem about childbirth. The paired perspectives are from the wife of a white plantation owner and an enslaved African-American woman. It reads in part:

My man is not here to hold my hand.
My man is not here to hold my hand.

He's out in the field.
He's out in the field.

with a whip in his hand.
with a whip at his back.

I lie here on my feather bed.
I lie here on the blanketed floor.

The pain comes. I push.
The pain comes. I push.

Someone, please come and help.
Someone, please come and help.

The midwife comes, the doctor, too.
The midwife comes, no doctor.

Silk sheets in my mouth.
A wood stick in my mouth.

To halt the screams.
To halt the screams.

I push some more.
I push some more.

I sigh relief. The child is born.
I sigh relief. The child is born.

Strikers battle the police during the 1934 West Coast longshore strike. As part of a unit on U.S. labor history, students role-play the strike.

Strong lungs scream.
Silence.

It squirms there, full of life.
It lies there, cold and blue.

It is a boy.
It was a boy.

Another born to be big and strong
Another one born to be laid in the ground.

A babe suckling at my breast.
This babe lying in my arms.

Tomorrow I will plan a party.
Tomorrow I will go to the field.

None of the improvs had been about childbirth, but this was where Diane found her passion.

There are no wrong answers here. Virtually every interior monologue or poem is plausible, even if students approach the same character's thoughts in very different ways. Chaunetta writes from the point of view of a woman whose children are sold off, Eric from that of a man contemplating escape, Monica from that of a plantation owner reflecting on his dissatisfaction with his overseers. Some of the pieces, like Diane's, are publishable, some not even close. But each student gains an insight with validity, and together their portraits form an emotional and empathic patchwork quilt. And again, the assignment challenges all students, regardless of supposed skill levels.

Untracking the Big Questions

Before students begin the read-around I ask them to take notes on three questions: 1) In what ways were people hurt text" created by the entire class.

Wrestling with a question like this is simply the next step. Everyone can succeed, and everyone is intellectually challenged. And because theory is

The read-around celebrates the diversity of students' experience, and in some cases their bravery or self-sacrifice.

by slavery? 2) How did people resist slavery? and 3) Explain why you think slavery could or could not have ended without a violent struggle. We circle-up for the read-around. I encourage, but don't require, everyone in class to share his or her writing. As students read their pieces they compliment each other, offer "aha's," and take notes on the questions. This is not an editing session, so critical remarks aren't allowed—thus students know they'll only hear positive comments if they choose to share. The read-around, or sharing circle, builds community as youngsters applaud each other's efforts and insights. The medium is the message: We all count here.

Afterward, people look over their notes and write on the questions. Unlike textbook questions, these encourage students to make meaning themselves, not to parrot back the meaning decided by some publishing company. The third question is a difficult one, calling for students to reflect on the obstacles to social change. It's a question that ordinarily might be set aside for the "advanced" class, but because of an anti-tracking pedagogy it can be approached by everyone: They all watched the improvs, they all participated, they heard my mini-lectures, they discussed their questions and insights, they climbed inside someone's head to write from his or her point of view and they listened to the "collective

grounded in students' in-class experience, the assignment doesn't privilege those students who may be more practiced at abstract thinking.

If we want our classes to be accessible to students regardless of academic background and confidence we have to discover ways of bringing concepts alive. Simulations are another show-don't-tell strategy. For example, in exploring the history of work in the United States, particularly "scientific management" or "Taylorization"—owners studying and then chopping up the labor process into component parts and assigning workers one repetitive task—a simple lecture would reach some students. But using paper airplanes and students as skilled workers to simulate changes in the production process provides all students access to a vital piece of history that can help them reflect on their own work lives.

We can tape off the floor and offer pieces of chocolate to simulate land and wealth distribution in different societies; unsharpened and sharpened pencils can represent raw materials and manufactured products to help us show the dynamics of colonialism; and with balls of cotton, shirts, wheat, "guns," and bank notes, we can walk students through pre-Civil War sectional conflicts. An untracked classroom can be both more playful and more rigorous than a traditional read-this/listen-to-this/write-this approach.

We can also allow kids to get out of the classroom and into the community, both as social investigators and change-makers. Students can visit a senior citizens' center to interview people about a particular time period. They might tour a factory to learn about working conditions, or travel to a Native American community to meet and talk with activists. Often, I conclude a major unit or a semester by encouraging students to become "truth-tellers"—to take their knowledge about an issue beyond the classroom walls. One year, a student of Linda's and mine choreographed and performed for a number of classes a dance on the life of Ben Linder, the Portlander murdered by the Contras in Nicaragua. Numbers of students rewrite children's books from a multicultural standpoint and use them to lead discussions at elementary schools. One group produced a videotape, cablecast citywide, about the erosion of Native American fishing rights on the Columbia River. One year, a student in a global studies class wrote and recorded "The South Africa Rap," questioning why corporations leave communities in the United States and invest in apartheid; it was subsequently played by several community radio stations around the country. A real-world curriculum aims to give students an equal opportunity to understand society—and to change it.

A New Teacher-Student Covenant

An anti-tracking pedagogy needs to offer alternatives to traditional teaching methods and critique these methods as well. The traditional teacher-student covenant proposes to rehearse students for alienation: I give you an assignment over which you have no or little control. It's not about you; it's about subject *x*. I think it up—or, more often, a textbook company thinks it up—I design it, you perform it, and I evaluate it. In exchange for successfully carrying out your part of the bargain I give you a reward: your grade. Neither the work nor the grade has any intrinsic value, but the grade has exchange value that can be banked and spent later for desired ends. Conception and execution are separate, and this dichotomy prepares young people for a life of essential powerlessness over the conditions of their labor and the purposes towards which that labor is used. An anti-tracking pedagogy needs to offer a new covenant, one that promises students an education rooted in their lives, with much greater initiative and participation.

In Linda Christensen's and my Literature and History course we constantly draw on students' lives as a way of illuminating both history and literature, and in turn draw on the history and literature as a way of illuminating students' lives. In the slavery and slave resistance unit, mentioned above, we read an excerpt from Frederick Douglass' autobiography in which a teenage Douglass defies and physically confronts his overseer (*Narrative of the Life of Frederick Douglass*, pp. 68-75.) We discuss the conditions in Douglass' life that propelled him into this confrontation, and growing out of the discussion ask students to write about a time in their lives when they stood up for what was right. The assignment gives a framework for students' writing but offers them lots of room to move, and as with the other assignments described, this one adjusts to a student's skill level. Some students may be able to write a personally probing, metaphorical piece while others may struggle to write a couple paragraphs—but the assignment offers all students a point of entry.

The read-around celebrates the diversity of students' experience, and in some cases their bravery or self-sacrifice: Nate writes about confronting a racist and abusive police officer, Steph-

Students discuss a role play.

anie about attending an anti-nuclear power demonstration, Josh about challenging a teacher's unfairness, Zeneda about interrupting an incident of sexual harassment. But the stories also give us the raw material to reflect on when and why people resist, and the relative effectiveness of some forms of resistance over others. And we can test our findings against Frederick Douglass' experiences.

In a unit on the history and sociology of schooling, students write about an encounter with inequality in education, and at a different point, about a positive learning experience. In a lesson on the Cherokee Indian Removal, they write about a time their rights were violated. After reading a Studs Terkel interview with C.P. Ellis, who quit his leadership position in the Klan and became a civil rights advocate and union organizer, students write about a significant change they made in their lives.

The personal writing and sharing

undercuts a curriculum designed to inure students to alienated work, as the assignment also equalizes students' opportunity for academic success and theoretical insight. Moreover, it is a key part of creating a classroom discourse that in both form and content tells each student: You matter; your life and learning are important here. That's another aim of breaking from a curriculum that is traditionally male dominated, and extols the lives of elites over working people and people of color. Unless we reorient the content of the curriculum to better reflect the lives of all our students, we implicitly tell young people, "Some of you are better than others; some of you are destined for bigger things."

An Explicit Critique of Tracking

Ultimately, an anti-tracking pedagogy needs to engage students in an explicit critique of tracking. As Jeannie Oakes and others have shown, one of the byproducts of tracking, even one of its aims, is that low-tracked students blame themselves for their subordinate position in the scholastic hierarchy; students come to believe that they are defective and the system is OK. Conse-

as they engage in a critical inquiry that subverts the apparent legitimacy of a system of privilege that benefits some at the expense of others.

We read excerpts of Jean Anyon's

> An anti-tracking pedagogy needs to engage students in an explicit critique of tracking. The unequal system of education must be examined.

quently, the unequal system of education, of which tracking is an important part, needs a critical classroom examination so that students can expose and expel the voices of self-blame and can overcome whatever doubts they have about their capacity for academic achievement. (Also see role play on tracking, p. 132.)

In our unit on the history and sociology of schooling, students look critically at their own educations. We start with today and work backwards in time to understand the origins of the structures that now seem as natural as the seasons. From David Storey's novel, *Radcliffe*, we read a short excerpt that poignantly describes the unequal treatment received by students of different class backgrounds and, as mentioned earlier, ask students to recall an episode of unequal schooling from their own lives. We use the novel excerpt and students' stories to talk about the hidden curricula embedded in school practices—the lessons students absorb about democracy, hierarchy, power, solidarity, race, social class, resistance, etc. Students make observations on their own educational experiences, both past and present, and informally inventory the building's resources: Who gets what kinds of equipment, facilities, class sizes and why? Our students' research is subversive in the best sense of the term

classic 1980 *Journal of Education* article, "Social Class and the Hidden Curriculum of Work," which attempts to demonstrate that schools' expectations of students vary depending on the social position of students' parents. For example, through her research Anyon found that schools in working-class communities value rote behavior and following directions; "affluent professional schools" value creativity and student initiative. The article, written for an academic journal, is a real stretch for a lot of students and might stay beyond their reach if we confined our conceptual exploration to reading and discussion. Instead, we test Anyon's theory by traveling to a wealthier, suburban school to make observations on classroom and school dynamics. We return to compare these to their observations of our own Jefferson High, a school in the center of a predominantly African-American, working-class community. Their firsthand experience makes theory student-friendly, and allows everyone to participate in the discussion as we evaluate Anyon's argument.

We read excerpts from the second chapter of Jeannie Oakes' *Keeping Track* on the history of tracking and a chapter on the history of the SAT test, "The Cult of Mental Measurement," from David Owens' *None of the Above*. From Paul Chapman's *Schools as Sort-*

ers, we review a 1920 survey (p. 126) conducted by Stanford University that found high school students had aspirations that were too high for the jobs available: Over 60 percent of them wanted professional careers, whereas fewer than 5 percent of jobs were in the professions. Concluded Stanford psychologist William V. Proctor: "For [students'] own best good and the best good of the nation a great many of them should be directed toward the agricultural, mechanical, and industrial fields." Could the "problem" of students' high expectations help explain some social groups' commitment to intelligence testing and tracking? My students react with some anger at this conscious attempt to deflate children's dreams.

Providing new information and ways to question the character of schooling is a vital component of untracking any school or classroom. As I've suggested, tracking is not just a bad idea, but is a practice linked to the legitimation and maintenance of deep social inequality. Undercutting the legitimacy of unfair privilege is thus another necessary piece in an anti-tracking strategy. As indicated in the classroom examples provided, the curriculum can offer students permission and encouragement to critique social inequities and to think about alternatives. Further, introducing into the classroom a legacy of resistance to injustice helps nurture an ethos of hope and possibility. Learning from individuals and movements working for democratic social change, both past and present, provides inspiration that not only can societies change for the better, but so can we. Because tracking rests on a premise that people's intellectual capabilities and potential for achievement are fixed, an anti-tracking curriculum needs to demonstrate a more hopeful—and realistic—view of human possibility.

Grades and Equity

At the end of the first quarter Linda and I taught together, Alphonso came to complain about his grade. "I don't think I deserve a C," he argued. "Maybe I can't write as well as Katy. But she came in writing like that, and I've worked really hard. Compare what I'm doing now to what I wrote when the year began. I think I deserve at least a B." Alphonso's complaint illustrates a dilemma of evaluating or, more precisely, grading students in an untracked class. Alphonso was right: Katy knew more history, wrote with more detail and clarity, and had a firmer grasp of course concepts. But Alphonso had worked hard, made important strides in his writing and comprehension, and regularly shared his insights with the class. Still, were we to grade on a curve or based on some fixed standard of achievement, a C would have been fair, even generous. However, we had told the class we wouldn't grade this way, but that their grades would be based on effort, openness, growth, consistency of written and oral participation, respect for one another, as well as clarity of analysis. Thus we gladly changed Alphonso's grade and confessed our mistake.

"Fair grading" is an oxymoron and I'd prefer not to give letter grades at all. I attended an ungraded college, Antioch, where professors wrote students end-of-the-term letters indicating academic strengths and areas needing work. Students responded with self-evaluations that commented on teachers' assessments. It all seemed to make more sense. Of course, Antioch professors didn't see 150 students a day. Nor were they ordered by school or state authorities to sum up a student's performance with a single letter grade.

An anti-tracking pedagogy needs a system of student evaluation that does not reward students based primarily on the knowledge with which they begin a class. A system of fixed criteria from the outset benefits some and penalizes others largely on the basis of class, race, gender, or nationality. An untracked class needs an egalitarian evaluation system that lets all students know they can succeed based on what they do in class, not on what they have or have not accomplished in the past.

Linda and I do not assign letter grades on individual assignments during the term. Instead, we write comments on students' papers indicating our evaluation and keep track of in-class participation and completion of written work. Students maintain folders of their work and at the end of each term write extensive self-evaluations analyzing all aspects of their achievement in class and present a case for a particular letter grade. Linda and I read their evaluations, review their folders, discuss their overall progress and conference with students. Only then do we assign letter grades.

As in Alphonso's case, sometimes we blow it. But students are always free to challenge us, call our criteria into question, and draw our attention to factors we may have overlooked. Every year we tell students about Alphonso to underscore our fallibility and to encourage their vigilance.

Ours is obviously not the only way to grade. But whatever system teachers adopt should derive from a broader anti-tracking philosophy and strategy. In evaluation, as with everything else, we must be bound by considerations of equity, not tradition or efficiency.

An Anti-Tracking Pedagogy

An anti-tracking pedagogy is more than just a collection of good teaching ideas strung together in a classroom with kids of different social backgrounds and educational histories. That may be a step in the right direction, but we still need to ask: Towards what? Is it enough to offer quality education in a heterogeneous setting, as some untracking proponents suggest? I don't think so. Once out of school, our students will still be "tracked" by jobs that require little decision-making and initiative, by high unemployment, by racism and sexism. We can't truly untrack schools without untracking society. Thus an anti-tracking pedagogy should equip educators and students to recognize and combat all inequity. Its organizing principle should be justice—in the classroom, in school, and in society at large. ■

Bill Bigelow (bbpdx@aol.com) has taught high school social studies in Portland, Ore., since 1978. He is an editor of Rethinking Schools *magazine.*

Some of the anti-tracking lessons mentioned here, and others, are described in greater detail in his curricula Strangers in Their Own Country *(South Africa) and* The Power in Our Hands *(U.S. labor history), available from Teaching for Change, www.teachingforchange.org, 800-763-9131.*

what the mirror said

By Lucille Clifton

listen,

you a wonder.

you a city

of a woman.

you got a geography

of your own.

listen,

somebody need a map

to understand you.

somebody need directions

to move around you.

listen,

woman,

you not a noplace

anonymous

girl;

mister with his hands on you

he got his hands on

some

damn

body!

Lucille Clifton is the former poet laureate of Maryland. She has been the Distinguished Professor of Humanities at St. Mary's College of Maryland since 1991. (See p. 212 for teaching ideas.)

SUSAN LINA RUGGLES

PART THREE

TEACHING IDEAS

Drop in to any large teachers convention and you're likely to find hundreds of publishers selling textbooks, manuals, and software which they insist will promote foolproof teaching techniques. You are unlikely to find resources to help you confront the corporate and political forces that shape students' attitudes and beliefs.

This chapter explores practical ways young people can critique powerful influences such as racism, sexism, and homophobia—and celebrate struggles to reclaim their full humanity.

Using Pictures to Combat Bias

By Ellen Wolpert

For many years, I separated my political work and my education work. Politics was something I did before and after work. Education was what I did at my job at the daycare center.

One of the benefits of the women's movement and educational awareness around multiculturalism is that they helped me bridge those worlds and better understand the politics of our everyday lives.

I gravitated toward pictures because I'm a visually oriented person and because young children are particularly sensitive to pictures: During the time they struggle to understand first the spoken word and then the written word, they spend their lives "reading" images to understand the world. Through visual images, I wanted to integrate cultural diversity and challenge the dehumanizing images that children receive.

At first I thought about using visual displays such as bulletin boards. But I found such displays unbearably passive. I wanted to create something the kids could play with, something that would become a part of their everyday activities. I began collecting pictures—from magazines, rummage-sale books, photographs taken by myself of the children's families, newspapers, discarded library books—you name it. Then I used those photos and pictures to make games that were the same kind of games the kids already knew and enjoyed: bingo, lotto, rummy, memory/matching games.

Catalogs are filled with such card games, generally using zoo animals,

Teachers can make "picture cards" to use in anti-bias activities and games.

endangered species, numbers, or stylized graphics. I decided to save the money I spent on such games and use it toward my own picture collection.

In order to make this project more real, let me go through the steps of collecting and using the photos.

First, I've developed three basic sizes of photos: 5 x 7, 7.5 x 8.5, and 7.5 x 11 inches (a full-page picture from *National Geographic*, for example). The smaller photos lend themselves to games such as concentration and rummy, while the bigger ones are good for sorting and counting games.

Second, I try to collect two of each. I then mount the photos on mat board and cover with clear contact paper. While two copies are essential for games such as concentration, rummy and puzzle-type games can be done with single copies.

Third, I try to organize the pictures

around various subjects: families, housing, sports, work, African Americans, Native Americans, women, food, transportation, ways of carrying things, and so forth. The more photos I collect, the better I am able to mix and match and develop a variety of possibilities.

Here's an example of how I use the picture cards for a concentration/memory game using pictures of Native Americans. For a good game of concentration with young children, it is best to have two copies of at least 10 different images. I go through my card collection and pick out 10 sets of pictures that counteract the usual stereotypes of Native Americans, for example, wearing feathers and living in teepees. Some of the pictures I have: a young girl playing football, a man getting on a subway in New York, a man in a pin-striped suit who heads a corporation, a family playing lacrosse, a young boy watching TV in a Seminole chikee, some kids who had set up a lemonade stand, and so forth. (For this collection, I was greatly helped by copies of *National Geographic* that showed Native Americans in contemporary situations.)

I don't permanently separate my collection into discrete groups. For instance, I also use some of the Native American photos in a concentration game with other themes. I might, for instance, use the picture of the man and the New York subway during a game with a transportation theme, or the picture of the girl playing football in a sports theme.

The most important thing is to use the cards to spark discussion. I find this is particularly easy during some of the sorting games, such as a form of rummy.

To make the rummy game, I use about 40 different images. I deal out three to a player, with a draw pile and a discard pile. The idea is to find something in common on three different cards. The players can determine the common attributes—whether it's food, men taking care of babies, women workers, people protesting injustice, housing, and so forth. As we play the game, I try to get the kids talking about what is in the picture and how they determined the common attribute. This not only develops specific language skills, but also forces the children to focus on what is in the picture.

Because I concentrate on images that counter bias, this also indirectly challenges stereotypes. But I also interject comments. For example, one of my children once kept referring to "sitting Indian style" whenever I asked children to sit in a circle on the floor. When we played with my Native American cards, I specifically pointed out cards showing Native Americans sitting on couches, chairs, and so forth.

It's important that teachers create

activities that elicit children's comments in order to pick up on stereotypes and assumptions mentioned in casual conversations. I use those everyday comments as the basis for a game. For instance, if a boy repeatedly mentions that girls can't play baseball, I might pull out pictures that show girls playing sports.

Similarly, when the movie *Aladdin* came out, I decided to collect photos of Arabs doing various things, whether an Arab father reading to his daughter, or an Arab doctor, or an Arab businessman in a "Western" suit. I used these cards to counter the movie's stereotypes of Arabs as hook-nosed, knife-wielding, turban-wearing, Jafar-like "bad guys."

Finally, I think it's important to add your own photographs to such collections. I've taken pictures of kids on the playground, taking special care to show girls playing sports and climbing, and boys playing with dolls or playing "dress-up." I've also encouraged children to bring in pictures, which is particularly useful when we do a unit on families. I have found that such photos are the most "real" to kids and the most valuable part of my picture collection.

They also provide a way for children to readily connect their family lives with their learning.

Pictures alone won't transform a classroom. But they can become a key element in a classroom that encourages tolerance, understanding, and self-respect. As children play with the pictures—as their own images are reflected back at them in positive ways, as their ideas and analytical thinking are encouraged, as they begin to understand that diversity exists everywhere—they will begin to develop pride, self-confidence, and respect for others.∎

Ellen Wolpert is the coordinator of the Cambridge Community Partnerships for Children, in Cambridge, Mass.

My Mom's Job Is Important

By Matt Witt

My mother is a cashier. She works at Zayre's. My mom said to be a good cashier you should be punctual, courteous, broad-minded, honest and accurate."

So begins 5th grader Antonia Guzman's account of her mother's job at a discount department store. But Antonia's account does not stop with the usual recitation of the skills and attitudes people need to fit into the world of work which so often emerge from classroom units on employment. Instead, Antonia goes on to explore her mother's dreams and reflects on the importance of her mother's contribution:

> My mom said that the job she wants if she could change her job right away is to become an entrepreneur. She would like to own a retail business like a gift shop. She would like to be an entrepreneur because she would like to be her own boss, and your income is not limited and you can work at your own pace.
>
> I think my mom's job is important because if there's no cashier no one would keep track of the prices when a customer buys an item or a product.

Antonia is a student at Oyster Bilingual Elementary School in Washington, D.C., a public school whose students come from a wide variety of racial, ethnic, and economic backgrounds. Parents and teachers at Oyster organized a year-long "Program on Work," which demonstrated some exciting approaches to teaching and learning about work.

Drawings by students from Oyster Bilingual Elementary School.

In the Oyster program, children critically examined slides of work situations, interviewed their parents, explored probing questions, entertained controversy, invited parents and other adults into the classroom to talk (and in one case, sing) about work, and constructed a display for parents featuring stories, poems, and drawings they had created. An understanding and respect for their parents' jobs was combined in the unit with the exploration of legal and historical issues.

Why study work? First, because it is a central aspect of our lives and our society. If a goal of education is to teach students to think critically about how our society is organized, their study of work-related issues cannot be limited to learning the difference between "goods" and "services," memorizing a few names like Samuel Gompers or George Meany, and soaking up donated corporate propaganda that paints an incomplete picture of the country's economic life.

Second, studying work is a good way to encourage interaction between students, parents, community residents, and teachers—either by bringing people from the community into the classroom to talk about their work or by sending students out to investigate.

Third, studying work provides stimulating subject matter with which to develop skills such as writing, interviewing, debating, drawing, and singing.

The program at Oyster School began with discussions about work in each class from 2nd grade through 6th, conducted by teachers and parent volunteers. To begin with a subject students could relate to easily, they were shown slides of child labor taken in the U.S. in the early years of this century.

"What are these children doing?" students were asked. When they established that the children in the slides were working—in coal mines, cotton fields, textile mills, and other industries—students were asked, "Why are they working and not in school?"

Exploring Child Labor

Through further discussion, students discovered that as recently as when their grandparents were children, many young people were employed in child labor. This led to many questions: "Why did child labor exist? Who benefited from it, and who opposed it? What did working people do to get it outlawed?"

Slides of modern-day child labor in other countries provoked comments from students from recent immigrant families. "They still don't have any laws against children having to work," said a student who came to the United States from Guatemala. "Children have to do a lot of hard work, especially on the farms."

Students were then asked whether children have a right to get an education instead of going to work, which provoked a discussion about who decides what is a right and what is not.

They were shown slides of people of different races, ages, and genders, and were asked whether they thought it would be legal for an employer looking to hire someone to pick among those people based on those differences. They also saw a slide of a pregnant woman and were asked whether it would be legal to fire her if she refused to do a task that might threaten the health of her unborn child.

After students gave their views, they learned that laws establishing what they considered to be obvious rights had been passed just since their parents were born. Asked how they thought workers got those laws passed, students drew on what they learned during a schoolwide program honoring Martin Luther King, Jr., and the Civil Rights Movement.

"Boycotts," they suggested. "Sit-ins. Strikes. Marches."

Historical slides showed some of these tactics being used, including sit-down strikes in the 1930s and equal rights rallies in the 1960s. Rights, students learned, are not given but won, and change with time as new social movements emerge.

Next, students saw slides of men doing traditionally "male" jobs—doctor, factory worker, coal miner—and women doing traditionally "female" jobs such as secretary, flight attendant, and homemaker. That prompted a discussion about whether both men and women could do those jobs.

The next slides showed men and women doing the jobs that are stereotyped as being only for the opposite sex. Discussion followed on whether all people should be able to choose jobs that suit them, or whether, as a few boys in each class would argue, "the only work women should do is at home."

Another discussion in all classes, including pre-K, kindergarten, and 1st grade, was based on slides of various Oyster parents doing their jobs. Construction workers and housekeepers are more common among the school's families—but the range is wide including a lawyer, a reporter, a dancer, a furniture maker, a cab driver, and aides to government officials. The occupations were discussed from many points of view. "What does the person shown actually do in his or her job? What would be satisfying about the work, and what would make it difficult, stressful, or dangerous? What makes the job important to society?"

In all classes, students were able to identify a number of reasons that each job is valuable to society. In some cases, that led to new questions, such as, "If each job is important, why are some jobs paid more than others?"

BY ALEXANDRA RUIZ
MY FATHER IS A PAINTER

What Do You Do at Work?

When shown slides of homemakers and asked what job these people were doing, a few students answered, "They don't have a job. They just stay home." This provoked lively discussions about the duties of homemakers and both the strains and satisfactions of childrearing.

With these classroom discussions as background, students were assigned to interview their parents or other adults about their work. "What do you do while I'm at school? What do you like about your job? What would you change if you could?"

What they learned from these interviews was as varied as the jobs their parents did. Many children learned that what their parents liked most about their jobs was a chance to meet or help people, while a common complaint was that customers or employers did not treat them with respect.

Some of the recent immigrants told their children they wished they had jobs like they had had in their native countries, instead of the less skilled work they were confined to in the United States.

Other parents talked about problems with shift work, mandatory overtime, and being denied benefits that were due them.

All classes from pre-K to 6th grade had discussions about what they had learned. In the pre-K through 1st grade classes, a parent brought in a guitar and sang with the children, "What does your mama (or papa, grampa, etc.) do? What

status jobs greatly appreciated both the recognition they received and the open discussion of issues of equity in the work world.

Another obstacle was the desire of some teachers to narrowly define the program as "career education." It took a great deal of discussion to convince some that the role of the school was to prepare students not merely to fit into

chance to experience or at least observe one or more jobs would be an obvious complement to discussions and interviews about adults' views of work. Parents from a fourth grade class at Oyster demonstrated the potential for "work experience" activities by arranging for students to work as teacher's aides in a nearby nursery school. When each had had a turn, the students had a lengthy discussion about what they had learned, and prepared an oral report which was given to the rest of the school during an assembly.

Parents with lower-status jobs greatly appreciated both the recognition they received and the open discussion of issues of equity in the work world.

does your mama do? What does your mama do when you're in school, you're in school?" The song would stop as a student explained what she or he had found out, and pick up again when it was time to give someone else a chance.

After all students did drawings and the second through sixth grade classes wrote reports or poems using what they had learned, their work was put on display at the school and compiled in a booklet. Parents were invited to the school one evening to see the display, get copies of the booklet, and take part in a community forum about work along with teachers, students, local union leaders, and local labor scholars.

Problems and Lessons

In carrying out the "Program on Work" teachers and parents at Oyster School encountered a number of problems. For example, when the program was first proposed, some of the white middle-class parents active in the PTA objected that "the poorer families are not going to want the fact that they are a housekeeper or a janitor plastered all over the walls." As it turned out, the opposite was true: Parents with lower-

the world of work as it exists, but to be able to analyze it and critique it.

In adapting the program for other schools, certain omissions would have to be corrected and some program elements could be developed further. For example, children of the few parents at this particular school who were without work were simply told to interview them about jobs they used to have or would like to have, or to interview an older sibling, neighbor, friend, or worker at the school.

In retrospect, more time should have been spent in classroom discussion on unemployment, disability, retirement, and other issues related to people without work. Students could have been asked to think of all the reasons why someone might be unemployed or unable to work, to consider what obligation society has to such people, if any, and to discuss possible solutions. Perhaps someone active in a community organization working to win expanded jobs programs could have been invited to talk with students about the causes of unemployment and proposed remedies.

Particularly for older students, the

Workplace visits are also recommended. They are most fruitful if a worker visits the school first and prepares students to think about the working conditions they will see, how conditions have changed over the years, how decisions are made when problems come up, and so on. Otherwise, such visits tend to focus almost exclusively on what tasks a worker performs at his or her job.

One final suggestion: Schools that need extra funds for materials, transportation, or other expenses to incorporate the world of work into the curriculum might consider asking local unions for help. They also may be able to help set up workplace visits. ■

Matt Witt was coordinator of Oyster Bilingual School's "Program on Work." He is director of the American Labor Education Center and its website, www.TheWorksite.org, which provides downloadable resources.

Father Was a Musician

By Dyan Watson

In the basement they played.
"Jam session" he called it,
halting only to mend a chord or two.

The house swayed from side to side
dancing freely, carelessly
while neighbors shut doors and windows.

Sometimes I would sneak into his bedroom
just to see it, touch it,
pluck a string or two.

At night, I dreamed
of concerts and demos.

I want to be just like him.

Dyan Watson wrote this poem as a student at Jefferson High School in Portland, Ore. She currently is a doctoral candidate in Learning and Teaching at the Harvard Graduate School of Education. (See p. 212 for lesson ideas.)

There's More to Heroes Than He-Man

By Marcie Osinsky

As part of a yearlong folktale curriculum, I began a study of heroes and heroines with my 1st- and 2nd-grade class. First we brainstormed about heroic characters. The Ninja Turtles and He-Man topped the list. The children's concept of heroism did not include people in their lives.

As a result, I decided to use oral history and storytelling to highlight the heroism of people close to them. Children need to see models of strength and courage in their own families and communities in order to identify such qualities in themselves. Oral history and storytelling also are wonderful ways to include parents in building a classroom community that respects differing perspectives and voices.

After making our own definitions of heroism using storybooks and folktales, we invited parents to a "story-sharing breakfast" to talk to us about people who were heroic in their lives.

To prepare the children, I modeled an interview where I made a lot of mistakes. I interrupted and asked questions out of the blue. The kids told me what I did wrong. We then did mini-interviews where I interviewed another adult about his or her heroic person.

Then we had our "story-sharing breakfast." The parents sat in groups with children and told stories and answered questions. The images of all the characters in the stories filled the room. One grandmother talked of how she stowed away on a ship to Europe in World War II to be a foreign correspondent. A man told how he delivered eggs early each day to put himself through college while raising his family.

As the stories progressed, the atmosphere became one of listening, telling, and questioning. Kids were involved in the conversation and learned what was dear to their parents.

Soon after the story-sharing breakfast, for example, Gabriel and Brent were chopping onions in class to make soup. Gabriel was having difficulty and Brent showed him his technique to cut onions, explaining: "This is how I chop onions. This is how my mom chops onions and my nana chops onions. This is how my whole family chops onions. We've been chopping onions like this since—since the cavemen."

The Parents' Stories

The stories connected the kids to another time in history when people also faced everyday hardships and difficult decisions, as some of the kids do now.

While quite a few parents told dramatic stories about war and conflicts from their home countries, others told stories that showed the heroism of difficult decisions and everyday struggles.

One parent, Lynne, told how she wanted to be a dancer and moved from the West Coast to Boston. She told of another dancer who encouraged her and gave her confidence. "I will always remember her," Lynne said, "because she gave me such strength to go after what I wanted to do." One student said of Lynne's story, "She was her own hero, because it was a scary thing to move from California and to become a dancer and live here, and she did it."

One parent told of a man saving her mother's life when she was hit by a car in Haiti. The accident occurred during curfew at a time of political unrest, and the driver did not stop. An ambulance was called but did not come. People were afraid the woman might die. "Then a man walked to her, grabbed her and put her on his shoulder," the parent said. "He carried her to the hospital. If he had not carried my mother, I would not have a mother right now. That man was not afraid to get killed on the street." The kids were upset after hearing the story. They asked, "Why couldn't you go out in the street? Who would shoot you? Why would you get shot by police if you had not done anything wrong?"

As we continued, I began to see how stories help connect the listener to a different time, place, and cultural context, giving the children a sense of belonging to a larger history. After learning that she had family roots in Africa and hearing more stories about the continent, Darlene said, "Oh yeah, I been to Africa, with my ancestors."

Through the project, I discovered the power of storytelling not only to create a curriculum respecting diverse perspectives but to allow parents and children to help shape that curriculum so that it reflects their realities.

The stories from our breakfast became an important part of life at our school. We illustrated and transcribed them and made a book. Throughout the year, the book was read over and over again by the kids and parents. ∎

Marcie Osinsky works with the Boston Teacher Residency Program in the Boston Public Schools.

The Military Recruitment Minefield

By Bill Bigelow

Emiliano Santiago. Not many of our students know his name. But they should. Santiago joined the Oregon Army National Guard on June 28, 1996, shortly after his high school graduation in Hermiston, Ore. He served honorably, became a sergeant, and was discharged in June 2004, after eight years in the Guard.

But in October of 2004, more than three months after his discharge, the government extended Santiago's termination date—to December 24, 2031. Yes, 2031; it's not a misprint. Santiago's unit was ordered to report on Jan. 2, 2005, to Fort Sill, Okla., where it would join other soldiers being sent to Afghanistan.

In November 2004, Santiago's attorney, Steven Goldberg of the National Lawyers Guild, filed suit in federal court in Portland, arguing that the military had no right to order Santiago to active duty months after he'd been discharged. During Santiago's hearing, Matthew Lepore, the Justice Department attorney, agreed that Santiago's activation had come after his discharge. But Lepore said that because commanders of Santiago's unit had been told earlier that under the military's stop-loss policy his unit might be mobilized, that was notification enough.

True, Lepore acknowledged, Santiago himself was never notified, but that made no difference. Lepore argued that the court was obliged to view this case through a "deferential lens"—to assume the military knew what was best for the military. Judge Owen M.

This poster was designed by Jessica Killops, then a senior at Franklin High School in Portland, Ore. It is based on an image by Charles Moffat.

Panner agreed. He ruled against Santiago, saying he believed the military would be harmed more than Santiago if the court ruled against the government. Goldberg's appeal to the 9th Circuit Court of Appeals was rejected.

High school teachers, counselors, students, and parents everywhere should know about Santiago's case. Think you're signing up for four years, or eight years? Think again. Santiago was 19 when he entered the military. When his new discharge date rolls around, he'll be 54—if the military doesn't extend it again.

No Child Left Unrecruited

Thanks to a provision in the No Child write about their experiences with military recruiters. I was astounded by students' stories. One hundred percent of O'Neill's students—three untracked classes of almost 40 students each—had been recruited in some manner by one or another branch of the military. Julie's students were typical of the high school as a whole: largely white and working-class, with a relatively small number of Asian Americans, Latinos, African Americans and Native Ameri-

Marines?" I told them no. He was, like, "You ever thought about having the Marines put you through college?" The Marines called my house at least twice a week. They asked me this year if I ever thought about wrestling for the Marines. I told him no, but he said, "The Marines can help put you through college and pay you to wrestle." One day I was waiting in line to get a bus pass. This Navy guy asked me what I had planned after high school. I told him I might kickbox. He said I could kickbox for the Navy. He handed me his card and walked away.

Thanks to No Child Left Behind, military recruiters have easy access to high school students these days.

Left Behind legislation, military recruiters have easy access to high school students these days. In Portland, where I teach, the school board in 1995 banned organizations that discriminate based on race, sex, or sexual orientation—including the U.S. military—from recruiting in the schools. NCLB overturned that ban, requiring that recruiters have "the same access to secondary school students as is provided generally to post-secondary educational institutions or to prospective employers of those students." The law also requires high schools to provide the military access to students' names, addresses, and telephone numbers—unless a parent or student contacts the school to deny permission to release this information.

It was against the backdrop of the Santiago ruling and increased recruiter access to students that Franklin High School teacher Julie O'Neill began a short unit on military recruitment with her senior political science students. As I was on leave from teaching, Julie invited me to collaborate on the unit.

We began by asking students to

cans. Recruiters had come into classes ranging from Foods ("You have to be in the military to cook for the President, ya know."), to Oceanography, to Band, to Weight Training. Recruiters had visited the Latino Club, played a key role in the annual Field Day activities, worked with the student program that links seniors and freshmen, and approached students in the halls.

They'd badgered students in malls, called them repeatedly, emailed them, visited them at home, bought them school supplies, drove them around town, mailed them videos and DVDs, and invited them to mini-boot camp weekends. Even students whose parents had asked the school in writing not to share information with recruiters reported being contacted multiple times. The recruiters' techniques were consistent: find out students' after-graduation aspirations and attempt to convince them that the military was the way to realize these. Channa's story was typical:

My 10th-grade year when I was
weight lifting, they asked me,
"You ever planned on joining the

The Marines have extraordinary access to students in Weight Training, offering a "Marine Challenge" curriculum where students do 13 pull-ups and bench press half their weight 13 times. Recruiters yell at students and give them orders. One student described being in the weight room, "doing a normal workout and all of a sudden three recruiters were at my side counting my reps. I was like, 'WHOAAH!!'"

Cynthia's story showed how recruiters take advantage of the scarcity of college financial aid in their sales pitches:

A few weeks ago a recruiter called
me, and I wasn't so much annoyed
that they were soliciting me. I was
disturbed by what the recruiter
revealed to me. They asked if I was
going to college, and I said, "Yes, I
am going to the University of Notre
Dame." The recruiter paused, then
fired another question. "Wow. That's
an expensive school. Do you have
money to pay for it?" I replied, "Yes,
they are giving me $30,000 every
year for four years." Dumbfounded,
the officer said, "Well, the Army can
offer you lots of experiences that
college can't." I told him I wasn't
interested, and the conversation
ended. Yet I was left with the impression that they prey on kids with

either no plans after high school and/or no money to pay for college.

A number of students used this predator and prey metaphor to describe recruitment experiences. Zussette wrote, "When I see them talking to high schoolers, they remind me of a pack of lions going in for the kill. They try to get them into a corner or up against a wall. They start to ask questions like, 'Have you ever thought about joining the army?' 'How old are you?' 'You know, the army can help pay for college.'"

The stories also generated grumbling from one or two students. Ben said: "These are so negative. Doesn't anyone have a good story about military recruiters?" But in his own story, Ben wrote about how annoyed he was by recruiters' pressure: "Recruiters are extremely pushy and opinionated. I was promised everything from tuition to guaranteed jobs to free housing."

I read all 100-plus recruitment stories. The more I read, the more overwhelmed I became by the sense that today's students live in a kind of parallel universe where they maneuver daily through a psychological minefield of quota-driven recruiters.

And there was another pattern: Recruiters lie. Claire went with a friend to the recruitment office to take a math test. "When she was done with her test, he told us about how the government pays for you to go to college and after you served you still get money. I think that was the main reason she wanted to join—that and they told her that she wouldn't have to to Iraq. How do they know?"

They don't; it was a lie. In a valuable article, "AWOL in America," in the March 2005 issue of *Harper's*, Kathy Dobie reports that the G.I. Rights Hotline has "heard hundreds of stories involving recruiters' lies." As Dobie reports, "One of the most common lies

told by recruiters is that it's easy to get out of the military if you change your mind. But once they arrive at training, the recruits are told there's no exit, period—and if you try to leave, you'll be court-martialed and serve ten years in the brig, you'll never be able to get a good job or a bank loan, and this will follow you around like a felony conviction." It's not true, but as Dobie speculates, the threats are likely effective in keeping some unhappy soldiers from trying to get out. In fact, the expectation that recruiters make promises they can't back up is acknowledged in the enlistment contract that prospective soldiers must sign. More on that extraordinary document later.

Fahrenheit 9/11

One of the striking segments in Michael Moore's documentary *Fahrenheit 9/11* is the few minutes the film spends with Marine recruiters Staff Sgt. Dale Kortman and Sgt. Raymond Plouhar (later killed in Iraq) as they troll for prospects in the Courtland Mall in Flint, Mich. Julie and I showed this segment in class so students could reflect on a number of the techniques that military recruiters employ to snare recruits. Recruiters' choice of the Courtland Mall in Flint instead of the suburban Genesee Valley Mall is emblematic of recruiters' choices around the country when they concentrate on high schools in working-class neighborhoods—like Portland's Franklin High School—but appear less frequently at high schools in more elite neighborhoods.

We wanted the *Fahrenheit 9/11* segment to reinforce students' own obser-

vations that recruiters probe for an individual's career goal and then link that to a future in the military, as in this exchange:

Sgt. Dale Kortman: Gents! You know we're looking at ya, right! You guys ever thinking about joining up?

John Kingston: I thought about going to college and playing basketball.

Sgt. Kortman: OK, OK. You any good?

Kingston: Yeah. Especially basketball.

Sgt. Kortman: Good. You can play ball for the Marine Corps, as well, you know, travel around the world, get on the Marine Corps basketball team. Um, David Robinson was in the military as well …

Kingston: Oh, was he?

Sgt. Kortman: So, yeah, so, you can definitely hook it up so.

Never mind that Robinson was in the Navy, not the Marines, went to the elite Naval Academy at Annapolis, and is about 7 feet tall. Moore concludes the segment with a poignant comment from a young black man, Martres Brown: "[O]ne would love to have that chance to experience college life, you know, stuff young people can do without having the risk of dying in the process."

Students were unfazed, chuckling at the recruiters' techniques they recognized. Frankly, I think the segment was more startling to me than to the students. They experience this all the time;

> A number of students used the predator and prey metaphor to describe recruitment experiences.

I see it in the movies. But it did reinforce our conversations about their recruitment stories. One student remarked, "It seemed the recruiters were hunting their prey." And another: "One of the all the Portland teachers and counselors who'd taken him up on this offer. "We'll put you up in a nice hotel on the beach." He was sincere, charming, and relentless. I got a taste of how good

Anything that promotes questioning is the enemy of recruiters.

things I notice is that they target people who have low self-esteem." This may or may not be true, but in discussions students agreed that recruiters seem to concentrate on individuals who do not have the highest grades. Interestingly, students also agreed that young women are more heavily recruited than young men.

In the segment from the DVD, Sgt. Plouhar comments to Moore, "It's better to get them when they're ones and twos. And work on them that way." His observation underscores the importance of a critical examination of recruitment practices. Recruiters seek to isolate people in order to "work on them." Anything that promotes questioning is the enemy of recruiters. By contrast, a study of recruitment is best engaged in collectively, as we share stories, look for patterns, patch together insights, and nurture habits of skepticism.

Dream Life of the Culture

Julie had asked students to bring in recruitment brochures, posters, videos, and DVDs that they'd received, so that we could use these to evaluate some of the propaganda techniques used by military recruiters. I'd gone to the local recruitment station to get some more posters and ended up a target of recruitment myself—an all-expenses paid several-day educators' trip to San Diego to learn more about the Marines. The recruiter, Sgt. Héctor Torres, listed

these guys are.

We taped recruitment posters and brochures around the room in ten "stations," and labeled these with Post-it notes one through ten. I introduced the activity by talking a bit about the history of propaganda and advertising. A number of 11th-grade global studies classes at Franklin watch the excellent video *The Ad and the Ego*, probably the best classroom resource on the history of advertising in the United States. I reminded students that *The Ad and the Ego* points out that advertisers' assessment of human motivation has radically shifted since advertising became a major U.S. industry in the 1920s. Then, typical ads were filled with text. Advertisers saw humans as essentially rational beings, who, if presented with sufficient evidence, could be convinced to buy their product. Thus an ad for, say, Pepsodent, would include lots of information on the product, why it's good, bad things that could happen if it's not used, and how to use it. But not any longer. Now, advertisers regard individuals as moved more by image and emotion and less by argument.

I shared with students a quote from University of Massachusetts professor Sut Jhally in *The Ad and the Ego:* "Advertisers don't really talk about things, they talk about these things [products] in relationship to other things which are important to us. So advertising, I think, is the dream life of the culture, because what it reflects is the things

that we really want." Julie and I asked students to pay attention to the deeper appeal in the recruitment materials. We wrote on the board, "What are the dreams that these ads speak to? What are they trying to 'sell' young people on a deep level?"

As a whole class, we practiced on a poster that shows a Marine who appears to be part human and part three-dimensional blueprint—very scientific and machine-like, holding an assault rifle. Students had wonderful insights, finding more dimensions to the ad than I'd considered. They talked about the power that it offers largely powerless high school students, compared it to movies like *The Matrix* and to video games they were familiar with, and pointed out that as part machine it promised indestructibility. As one student commented, "It says, 'I can stand up for myself and no one will hurt me.'"

We divided students into ten groups, and asked each group to go to an assigned poster or brochure displayed around the classroom. We asked them to take notes on the questions we raised and to make any additional observations on the materials. After students spent about four or five minutes at one station, we asked them to move to the next poster and repeated this so that each group was able to view and discuss five of the ten recruitment materials. It was a lively activity, and the students seemed to enjoy peeling back the layers of meaning in the ads.

Afterward, we discussed some of their insights. "This Marine poster is like an invitation to all the weak kids who get picked on: You can defend yourself when you're a Marine. The men are so quick in the picture, it's actually blurred." One of the ads showed young men grimacing as they did pull-ups, with the caption: "Pain is weakness leaving your body." One student commented, "This one is saying that the

Marines will help you rise above pain. You can get away from a bad or abusive childhood and get past it."

We followed up by viewing a short promotional video from the National Guard. (By the way, these are easy to come by as recruiters hand them out like candy to students.) It promises teamwork—"There is no 'I' in 'team'"—and ticks off all the qualities that someone will acquire or develop in the Guard: loyalty, respect, duty, self-less service, honor, integrity, personal courage, and education. As one student pointed out afterward, "It looks like so much fun, it's not even a job. Like all your dreams can come true. Like summer camp for the government."

The 'Contract'

It took me weeks to locate a copy of the enlistment contract that recruits sign when entering the military. [Download a PDF at www.rethinkingschools.org.] Recruiters don't let prospects take it home, they don't let teachers have copies, they don't let parents have copies. No wonder. It's a scary document. Ask Emiliano Santiago.

For some of our students, this document will be the most important contract they sign in their entire lives. Joining the military is a life-altering

---

10 Points to Consider Before Signing a Military Enlistment Agreement

From www.unitedforpeace.com

1. Do not make a hasty decision by enlisting the first time you see a recruiter or when you are upset. A recruiter is a salesperson who will give only a positive, one-sided picture of life in the military. Don't make this important decision when you are depressed, hard up for work, confused or unsure about your future, or pressured by your family. This decision affects many years of your life; don't make it lightly.

2. Take a witness with you when you speak with a recruiter. There is a lot of information to take in. A friend can take notes and help you ask questions.

3. Talk to veterans. Veterans can give you their view of military life, good and bad.

4. Consider your moral feelings about going to war. The mission of the military is to prepare for and wage war. If you cannot in good conscience engage in war or in killing, you should not consider enlisting. If you become opposed to war after you join, you have the right to seek a discharge, but it is a long, difficult, and uncertain process.

5. Get a copy of the enlistment agreement. Read the fine print carefully, especially the part about what the military can order you to do. You do have a right to take this home, look it over, and ask others about it.

6. There is no "period of adjustment" during which you may request and receive an immediate honorable discharge. Once you have left for basic training, you must fulfill the full number of years (usually eight, with some of these in the reserves) on your enlistment contract. You cannot leave of your own free will. The military, however, may decide you are "unsuitable" and discharge you without your consent.

7. Get all your recruiter's promises in writing, but also remember that the military can change the terms (such as pay, job, or benefits) of your work. Though there are no guarantees, a written statement may offer you (as a service member) some protection if promises are not met. However, the contract is more binding on you than on the military. You are ultimately responsible for information on the form, so don't tell lies, even if pressured.

8. There are no job guarantees in the military. The military is not required to keep you in the job you trained for on a full-time or permanent basis. In fact, most recruiters were involuntarily reassigned to their jobs. Placements are mostly dependent on what the military perceives it needs. Most military jobs are in areas that account for only a small percentage of civilian jobs.

9. Military personnel cannot exercise all of the civil liberties enjoyed by civilians. You do not have the same constitutional rights. Your rights to free speech, assembly, petition, and exercise of individual expression (such as clothing or hairstyle) are restricted. You must follow all orders given to you, whether you agree with them and consider them right or fair.

10. Many opportunities exist for you to serve your community and enhance your skills. Before you decide to enlist, check out other options that would help you "be all you can be." Travel, education, money for school, job training, and adventure can all be found in other ways. Your local community may even have opportunities that you hadn't considered.

Check out UFPJ's counter-recruitment website, www. unitedforpeace.org. Click on Campaigns, then click on Anti-Military Recruitment. The 10 Points are also posted in Spanish.

Call the G.I. RIGHTS HOTLINE at 800-394-9544.

decision, and one that the government urges—indeed bullies—young people to make before they're deemed mature enough even to buy a bottle of beer. A critical examination of this document should be part of the core curriculum

friend was told that she wouldn't be sent to Iraq. It reads: "The agreements in this section and attached annex(es) are all the promises made to me by the Government. ANYTHING ELSE ANYONE HAS PROMISED ME IS NOT VALID

the Army focus so much on honor, but not agree to honor agreements?"

As we were teaching this unit, Steven Goldberg, Emiliano Santiago's attorney, offered a workshop for Portland teachers during a districtwide inservice day. In a room full of veteran social studies teachers, Goldberg opened: "So, are we at war?" It wasn't merely an academic question. Section 9c says: "In the event of war, my enlistment in the Armed Forces continues until six (6) months after the war ends. ..." So one's length of service in the military turns on the issue of whether the United States is at war. Some teachers argued that Congress has not declared war since 1941; so, no, we're not at war. Others said that President Bush had pronounced a War on Terrorism, for which Congress voted funds, so that did constitute "war." And U.S. soldiers are dying in combat in Afghanistan and Iraq, so aren't these wars—in fact, if not in title? If 40 teachers with advanced degrees couldn't agree on such a key question, how could one expect an 18-year-old to interpret this part of the document?

It took me weeks to locate a copy of the enlistment contract. No wonder. It's a scary document.

in every high school in the United States. It's not hyperbole to say that this study is a matter of life and death.

The "Enlistment/Reenlistment Document—Armed Forces of the United States"—its official title—is anything but straightforward. In fact, its interpretation was at the center of the Santiago case that went before the 9th Circuit Court of Appeals. In small groups, we distributed colored highlighters to students and asked them to mark passages that they found vague, disturbing, or confusing. We also asked students to circle the four items in the document that they thought were the most important for an individual considering joining the military, and to come up with six questions about the enlistment document.

When we regrouped for discussion, we went page by page. On page 1, Section 8a deals with the delayed entry/enlistment program, which applies to many of our students who join even before they leave high school. Recruits agree to "keep my recruiter informed of any changes in my physical or dependency status, moral qualifications, and mailing address." Students wondered about the definition of moral qualification. Did this mean one's religious affiliation, sexual orientation?

Section 8c implicitly acknowledges that some recruiters may have made false promises—like when Claire's

AND WILL NOT BE HONORED." [emphasis in original] Section 8c has a ring of full disclosure, and implies that if a recruit does get something in writing then it will be honored.

Section 9 tells recruits: "Many laws, regulations, and military customs will govern my conduct and require me to do things a civilian does not have to do." The section states that a recruit will be subject to laws "which I cannot change but which Congress can change at any time." Reading this section prompted one student to ask, "How can one sign a contract that is always changing?"

Arguably the most important part of the contract is section 9b— it makes all promises in the document irrelevant:

> Laws and regulations that govern military personnel may change without notice to me. Such changes may affect my status, pay, allowances, benefits, and responsibilities as a member of the Armed Forces REGARDLESS of the provisions of this enlistment/reenlistment document. [emphasis in original]

Congress must pass laws, but regulations are military matters, and changes in these could nullify other parts of the document. One student said, "Anything they promise you is BS. Look at it." Another added: "All this needs to say is, 'You're the military's. Sign there.'" Another wondered: "How can

Shoot a Bird

Following our examination of the Enlistment Document, we asked students to offer several pieces of advice to prospective recruits based on their reading of the enlistment contract. A few pieces of their advice:

- Read the contract thoroughly.
- Read the Uniform Code of Military Justice.
- Don't sign up for the military because you're mad at your parents; you might never see them again.
- Take a friend to the recruiters.
- Take a lawyer.
- Don't sign unless you're 100 percent sure, 100 percent of the time.

Although from the beginning of the unit we'd emphasized that this was not a study of the war, or even of military service, some students naturally had a hard time uncoupling recruitment from military service itself—as revealed in this piece of advice from Jasmina, a young woman who had suffered through war in Bosnia: "Shoot a bird, and then think about whether you can kill a human."

We distributed a list of 10 pieces of advice from United for Peace & Justice (UFPJ), the organization that sponsors the G.I. Rights Hotline. And we asked students to compare the 10 points with the advice they suggested. Much of students' advice echoed the 10 points, including: take a witness when talking with recruiters, carefully read a copy of the enlistment agreement, and don't make a hasty decision when you're upset. To some of us the items in the UFPJ document might seem to be common sense, but these bits of wisdom may be vital as students make key choices about their futures.

Phony Memo

In class, we had not yet talked about the Santiago case. Julie had a brilliant idea to introduce it. She wrote up a phony memo from the principal full of dire language about how "early data indicate that Franklin is falling far behind projected goals," and is in danger of being labeled a failing school under No Child Left Behind. Thus, the memo read, Franklin's school year will be extended an extra month and graduation will be postponed to June 30. "I apologize for any inconvenience this may cause, but take comfort in the shared vision of Portland Public Schools and Franklin High School to educate all its children," blah, blah, blah. It was pitch-perfect memo-speak. Julie put it on the principal's letterhead (with permission), used his signature stamp, and asked a colleague, Jim Dyal, to feign agitation and deliver the document to her. When he arrived at the door, Julie pretended that she was too busy to deal with it and when Dyal persisted, she asked a

student to read it aloud to the class.

Students bought the charade and were dumbfounded. I took notes as they voiced their anger at this month-long extension of their school year:

"They can't do that, I have plans."

"Can I sue for the plane ticket I bought?"

"Let's walk out. Who's down?"

"Can they do that? This will put so much stress on seniors going to college."

"That's the administration's problem. It's not our problem."

"That's not fair. We've had to make plans for the summer. Can they legally do that?"

It was only when Julie put a transparency of the "memo" on the overhead and asked students to list their arguments against graduation postponement that they realized it was a hoax.

How students react to the lure of the uniform depends, in part, on our curriculum.

We distributed an article on the Santiago case. His enlistment had been extended 27 years. Their school year had been—momentarily—extended 27 days. Julie wanted to give students a small dose of what it would feel like to have one's expectation of freedom ruptured. A number of students were a bit sheepish when they compared their outrage at a delayed graduation with how Santiago must feel as he faces a much greater, and more perilous, delay in his discharge.

We wanted students to understand the government's argument in the Santiago case, as it's a position that anyone considering enlistment should be aware of. Steven Goldberg had faxed us a part of the U.S. government's brief defending its cancellation of Santiago's discharge. It is grounded in the government's interpretation of the "contract" between

the government and an enlistee. Here's a key passage from the brief filed with the 9th Circuit Court of Appeals:

> Enlistment in the armed forces does not constitute merely a bargain between two parties, but effects a change of status by which "the citizen becomes a soldier": "no breach of the contract destroys the new status or relieves . . . the obligations which its existence imposes." Bell v. United States, 366 U.S. 393, 402 (1961) (quoting In re Grimley, 17 U.S. 147, 151-152 (1890)).

In other words, it doesn't make any difference if the government violated the enlistment agreement with Santiago regarding his date of release from military service. Once he signed that contract, he no longer was merely a citizen but was a soldier, and when you're a soldier you're subject to military rule and laws governing the military.

Advertising the Truth

For the final assignment in the unit, Julie asked students to design truth-in-advertising pieces about military enlistment. Each had to have a specific target audience, include a clear message drawing on something studied in class (for example: the Santiago case, the enlistment contract, students' recruitment stories, additional enlistment/military stories that students read, United for Peace & Justice's 10 points). She required them to be visually effective, to be publishable, to provide sources—and to be truthful.

A number of students patterned their alternative ads after actual military recruitment ads or brochures and downloaded images from military websites. Many looked professional and had to be read to recognize the satire, as in Garrett Ross's ad for the U.S. Army Reserves:

> When it comes to strength & security
>
> … No, no, don't bother reading that fine print. It's just legal gibberish. Just sign there. Don't worry, we'll take care of this stuff. We've got lawyers and crap like that. Y'ever shoot a gun, kid? It's really cool.

Emily Beloof's brochure kept the Army's original language on the cover:

> There is another girl inside of you. When you wanted to stop, she pushed you harder. When you needed rest, she ran farther. She knows no bounds and tests all of the limits. She is stronger than you allow yourself to be. There is a girl inside of you who always wanted to run with the big dogs. She will not settle until she has become the best she can be. There is another girl inside you …

Open the brochure, and Emily's text takes a deeper look at "the girl inside of you":

> Can she go the distance when her orders contradict her morals or ethics or what she knows to be right and good? Is she willing to live with broken promises? The Army can change your contract at any time without your permission. Be aware. Know what you do when you join up. She needs your direction. When she considers the military, make sure you ask a few questions.

On the Internet, Jessica Killops found a startling image by Charles Moffat of a woman being gagged by an American flag. She incorporated this into a poster denouncing militarism as an attack on women (see p. 85). Without a doubt, Jessica's statistics that 90 percent of recent women veterans had experienced sexual harassment of some kind in the military, and almost one third of these reported being raped, sent shock waves through the classroom.

First-Time Effort

This was a first-time effort for both of us, so there are some things we would do differently. Ultimately, the fullest evaluation of military service needs to be grounded in an examination of what the military is actually doing. There are essential critical tools students can develop from a unit like this, but it would be more powerful were it connected to a broader look at the role of the U.S. military in the world, particularly in Afghanistan and Iraq. In fact, in our final activity, asking students to discuss their alternative ads in small groups, the discussions that I heard centered on why the United States is involved in Iraq. What's on students' minds is not just recruitment, but the military itself and the Iraq war.

As implied in Ben's earlier comment about wanting to hear a "good story" about military service, a few students thought that by raising questions about the military we were beating up on the United States. They worried that we were attacking decisions that their family members had made, or even challenging their future career choices. These students thought we should have featured stories of vets who had enjoyed and benefited from their service. I can understand how our critical stance could have felt "one-sided" to some students. But our aim was not "balance." This was not a unit on "here's some bad stuff about the military and here's some good stuff." During their senior year of high school, students are massively assaulted by military propaganda. Much is dishonest, much is manipulative. Helping students develop the capacity to question recruitment materials could literally save someone's life. That's what we were after.

If we don't help students nurture this skeptical sensibility about military recruitment and enlistment, then our hidden curriculum is "Do as you're told," "Trust the authorities," "Government knows best." This is profoundly undemocratic. It's a curriculum of ignorance. How we teach about vital issues like recruitment says something about the kind of world we want to help create: Do we want people to be active, questioning, and engaged, or simply to be consumers of other people's plans?

In a recent segment of PBS' *News Hour with Jim Lehrer*, Emiliano Santiago's mother said that as a high school junior Santiago had been "lured by the uniform of the recruiters." How students react to the lure of the uniform, finding "the other girl inside you," or any other recruitment ploy depends, in part, on our curriculum. As military authorities find it increasingly difficult to convince youngsters to enlist, they have begun to send even more recruiters into the field and to authorize larger payments to those who will sign up. We owe it to our students to help them critically evaluate the hard-sell and the lavish promises. ■

Bill Bigelow (bbpdx@aol.com) has taught high school social studies in Portland, Ore., since 1978. He is an editor of Rethinking Schools *magazine.*

Coping with TV: Some Lesson Ideas

By Bob Peterson

"One thousand and ninety-five hours!" Elizabeth shook her head in disbelief as she announced to the class the amount of time she would "have for herself" each year if she reduced her TV watching from five to two hours a day.

"That's over 45 days of time!" added Dennis, as he quickly figured it out on the calculator. The class brainstormed what a kid could do with that much time—learn to juggle or to play a musical instrument, read scores of books, write their own book, get good at a sport. Of course, several in the class proudly proclaimed that if they had that much extra time, they'd do what they liked best to do—watch TV.

For years I chose to ignore TV, on the one hand blaming it for many of my students' problems but on the other feeling it was beyond my control. Yet I came to realize that because of TV's negative impact on children, we must teach children how to cope with television. At La Escuela Fratney, the kindergarten through 5th grade school where I teach, the staff decided to tackle the problem head on and sponsor an annual No-TV Week. Our goal was not only to decrease the amount students watch television but to increase students' skills in critically analyzing television and other media.

Limiting the Habit

Students need to recognize that TV watching can develop into an addiction. Students often are familiar with the word "addiction" and link it to drugs. The anti-TV addiction commercials available on video from the Media

Foundation are useful for sparking discussion of TV addiction (see resources, next page). The commercials show entranced children watching television, and explain how the child is addicted. In follow-up discussions, students can explore the meaning of addiction, different types, and how people overcome their addiction.

Statistics can be helpful. According to Nielsen Inc., children on the average watch about 24 to 28 hours of television per week. The average 5-year-old will have spent 5,000 hours in front of the TV before entering kindergarten, more time than he or she will spend in conversation with his or her parents for the rest of their lives and longer than it would take to get a college degree.

Part of Fratney's success at reducing kids' TV watching was because we worked closely with our students' families. No-TV Week is not aimed just at students and staff but also at family members. During the week, everyone—staff, students, and family members—are asked to voluntarily pledge not to watch TV.

To prepare students for the week, teachers try to raise the students' awareness of how much time they spend watching television. Students keep a weeklong log of the TV they watch, including the names and times of the programs.

Some of the teachers then have each child tabulate the number of hours they watched TV, making comparisons and reflecting on the differences. Some classes rank their favorite shows and discuss why they are popular. For older students, the No-TV Week can be tied to math lessons. The students figure out the average hours of TV watched daily, weekly, annually, or from the time they were 5 years old to age 18.

Some classes prepare "No-TV Week Survival Kits" with alternative home activities such as playing games, going on a bicycle ride, making cookies, or reading a book. One year my class coordinated a schoolwide campaign to come up with 500 things to do instead of watching TV. Another year my 5th graders went to each class and surveyed the students about the types of media/communication devices in their homes—from TVs to computers, from phones to video games. They tallied the data, figured out the percentages, and made bar graphs to display the survey's results.

Because many children have difficulty conceptualizing "life before TV," I have children interview a family member or friend who grew up without television. Questions include: How did your life change after you got a television set? What did you do instead of watching TV?

Parent response to No-TV Week has ranged from wildly enthusiastic, to highly supportive, to nonchalant. Although most of the families fall in the middle, there are a number who tell wonderful stories about how the week forced them to reconsider their television habits. One parent, for example, explained how previously her family had always watched TV during dinner. While she didn't like the habit, she wasn't sure how to change it. After the No-TV Week, she said, she felt confident enough to ban the television during dinner and call for family conversation instead. Another parent said that after the week, she started a practice of telling her kids at breakfast several times a week that it would be a No-TV Day. A third parent said her children even ask for No-TV evenings because they like to play games with Mom and Dad.

Critique

After the first No-TV week, parents suggested we put more emphasis on helping children critique and analyze television. They were concerned not only about the shows but the commercials.

The teachers started by focusing on commercials. On the average, children see 20,000 TV commercials a year—over 350,000 by the time they are 18, according to Action on Children's Television. One of my homework assignments asks students to "Add up the Ads" and to keep track of all the TV ads they saw in one night—both the number and the minutes. This gives the children an understanding of how commercials saturate our lives and gets them to begin thinking how the television industry rests on advertising dollars.

For one lesson plan on commercials, teachers videotaped certain commercials and later watched them with their students. Teachers posed the question, "What messages are sent by the commercial and why?" They also explained the difference between implicit and explicit messages. After watching and discussing various commercials, students wrote about the ads' explicit and implicit messages. As Maria noted, "You seem to be always happy if you eat that cereal." John concluded, "There always are pretty ladies next to new cars. It must be so men come in to look at them."

TV shows can be critiqued in the same way. I have taped segments of cartoons and sit-coms to show in class. We analyze the messages and ask: How are problems solved? Who does most of the talking? What race, gender, and age are the characters in the shows—or commercials? How many instances of violence does one observe? How many put-downs are there? As a follow-up homework assignment, students interview a family member about the positive and negative messages of TV shows. One parent answered, "Children tend to believe that violence is the way to solve problems like in violent TV shows." Another responded, "TV has a bad effect because it absorbs much of the brain."

How much of our kids' brains TV will "absorb" is an open question. But media literacy projects like our No-TV Week present the question for discussion and allow collective reflection on one of the most powerful influences on our children's lives. ■

Bob Peterson (REPMilw@aol.com) teaches at La Escuela Fratney in Milwaukee and is an editor of Rethinking Schools *magazine.*

No-TV Resources

www.tvturnoff.org
This non-profit organization promotes the national TV Turnoff week each April. Includes quotations, statistics, and teaching ideas.

www.whitedot.org
A thoughtful collection of articles about TV and its effect on children.

www.adbusters.org
Produces an excellent print magazine and the Jammers Video/DVD ("The Production of Meaning") that includes startling "commercials" about TV addiction and overconsumption.

Winn, Marie, **Unplugging the Plug-In Drug** (New York: Penguin Books, 1987). Gives a detailed description of how to run a No-TV campaign.

Lappé, Frances Moore and family, **What to Do After You Turn Off the TV** (New York: Ballantine Books, 1989). Hundreds of great ideas.

What Do We Say When We Hear 'Faggot'?

By Leonore Gordon

Alice is 11. She walks down the school halls with her arm around her best friend, Susan. During lunch, they sit on the floor holding hands or combing each other's hair. Lately, Alice has been called "dyke," and boys have been told not to be her friend.

Brian refuses to take part in a fight on his block. As he makes his way home, he hears cries of "faggot" and "sissy." Suddenly he begins to run, realizing that the other children may now attack him.

Carl is gifted musically; he would like to join the elementary school chorus. Although he hesitates for several weeks, the music teacher persuades him to join. One morning soon after, he enters the classroom tense and angry after chorus, muttering that several boys have called him "gay."

Some children play a "game" called "Smear the Queer," in which one child suddenly attacks another, knocking him to the ground. The attacker shouts "Fag!" and then runs away.

Homophobic name-calling is pervasive. Even 1st graders are now using such terms as "faggot" to ridicule others, and such name-calling is increasingly common in the older grades. Homophobic name-calling is devastating to young people experiencing homosexual feelings. For youngsters who are not gay, such name-calling creates or reinforces hostility towards the gay and lesbian population. And it forces all children to follow strict sex-role behaviors to avoid ridicule.

Because homosexuality is such a charged issue, teachers rarely confront children who use homophobic name-calling to humiliate and infuriate other children. Many teachers do not realize that this sort of name-calling can be dealt with in much the same way as other kinds of bigotry and stereotyping.

Teaching children to be critical of oppression is teaching true morality, and teachers have the right, indeed the obligation, to alert their students to all forms of oppression. Educating children not to be homophobic is one way to show the difference between oppressive and non-oppressive behavior.

Challenging homophobic name-calling by teaching children nonjudgmental facts about homosexuality and by correcting myths is also intrinsically connected to anti-sexist educational values, since homophobia is used to reinforce rigid sex roles. Furthermore, if adults criticize other forms of name-calling but ignore antigay remarks, children are quick to conclude that homophobia is acceptable.

Boys are far more likely to be the object of homophobic name-calling than girls, perhaps because sex roles for boys remain, to some extent, more rigidly defined. A boy involved in a traditional "female-only" activity such as sewing or cooking risks out-and-out contempt from his peers, as well as the possibility of being called "faggot" or "sissy." Girls are more able to participate in activities that have traditionally been for boys, such as sports or shop, without loss of peer approval.

At the late elementary and junior high school levels, physical affection between girls is far more acceptable than between boys, but a girl will be called a "dyke" if she does not express, by junior high, a real interest in pleasing boys or in participating with other girls in boy-centered discussions.

As an elementary school teacher, I have made an awareness of oppression and of the concept of "majority" and "minority" a focus of current events, history, and social studies. Throughout the year we discuss those who are not in the majority in this country: Native Americans, Puerto Ricans, blacks, Chicanos, disabled people, older people, and many others. We also discuss women, a generally powerless majority.

If oppression is being discussed, it is impossible to ignore lesbians and gay men as a group that faces discrimination. Children in the middle grades have a strong sense of justice, and they can understand the basic injustice of people being abused because they are different from the majority. They can also identify with the powerlessness of oppressed groups because children themselves are often a verbally and sometimes a physically abused group.

Types of Name-Calling

Group-biased name-calling can be handled in a variety of ways. Sometimes children do not truly understand why a word is offensive. If a teacher simply takes the time to tell the class that a particular word insults or demeans a group of people, children will often stop using the word. (Occasionally, children do not even know what a term means. One New York City 10-year-old who frequently called others "faggot" told me that the word meant "female dog." A 12-year-old said that a lesbian is a "Spanish Jew.")

Discussions about the meaning of homophobic words can often be quite consciousness-raising. When I hear a child use the word faggot, I explain that a "faggot," literally, is a stick used for kindling. I also explain that gay people used to be burned in medieval times simply for being gay, and they had to wear a bundle of sticks on their shirts to indicate that they were about to be burned. (At times, gay men were used as the kindling to burn women accused of witchcraft.) After the discussion that ensues from this revelation, I make it clear to my students that the word is not to be used again in my classroom, and it rarely is.

When I talk about the words "lesbian" and "gay men," there is always a stir of discomfort, so I ask what those words mean. I am also usually told that a gay man is an "effeminate" man. We discuss the stereotyping inherent in that myth, as well as the fact that "effeminate" means "behaving like a woman," and the class begins to realize that "behaving like a woman" is viewed negatively.

When asked what it really means to be called a "faggot" and why it is insulting for a boy to be called "gay," students will often respond that saying a boy is like a girl is the worst insult imaginable. At this point, girls are likely to sense that something unjust has been touched upon, and they will often take up their own defense, while simultaneously having their own consciousness raised.

Before we go on with the lesson plan, I usually attempt to reach a consensus on definitions. Here are some that have

seemed acceptable: "Someone who loves someone of the same sex, but can be close to people of the opposite sex if they want to" and "Someone who romantically loves someone of the same sex." We added the word "romantically" in one class after a boy commented in a confused tone, "But I love my father ..." When discussing definitions, it is important to tell children that gays and lesbians are as different from one another as are heterosexual men and women. There is no such thing as a "typical" lesbian or gay man.

Imagining Names

When we continue with the lesson plan and students are asked to imagine being called names as they walk with a close friend of the same sex, they describe feeling "different," "dumb," "weird," "afraid," and " embarrassed." (One very different response was, "I'd feel loved, because the main thing would be walking with someone I loved.") When asked how they would feel as one of the name-callers, children usually admit that they "would feel like part of the group."

Suggested responses to homophobic attacks have included, "It's my choice," "We like each other, and for your information, we're not homosexual," "I'm not ashamed," "I'm just as different as you are," "I don't care," and "So what!"

I have also used the music of Holly Near to teach about oppression. Songs are an effective tool in reaching children, who seem to retain information presented in this mode quite easily. Near sings about the oppression of many different groups and her songs help students make linkages between their struggles.

Another way to combat homophobia—particularly for older students— is to invite a speaker from a gay organization to talk to the class. Listening to a gay or lesbian who is also a living, breathing human being—someone

who has parents, siblings, and looks a little nervous in front of a group—is often a decisive factor in breaking down homophobic stereotypes.

Homophobic attitudes can also be countered in discussions about sex roles. Students can be asked, "What does a boy have to do to 'act like a girl?'" (and vice versa). The stereotypic behaviors that are mentioned can usually be quickly discounted by asking children to consider their own home lives. Many children, particularly those with single or divorced parents, have seen their mothers working and their fathers cleaning the house.

Another classroom activity is to ask students to look in any standard dictionary or thesaurus for the definitions of "male" and "female," "masculine" and "feminine," "husband," "wife," etc. The definitions are often so blatantly offensive and stereotypic that they create a small sensation when read aloud, thus challenging children to rethink their own definitions.

Discussing homophobic concepts is one thing; enduring homophobic name-calling is an entirely different matter. The pressure to conform is especially overwhelming within the school/peer structure, and it is vital that teachers try to instill the courage needed to function independently when one is the object of ridicule.

I attempt to teach my students to be willing to defend not only their own rights but the rights of others. Because name-calling is so common among children, and because it embodies the bigotry learned from adults, it is a good place for educators to begin. ∎

Leonore Gordon is a poet, teacher, and family therapist.

This article is adapted from The Bulletin of the Council on Interracial Books for Children, *Vol. 14, Nos. 3 and 4.*

Learning from Worms

By Rachel Cloues

Each September the reaction in my 4th-grade classroom is predictable: "Worms? Gross! Why can't we have a real classroom pet, like a rabbit or a guinea pig?"

Rabbits, guinea pigs, turtles, and other more conventional pets are fine, but there are many reasons why I prefer setting up a redworm compost bin in my classroom each year. Worms require much less daily care and they provide endless opportunities for learning about cycles, systems, decomposition, food, soil, science inquiry, and basic ecological connections.

More important, I find that having a worm bin helps children develop empathy, combat stereotypes, and gain respect for all forms of life on earth.

Our classroom "vermicomposting system," which is simply a five-gallon plastic box with a lid and holes drilled in the bottom, sits off the floor a few inches over another lid that collects drips. The bin provides a home for more than 1,000 California redworms, a variety of earthworm that can be ordered online from a number of different worm farms (see resource list) or purchased at a local plant nursery.

During the first week or two of school, the students and I prepare the bin for the worms and make predictions about what will happen in the worm bin. I ask students what facts about worms they already know, and I make a chart for the wall. I also write down what they are interested in finding out. Inevitably, someone states that worms can be cut in half to make two new worms; I respond by saying I have heard cutting worms kills them, and we agree to write the child's statement instead in the question

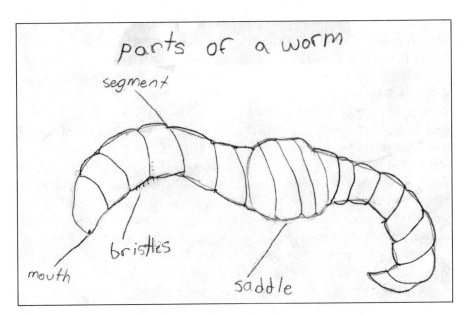

column of the chart. Later I will bring in books that teach the children that, in fact, cutting worms in half results in the death of the worm.

The day I bring the worms to school we sit in a circle and shred enough newspaper to fill the box. Then we add water, mixing with our hands until it feels as moist as a damp sponge. This serves as bedding for the worms and also as a source of carbon. In front of the students I create the first nitrogen-rich food supply—a "worm sandwich"—with moldy bread, wilted spinach, cucumber peels, old bananas, coffee grounds, apple cores, and anything else suitable for a compost pile. Later, the students will bring their own fruit and vegetable compost from home or supply the worms with leftover lunch scraps, but at the beginning I model what is appropriate for the worms to eat.

Adding the worm sandwich to the bin is a dramatic prelude to introducing the redworms. The children wonder out loud whether or not the worms

can see and smell, how they eat, and if they have teeth. They generate other thoughtful questions like, "How do the worms find the food if they don't have eyes?" and "Can you tell the difference between a male and a female worm?" I add their questions to our wall chart.

At this point, we also discuss respect. I ask them what they already know about respecting people and how that translates to respecting other living things. I tell the students that worms are sensitive to noise, vibrations, and bright light. We talk about how the worms will be living in our classroom community and how we should respect them. I ask students how they think the worms should be handled and together we make a commitment to hold them gently. Most of the children are curious about the worms, and their initial reactions range from revulsion to fascination.

Once everyone has had a chance to observe the worms, to hold one if they wish, and to comment, we carefully place them in the worm bin and gently cover them with the newspaper bedding. In six years of having worms in my classroom, I have never observed a student mistreating a worm.

Most of my students come from low-income families and live in apartment buildings. They are the children of immigrants—and often immigrants themselves—from Mexico and Central America. Although many of them have spent scattered time in rural farming communities, and their parents and grandparents have perhaps even farmed, I find that they usually have little experience with gardening, composting, or observing insects and invertebrates in the soil.

I find that the worms in our classroom model healthy eating habits, which is important because my students eat a lot of cheap fast-food meals. Worms thrive on fresh fruits and vegetables. I teach the students that we must avoid putting sugary, salty, and fatty foods in the worm bin because they are not particularly healthy for the worms.

Redworms work quickly, and over the course of the first few weeks of school they eat the newspaper bedding and food scraps we provide and convert them to a dark, nutrient-rich, and odorless compost (this is called "vermicompost," or "worm castings"). The children are amazed when the first worm cocoons appear—tiny but visible lemon-colored globes, half the size of a grain of rice. With patience, we begin to examine baby worms hatching from the egg cases.

When we add food to the worm bin I bring up the concept of recycling. We begin the conversation, which will last all year, on what recycling means both for people and in the natural world. Cycles, in general, are an important curricular theme in 4th grade, and we look critically and in depth at the process of recycling commodities. We examine the water cycle and life cycles of familiar animals and plants, including humans. There are many connections to our worm bin and endless opportunities for comparing and contrasting cycles.

Changing Attitudes

At the beginning of the year many students are reluctant to touch the worms or even look closely at them, but by June the children have come to respect, care for, and sometimes even love our classroom worms. I find that the worms provide an ideal opportunity for teaching about animal stereotypes. Like snakes, spiders, or bats, worms have a negative image. At first, many children refer to the worms as "gross," "ugly," "disgusting," and "slimy." But after they learn about the hard work worms do in the natural environment, they come to appreciate them.

"Did you know," I ask my students, "that earthworms are constantly digging through and eating dead plant material, like leaves, so that all of that stuff doesn't pile up and rot around us outside?" I also tell them how the vermicompost is full of nutrients for the soil, and we can even add it to our classroom plants or schoolyard vegetation. One student wrote about the worm bin:

> When we first got the worms I thought ICKY and I also thought that it was going to be stinky and slimy! But my teacher proved me wrong. She said that [the worm bin] was not smelly or gooey or mushy. She also said that it was damp and a decomposing habitat. So now we still think it is strange but cool at the same time!

On our classroom wall, the students post a colorful construction paper mural they made that shows worms in their underground tunnels. The students are quick to explain to visitors that outside worms dig tunnels underground, allowing water and air to reach the roots of trees and other plants. The children have examined different components of soil like sand, gravel, clay, and decomposing plant material, and they have learned about minerals. They demonstrate a new framework for thinking about soil, what makes it healthy, how it supports life on our planet, and the critical role worms play in that process by breaking down organic matter.

In this era of intense testing and increased desk work in public schools, as well as excessive television and video watching at home, it is becoming more and more difficult to endow students with any ecological understanding or sense of place. In my classroom I try to integrate these concepts into the curriculum as much as possible; I worry that if they are left out, we may end up with a generation of kids completely disconnected from the natural world, and from each other. There is incredible opportunity for hands-on learning about ecology when a worm bin is part of a classroom. It naturally motivates

---

Resources on Worms

Children's books:

Worms Eat My Garbage, by Mary Appelhof.

Worms Eat Our Garbage, also by Mary Appelhof. Classroom teaching guide for all ages with reproducible worksheets and activity ideas.

The Worm Café: Mid Scale Vermicomposting of Lunchroom Wastes, by Binet Payne.

Wriggling Worms, by Wendy Pfeffer.

Vermicomposting for kids:

www.niehs.nih.gov/kids/worms.htm

Redworm suppliers:

Earth Angel Worm & Garden; www.buyworms.com, 888-BUY WORMS
www.happydranch.com
www.wormswrangler.com

children to be interested in science and to think critically.

A book by Mary Appelhof, *Worms Eat Our Garbage,* is a wonderful classroom resource for all ages with non-harmful worm experiments, observation ideas, and reproducible worksheets. But I incorporate our worm bin into lessons ranging from science and math (how does one measure a worm?), to nutrition and health, to language arts. A challenging assignment is to ask students to describe in detail what they see, smell, and hear when they observe the worm bin closely. A group of students one year wrote, "The worm bin smells like soil, wet wood, the ground after it rains, and pine cones."

Foss and Science Ethics

My worm curriculum contrasts in some important ways with the packaged science curricula supplied by the school district. For example, the Foss 2002 edition of the *Insects* curriculum aims to teach 1st and 2nd graders about the life cycles of mealworms, waxworms, milkweed bugs, silkworms, and butterflies. The curriculum instructs teachers to order the insects from a science supply company, create habitats for them in the classroom, teach students about the respective life cycles, and then discreetly kill the insects at the end of the unit.

In the "Plan for the End of the Life Cycle" instructions, the teacher's guide states: "The humane way to end the cycle of waxworms is to put the culture in a freezer overnight and then dispose of the medium in the trash." While I understand that the curriculum and the instructions within are intended to be an easy method for busy teachers to teach students science concepts, I believe educators have a responsibility to teach more authentically. It is hypocritical to pretend to establish a "real" life cycle for students to observe, and then to put an end to that cycle artificially. Not only do students and teachers gain a false impression of the

life cycle of that insect, they learn that the lives of insects are disposable. The unspoken result of the lesson is that the teacher, in fact, controls the life cycle.

The Foss unit on painted lady butterflies is also disturbing, for a different reason. The teacher's guide makes a weak attempt at addressing the problem of introducing nonnative species to an environment, but it then instructs the teacher to do just that:

> After a month the [butterflies] will die, not because of any ill effects caused by captivity, but because that is their normal life span. Even though it is never advisable to release study organisms into the environment, if a painted lady butterfly 'escapes,' it will not be an environmental disaster—painted ladies are already well established throughout the country.

I recently learned that most species of earthworm are not native to the temperate deciduous forests of the Northeastern and Midwestern United States; the native worm population was killed off by glaciers during the Ice Age. European species were later brought over by settlers and have, in fact, been harmful to the forests in that part of the country—especially to some maple trees. This could be an interesting and important issue to bring to the attention of students, particularly in the states where invasive worms are affecting forests. The causes and effects of nonnative species introduced to new ecosystems can be explored in any bioregion, and certainly could be incorporated into a unit of study about earthworms.

Within the classroom, a worm bin is a harmless model for studying many kinds of life cycles, including plant, worm, and a diverse variety of decomposer organisms. The worms continue to live year after year, producing egg cases and dying in the worm bin. I always take my bin home for the summer months, but someone unin-

terested in that possibility could easily find a family or co-worker to adopt the worms, even someone who lives in an apartment. Another benefit of raising worms is that the resulting compost provides an outstanding natural fertilizer for classroom plants or a school or community garden plot. I have even sent vermicompost home with students in resealable bags, with a note to parents explaining its use for houseplants.

Although a weekly farmers market is set up within a mile of the school, none of my students' families shop there. The local, organic produce is too expensive. With our worm castings from the classroom bin, we have been able to start our own vegetable seedlings at school. Last year, for the first time, we began a small classroom garden in some available soil in the courtyard. In the springtime, we harvested and ate organic snap peas, radishes, carrots, and broccoli. The farmers market may still be too expensive for my students' families, but they have gained an awareness of how food can be grown, and what "organic" means. They have begun to learn about sustainable agriculture.

I have found that a worm bin is a simple and powerful learning tool. Balanced vermicomposting in the classroom requires that teachers and students work together as a team. Along with my students, I find myself challenged to think deeply about the connections between our daily lives—especially what we eat—and the earth that provides our food. The worms help my students examine stereotypes, biases, and fears, as well as to confront their own actions and how they affect the planet. Each year, the students stop asking for a pet rabbit or guinea pig. Instead, they put their ears close to the worm bin and listen carefully to hear the worms eating. ∎

Rachel Cloues teaches 4th grade at Sanchez Elementary in San Francisco.

The Organic Goodie Simulation

By Bill Bigelow and Norm Diamond

This activity is about power. Set in an imaginary society, it poses students a challenge: Can you overcome divisions and unite to create needed changes? If so, what circumstances encouraged this unity? If not, why not? Unfortunately, these days many students are cynical about their capacity to work together—for a better school, a better community, a better society. Without confronting that cynicism, students run the risk of dismissing much of the history from which they could draw hope for the future. This lesson lets them experience some of the pressures that lead workers to organize. Depending on what happens in class, students either glimpse the possibility of organizing and practice overcoming cynicism, or gain an experience out of which their attitudes can be directly discussed. It's also a lot of fun.

Grade Level

Middle school to adult.

Materials Needed

One large machine-like object, e.g., a TV or an overhead projector.

Time Required

One class period (at least 45 minutes) to "play," and time for a follow-up discussion.

Procedure

1. Close the door and pull the blinds in the classroom. Tell students to imagine that we are going to have to live in this classroom for the rest of our lives (many groans). Explain that there is no soil for farming but we are in luck because we have a machine that pro-

duces food—organic goodies. Correct yourself, and point out that actually *you* own the machine. Put the projector or whatever machine you've selected in the front of the classroom.

2. Tell students that you need people to work for you producing organic goodies. Workers will receive money to buy enough food to live on—those not working will find it hard to survive. Ask for volunteers who want to work, eat, and survive. (On those occasions when additional coercion is necessary, we tell students that to receive credit for the activity they must not starve.) Choose only half the class as workers. The other half will be unemployed. Sit the two on opposite sides of the room, one group facing the other.

3. Now explain the economics of your society. Put the "Organic Goodie Economy" chart (see below) on the board. (You might want to have the chart up earlier, covered with a map or a screen.)

Explain that five organic goodies a day are necessary to survive in a fairly healthy manner. Those receiving less, the non-workers, will gradually get sick and starve. Go over the chart with students: Each worker *produces* eleven (11) goodies a day. All workers are *paid* $6.00 a day. A goodie costs $1. One dollar is deducted from the pay of each worker to make small welfare payments to the unemployed. So, after taxes, a worker can buy five goodies a day, enough to survive. Explain that as the owner, you of course deserve more because it's your machine, and without your machine everyone would starve.

4. Show the unemployed that, as the chart indicates, they only receive $2 a day in welfare payments. This means they can only buy two goodies a day—they are slowly starving to death. They desperately need work.

5. Make sure each student under-

stands his or her position. Now the "game" begins. Your goal is to increase your profits—that's all you're after. The way you can do this is through cutting wages. *Note:* No money or goodies are actually exchanged. We generally begin by telling students to imagine that a number of weeks have elapsed and then ask members of each group how they have been eating, how they're feeling. (By the way, everyone *could* be employed to produce goodies—eleven a day, as mentioned—but we don't tell that to students unless they ask.)

6. There is no "correct" order in which to proceed, but here are some techniques that have worked for us:

■ Ask which of the unemployed people wants to work. Offer someone $5.50 a day—less than other workers but more than the $2 they're getting now in welfare payments. After you have a taker, go to the workers and ask who is willing to accept $5.50. Fire the first person who refuses to accept the lower wage and send him or her across the room to sit with the unemployed. Hire the unemployed person who was willing to accept the lower wage. Con-

tinue this procedure, trying to drive down wages.

■ Occasionally you might ask workers to repeat after you, "I am a happy worker." Fire those who refuse and hire someone who is unemployed.

■ We often make derogatory comments about the "welfare bums" and invite workers to do the same. (Later we can talk about why the people were on welfare, and who was the real bum.)

■ Anyone who mentions "union" or striking or anything disruptive should be fired immediately. Get all workers to sign "yellow dog" contracts promising never to join a union as long as they work for you.

■ Sometimes we hire a foreman (a spy), for a little more money, who will turn in "subversive" workers. Occasionally we whisper something in a worker's ear, to encourage suspicion and division among workers. Someone usually threatens to take over the machine. When this happens we hire a policeman or two to protect it. We explain that she or he is here to protect "all our property equally, not just my machine." Having someone physically protect the machine also alerts students to the fact

Organic Goodie Economy

Production = 11 x number of workers

	Per Day		
	Workers	*Unemployed*	*Owner*
Wages	$6 x no. workers	Nothing	Nothing
Taxes	–$1 x no. workers	+$2 x no. unemployed	–$1 x no. unemployed (see note)
Consumption	5 Organic Goodies x no. workers	2 x no. unemployed	6 Organic Goodies
Surplus	Nothing	Nothing	4 x no. workers, minus 6 for daily consumption

Example: If there were 10 workers and 10 unemployed, a total of 110 goodies would be produced. After taxes, the workers would be able to consume 50. From welfare payments, the unemployed would consume 20, leaving a total of 40 for the owner—34 after consuming his or her six.

Note: Workers' and owner's tax needs to provide $2 to each unemployed person (taxes paid in goodies).

that they could take it over.

■ It's important to keep workers and unemployed from uniting to strike, or worse, to take control of your machine. You can offer privileges to people to prevent them from seeing their common interests—differential wages, shorter work days, perhaps even profit sharing.

■ If they are successful in uniting and stopping production, you have a couple of options: 1. You can wait them out, indicating your surplus, and how quickly they will starve (use the chart to remind them how much you have left over everyday); or 2. Give in to their wage demands and a little later raise the price of organic goodies. After all, you can justify your need for more income to meet your higher costs.

■ Sometimes we announce that every three minutes an unemployed person will die of starvation. This emphasizes to the entire class that should they fail to act there will be consequences.

7. The game is unpredictable, and a range of things has happened while playing it. What *always* happens, however, is that people try to get organized. The game ends when students have had ample opportunity to get together—successfully or otherwise. Participants may be totally demoralized or they

may have taken over the machine and decided to run it collectively.

8. For homework, we ask students to write on the experience. Questions might include: What did you personally do to try to stop my efforts to divide people? How effective were you? Were there actions you considered, but didn't take? Why not? If we were to do this simulation again, what different actions would you take? We also ask students to comment on the Fred Wright cartoon (see p. 100), and how it relates to our activity.

Additional discussion and/or writing questions include:

■ What methods did I use to try to keep people from getting together to oppose me? When was I successful? When unsuccessful?

■ At which points were you most successful in getting together? When were you least successful?

■ What kept you from immediately calling a meeting and demanding equal treatment, or simply walking over to the machine and taking it over? Here we try to get at students' preconceptions about people's capacity to stick together. Did they think that efforts to unite all workers and unemployed would eventually be betrayed? Why? We want to explore with students what in their lives would leave them hopeful

or skeptical. Have they had experiences that convinced them that people could unite and act together for important goals?

■ As the owner, what kind of attitudes would I want you to have about your ability to work together as a unified group? What attitude would I want you to have about property rights? About respect for authority?

As a follow-up activity, sometimes we ask students to think of a time when they were able to work successfully with others toward a common objective. We ask them to write this up as a story. We then share our stories in class and take notes on the circumstances that allow people to unite—creating what we call a "collective text," the wisdom we can draw from each other's lives.

Does all this sound too complicated? It's not. A number of teachers have told us, "I didn't want to do that activity because I wasn't sure I could remember everything, and I didn't know if it would work." As they discover: It works.■

Bill Bigelow (bbpdx@aol.com) has taught high school social studies in Portland, Ore., since 1978. He is an editor of Rethinking Schools *magazine. Norm Diamond is active on education and labor issues in Portland, Ore., where he taught at the Pacific Northwest Labor College, an institution of higher education geared toward workers and their families.*

This article is adapted from Bigelow and Diamond's The Power in Our Hands: A Curriculum on the History of Work and Workers in the United States *(Monthly Review Press, 1988), available from Rethinking Schools, 800-669-4192 or www.rethinkingschools.org. The inspiration for this lesson came from Mike Messner's article "Bubblegum and Surplus Value,"* The Insurgent Sociologist, *6 #4 (Summer 1976): 51-56.*

This article is reprinted by permission of Monthly Review Foundation.

World Poverty and World Resources

By Susan Hersh and Bob Peterson

An important part of a person's understanding of global issues is the recognition of the dramatic inequalities between nations and social classes within countries. Math is an essential tool for acquiring this understanding.

The purpose of this activity is to demonstrate graphically the vast differences in wealth between different areas of the world. It combines math, geography, writing, and social studies.

We remind students of some of the things we learned about colonialism, such as how great quantities of silver and gold were stolen from the Americas and taken to Europe. We also explain that current relations between countries and international organizations, such as the World Trade Organization, also affect how much wealth countries possess. We make sure that students know the following terms: resources, GNP, wealth, distribution, income, power, and colonialism. (Additional teaching ideas that help set the context for this lesson can be found in *Rethinking Globalization*. See Resources, p. 226.)

Materials Needed

■ 11" x 17" world maps for each student or pair of students.

■ 50 chips (25 of one color and 25 of another) for each map.

■ 25 slips of paper with "I was born in [name of continent, based on chart]."

■ 25 chocolate chip cookies.

■ World map laid out on playground, or signs with names of continents and yarn to distinguish boundaries.

■ Transparency of "World Population and Wealth" table (p. 104).

■ Six "negotiator" signs with yarn to hang around students' necks.

■ Writing paper and pens or pencils.

■ Additional cookies for students

who don't get any during the simulation (optional).

■ Worksheets (optional) for students to write down their estimates (available at www.rethinkingschools.org/math).

World Population and Wealth

Continent	Population (in millions)	% of World Population	# of Students (in a class of 25)	Wealth (GNP) (in billions of dollars)	% of World GNP	# of Treats (out of 25)
Africa	906	14.0	4	495.4	1.8	0.5
Asia	3,905	60.4	15	7,172.6	25.5	6
Oceania	33	0.5	0	442.4	1.6	0
Europe	728	11.3	3	9,606.3	34.2	9
U.S. and Canada	331	5.1	1	8,933.6	31.8	8
Latin America	561	8.7	2	1,430.7	5.1	1
World Total	6,465	100.0	25	28,081.0	100.0	24.5

Sources: World population figures are from the U.N. Population Division, www.un.org/esa/population, based on estimates from July 2005. GNP figures are from the World Bank, quoted in the Universal Almanac, 1994. GNP is the total national output of goods and services. Percentage of world wealth is an estimate based on total GNP.

For the purposes of this chart, one third of Russia's GNP is attributed to Asia and two thirds to Europe. Latin America includes Mexico, the Caribbean Islands, and South America.

Suggested Procedure

1. Give each student or pair of students a world map. Have them identify the continents and other places you have been studying.

2. Ask students how many people they think are in the world. After students have guessed, show them an almanac or a website with a current estimate. Ask: If we represent all the people in the world with 25 chips, how many people is each chip worth? (For 6.5 billion people, for example, each chip would represent 260 million people.)

3. Give 25 chips to each student/group and have them stack them on the continents, based on where they think people live. Have students write down their estimates using the worksheets mentioned in the materials list or on a piece of paper. Discuss student estimates and then tell them the accurate figures. Have them rearrange their chips to reflect the facts. Ask students what the differing stacks of chips tell them about the world's population.

4. Explain that you are now going to give them another 25 chips of a different color and that they represent all the wealth produced in the world (the monetary worth of all the goods and services produced every year, from health care to automobiles). Each chip therefore represents 1/25 of the world's total amount of goods and services produced. Tell the students to put the chips on the continents to indicate their estimate of who gets this wealth.

5. Discuss student estimates and record them on the chalkboard. Have students reflect on the sizes of the two different sets of chip stacks, representing population and resources. Collect the chips.

6. Tell students you are going to demonstrate how population and wealth are distributed by continent. Have each student pick an "I was born in…" slip from a container labeled "chance of birth." Students may not trade slips. (As you distribute the slips, listen for stereotypical reactions to the conti-

nents—these will be useful in the follow-up discussion and will indicate possibilities for future lessons.)

7. Have students go to an area that you have designated to represent that continent. (Playground maps work great for this.) After students are in their areas, remind them that they each represent about 260 million people and that you are going to distribute the world's wealth. Have each continent/group designate one person to be a "traveling negotiator" and distribute a traveling negotiator sign to those people.

8. Explain that once the bag of resources is passed out to a representative from each continent, each group needs to sit in a circle and discuss their situation. Tell the students there will be a cross-continent negotiation session, then a time for the traveling negotiators to return to their home base to discuss their negotiations with the rest of their group, and finally a time for any trading or donating of resources. Students on each continent are to talk about how

many resources they have compared to people of other continents and to discuss ways they might negotiate to increase their resources. They may plead and/or promise. (Note: Every continent, except North America, will have at least one "stay-at-home negotiator" and one traveling negotiator. The North American person can stay put or travel throughout the world. Also note that because Mexico is by most definitions part of North America, I explain to the students that for the purpose of this simulation we will be using "Latin America," which includes South America, Central America, and Mexico; instead of "North America," we will use "United States/Canada.")

9. Use a popular treat—such as chocolate chip cookies—and distribute them according to the percentages noted in the chart. Announce the number of treats you are giving to each continent as you do so. Provide a paper bag for each continent to keep their treats in. As you dramatically place each of the resources into the bag, remind students they are not to eat the treats until after the negotiation session.

10. Announce that the negotiation session is to begin. Only traveling negotiators may move to a different continent. When they come, they should sit in a circle with the stay-at-home negotiators and discuss the distribution of wealth and what should be done about it.

11. After five or 10 minutes, tell all traveling negotiators to return to their home continents. Each group should then discuss the negotiations. After a few minutes, announce that the trading session may begin, and if a continent wishes to trade or donate resources, they may. After that, instruct the people holding the resource bags to distribute the resources to people in their group.

12. Give each continental group tag board and markers. Tell them to make

some signs that describe what they think of the way the resources were distributed.

13. Bring students back together for a whole-class discussion. Have each group share their posters and perspectives. Show students the information from the world wealth chart via a transparency or handout. Connect their emotions and feelings of fairness to the information on the chart. (At this time, a teacher might give out additional treats to those students who did not get any.)

Questions Worth Posing if the Students Don't Ask Them Themselves

■ How did the distribution of wealth get to be so unequal?

■ What does the inequality of wealth mean in terms of the kinds of lives people lead?

■ Who do you think decides how wealth is distributed?

■ Should wealth be distributed equally?

■ Do you think that, within a particular continent or nation, wealth is distributed fairly?

■ How does the unequal distribution of wealth affect the power that groups of people hold?

■ Within our community, is wealth distributed fairly?

■ What can be done about the unequal way wealth is distributed?

■ Who can we talk with to find out more information about these matters?

If your students have studied colonialism, ask them what role they think colonialism played in creating this inequality.

After the discussion, have students write about their feelings, what they learned, what questions they continue to have, and what they might want to do about world poverty. Some students might also make wall posters that graphically depict the inequality of wealth.

Follow-Up Activities

A few days after this simulation, "Ten Chairs of Inequality" (included in *Rethinking Mathematics*) is a useful activity to help students understand that wealth is also unequally distributed in individual countries.

Students also can do follow-up research on related topics, such as: the role colonialism played in the wealth disparity; how current policies of U.S. corporations and the U.S. government affect people in poorer nations; the role of groups such as the WTO and the International Monetary Fund; and what different organizations and politicians are doing about world poverty. (Refer to the list of "Organizations and Websites for Global Justice" in *Rethinking Globalization*. See Resources, p. 226.)

Three notes of caution with this activity: First, as with any simulation (or role play) this should be understood to be just that—a simulation. We can in no way reenact the violence of poverty and hunger that kills tens of thousands of children daily. We are providing a mere glimpse. Second, while Africa and other areas south of the equator do not have lots of wealth as defined by GNP, those areas have great human and natural resources and this fact should not be lost on the students. Finally, in this simulation we seek to describe rather than to explain current power and wealth arrangements. They can, however, be powerful tools in motivating students to want to figure out the answer to the essential question: Why?■

Susan Hersh developed this lesson while teaching 5th grade at La Escuela Fratney in Milwaukee.

Bob Peterson (REPMilw@aol.com) teaches 5th grade at La Escuela Fratney in Milwaukee and is an editor of Rethinking Schools *magazine.*

Math, SATs, and Racial Profiling

By Eric Gutstein

In our classrooms, we may not often think of technology as a tool for teaching for social justice. But in my experience of teaching middle school mathematics, I've found that technology can be a powerful asset.

Although I am a university-based mathematics educator, I regularly teach at Rivera school, located in a Mexican immigrant community in Chicago. The following are examples of how my students and I have used technology to investigate racial profiling and to analyze the relationship of family income level to scores on standardized tests.

In particular, I want to show the potential of using graphing calculators with students. (A graphing calculator is basically a hand-held computer that can do sophisticated mathematics, display various types of graphs and create tables from data, and perform various types of statistical analyses. While they are still too expensive for many students, many high school and middle school math departments have them.)

Mathematics plays a central role in understanding racial profiling. The essence of profiling is proportion and expected value: A higher proportion of African Americans (or Arabs/Arab Americans today) are stopped and searched than would be expected given their percentage in the population—assuming random (i.e., fair) searches or stops.

Driving While Black

In 2001, I did a project with my 7th-grade class called, "Driving While Black/Driving While Brown: A Mathematics Project About Racial Profiling." I gave students data about percentages of stops of Latino drivers and the percent of Latino drivers in Illinois. This was a difficult project conceptually because students had little experience with the mathematical ideas of expectation.

In mathematics, expected value is based on theoretical probability. If 30 percent of drivers are Latino, we would expect that 30 percent of random stops would be of Latinos—but only in the long run. This does not mean that if police made 10 stops and five were of Latinos something is necessarily out of line, but it does mean that if they made 10,000 stops and 5,000 were of Latinos, something is definitely wrong.

Technology comes in handy to show how actual results tend to converge with theoretical probability as the number of events increases. I used a graphing calculator in class to demonstrate this on a graph called a histogram, which can visually display the results of probability events. I used a simple computer program (written for the calculator) that simulates a dice-tossing situation. If you throw two dice, the probability of throwing a seven is 1/6, while the probability of throwing a two is 1/36. However, if you toss two dice and do this just six times, there is good chance (about 1 in 3) that you won't even get one seven!

With the calculator and program, I simulated 10 tosses, then 100, 1,000, and finally 10,000, and we looked at each resulting histogram (shown on an overhead projector that displays the calculator screen). As the number of tosses increased, the histogram began to take on the "ideal" shape as predicted by the theoretical probability (for example, 1/6 of 10,000 is about 1,667, and we had quite close to that number of sevens). These gradually converging "shapes" helped students realize that the greater the number of "trials," the closer to the theoretical probability the results should be.

Students learned important mathematical ideas about probability through considering actual data about "random" traffic stops and compared these to the theoretical probability, what we should "expect." Graphing calculators can easily simulate large numbers of random "traffic stops," since they have a built-in "random" number generator.

Without calculators, one can still do the simulation, albeit with fewer repetitions and more effort. I had students pick cubes from a bag (without looking) where three of 100 were brown (Latino), and the rest white (because in that part of Illinois, three percent of the drivers were Latino.) Each group's record of 100 picks simulated how many Latinos should have been stopped out of 100 random stops. We then combined all the groups' data and had a larger number that came fairly close to 3 percent, although individual groups' data ranged from 2 percent to 7 percent. But in real life, the percentage of Latinos actually stopped was about 21 percent. Students saw through their own simulations that what they "expected" was not what the Illinois State Police actually did.

At the end of the project, students had a range of responses, but most reached the conclusion that the disproportionate number of traffic stops for

Latinos was related to racial discrimination. A fairly typical response was:

> I learned that police are probably really being racial because there should be Latino people between a range of 1-5 percent, and no, their range is 21 percent Latino people and also I learned that mathematics is useful for many things in life, math is not just something you do, it's something you should use in life.

But not everyone saw it that way. One student commented:

> Police are maybe just stopping people because they might look suspicious, drunk, or something. They don't just stop you for anything. I think that this project was not accurate to prove anything. I mean what is it proving, it is not accurate in the cubes.

In hindsight, a weakness in the project was that although students understood that the data showed something was amiss, we spent insufficient time discussing and analyzing the complexities of racism. What did emerge was students' sense of justice ("Why do they make random stops? … just because of their race and their color?") and sense of agency, as well as perhaps a sense of naivete ("And Latinos shouldn't let them [police], they should go to a police department and tell how that person was harassed just because of a racial color").

Bias in SAT Scores

This issue of the complexity of the social issues also surfaced in an earlier project I did with an 8th-grade class in 1998-99. In this project, students investigated the relationship between race, gender, and family income and ACT and SAT scores (see table). We were studying data analysis and creating scatterplots, a type of graph one can use to visually inspect the correlation of two variables (e.g., test scores and family income). Students had to create a scatterplot from data that I downloaded from FairTest's web site (www.fairtest.org). We did not use graphing calculators for two reasons—individual scores and income levels were not available (the FairTest data aggregated the 1,127,021 students who took the test in 1997 by income level ranges of $10,000 or $20,000) and at the time, Rivera had no graphing calculators (they have since bought a classroom set). But if individual data were available and we had calculators, I would have had groups of students input 500 pairs of data and inspect the graphs. At Rivera, due to circumstances, students made hand plots.

For the SAT, the raw data themselves make the correlation pretty clear (since the data set is so small), but the graphs students created made it even clearer to them. SAT scores go up in an almost lockstep correlation with family income. Students, who also saw Mexican Americans near the bottom of the listed racial groups and males above females, had plenty of questions. In Part 2 of the project, I had students write letters to Educational Testing Service (ETS) about the data, asking any questions and making any points they wanted to. Their responses ranged, but many asked pointed (and sometimes confused) questions about inequality and about the interrelationships of race and class. Samples from two letters follow:

> Both the SATs and the ACTs had a low score if their income was low. I think this really isn't giving anyone a chance. You see, what if you have a really smart student that only [has] an income of $9,000, would he/she

1997 SAT Scores by Race

Total Test-Takers = 1.1 million (1997 data)

	Verbal	Math	Total
American Indian or Alaskan Native	475	475	950
Asian, Asian Amer., or Pacific Is.	496	560	1056
Black or African American	434	423	857
Mexican American	451	458	909
Puerto Rican	454	447	901
Hispanic/Latino	466	468	934
White	526	526	1052
Other	512	514	1026
Males	507	530	1037
Females	503	494	997
All Test-Takers	505	511	1016
less than $10,000/year	428	448	873
$10,000 - $20,000/year	454	464	918
$20,000 - $30,000/year	480	492	972
$30,000 - $40,000/year	496	497	993
$40,000 - $50,000/year	507	508	1015
$50,000 - $60,000/year	515	518	1033
$60,000 - $70,000/year	522	526	1048
$80,000 - $100,000/year	540	544	1084
more than $100,000/year	559	571	1130

Source: 1997 Profile of College-Bound Seniors, College Board

not get much of an education? Is it just a stereotype or do you give a better education to people that pay more? If this is true, I hope you can make a change.

I have noticed that the people and genders who have been "oppressed" are doing worse than the "whites." I have noticed that many books used at my curriculum (8th grade) have not been related to me in any way because I'm a Mexican-American. I don't believe that they relate to anyone except "whites." For some reason I believe that's the reason, but not the whole reason. ... Minorities—when you hear that word, what does it mean? It means poor African Americans, Mexican Americans, Puerto Ricans and other poor non-white people. You don't hear a lot about poor whites and minorities! You hear about rich whites. So who do you think has the high scores with the high salaries? Who? Why?

This story would not be complete without raising a few other issues. For three full class periods, we sat in a circle, and students read and discussed their letters with each other. This was difficult and emotional, since students saw themselves at the bottom of the data. But this was an honors class, and students were strongly college oriented. They wanted an answer to their key question: Why are we on the bottom?

I tried to help them understand that there were multiple, interconnected reasons: that schools in general and the tests in particular did not value (nor assess) their "cultural capital"—their home language, culture, ways of communicating, and experiences—but were instead geared to that of white, middle-class families. We talked about how schools in wealthier areas usually had more resources, smaller classes, more experienced teachers, and more challenging curricula, and that in the United States,

the overall educational opportunities for urban students of color tended to be inferior to those of white students.

But some of these ideas were abstract to students who rarely experienced other communities or cultures, and we did not end the discussion with a definitive answer—nor was that my intent.

And different students reached various levels of awareness, including some who tended to explain away what appeared to other students to be unjust situations (e.g., espousing the view that immigrants expected to be at the bottom in a new country to justify why Mexicans so often wound up with the jobs no one else wanted.)

Read the World

Paulo Freire, the noted Brazilian educator, stressed the idea of teaching students to not only read but to "read the world." In my lessons, I did not try to answer their questions about the world (nor could I always do so), because my focus was more on helping them develop the orientation to raise questions and critique rather than satisfying them with answers. But in this case, their reading of the world had the real potential to paralyze and demoralize them. This raises a question about the relationship of students reading the world to their self-perceptions and points out our responsibilities when we attempt to teach for social justice. That is, how do we help students develop a sense of agency, confidence, and determination while at the same time helping them learn about concrete examples of racism, classism, and injustice that may be outside their immediate experience? There is no room to address this here, but I leave readers with a comment from a student I taught for close to two years as she reflected on what she had learned at the end of our time together:

With every single thing about math

that I learned came something else. Sometimes I learned more of other things instead of math. I learned to think of fairness, injustices and so forth everywhere I see numbers distorted in the world. Now my mind is opened to so many new things. I'm more independent and aware. I have learned to be strong in every way you can think of it.

These examples may serve as food for thought as we consider how technology and mathematics—neither of which many of us immediately link to social justice—can be used to help students read the world and begin to make sense of things like racism and classism. Clearly, initial explorations should not serve as final explanations, as these are complex issues that even adults are often trying to make sense of and connect to other aspects of society. They cry out for further and ongoing investigations, to be returned to again and again. But the possibilities exist to help young people develop the orientation to seek ever-deeper answers to these types of questions, and we can take advantage of available technology and turn it to uses for social justice. Students, as young people and as they become adults, can and will raise their own voices in the world. Ultimately, it is how we structure society—for what purposes and in whose interests—that determines how science and technology are used.■

Eric Gutstein teaches in the College of Education at the University of Illinois-Chicago and is active in Teachers for Social Justice (Chicago). He would like to acknowledge the work of Marilyn Frankenstein regarding math and social justice.

The Day Sondra Took Over
Helping students become self-directed

By Cynthia M. Ellwood

I f you write that big, you're never gonna be able to get them all up there," said Sondra, voicing her third critique of my teaching in five minutes. With that, I deposited the chalk in her hand.

"Take over," I said.

"Oh, my fault, Ms. Ellwood," she apologized.

"No, really, go for it. I want you to."

She looked doubtful, not sure whether she was being admonished.

"Try it. I think you'd be great."

After a minute or so of this back-and-forth, Sondra stood up, and I moved to a seat near the back of the room.

We had just read "Little Things Are Big," by Jesús Colón, in my fifth-hour American Ethnic Literature class. (See p. 113.) Set in New York during the 1950s, the short story is about a young, black Puerto Rican fighting an internal battle as he tries to decide whether he should offer to help a white woman loaded with luggage and children as she disembarks from the subway. "Courtesy is a characteristic of the Puerto Rican," the protagonist reports. "And here I was—a Puerto Rican—hours past midnight, a valise, two white children, and a white lady with a baby on her arm palpably needing someone to help her at least until she descended the long, concrete stairs." But he holds back, afraid that this white woman might misinterpret the intentions of a black man approaching her in a deserted subway so late at night. Later he is tortured by his choice: "I failed myself to myself,"

SKJOLD

he muses. He vows that if he ever again faces such a situation, he will offer aid no matter how it may be received.

I asked each student to write down three questions for discussion and had just begun to list their questions on the board under two categories: "plot/fact questions" and "thought/opinion questions," when I handed Sondra the chalk.

Once up, Sondra took firm command of the class. She abandoned my approach. "Anthony, just tell me your best question," she said. Then rather than putting it on the board, she posed it to the class for immediate discussion. When it seemed as if a topic had been plumbed, she moved to the next student and asked again only for that student's best question. Whenever I tried to direct

things, or other students tried to intervene, Sondra said firmly, "This is my class." She refused to recognize me unless I raised my hand like everyone else. At one point, when I forgot and simply spoke out my opinion, she did such a magnificent job of ignoring me that Ernesto took pity: "That's OK, Ms. Ellwood. Tell me what you want to say, and I'll say it," he offered magnanimously.

It was a fine discussion. We talked about what the author meant to convey, how the characters must have felt, whether it could happen today, where racism comes from, and both the obvious and subtle ways racial prejudice still affects our lives. We struggled with some tough questions. One student said he could do anything if he tried hard enough, so racism wasn't an issue. "Well, you're just blaming a person that doesn't make it, then, just saying they didn't try hard enough when it might be because of racism," another countered. We agreed that it was important to believe in yourself and never give up. But we also agreed that inequality was real. Were these ideas contradictory? The students didn't reach consensus on that one, but I think we had a chance to talk and think hard about an issue that struck a deep chord.

As I listened and participated, I also learned. I was reminded that my students must hold fiercely to the conviction that they can "make it." The easy money of drug sales, the instant power of gang affiliation, the adoring neediness of a new baby are not trivial temptations if a young person—impatient to "become someone" as most teenagers are—has trouble believing the American dream. I've always tried to present them with examples of people who strove for their dreams, who acted heroically in everyday life, who fought oppression and pursued high ideals individually and collectively.

I've also encouraged students to critically examine our world and the problems we confront. Yet, while I'd always thought of this social critique as empowering, I realized as I listened to the discussion that day that for some of my students, such analysis might be feeding feelings of hopelessness and despair. The connection I made that day (or rather my students made for me) was subtle but important. In the future I'll try to confront this tension more directly: How do you maintain hope if you see the world as troubled and even systematically unfair? I'll be more careful to match our analysis of problems with an immediate exploration of the large and small steps people can take, and are taking, toward their solution.

That Monday in April was a triumph for me. For while this penetrating, stu-dent-led discussion seemed almost to occur spontaneously, through some quirk of chemistry and circumstance, I had been trying to make this happen from the beginning of the year. (We were to study Mythology and Folklore the first semester, followed by American Ethnic Literature the second.) I had articulated three goals at the beginning of this course. First, I wanted my students to see themselves as learners, people who felt invested in and responsible for the learning (their own and others') in the classroom. Second, I wanted them to see literature as open to interpretation, and I hoped to train them to "unpack" a piece of literature. Third, I wanted them to learn to engage in "academic discourse," which I define briefly as arguing using evidence.

That day, my fifth hour seemed to fulfill all three goals as they had never done before. We had had many good discussions before, but never ones that were so clearly directed by the students themselves.

No Accident

That the events that day were not simply happenstance set off by an interaction between Sondra and me was later reinforced when I formalized in my eighth hour the student leadership that had seemed to arise spontaneously in fifth hour. I explained that I wanted them to run this discussion and we appointed a student facilitator. The eighth hour discussion had a different rhythm and elaborated on different themes than in fifth hour. And without Sondra's commanding leadership, I had to exercise more self-discipline to keep from controlling the discussion while still attempting to pose issues that might push students to dig deeper and think harder. But as in the earlier class, my eighth hour students willingly assumed responsibility for the discussion and, I felt, moved toward particularly thoughtful analyses of the short

story and related themes in our lives. In the final months of the school year, both classes continued to build, albeit unevenly and imperfectly, on the abilities students showed that day.

Nor was this triumph the result of finally hitting upon the magic recipe, the perfect approach. I knew it couldn't have happened in the first month of class; we had all learned a lot to bring us to this point. I set about trying to analyze what exactly had worked to bring about the fulfillment of my goals, and how I might learn from it to become a better teacher.

Laying the Groundwork

From the first day, I had attempted to train students in my three rules of "academic discourse." Whether you're discussing or writing, I said over and over, you must: (1) have a point (in an essay, this main point is called a thesis), (2) provide evidence to back it up, and (3) anchor your point (in discussion that usually meant drawing an explicit connection between your point and what had already been said; in an essay one often anchored one's thesis with reference to another written piece or to "common wisdom.") We had practiced these skills endlessly over the year and had made substantial progress before what I call "the day Sondra took over."

I had also constantly worked to confront students with serious, open-ended questions. As I see it, the main reason for studying literature is to discover more about humanity and oneself. And the main reason we learn to write is to be able to express our convictions powerfully. That means that moral controversies, searching questions, and even deeply personal dilemmas are not only admissible in my classroom, they are central. So I had attempted, with everything we studied, to bring these kinds of questions to the fore, and especially to forge a connection between the daily concerns of my students and age-old human questions, between their individual experiences and universal experience.

During the first semester, in Mythology and Folklore, we tried to identify the values implicit in Greek literature and compare Greek beliefs with our own views about fate, the role of women, family relationships, religion, right and wrong. We recalled how fantasies—myths—appeared to us as children and argued about whether children should be scared into obedience with threats of the boogie man, or taught to be good with the promise of presents from Santa. We identified archetypes—themes, symbols and story lines that come up again and again in the stories of cultures separated by time and distance—and tried to figure out why they recur.

As I look back, I can see that the groundwork we laid in the first semester and the first part of the second semester contributed to that moment in April when Sondra took over the class and my students began taking greater responsibility for their own learning. At the end of the first semester I had asked each student to evaluate the class in the form of an anonymous "letter to a friend" describing the course. While many letters complained that the course demanded too much writing, almost every letter noted that students were expected to think hard and formulate their own opinions. A typical comment was: "The fact that we are able to discuss our own point of view rather than always having to listen to the teacher's point of view ... is a very positive and important part of this class." Another said simply, "She'll ask you your opinion whether you want to give it or not." A third student wrote, "You read stories to dig deep into what the characters are thinking and how they are alike and different from today's world."

As I reread these papers today, I see

that by the end of the first semester we had not resolved the issue of who was responsible for the success of the class, the teacher or the students. Some students saw it as my responsibility to keep the class exciting at all times: "But sometimes this class is so boring. Sometimes

Students knew they were expected to articulate their views, but the responsibility for posing provocative questions and guiding the discussion to thoughtful conclusions seemed to fall entirely on my shoulders. I wrote in my journal during the March spring break:

> While this penetrating, student-led discussion seemed to occur spontaneously, I had been trying to make it happen all year.

you have to pep us up or something. Like writing paragraphs—I hate it!"

Another at least recognized how demanding the teacher's role was:

> The most important aspect of all is the leader (or the teacher). She has to prepare herself for weeks in order to make the class interesting and not bore the whole class. What I'm trying to say is you need to have GANAS [Spanish for 'desire'] in order to make the class interesting.

One seemed possibly to be expressing ambivalence about whose responsibility the class was. This student wrote cryptically: "I've learned that the teacher can influence how you act in class or what you learn in class is up to you."

Giving Students Responsibility

For all our circle discussions, essays, dramatizations, group work, freewrites, surveys, debates, mock "Oprah shows," more discussions, and more essays—and in spite of the tremendous progress we had made in the first semester and the beginning of the second—it was not until Sondra took over the class in April that I felt my goals were met. By late March, I had been feeling exhausted, and yet I felt I wasn't demanding enough of my students. It seemed like the burden of learning fell more heavily on me than on them!

They [students] still don't get the purpose of academic discourse to the point of feeling truly invested in the process. They engage in it because they like me and want to please me, or because I've managed to awaken their interest by coming up with an angle that speaks to their concerns, or to get a good grade, or when they're feeling generally agreeable. But the class is still heavily teacher-propelled.

In my more cynical moments, I felt as if I were up there performing like a maniac to win their engagement or running myself ragged to contrive situations that led them to "discover meaning for themselves" only to have them view our analytic dialogues as "conversating," as a student put it once.

My friend Grace listened to my whining and then said simply, "Why did you participate in high school?" She was right. Somehow I hoped that I could teach my students to pick up a piece of literature and plumb it on their own, to find for themselves the universal themes, the ideas that speak to their experience—just for the pure joy of learning. Yet I didn't do that in high school, or even consistently in college. I participated to get a good grade, because I liked the teacher, because the teacher or a particular text raised issues I found interesting or useful.

Finally: the Breakthrough

So how did it happen that one week later (the week after spring break), Sondra stepped to the front of the class, and I saw my students take more responsibility for raising questions and directing discussion? I think it happened, first, because we had laid the groundwork in previous months. Second, an article by Grant Wiggins entitled "Enabling Students to Be (Thoughtful) Workers" offered some useful suggestions at a key time. A friend showed me the article in February, and I went back to it over spring break as I pondered how to make my class less teacher-centered.

Wiggins says we should organize our courses—regardless of the subject area—around "essential questions." Instead of thinking about what content we want students to cover, we ought to identify large, overarching, higher-order questions which "go to the heart of the discipline" and which are open-ended enough to allow students to pursue their own answers. In this scheme, "the textbook, rather than providing the logic of the syllabus, becomes a reference book for posing and solving problems." I realized that Wiggins' "essential questions" were much like the questions I posed again and again to my students. I organized my courses around major themes or problems, which I presented at the beginning of every semester. And as we explored those themes I constantly confronted my students with open-ended questions designed to help them formulate their own understandings of the larger issues.

But I realized as I read Wiggins that I was asking most of the questions. Having students pose questions was part of my repertoire, something we did sometimes, the way I sometimes gave surveys to awaken their prior understanding of an issue or the way we sometimes staged debates to get students involved in articulating their opinions. Wiggins suggested that "students write down at least three questions for each lesson and reading." While students posing questions was an occasional part of my class, Wiggins was suggesting it should be a routine assignment for every reading.

Starting the first day after spring break, I asked students to write questions about everything we looked at in the class. (I found, incidentally, that grading these questions is not difficult. Students and I were clear on the criteria for a "good" question: It was one that was open-ended—having no right answer—meaty, and thought provoking. Such questions were easily recognizable, though not easy to produce. I gave C's for producing three relevant questions that showed a student had done the reading and A's when they produced two or more truly thought-provoking questions.) The following Monday we had our breakthrough, when Sondra took over the class.

Qualifying Conclusions

Of course, to say that Sondra "took over the class" that Monday in April or the students "took responsibility" for posing questions and running discussions from that day forward stretches the truth. In fact, I never once relinquished control over the class—even on the few occasions when I sat on the sidelines and steadfastly refused to take part in a discussion. Though we played at changing roles on that day and subsequently, I never stopped being the teacher and the authority.

Nor do I think giving up my authority is something worth striving for. I believe I have things to teach my students—I actively trained them to argue with evidence orally and in essay form. For example, I organized the course around themes which my experience tells me are "big ideas" they will encounter in college and adult life generally; I tracked down and introduced litera-ture, essays, films, and other resources that I felt would be fertile ground for thought; and even as I sat in a discussion as "just another participant," I was constantly trying to pose questions and bring up issues that would focus the discussion and deepen students' thinking. I do, however, learn constantly from my students. They have helped me to see things from entirely new angles and have introduced questions that set me off on personal searches extending beyond the end of any particular school year. As I've learned about their views and experiences, the questions I pose to them and the way I pose them have also changed.

At times students may assume full, responsible, eager control over their own learning. My experiences this year suggest that I should see such moments as goals and triumphs but not the absolute measure of success. My day-to-day job is to try to provide the training, skills, atmosphere, and conditions that will enable us to share the responsibility more and to change places from time to time—a job that remains exhausting.

We have not abandoned our roles as teacher and students. But I believe my students and I have learned more by changing the parameters of those roles.∎

Cynthia Ellwood is a principal in the Milwaukee Public Schools.

Little Things Are Big

By Jesús Colón

It was very late at night on the eve of Memorial Day. She came into the subway at the 34th Street Pennsylvania Station. I am still trying to remember how she managed to push herself in with a baby on her right arm, a valise in her left hand, and two children, a boy and girl about 3 and 5 years old, trailing after her. She was a nice looking white lady in her early 20s.

At Nevins Street, Brooklyn, we saw her preparing to get off at the the next station—Atlantic Avenue—which happened to be the place where I too had to get off. Just as it was a problem for her to get on, it was going to be a problem for her to get off the subway with two small children to be taken care of, a baby on her right arm and a medium sized valise in her left hand.

And there I was, also preparing to get off at Atlantic Avenue, with no bundles to take care of—not even the customary book under my arm without which I feel that I am not completely dressed.

As the train was entering the Atlantic Avenue station, some white man stood up from his seat and helped her out, placing the children on the long, deserted platform. There were only two adult persons on the long platform some time after midnight on the eve of last Memorial Day.

I could perceive the steep, long concrete stairs going down to the Long Island Railroad or into the street. Should I offer my help as the American white man did at the subway door placing the two children outside the subway car? Should I take care of the girl and the boy, take them by their hands until they reached the end of the steep long concrete stairs of the Atlantic Avenue station?

Courtesy is a characteristic of the Puerto Rican. And here I was—a Puerto Rican—hours past midnight, a valise, two white children, and a white lady with a baby on her arm palpably needing somebody to help her at least until she descended the long concrete stairs.

But how could I, a Negro and a Puerto Rican, approach this white lady who very likely might have preconceived prejudices against Negroes and everybody with foreign accents, in a deserted subway station very late at night?

What would she say? What would be the first reaction of this white American woman, perhaps coming from a small town, with a valise, two children, and a baby on her right arm? Would she say: Yes, of course, you may help me. Or would she think that I was just trying to get too familiar? Or would she think worse than that perhaps? What would I do if she let out a scream as I went toward her to offer my help?

Was I misjudging her? So many slanders are written every day in the daily press against the Negroes and Puerto Ricans. I hesitated for a long, long minute. The ancestral manners that the most illiterate Puerto Rican passes on from father to son were struggling inside me. Here was I, way past midnight, face to face with a situation that could very well explode into an outburst of prejudices and chauvinistic conditioning of the "divide and rule" policy of present day society.

It was a long minute. I passed on by her as if I saw nothing. As if I was insensitive to her need. Like a rude animal walking on two legs, I just moved on half running by the long subway platform leaving the children and the valise and her with the baby on her arm. I took the steps of the long concrete stairs in twos until I reached the street above and the cold air slapped my warm face.

This is what racism and prejudice and chauvinism and official artificial divisions can do to people and a nation!

Perhaps the lady was not prejudiced after all. Or not prejudiced enough to scream at the coming of a Negro toward her in a solitary subway station a few hours past midnight.

If you were not that prejudiced, I failed you, dear lady. I know that there is a chance in a million that you will read these lines. I am willing to take that millionth chance. If you were not that prejudiced, I failed you, lady, I failed you, children. I failed myself to myself.

I buried my courtesy early on Memorial Day morning. But here is a promise that I make to myself here and now; if I am ever faced with an occasion like that again, I am going to offer my help regardless of how the offer is going to be received.

Then I will have my courtesy with me again. ∎

Jesús Colón (1901-1974) was a social activist who wrote about the Puerto Rican community in New York.

Reprinted with permission from International Publishers, New York, from the book A Puerto Rican in New York and Other Sketches, *1982.*

Haiku and Hiroshima

Teaching about the atomic bomb

By Wayne Au

As teachers know, some classroom materials invariably work, no matter the group of students. *Barefoot Gen* is one of them.

Barefoot Gen, a Japanese animation full-length feature, tells the story of Gen (pronounced with a hard "G"), a young boy who, along with his mother, survives the bombing of Hiroshima.

The story chronicles their struggles as they try to rebuild their lives from the bomb's ashes. It is based on the critically acclaimed, semi-autobiographical Japanese comic book series *Hadashi no Gen,* by Keiji Nakazawa. Both the comic strip and the feature film oppose the Japanese government's actions during World War II and include criticism of the intense poverty and suffering forced onto the Japanese people by their government's war effort.

The film's critical eye points to one of the lessons I want students to draw from *Barefoot Gen:* that it is important to scrutinize the relationship between the people of a country and the actions of their government—ours included. I want my students to understand that as thinking human beings, we have the right to disagree and protest when a government's actions are not in the interests of humanity, as Gen's father does or as many U.S. people do in condemning the bombing of Hiroshima and Nagasaki.

I also find the film useful to help students look beyond the demonized and often racist images of the Japanese, particularly in the context of World War II,

"One of the most important animated films ever made!"
—Richard von Busack, SAN JOSE METRO

BAREFOOT GEN

and see actual people living, dying, and protesting their government's actions.

High school students enjoy the disarming and playful nature of *Barefoot Gen*'s cartoon medium. Some students are familiar with the film genre of Japanese animation, or anime, which has gained popularity in the United States.

The film's effect is hardly playful, however, and students quickly realize that this is a serious film with character development, plot, and real emotion. Its animation allows the intense imagery of the atomic explosion and its aftermath to take shape on screen, in front of our eyes.

The atomic detonation of the bomb named "Little Boy" over the city of Hiroshima killed almost 120,000 civilians and 20,000 military personnel. The explosion reached into the millions of degrees centigrade and obliterated an area of 13 square kilometers. Three days later, "Fat Man" was dropped on Nagasaki, killing 74,000 people. These astounding numbers do not include the estimated 130,000 who died within five days of the bombings or those who survived the initial explosion but suffered or died from long-term genetic damage and radiation sickness. [(In offering students a broader context for the events of August 1945, I've found historian Howard Zinn's work especially valuable. See the chapter "Just and Unjust Wars" from his book *Declarations of Independence* (HarperPerennial, 1990) and his article "The Bombs of August," in *The Progressive* magazine, August 2000.]

The images in *Barefoot Gen* are powerful and devastating to watch. Thankfully, the film ends on an upbeat note of survival, because like Gen, humanity can and will triumph over devastation.

For the post-film discussion, I mainly ask students to share their feelings and thoughts about the movie. Some say that they've never cried watching a cartoon before, and most remark that they can relate to Gen's personal struggles of losing loved ones or fighting to survive in a harsh world. Across race, gender, and nationality, students consistently exhibit emotional empathy with Gen.

I like to follow the discussion with the class using the traditional Japanese poetry forms of haiku and tanka to express their responses to the film. This works best if these can be assigned the same day as watching the movie. First we read aloud some haiku and tanka written by survivors of the bombings from *White Flash/Black Rain: Women of Japan Relive the Bomb* (Milkweed Editions, 1995).

Reality
is this and only this—
the one bone
I place in the bent and burned
small school lunch tin.
　　　　　—*Shoda Shinoe*

grabbing sand
beneath the flaming sky
is to be alive
　　　　　—*Kingyo Humiko*

looking for her mother
the girl still has strength
to turn over corpses
　　　　　—*Shibata Moriyo*

After discussing the imagery and themes of the haiku and tanka examples, I describe the syllabic requirements of these traditional Japanese forms. Haiku requires three lines, with five, seven, and five syllables in each line respectively, totaling 17 syllables. With five lines, tanka similarly requires five, seven, five, seven, and seven syllables respectively, totaling 31 syllables. The examples are translated from Japanese, so they do not make good syllabic models in English, but their content is powerful enough for students to get the idea.

From there, we write. Expressing emotions through poetry is hard work, and trying to make poetry fit into a limited syllable space is even harder. Fortunately, because haiku and tanka are relatively short compared to essays or other writing assignments, students don't feel too intimidated and, however frustrating, have fun fitting their words into the puzzle that the traditional forms present. Students' writing has been outstanding, demonstrating their abilities to empathize with the Japanese people who suffered the bombing.

screams the sound of souls
being devoured, banished
from all existence
　　　　　—*Joseph Tauti*

red sky floats above
starts to drip the blackness down
towards the drying deathbed
now scorched by the liquid fire
bleak chariots move the dead
　　　　　—*Amanda O'Conner*

Little children scream
They look for their families
which they will not find
　　　　　—*Shanique Johnson*

Understandably, the feeling of dread and despair evident in the student examples underscores the immense human suffering. Dropping an atomic bomb on real, live people is serious, and it is important that students recognize this fact.

In the end, the mushroom clouds left by "Little Boy" and "Fat Man" towered over more than just the two cities of Hiroshima and Nagasaki. Those explosions cast their shadows over Asia and Europe, signaling to the rest of the world, especially the Soviet Union, that the United States was indeed the dominant global military power with the devastating firepower to back it up. More important, and more frightening, U.S. officials were willing to use that firepower. ■

Wayne Au (wayne.au@sbcglobal.net) is an editor of Rethinking Schools *magazine and is an assistant professor of secondary education at California State University, Fullerton.*

Students as Textbook Detectives
An exercise in uncovering bias

By Bill Bigelow and Bob Peterson

Many school districts rely on textbook series to shape curricula in social studies, science, math, and other subjects. Such texts may have useful background information, photos, maps, and graphs. But often they contain harmful biases and omissions. Thus, textbooks can be valuable resources to help sharpen students' critical reading and analytical skills. We include the lesson described below as an example of teaching critical literacy—offering students some tools to question basic assumptions of the material they read, to "talk back" to their texts.

Grade Level: 5–12

Procedure

1. For background information on the causes and consequences of the U.S. war with Mexico, see the tea party activity in Bill Bigelow's *The Line Between Us: Teaching About the Border and Mexican Immigration;* Chapter 8, "We Take Nothing by Conquest, Thank God," from Howard Zinn's *A People's History of the United States,* also included in *The Line Between Us;* Ronald Takaki's *A Different Mirror* (Chapter 7: "Foreigners in Their Native Land"); and Elizabeth Martínez's *500 Años del Pueblo Chicano/500 Years of Chicano History in Pictures.* Also see the interview with Howard Zinn on pp. 179–185 in this volume. Useful first-person accounts of participants can be found in Milton Meltzer's *Bound for the Rio Grande.* As a follow-up activity you might use Henry David Thoreau's essay "On Civil Disobedience."

2. If possible, share with students activities and excerpts from these books—representing perspectives not included in the textbooks produced by major publishing corporations. The more background students have on the war with Mexico, the more easily they will be able to complete the assignment included here. However, this is also a useful introductory activity that can alert students to issues of point of view and bias.

3. Distribute to students the selection from Glencoe McGraw-Hill's *American Odyssey,* "Thinking Deeply" questions, and map of territory that Mexico lost to the United States—all on the following page.

American Odyssey is a high school text. Although the main focus is the 20th century, the book includes 249 pre-20th century pages. Note that the two-paragraph section reproduced at right is the book's entire discussion of the U.S.-Mexico War. (As an alternative to using the excerpt provided, ask students to use their own textbooks, or distribute several different texts so they can compare coverage.)

4. Divide students into small groups and ask them to read the textbook excerpt, discuss the questions and answer them in writing.

5. Bring students back together to share their insights. Be sure to ask the bigger "why" questions, such as:
■ Why do you think this textbook leaves out important information?
■ Why do you think some school districts use textbooks that present such an incomplete story?
■ Why is it important when textbooks fail to tell students about individuals and movements in history that opposed government policies?
Also ask:
■ How do you think books like these affect the way students think about wars the United States has been involved in?
■ How do the books affect the way students view the world today, for example, "illegal" immigration from Mexico to the United States? (Our students are often surprised to learn that Texas, California, New Mexico, Arizona, etc. were once Mexican territory, and were acquired by the United States through deceit and invasion. For some, this puts the legitimacy of the border and the issue of so-called illegal aliens in a new light.)
■ In the Glencoe McGraw-Hill text, the entire section on the U.S.-Mexico War consists of two paragraphs. What message does that send to readers about the importance of this period?

6. Allow students to act on what they find. They might write letters to a textbook company or a school district textbook selection committee, rewrite sections of the text or write critiques to be left in the book for the following year's students, and/or lead workshops with other students and young children about the biases they uncovered.

Note: While the "Thinking Deeply" questions here are aimed at critiquing representations of the U.S. war with

Mexico, this format can be used with virtually any textbook account of any historical period, or with children's literature. For example, in examining stories or descriptions of the "discovery" of America, elementary students could be asked: How many times does Columbus talk? How many times do we get to know what he is thinking? How many times do the Native people have names? How many times do the Native people talk? How many times do we get to know what the Native people are thinking? Or on the high school level, students might be encouraged to ask: What kinds of things do you learn about Columbus, his background, why he's sailing west and what he wants? What do you learn about the Taíno people he encounters in the Caribbean? Whom does the book get you to root for and how does it accomplish that? (For example, are the books horrified at the treatment of the Taínos or thrilled that Columbus makes it to the "New World"?)

Thinking Deeply

1. What do you learn about the causes of the war with Mexico? What doesn't the book tell you about the causes?

2. What does the textbook tell about opposition to U.S. involvement in the war?

3. What does the textbook include about the lives and thoughts of African Americans, Mexicans, or women?

4. What questions do you have about the U.S. war with Mexico that are not addressed in this textbook passage?■

Bill Bigelow (bbpdx@aol.com) has taught high school social studies in Portland, Ore., since 1978. He is an editor of Rethinking Schools *magazine.*

Bob Peterson (REPMilw@aol.com) teaches 5th grade at La Escuela Fratney in Milwaukee and is an editor of Rethinking Schools *magazine.*

A map of territory Mexico lost to the United States.

War with Mexico

In 1836 when Texas declared its independence from Mexico, white Southerners hoped to acquire Texas as a new slave state. Northerners feared that the admission of Texas to the Union would not only increase the South's power in Congress but would also embroil the United States in a war with Mexico. Nevertheless by 1845 enough politicians were caught up in the fervor of westward expansion—believing that it was the destiny of the nation to reach from shore to shore—that white Southern politicians were able to prevail in getting Texas admitted to the Union as the 28th state. Mexico was outraged at this action. After a border skirmish between American troops and Mexican troops, the United States declared war on Mexico in May 1846.

On Feb. 2, 1848, after almost two years of fighting, the nations ended the war by signing the Treaty of Guadalupe Hidalgo. This treaty gave the United States vast new regions that today include California, Arizona, New Mexico, Utah, Nevada, and parts of Colorado and Wyoming. The fear that these territories would organize into states intensified the sectional conflict between the North and the South. Many Northerners opposed the extension of slavery even into the newly acquired lands that lay south of the line established by the Missouri Compromise.

From Glencoe McGraw–Hill's American Odyssey.

What Can Teachers Do About Sexual Harassment?

By Ellen Bravo and Larry Miller

Theresa was the only girl in the metalworking class. When a teacher asked her how things were going with the boys, Theresa replied, "Oh, it's much better. They don't grab my breasts and butt anymore. They just call me all those names."

* * *

Paula hated walking past Leon and his friends. They would grab themselves and say things like, "Come on, now, you know you want it." Some of her friends yelled comments back, but Paula never knew what to say.

* * *

Anton took the long way to class. He didn't want to pass a certain group of girls who always made fun of him for being a virgin.

* * *

The 8th-grade girls didn't like the way the teacher would fondle their hair and then let his hand skim across their bodies. But because this had been going on for awhile, they were afraid to tell their parents. And they didn't know who to tell at school.

These are just a few of the types of sexual harassment problems in our schools. Despite the headlines and well-publicized court cases, most administrators have focused little attention on the problem. But teachers don't have to wait for a directive that may be years in coming; we can take action right now in our classrooms.

Sexual harassment isn't the only problem kids face in school and for many, it's not the worst problem. But it's an area where a lot of confusion exists—confusion that's been cultivated by many people in authority who have trivialized the issue, criticized those who have raised it, and distorted proposed solutions.

For high school students, the situation is further complicated by adolescence. If being preoccupied with sex makes someone a harasser, most teenagers would have to plead guilty. Where's the line between appropriate and inappropriate behavior—and who's drawing it?

Last year, when Larry Miller did a seven-day unit on sexual harassment, students afterward remarked that it was one of the highlights of the school year. He found that developing a unit on sexual harassment has several advantages:

■ **The students love it.** Students repeatedly said throughout the year, "Why can't class always be as interesting?" Sexual harassment is also a subject on which students are eager to talk and have a great deal to say. What adolescent hasn't spent an inordinate amount of time contemplating the complexities of intimate relations?

■ **The students need it.** Most students don't understand the issue of sexual harassment and have lots of misconceptions. They need guidance and support to help figure out what is and isn't appropriate behavior.

■ **The students benefit from it.** The benefits occur on a number of different levels. First, a sexual harassment unit empowers those individual girls and boys who may have been harassed. (For boys, it's almost always for being gay or

not "manly" enough.) Such students urgently need validation that harassment is wrong, that they're not crazy, and that they're not at fault. They need to hear that someone in authority cares about the problem and isn't blaming them or dismissing their pain.

Second, it makes clear that harassment is unacceptable behavior—thus helping to create a classroom culture in which students will have a stronger understanding that their rights will be respected and defended, regardless of whether they have ever been harassed. While it is essential to go beyond dealing with harassment on a classroom-by-classroom basis, individual discussions of the issue are often an essential first step (see article p. 121).

Third, it helps clear up confusion among boys who think they'll be in trouble for flirting or consensual joking. Larry found that while many boys initially felt hostile and suspicious during the unit (they feared the unit would demonize all boys and portray all girls as innocent victims), such attitudes changed when they found the focus was on inappropriate behavior and not on boys in general.

Fourth, it helps raise broader relationship and gender issues that the students need to talk about. One incident underscored this point to Larry. After the unit, a 16-year-old male student came up to him one day and asked to talk privately. It turned out the student had a common but simple biological question about sex—but had no adult male he felt comfortable talking to.

A Good Curriculum

A good curriculum makes clear that while most harassers are male, most males are not harassers. It also encourages students to intervene when harassment occurs, to speak out not as champions of the "poor victims" but as people offended by such behavior.

At its minimum, the curriculum should have three goals. First, it must help the majority of students to understand why harassment is wrong. Second, it must help the harassers to stop their behavior. Third, in what is a more complex issue, it must address larger issues of gender stereotypes and power. Students need to understand that sexual harassment is part of a continuum of sexual misconduct that has to do with domination rather than sex. This takes the issue out of the battle-of-the-sexes mode and helps students better understand patterns of sexual discrimination.

It is also essential to deal with the perspective that those who challenge sexual harassment are merely whining "victims" rather than people with a legitimate anger. Some critics argue that sexual harassment awareness training contributes to a nation of "victims." Like any unit dealing with situations of oppression, the curriculum's purpose is not to create a sense of hopelessness but of understanding and power—the knowledge that each of us is important and deserves to be treated with dignity. We don't prevent or stop harassment by ignoring it any more than we do by condoning it. In fact, ignoring sexual harassment sends a powerful message that no one cares. This "hidden curriculum" can leave girls with a sense of powerlessness and, in essence, teaches girls to accept sexual inequality.

Teaching Techniques

Obviously, good teaching is central to the unit's success. Teachers can use a variety of techniques, from videos to role plays, small-group discussions, and student essays. It is useful to begin with a "safe" lesson idea that encourages students to share their feelings, such as an anonymous survey asking students both their definition of sexual harassment and whether they have ever been harassed.

It's a good idea to include at least one lesson plan that helps students distinguish between flirting and harassment. (See sample plan, p. 121). In helping students distinguish between the two, Larry found that two questions were essential: Was the behavior unwelcome? Did the behavior make the recipient feel uncomfortable? If the answer is "yes" to the questions, the line is usually crossed between flirting and harassment.

Role plays and scenarios are a particularly useful technique. In his unit, Larry took a male and a female student that he knew were mature enough to act out what was, from their own experiences, the difference between flirtation and harassment. For example, the young man would look the girl up and down, make comments such as, "Hey, you want some of this," or grab

---

The Need for Districtwide Changes

Classroom lessons are the core of any sexual harassment policy. But classroom activities are not enough. To effectively combat sexual harassment, there must be schoolwide and districtwide changes. All school and district staff should receive the training necessary to help create a school and district climate where sexual harassment is dealt with quickly and forcefully. Some of the essential components to help create such a climate include:

■ **Commitment from the top**. A clear acknowledgment that sexual harassment is a problem and won't be tolerated.

■ **Policy**. Procedures need to be clear and familiar. Information should be distributed to each student in a way that will get their attention.

■ **Definition**. The policy should describe, concisely and with specific examples, what sexual harassment is and what kinds of behavior are prohibited.

■ **Complaint procedures**. Students and school personnel should be given several channels for reporting a complaint and a timetable for its handling. The policy should make clear that due process will be observed.

■ **Discipline**. The policy should specify what the consequences are for engaging in prohibited behavior.

■ **Protection**. Those reporting harassment need assurances that there will be no retaliation.

■ **Confidentiality**. Every step should be taken to preserve confidentiality for those involved. The procedures should include a telephone number students can call if they want to discuss the situation anonymously with a trained professional.

■ **Investigations**. Impartial and well-trained investigators should be provided to pursue any formal complaints.

■ **Education**. All students, teachers, and staff should receive training.

■ **Healing**. Those who have been harassed may need access to trained professionals or a support group to help them heal.

■ **Assessment**. Schools should monitor their progress and step up education and intervention if necessary.

himself in his private parts. The girl would respond, "Go away, boy, I don't need that crap." It was clear from the class's response to the role plays that the students, whether or not they could articulate it, often knew the difference between flirting and harassment.

Scenarios, in which the teacher describes a situation and asks for students' responses, are a useful way to open up discussion. Larry developed the following activities and also used some from the resources listed on this page.

In one scenario, boys "rate" girls as they walk past them in the hallway ("She's a 10"; "She's so ugly she'd be pretty if she were a dog"). During a discussion of such "ratings," some boys argued that rating girls can be a compliment. "It's just ugly girls who are offended," one said.

Some girls had a different view. "I don't care what I'm rated; it makes me uncomfortable," Betty replied. "I don't like it." Other girls backed her up and made the point that such ratings are degrading and make a woman feel less than a human being. Larry found that such conversations were much-needed. Whether or not every student took Betty's comments to heart, her point was made.

Another scenario focused on how boys "eye" girls. James, for instance, argued that he can look at anything he wants. "These are my eyes," he insisted. But another student responded, "If I feel disrespected, then you're out of order"—picking up on a common student concern with "respect" as a key

factor in determining what's right and wrong.

In doing such scenarios, it is important that at least one deal with the most evident form of harassment: the use of abusive words such as "bitch" and "whore." In the discussion following such a scenario in Larry's class, one female student reflected a common

> It was clear from the role plays that the students, whether or not they could articulate it, often knew the difference between flirting and harassment.

view that, "If a girl is not a 'whore' then she should be tough enough not to be offended by these words."

Her view sparked a lively debate. A number of both young men and women shot back with comments such as, "We shouldn't have to put up with that kind of nonsense."

The power of the unit was most clear in the summary essays written by Larry's students. Many of the students came to clearly understand not only the difference between flirting and harassment, but the issue's importance.

Reflecting on flirting and harassment, Jamela wrote in her summary essay: "Flirting and sexual harassment are two different things. Flirting is when two people are joking and kidding around and none of them mind. But sexual harassment is when two people might be joking around and kidding around and one goes too far. Another form may be when two people are talking or playing and one of them touches the other in a way they don't like, or grabs the other in a way they don't like."

Jason, meanwhile, focused on the many responses to sexual harassment. Articulating a range of responses that

most students were unaware of before the unit, he wrote, "Sometimes you can handle sexual harassment by ignoring it or asking the person to stop it, especially when it is name-calling, rumors, light touching, or gestures. If it continues you need to go to someone in authority, either a teacher, parent, boss, or head of the department. If it still continues you need to keep taking action and not let them get away with it. Don't be afraid to talk to other students or co-workers about it. Perhaps it is happening to them too and you could build a better case against that person. Sexual harassment should be an important issue in all communities. Looking the other way and doing nothing about it is saying that sexual harassment is OK." ∎

Ellen Bravo is former director of 9to5, National Association of Working Women. She teaches women's studies at the University of Wisconsin–Milwaukee, including a graduate-level course on sexual harassment. Her most recent publication is Taking on the Big Boys, or Why Feminism Is Good for Families, Businesses and the Nation *(Feminist Press, 2007).*

Larry Miller taught high school in Milwaukee Public Schools for 15 years. He is administrator of W.E.B. DuBois High School, a small public school focusing on communications technology, and is an editor of Rethinking Schools *magazine.*

Flirting vs. Sexual Harassment
Teaching the difference

By Nan Stein and Lisa Sjostrom

Objectives

To raise student awareness about the kinds of sexual harassment which take place all the time; to discern the fluid, subjective line between flirting and sexual harassment; to encourage open student discussion of a complicated topic.

Preparation

■ Prepare three lists with headings and subheadings either on the blackboard or on big sheets of newsprint (these sheets may provide great reference points in later lessons). The titles of the first three lists should read "Verbal or Written," "Gestures," and "Physical." Under each heading write the two subheadings "Flirting" and "Harassment." During the discussion, anticipate creating a third subheading on each of the three lists titled "Depends." At this point, the three lists should be titled like this:

Verbal or Written
Flirting   Harassment

Gestures
Flirting   Harassment

Physical
Flirting   Harassment

■ Decide beforehand if you will allow students to use profanity or if they should speak in euphemisms. Another alternative is for students to write their answers on paper and hand these lists to you to decide what to record on the main lists.

SUSAN LINA RUGGLES

■ If possible, ask students to arrange their chairs in a circle.

■ Decide upon ground rules; e.g.,

1. Everyone must listen when someone is speaking.

2. Don't get personal by mentioning anyone's name when telling about a specific incident.

3. Ask students to determine other rules, such as "What's said here, stays here."

■ Encourage younger students, in particular, to be in their most "mature" behavior mode.

Introduction

"This activity is pretty simple and fun. We're going to talk about the difference between flirting and sexual harassment. Before we begin, I want to state from the outset that we're not here to demonize or blame boys. Many of us may never be either targets of harassment or perpetrators. But all of us are *witnesses and bystanders* who see harassment happening, and we need to learn to say, "Hey, cut it out, that's not funny!" or "What would you do if this were your sister, your mom, or your brother?" So, we're not just trying to change boys and men. We're trying to change *all* of us—so we'll have the courage to actively respond when we see sexual harassment go on.

"You are the best anthropologists of your own culture—and 'subcultures' (cliques, who you 'hang' with). All the time you are observing other kids' behavior in school, and seeing how behaviors differ depending on where you are and whether there are adults around or not—in classrooms, locker rooms, the cafeteria, the parking lot, the hallways. In this discussion, I want you to draw upon what *you* already know and see. You are the experts and sophisticated 'critiquers' of your subcultures.

"In this exercise, we're going to talk about how you all interact with each other and what you observe, how you make sense between what is sexual harassment and what is flirting ('hanging out,' 'getting to know someone').

"First we'll focus on verbal and written exchanges, such as comments and notes. Then we'll focus on gestures like winking, waving, and other ways you communicate without speaking or touching. Lastly we'll consider physical interactions. For each category, we'll talk about examples of flirting and then instances that cross the line into sexual harassment. I don't expect everyone to agree. What's most important is that we start talking. ... Can anyone give me an example of a comment or a note that's flirting and nice?"

Activity

- To avoid confusion, walk students through the lists one at a time.
- Write down student answers under the appropriate subheading.
- Encourage students to stay with specifics they know from a school setting and not stray to hypothetical or out-of-school situations.
- If one column isn't being addressed, ask students specific questions; e.g., "Can you give me examples of physical ways people flirt?"
- When students disagree upon the nature of a particular behavior or comment, ask them what they are basing their criteria upon and enter this under the heading "Depends." For example, perhaps the nature of a comment *depends* upon whether the speaker is a

friend or a stranger, or upon his or her tone of voice. Write these dependent variables right on the three lists.

- If one behavior falls under both "Flirting" and "Harassment," note this by drawing an arrow from one column to the other like this:

Verbal or Written

Flirting	Harassment
You look nice ➡	nice ass
Like your hair	'ho

Depends on:
tone of voice
how they look at you

Gestures

Flirting	Harassment
blowing kiss ➡	grabbing crotch
waving	lip licking

Depends on:
friend or stranger
how old they are
who else is around

Physical

Flirting	Harassment
hugs ➡	pinching
holding hands	grabbing

Depends on:
friend or stranger
where you are

Questions to Raise Afterward

After students have completed the activity, the following discussion questions can help them make sense of the lists.

- Why do people define sexual harassment differently?
- If sexual harassment is illegal, how come it goes on?
- Who allows sexual harassment to go on?
- What are some common forms of sexual harassment that often go unnoticed in schools?

- Do girls sexually harass other girls?
- Who harasses boys?

Troubleshooting

Discussion often gets heated and students can raise many challenging questions. Here are some typical questions and scenarios, along with suggested responses.

1. Boys raise the argument that girls are asking to be harassed by the way they dress.

"All of our opinions about temptation are shaped by the times we live in. Did you know that in Puritanical New England in the 1600s if a woman wore a dress and her ankles or wrists showed, men would walk on the other side of the street and turn their eyes away in horror? They believed the Devil was tempting them."

"Sometimes we—both males and females—do dress to look and feel good about ourselves. Yes, we may want attention, but that doesn't mean we want to be *harassed*."

2. Students ask: "But how do we know which is which? We won't be able to say anything to one another!"

"We're figuring this out all the time—silently. You don't ever go up to someone and say, 'Hi, can we flirt now?' This is why we need to keep talking and openly discussing our intentions, feelings, and interpretations of each other's words and behaviors."

3. Students ask about other hassles which don't fall under the category of sexual harassment.

- Crank calls: "Against the law. It is a crime under both state and federal laws for anyone to make obscene or harassing phone calls. Look in the front section of the telephone book—it's spelled out there, and tells you to call the phone company if these calls persist."

- Knocking books out of someone's

hands: "Someone's provoking you, but it isn't sexual in nature, so it isn't covered by federal law. Of course, the school may have its own rules about student behavior, like rules against cheating and fighting. And remember, something doesn't have to be illegal for you to say 'This is making me uncomfortable!' or 'You're acting like a jerk!'"

■ Being harassed by a family member at home: "Federal laws on sex discrimination and sexual harassment only apply to two places: one law covers school and school-sponsored events, and a second law covers the workplace. Of course, sexual assault at home or in the streets is just as serious. So speak up, say 'no,' tell someone you trust and keep telling until you find someone who believes you and will help you."

4. "Can a harasser get sued?"

"Yes and no. Under federal law Title IX, you bring a complaint against the school district and ask for monetary damages. Why? Because it's the school district's responsibility to enforce the rules and explain what's legal and illegal in school. Under law, the school district has to provide you with an environment that is safe and equal for learning for both girls and boys. So, the school district is responsible for maintaining a school climate and environment that is conducive to learning and one which allows everyone to participate without fear of sexual harassment. Though an individual cannot get sued under Title IX, if the person has done something that is also criminal (like assault), then the district attorney may choose to sue the individual in criminal court."

5. A student relates an incident of teen dating violence that occurred away from the school.

"Violence is a separate category from sexual harassment. Violence in teen relationships or domestic violence is a form of assault and is covered by criminal law. For that, you need to make a complaint through the police and the district attorney." ■

Nan Stein works with the Center for Research on Women at Wellesley College, in Wellesley, Mass. Lisa Sjostrom is director of Helping Kids Thrive, www. helpingkidsthrive.org.

This article is adapted from Flirting or Hurting? A Teacher's Guide on Student-to-Student Sexual Harassment in Schools (Grades 6 through 12), *published by the National Education Association (see below).*

Sexual Harassment Resources

Bullyproof: A Teacher's Guide on Teasing and Bullying for Use with Fourth & Fifth Grade Students. Stein, Nan and Lisa Sjostrom. Wellesley College Center for Research on Women and National Education Association, 1996. www.wcwonline.org > Our Publications. http://store.nea.org/NEABookstore/control/main.

Classrooms and Courtrooms: Facing Sexual Harassment in K-12 Schools. Stein, Nan. Teachers College Press, 1999. www.teacherscollegepress.com.

Flirting or Hurting? A Teacher's Guide on Student-to-Student Sexual Harassment in Schools (Grades 6–12). Stein, Nan and Lisa Sjostrom. National Education Association, 1994. http://store.nea.org/NEABookstore/control/main.

Gender Violence/Gender Justice: An Interdisciplinary Teaching Guide for Teachers of English, Literature, Social Studies, Psychology, Health, Peer Counseling, and Family and Consumer Sciences (Grades 7–12). Stein, Nan and Dominic Cappello, with Linda Tubach and Jackson Katz. Wellesley Centers for Women, 1999. www.wcwonline.org > Our Publications.

Hostile Hallways: Bullying, Teasing, and Sexual Harassment in School. American Association of University Women, 2001. www.aauw.org/research/girls_education/hostile.cfm.

The 9to5 Guide to Combating Sexual Harassment: Candid Advice from 9to5. Bravo, Ellen and Ellen Cassedy. 9to5 National Association of Working Women, 1999. www.9to5.org/pubs.

Stop Student Sexual Harassment Now! National Education Association, 1997. www.nea.org/titlenine/images/harass.pdf.

Celebrating the Student's Voice

By Linda Christensen

When Lawson Inada, a Japanese-American poet and professor of literature at Southern Oregon College, came to my class, we were in the middle of a unit on the history of education. One of the poems he pulled from his book *Legends from Camp* was about a classroom experience. When Lawson read "Rayford's Song" (see next page), I realized it was an opportunity for students to remember and explore their own history as students.

In "Rayford's Song," Inada remembers one of his classrooms in the 1930s in Fresno, a town in California's San Joaquin Valley where many people of African, Chinese, Filipino, Japanese, and Mexican descent worked in the fields and canneries. "Our classroom was filled with shades of brown," he recalls.

> Our names were Rayford Butler,
> Consuela and Pedro Gonzales, Susie
> Chin, and Sam Shimabukuro. We
> were a mixture. The only white person
> in the room was our teacher. Our
> textbooks had pictures and stories
> about white kids named Dick and Jane
> and their dog, Spot. And the songs
> in our songbooks were about Old
> Susanah coming 'round the mountain
> and English gardens—songs we
> never heard in our neighborhood.

Some of the songs mentioned in the poem may not be familiar to today's students ("Old Black Joe" is a Stephen Foster song written in 1860 that evokes nostalgic memories of the days of slavery). Nonetheless, the poem stirs up strong emotion in students because it speaks to the process that sometimes happens in schools of dampening our hopes and expectations. Many of us have experienced the loss of our voices, our songs, our stories. We've been told that we are not important, our people are not important, our gender is not important. Inada's poem dares to speak about that silencing.

Following are some ways a teacher might use the poem in class.

Group Poem

- Ask students to reread the poem and underline the words, lines, or phrases that strike them for some reason—perhaps because these seem important to the poem, maybe because they like the sound or because they can relate the line to something in their lives. (e.g., "Where did our voices go? … I must correct you. … One song. … One voice.")

- Tell students that they are going to create an oral group poem with the words, phrases, or lines they've selected. Each student can say his or her addition to the oral poem when there is a pause. They might want to use some of the devices of poetry and song—repeating a line or word, echoing. Sometimes students like to experiment with the call and response more typical in sermons. Encourage students to call out lines or words to form the new poem, in what might be described as the literary equivalent of an improvisational musical composition. To give students the idea, have eight or 10 students come in front of the room and experiment as an example.

Sometimes it takes a few times to get this going. Have patience. It's worth it. As students rewrite and reread the poem or any written text, they come to new understandings about the piece. Sometimes I have students begin singing "Swing Low, Sweet Chariot" as background to the poem—or play a recording.

Reflections on the Poem

- Ask students to write for five or 10 minutes about the poem; they might want to describe how the poem made them feel, their reactions to the poem, or memories that the poem prompted. There are no wrong answers.

- After students have written, begin the discussion. Some students might want to read their responses while others might want to use it as a springboard for their contribution to the class talk.

Student Writing

- Inada speaks of schools silencing students, but he also speaks more broadly about whose lives are included in the curriculum and whose are excluded. Ask students to write about a time when their voices were silenced or they felt their history or stories were silenced or left out of the classroom. They might want to write this as a story or a poem.

Read-Around/Collective Text

- Before students read their papers out loud, ask them to take notes on their classmates' papers. They might note how people felt about being silenced, who was silenced, who silenced them, and how they responded. After all the students have read who want to read, ask them to review their notes, think about the stories/poems, and write a paragraph or two on the ideas that emerged from the stories. They might want to mention specific people's stories. See p. 213 for more information on using read-arounds. ■

Rayford's Song

By Lawson Inada

Rayford's song was Rayford's song,
but it was not his alone, to own.

He had it, though, and kept it to himself
as we rowed-rowed-rowed the boat
through English country gardens
with all the whispering hope
we could muster, along with occasional
choruses of funiculi-funicula!

Weren't we a cheery lot —
comin' 'round the mountain
with Susanna, banjos on our knees,
rompin' through the leaves
of the third-grade music textbook.

Then Rayford Butler raised his hand.
For the first time, actually,
in all the weeks he had been in class,
and for the only time before he'd leave.
Yes, quiet Rayford, silent Rayford,
little Rayford, dark Rayford —
always in the same overalls —
that Rayford, Rayford Butler, raised his hand:

    "Miss Gordon, ma'am —
    we always singing your songs.
    Could I sing one of my own?"

Pause. We looked at one another;
we looked at Rayford Butler;
we looked up at Miss Gordon, who said:

    "Well, I suppose so, Rayford —
    if you insist. Go ahead.
    Just one song. Make it short."

And Rayford Butler stood up very straight,
and in his high voice, sang:

    "Suh-whing a-looow
    suh-wheeeet ah charr-ee-oohh,
    ah-comin' for to carr-ee
    meee ah-hooooome ..."

Pause. Classroom, school, schoolyard,
neighborhood, the whole world
focusing on that one song, one voice
which had a light to it, making even
Miss Gordon's white hair shine
in the glory of it, glowing
in the radiance of the song.

Pause. Rayford Butler sat down.
And while the rest of us
may have been spellbound,
on Miss Gordon's face
was something like a smile,
or perhaps a frown:

    "Very good, Rayford.
    However, I must correct you:
    the word is 'chariot.'
    'Chariot.' And there is no
    such thing as a 'chario.'
    Do you understand me?"

    "But Miss Gordon ..."

    "I said 'chariot, chariot.'
    Can you pronounce that for me?"

    "Yes, Miss Gordon. Chariot."

    "Very good, Rayford,
    Now, class, before we return
    to our book, would anyone else
    care to sing a song of their own?"

Our songs, our songs were there—
on tips of tongues, but stuck
in throats—songs of love,
fun, animals, and valor, songs
of other lands, in other languages,
but they just wouldn't come out.
Where did our voices go?

Rayford's song was Rayford's song,
but it was not his alone to own.

    "Well, then, class—
    let's turn our books to
    'Old Black Joe.'"

Promoting Social Imagination Through Interior Monologues

By Bill Bigelow and Linda Christensen

One of the most important aims of teaching is to prompt students to empathize with other human beings. This is no easy accomplishment in a society that pits people against each other, offers vastly greater or lesser amounts of privileges based on accidents of birth, and rewards exploitation with wealth and power. Empathy, or "social imagination," as Peter Johnson calls it in *The Reading Teacher*, allows students to connect to "the other" with whom, on the surface, they may appear to have little in common. A social imagination encourages students to construct a more profound "we" than daily life ordinarily permits. A social imagination prompts students to wonder about the social contexts that provoke hurtful behaviors, rather than simply to dismiss individuals as inherently "evil" or "greedy."

One teaching method we use to promote empathy, and return to unit after unit, is the interior monologue. An interior monologue is simply the imagined thoughts of a character in history, literature, or life at a specific point in time. After watching a film, reading a novel, short story, or essay, or performing improvisation skits, the class brainstorms particular key moments, turning points, or critical passages characters confronted. During a unit on the Vietnam War, we watch the documentary *Hearts and Minds*. The film weaves interviews with U.S. soldiers and Vietnamese with newsreel footage of the war and unexpected scenes of daily life in the United States.

Student suggestions included writing from the points of view of an American pilot who has become critical of his role in the war, a North Vietnamese man whose entire family has been killed in a bombing raid, and a Native American Marine who was called "blanket ass" and "squaw" by commanding officers.

The monologue technique gives structure to the assignment, but the freedom to write from anyone's point of view allows students to mold the piece to the contours of their lives and interests.

Jetta chose the point of view of a Vietnamese prostitute, and wrote in part:

> I sell my body because it's the only way to stay alive. They say my people are disgraceful, but they

have disgraced us. ... We are forced to sell our bodies. ... but who forces them to pay, to strip the dignity from someone's daughter? Do they not have daughters at home? Do they not have mothers? Where did they learn this? What kind of place teaches this?

In our classroom circle, students read their pieces aloud and give positive comments on each other's work. Listening to the collection of writings offers students an intimate portrait of the social consequences of the war. We feel, rather than observe from a distance. These portraits provide us a way to talk about the film without writing out typical discussion questions. The different lives that students imagine and their different interpretations give us opportunities to explore the film or reading more thoroughly.

As is true anytime we wonder about other people's lives, our monologues are only guesses, at times marred by stereotype. But the very act of considering, "How might this person experience this situation?" develops an important "habit of the mind" and draws us closer together. We write the monologues along with our students and can testify at the startling insights and compassion that can arise. Usually, we—students and teachers—tap into our own well of pain, pride, sorrow, confusion, and joy. Although we may never have experienced war, we know the pain of losing a family member or friend; we have experienced the difficulty of making a tough decision. Likewise, we have felt joy. From these shared emotions we can construct a piece that allows us to attempt a momentary entrance into another person's life.

In our Literature and U.S. History class, we read "A Jury of Her Peers" by Susan Glaspell, a 1917 story about rural women's lives. In the story, Minnie Wright, who lives on an isolated farm, strangles her husband in desperate retaliation for his strangling her bird, the creature that brought her the only piece of joy in an otherwise bleak life. We suggested students might begin their monologue or poem with "Write that I …" Maryanne assumes the persona of Minnie Wright and tries to imagine what in her life would lead her to commit such a horrid crime:

Write that I was young,
tender like the gardenia blossom …

I know that you think
I killed my husband,
my keeper, protector.

I stayed in that house, broken
chairs beneath me, husband on top
pushing his fury through me …

Please don't forget the bird.
You must tell them about its voice.
It was strangled.
We were strangled.

Interior monologues tap other people's pain, but they also tap people's hope. After watching *The Killing Floor*, about World War I black migration to Chicago and union organizing in the stockyards, Debbie wrote an interior monologue from the point of view of Frank, a black worker recently arrived from the South:

I sit and listen to the unfamiliar air of music drifting in through my window. Crickets had made music in the South, but never in a tune like this one. I want Mattie to hear this new music. The sound of white men's feet on the dirt avoiding our black bodies on the sidewalk. Oh, to share the sounds of coins clinking together as I walk.

As students read their pieces aloud in the circle, we ask them to take notes on the "collective text" they create, to write about the common themes that emerge, or questions they're left with. Or we might pose a particular question for them to think about. For example, recently we finished watching the film, *Glory*, about a regiment of African-American soldiers who fought in the Civil War. We wrote a dictionary definition of the word "glory" on the board and asked students as they listened to each other's interior monologues to notice: "Where is the 'glory' in the film *Glory*?" Students' own writings and observations became different points of entry to explore the interesting contradictions in the film and the events it depicts. For example, Eugene wrote: "In our class reading it was commented that there was mostly pain and not much glory. I think that their pain was their glory, the fact that they were willing to be martyrs. They were fighting for a freedom that they knew they would never have, because most of them would die in the war."

Empathy and sympathy are quite different. When Ghantel writes her *Color*

Purple interior monologue from the point of view of Mr._____, Celie's uncaring husband, she shows empathy; she tries to imagine how he looks at the world and wonders what experiences made him who he is. But she's not sympathetic; she doesn't approve of his behavior. In fact, she detests him. Interior monologues, by encouraging students to empathize with other people, no matter how despicable, invite kids to probe for the social causes of human behavior. People are not inherently sexist or racist; and while interior monologues are not analytical panaceas, they can be useful tools in nurturing insight about why people think and act as they do.

In our experience, success with interior monologues depends on:

■ Drawing on media or writing that is emotionally powerful.

■ Brainstorming character and situation choices so most students can find an entry into the assignment.

■ Allowing students the freedom to find their own passion—they might want to complete the assignment as a poem, a dialogue poem, from the point of view of an animal or an object (Minnie Wright's dead bird, for instance).

■ Giving students the opportunity to read their pieces to the entire class.

■ Using the collective text of students' writing to launch a discussion of the bigger picture.

Writing interior monologues won't necessarily have students hugging each other as they sing "We Shall Overcome," but they are a worthwhile piece in our attempt to construct a critical, multicultural curriculum. We want kids to think deeply about other people—why they do what they do, why they think what they think. We want students to care about each other and the world. Interior monologues are a good place to start. ■

Two Women

This poem was written by a working-class Chilean woman in 1973, shortly after Chile's socialist president, Salvador Allende, was overthrown. A U.S. missionary translated the work and brought it with her when she was forced to leave Chile. This is to be read by two people, one reading the bold-faced type and one reading the regular type.

I am a woman.
I am a woman.

I am a woman born of a woman whose man owned a factory.
I am a woman born of a woman whose man labored in a factory.

I am a woman whose man wore silk suits, who constantly watched his weight.
I am a woman whose man wore tattered clothing, whose heart was constantly strangled by hunger.

I am a woman who watched two babies grow into beautiful children.
I am a woman who watched two babies die because there was no milk.

I am a woman who watched twins grow into popular college students with summers abroad.
I am a woman who watched three children grow, but with bellies stretched from no food.

But then there was a man;
But then there was a man;

And he talked about the peasants getting richer by my family getting poorer.
And he told me of days that would be better, and he made the days better.

We had to eat rice.
We had rice.

We had to eat beans!
We had beans.

My children were no longer given summer visas to Europe.
My children no longer cried themselves to sleep.

And I felt like a peasant.
And I felt like a woman.

A peasant with a dull, hard, unexciting life.
Like a woman with a life that sometimes allowed a song.

And I saw a man.
And I saw a man.

And together we began to plot with the hope of the return to freedom.
I saw his heart begin to beat with hope of freedom, at last.

Someday, the return to freedom.
Someday freedom.

And then,
But then,

One day,
One day,

There were planes overhead and guns firing close by.
There were planes overhead and guns firing in the distance.

I gathered my children and went home.
I gathered my children and ran.

And the guns moved farther and farther away.
But the guns moved closer and closer.

And then, they announced that freedom had been restored!
And then they came, young boys really.

They came into my home along with my man.
They came and found my man.

Those men whose money was almost gone.
They found all of the men whose lives were almost their own.

And we all had drinks to celebrate.
And they shot them all.

The most wonderful martinis.
They shot my man.

And then they asked us to dance.
And they came for me.

Me.
For me, the woman.

And my sisters.
For my sisters.

And then they took us.
Then they took us,

They took us to dinner at a small, private club.
They stripped from us the dignity we had gained.

And they treated us to beef.
And then they raped us.

It was one course after another.
One after another they came after us.

We nearly burst we were so full.
Lunging, plunging—sisters bleeding, sisters dying.

It was magnificent to be free again!
It was hardly a relief to have survived.

The beans have almost disappeared now.
The beans have disappeared.

The rice—I've replaced it with chicken or steak.
The rice, I cannot find it.

And the parties continue night after night to make up for all the time wasted.
And my silent tears are joined once more by the midnight cries of my children.

And I feel like a woman again.
They say, I am a woman.

The period of rice and beans for the poor woman in the poem occurs after the election of the socialist Salvador Allende as president of Chile. Allende was elected in 1970. He was overthrown in a military coup in September 1973 after a long period of destabilization launched by the wealthy classes and supported by the U.S. government and U.S. corporations such as International Telephone and Telegraph. Along with thousands of others, Allende was killed by the military. The coup, under the leadership of Gen. Augusto Pinochet, launched a period of severe hardship for the working and peasant classes. (See p. 212 for lesson ideas.)

Role Plays: Show, Don't Tell

By Bill Bigelow

My lecture had put kids to sleep. As I looked out over the classroom, students' faces had that droopy, how-many-minutes-'til-the-bell-rings look. "But how can this be boring?" I silently protested. "We're talking about the Vietnam War." As students filed out of the classroom, I shook my head and pledged to find a way to ignite their interest. I was just a first-year teacher, but I knew there had to be a better approach.

Over the years, I've concluded that lectures have their place—but only when directly linked to activities that draw students into the intimacy of social dynamics. For me, the teaching strategy that most consistently enlightens and brings students to life is the role play. There are all kinds of role plays, but the best of these raise critical questions that require student initiative and creativity. At times students may roam the classroom, building alliances with other groups, or debating whether the U.S. government should recognize the independence of a united Vietnam at the end of World War II, or whether logging should be allowed in old-growth forests. A good role play invites students to enter the personas of contemporary or historical social groups to learn about issues in their characters' lives from the inside out.

I'm talking like the social studies teacher that I am, but role plays are valuable in just about every class—science, math, English—and at just about every grade level. Any time there is a division of opinion on an important issue, a role play can help students to understand the source of conflict and

CLEO PHOTOGRAPHY

to imagine possible resolutions.

I start with a controversial contemporary or historical problem: Should the Cherokee people be uprooted and moved west of the Mississippi River? Should the United States government build the Dalles Dam on the Columbia River? In a role play on the election of 1860: Do you favor banning slavery from the western territories? Should there be a Palestinian state? Should nuclear weapons be banned? Who is to blame for the 1968 massacre at My Lai? In a music class: Should rock 'n' roll and rap be regulated by the government? In an English class, students might represent different community groups debating whether Standard English should be spoken at all times in school. In a science class, students might examine the ecological complexities of logging old-growth forests by role-playing the interests of timber companies, loggers, and environmental activists, but also the salmon, owls, rivers, and trees themselves. Each group could propose answers to the question, Should logging be restricted?

Developing a Role Play

Stage one is conceiving substantive questions like these. Stage two entails selecting groups that will give voice to a range of perspectives on a particular issue. For example, a role play on land reform in Central America divides students into five groups: tenant farmers, the management of an instant coffee factory owned by a U.S. company, landless peasants, urban unemployed workers, and coffee planters. In the role play, each group has a somewhat different perspective on whether there should be land reform, how much land should be involved, and who should receive it. As in real life, strategic alliances between various groups are possible, and in the course of the role play students usually discover these and work together. The vitality of a role play depends on ensuring that actual social conflicts come to life in the classroom.

In a mock U.S. Constitutional Convention, I include roles for groups that weren't represented at the real convention. So instead of only lawyers, financiers, and plantation owners in attendance, I also invite poor farmers, workers, and enslaved African Americans. Students debate questions from each group's standpoint: whether to abolish slavery and/or the slave trade, whether to allow debt relief to farmers by permitting payment "in kind," and how political leaders should be cho-

Suggestions for a Successful Role Play

1. Introduce the role play and give students a sense of why the class is participating, and what the general guidelines will be. Break students into groups, roughly equal in size. It's vital that the question(s) each group will address are clear and understood by all.

2. Allow students to connect with the roles they've been assigned. You might encourage students to read their roles aloud in their small groups. I usually ask students to answer questions in writing based on their role: "How do you make your living? Why do you put up with such rotten working conditions?" Or I might ask them to write interior monologues—their inner thoughts about hopes and fears. Students can read these to each other in the small groups. Have each group make a placard so they can see who's who. You might interview students in front of the class or even bait them devil's-advocate fashion: "How do you really feel about that poor farmer in that group over there?" As mentioned earlier, be sure that students' roles are not too prescriptive. I've seen many role plays that tell students exactly who they are and what they think. What's left for the kids? Likewise, some role plays don't give students enough information to participate thoughtfully: "You are a Mexican farmer." That's not much to go on. Also, try not to mix up roles by having some economic and some moral, e.g., steel workers and liberals; steel workers may be liberals.

3. It's the students' show, but the teacher's participation is vital. I circulate in the classroom making sure that students understand their roles. I help them think of groups they might want to ally with. I also instigate turmoil: "Do you know what those middle-class people are saying about you immigrants?" It makes for more lively exchanges.

4. Each role should include at least some information that other groups don't have. This requires students to teach and persuade one another. So they need an opportunity to meet. After they have read and considered their roles and positions on issues, I tell students to choose half of their group to be "traveling negotiators."

The travelers may only meet and "wheel and deal" with non-travelers, to ensure that the whole class is involved at any given time.

5. It's important that students have an opportunity to present their points of view and hear from the other groups. I often structure these gatherings as "community meetings" assembled to discuss the burning issue under consideration. As with the small group negotiation sessions, I encourage students to use the information in their roles in their presentations to teach others. I usually play a role myself, sometimes as a partisan. For example, in a role play on whether "Mother Country" will grant independence to its Asian colony, "Laguna," I play the colonial governor and chair the assembly. I know some teachers will disagree, but in my experience, it hasn't been a great idea to have students actually run the meetings, as discussion is often heated and students will jump on each other for seeming to play favorites in whom they recognize. However, at times I'll conduct a meeting with a simplified version of Roberts' Rules of Order which offers students a good deal of say-so in the pacing of discussion. In some role plays, a major aim is to give students practice in making decisions without the presence of an authority figure. For example, a role play on the 1912 Lawrence, Mass., textile strike, asks students in a large group format to confront strategic and tactical issues on their own: "With thousands of workers out on strike, how will we make decisions? Should our commissaries feed non-striking workers?" In this role play, students simulate the euphoria and frustration that accompanies grassroots democracy.

6. It's essential to debrief. No activity stands on its own. Before we discuss, I usually ask people to step out of their roles by asking them to write for a few minutes. I might ask them to speculate on what actually happened in history. Sometimes I'll ask them to critique their own positions to give them permission to distance themselves from the points of view they espoused in the role play debates.

sen. This more representative assembly allows students to experience some of the underlying conflicts that were suppressed in the actual Constitutional Convention.

But a role play wouldn't work, or at least wouldn't work as well, if I simply said to students, "You play a poor farmer; you play a plantation owner." They'd have nothing to go on beyond their own preconceptions, often stereotypical, of farmers and plantation owners. So I have to do some research in order to provide students with information on the circumstances in different social groups' lives—circumstances that would contribute to shaping these groups' attitudes on a given issue. Students can do some of this work, of course, but my experience is that they need a base to work from. This is especially true because many of the groups I want to include in a role play have been written out of traditional history books. For example, it's not that easy to find information in a high school library on the problems of farmers after the American Revolution, or about the Unemployed Councils of the 1930s.

That said, involving students in researching different groups can sometimes make them more engaged in a role play. Earlier this year, in a somewhat different kind of role play, I told students that each of them would be representing members of the Cherokee Nation and that the U.S. government was proposing to move them off their land and relocate them hundreds of miles to the west. I provided a role sheet with some historical background, but before beginning the role play we spent time in the library researching the Cherokee in greater depth. In class, I played President Andrew Jackson at a gathering with the Cherokees. Although the meeting was imaginary, I read actual excerpts from Jackson's 1830 message to Congress on Indian Removal (*The Annals of America*, Ency-

clopedia Britannica, Vol. 5, pp. 418-421). After the speech, students pelted me with questions and criticisms based on their research. Following this exchange, their assignment was to write a critique of Jackson's speech.

Role Plays and Learning

In this and other role plays, amidst the deal-making, arguing, and oratory, students absorb a tremendous amount of information. But they absorb it in a way that reveals underlying social conflict and solidarity, so they can make sense of that information. In large measure, the process itself is the product. To be effective, the results of a role play needn't repeat history. Some of our best debriefing sessions concentrate on discussing why students made different choices than did the actual social groups they portrayed. Role plays allow students to see that history is not inevitable, that had people understood their interests more clearly, or had they overcome prejudices that kept them from making alliances, events might have turned out very differently. I want students to see themselves as social actors, to realize that what they do in the world matters—they are not simply objects to be thrown about by some remote process called History. When they succeed, role plays can help chip away at students' sense of predetermination, their sense of powerlessness.

In a different version of the Cherokee Removal role play, I include plantation owners, Atlanta bankers, the Andrew Jackson Administration, and the Cherokee. In this, as in other role plays, the intent is never to suggest that all points of view are equally valid. Andrew Jackson and Southern plantation owners can't propose stripping the Cherokee and other Southeastern Indian nations of their homelands without resorting to racist arguments. The role play allows students to see that. It's essential that key interests in

a particular issue be represented, not necessarily so students can hear "all points of view," but so they can dissect the relationship between people's social conditions and their ideas.

A final note: A role play aims at nurturing students' appreciation of why people in history and the world today think and behave as they do. But I never want students to sympathize with individuals who behaved in hurtful or exploitative ways, that is, to have some emotional identification or agreement with these people. In my experience, kids are able to make the distinction. This is especially so when in follow-up discussion we critique positions espoused by various groups in a role play, including their own.

In his book *A People's History of the United States*, Howard Zinn critiques traditional nationalistic approaches to history:

> Nations are not communities and never have been. The history of any country, presented as the history of a family, conceals fierce conflicts of interest (sometimes exploding, most often repressed) between conquerors and conquered, masters and slaves, capitalists and workers, dominators and dominated in race and sex. And in such a world of conflict, a world of victims and executioners, it is the job of thinking people, as Albert Camus suggested, not to be on the side of the executioners.

Role plays should bring that world of conflict to life in the classroom and allow students to explore the underlying premises of arguments and to decide: What is just? ■

Bill Bigelow (bbpdx@aol.com) has taught high school social studies in Portland, Ore., since 1978. He is an editor of Rethinking Schools *magazine.*

Testing, Tracking, and Toeing the Line
A role play on the origins of the modern high school

By Bill Bigelow

What we don't teach in school can be more important than what we do teach. When we fail to engage students in thinking critically about their own schooling, the hidden message is: Don't analyze the institutions that shape your lives; don't ask who benefits, who suffers, and how it got to be this way; just shut up and do as you're told.

Several years ago, Linda Christensen and I began teaching a unit on the history and sociology of schooling. In the unit, students wrote and shared stories about their own school lives—both good learning experiences as well as times they encountered unfairness or abuse. We invited students to probe the hidden curricula in their own classes, including ours, asking them to reflect on what they were learning about authority, bosses and democracy; solidarity and resistance, people's capacity to stand up for themselves and each other; knowledge, what kind is valued and where it comes from; and self-respect. Our class traveled to a high school in a wealthy Portland suburb to compare the hidden curriculum there with that at Jefferson, a school serving a predominantly working-class, African-American community.

Roots of Modern Schooling

To explore some of the historical roots of the modern high school I wrote a role play that I hoped would allow students to question aspects of schooling they often take for granted, such as

This role play places some students in the role of Hungarian immigrants at the turn of the century. Here, immigrants eat their first Christmas dinner in the U.S.

tracking ("ability grouping"), standardized testing, guidance counseling, student government, the flag salute, bells, required courses with patriotic themes, and extracurricular activities like athletics and the school newspaper. These now commonplace components of high school life were introduced in the early years of the 20th century, a time of growing union militancy and radicalism, and large-scale immigration from southern and eastern Europe, accompanied by vastly increased high school enrollment.

Underlying the new reforms was a consensus among leading educators that social class stratification was here to stay, and that high schools should abandon a single academic curriculum for all students. Charles Eliot of Harvard, for example, argued that classes were "eternal," with an elite "guiding class" at the top and on the bottom, a "thick fundamental layer engaged in household work, agriculture, mining, quarrying, and forest work." Schools, the educational establishment concluded, must be "realistic" and train children for specific roles in the social hierarchy. Intelligence testing would allegedly ensure students' accurate placement in differentiated curricular tracks. Simultaneously, as one school board president complained, "Many educators have failed to face the big problem of teaching patriotism. ... We need to teach American children about American heroes and American ideals."

Instead of just lecturing about the profound changes in schools occurring in the early years of the century, I wanted students to encounter them as if they were members of different social classes and ethnic groups, learning of proposed reforms for the first time. Through argument and negotiation, students-as-different-social-groups would need to decide whether they supported the then-new reforms in public education.

In the activity, I portray a gung-ho superintendent, newly arrived in "Central City," determined to modernize— i.e., stratify and "Americanize"—the curriculum. Each student portrays an individual in one of five social groups: corporate executives, members of the Industrial Workers of the World (IWW), middle-class people, Hungarian immigrants, and black activists.

Everyone is posed a series of questions about their views on schooling and is invited to advise the superintendent at a community meeting. In preparation, each group has a chance to consult and build alliances with any of the others. Through participating in the role play I hoped students might see firsthand that the school reforms were not simply benign, value-free changes, but were deeply political, benefiting some people at the expense of others. (See also the section "An Explicit Critique of Tracking" in "Getting Off the Track: Stories from an Untracked Classroom," p. 68.)

Role Play Instructions

Materials Needed

Enough for all students: copies of "Superintendent's Statement," "School Reform Meeting Questions," and "Mental Ability Test." Enough role sheets so that each student has a role (pp. 138–140) .

Procedure (Also see "Suggestions for a Successful Role Play," p. 131.)

1. Write on the board: "Place: Central City, U.S.A.; Time: Early 1920s." Also list the names of the five social groups. (Note: "Central City" represents numerous Midwestern and Eastern U.S. cities; I set the role play in the early 1920s because this is when standardized testing took off, but the social and educational trends described in the role play began earlier, in the beginning years of the 20th century.)

2. Divide the class into five groups, of roughly equal numbers. Distribute a different role sheet to students in each of the groups: i.e., all the members of one group portray Hungarian immigrants, etc. Ask students to read these carefully, and, in their role, to think about the kind of schooling they want for their children. Encourage them to mark important sections. After they've finished reading, you might ask them to write a brief interior monologue—their inner thoughts—on what kind of education they hope for their children; or they might write on their fears. Afterwards ask them to read these to others in their group. The goal here is simply to prompt students to internalize the information in their role sheets, and to encourage them to imagine these individuals as real people. Ask students to make placards or name cards indicating their social group.

3. Tell students that Central City has hired a new superintendent who is proposing a series of reforms in Central City high schools. To each student, hand out the "Superintendent's Statement" and the "School Reform Meeting Questions." As mentioned, the teacher plays the superintendent. Before my "speech," I generally ask a student to introduce me as Superintendent Quincy P. Aldrich or another similarly aristocratic sounding name. I read the statement aloud, with a good dose of pomp, stopping along the way to emphasize a point and to make sure students understand each proposed reform. (Note that the four tracks—feebleminded, dull, etc.—come from a quote by Lewis Terman of Stanford, who suggested that these categories of students would never change. I tell students that if they don't like those designations, perhaps they'd prefer the tracks suggested by Professor George Strayer of Teachers College: bright, slow, backward, and deficient. Clearly, I am hoping to provoke students by using these terms. For public consumption, the educational elite preferred designations such as college, general, commercial, and vocational.) I assure the gathering that all tracking will be based on scientific evidence and I have a sample test to prove it. Students always want to see the test, so at this point I distribute "Mental Ability Test," (developed by Lewis Terman, p. 136). "What does knowing the color of emeralds have to do with your intelligence?" an inquiring immigrant or black activist might ask. I encourage students' critical questions, but don't respond to them all as I want to conserve their defiant energy for the community meeting.

After the superintendent's proposal on guidance counseling, I emphasize that this is especially important considering the increased number of females in school these days: "Why, suppose a girl were to score high on a science test. It would be senseless to place her in a chemistry class. There are few if any female chemists in the country. It would be more sound to place her in an advanced domestic science course, which will help prepare her for the actual challenges she'll face in her life." After my presentation, I tell people that I don't want to argue about the reforms I've proposed, that right now all I want are questions about my speech, and later, in the community meeting, they'll have a chance to argue all they want. Generally, students in several of the groups will pay no attention to this plea and will argue anyway. Again, at this stage it's good to get their critical juices flowing, but not to exhaust their arguments.

4. In preparation for the community meeting, in their small groups, students should discuss the "School Reform Meeting Questions" and, at least tentatively, decide what they think. These opinions may change based on their negotiations with other groups.

5. After they've had a while, probably 15 minutes or so, to discuss the questions, I say something like: "Choose half your group to be 'traveling negotiators.' These people will meet with individuals in other groups to discuss the questions. This is your chance to find people who agree with you about the superintendent's reforms, or to convince others. Remember, there is power in numbers; the more united you are in the community meeting, the more likely it is that the superintendent will be convinced— or forced—to agree with you. One rule: travelers can't meet with other travelers, otherwise people left sitting in their groups will be left out."

6. This is the part I enjoy the most. As students dart around the classroom arguing points and finding allies, I listen in (as teacher, not superintendent), sometimes prodding people to meet with other groups or raising points they may not have considered. There is no "correct" amount of time to give this phase, but I don't want students' enthusiasm to wane, so I call a halt before they're talked out, perhaps 20 minutes or so.

7. Students should return to their small groups to prepare a presentation, however informal, on the various questions. I ask each group to choose a member to write on the board their response to question 1, on the purpose of schooling.

8. I seat the entire class in a circle (people should remain seated with their social group, each indicated with a placard) and begin the meeting by asking each group to respond to the question on the purpose of schooling. Again, there is no right and wrong way to run the meeting. The aim is to encourage the most spirited and democratic participation possible. As superintendent, I'm able to provoke people, point out contradictions, and raise questions. By the way, sometime during the community meeting I remind them that this is only an advisory meeting, that there is a school board, elected citywide, to decide educational policy. I'm just seeking "input." We wouldn't want to give students the false impression that all social groups affected by school reform actually had any say-so.

9. After the meeting, it's important that students have a way to distance themselves from their roles so the debriefing discussion is not simply a continuation of the community meeting. Sometimes I ask students to write about who they think "won" in real life, and to think about how things work in our high school today, to get clues on whose vision of schooling prevailed. Students might write a critique of the superintendent's position or of the position of one of the groups, including their own. Alternatively, they might remain in character to write an interior monologue on how they feel about their child's future in Central City Schools. Afterwards they might read these to the class.

10. Discussion questions include:

- Who do you think "won" in real life?

- Which of the reforms do you think were adopted in U.S. schools?

- If a majority of the groups opposed the superintendent's plan: If most of you opposed the reforms, why were they put into effect? What power did the different social groups have? What power didn't they have?

- Which of the alliances you built might not have happened in real life? Why not?

- Which of the superintendent's proposals do you see in our school today? (Note: When Linda Christensen and I did this role play with our untracked Literature in U.S. History class one year, we noticed that students who had previously been in the top track "scholars" program recognized immediately that our school is tracked. Other students, the majority, who had not experienced life at the top were unaware of how stratified our school is. One girl said, "We're mixed in here. The immigrants must have won.")

- Draw students' attention to the five purposes of schooling on the board: Which of these do you personally find most appealing? Why?

- Which of these seems closest to the kind of schooling you've had? Which of these do you think guides the way our school is set up today?

- What did the "intelligence test" measure? What didn't it measure?

- If you haven't already done so, it might be valuable to have students write about their personal experiences with standardized testing and/or tracking. ■

Bill Bigelow (bbpdx@aol.com) has taught high school social studies in Portland, Ore., since 1978. He is an editor of Rethinking Schools *magazine.*

Thanks to Robert Lowe, Sarah McFarlane, and Deborah Menkart for their help with this article.

Useful Background Materials

Some background materials I've found useful include:

Paul Davis Chapman, *Schools as Sorters*, New York University Press, 1988 (especially Chapter 5, "The Use of Intelligence Tests in Schools: California Case Studies").

David Tyack, *The One Best System: A History of American Urban Education*, Harvard University Press, 1974.

Joel Spring, *The American School, 1642-1985*, Longman, 1986 (especially Chapter 7, "Education and Human Capital").

Robert S. Lynd and Helen M. Lynd, *Middletown*, Harcourt, Brace, 1929 (especially part III: "Training the Young").

Jeannie Oakes, *Keeping Track: How Schools Structure Inequality*, Yale University Press, 2005 (Chapter 2, "Unlocking the Tradition").

Samuel Bowles and Herbert Gintis, *Schooling in Capitalist America*, Basic Books, 1976, (Chapters 5 and 6, "The Origins of Mass Public Education" and "Corporate Capital and Progressive Education").

ACTIVITY TOOLS

MENTAL ABILITY TEST
STANFORD UNIVERSITY   TEST 1   INFORMATION

Draw a line under the ONE word that makes the sentence true, as shown in the sample.

Sample:
Our first president was: Adams   Jefferson   Lincoln   <u>Washington</u>

1. Coffee is a kind of
   bark   berry   leaf   root

2. Sirloin is a cut of
   beef   mutton   pork   veal

3. Gasoline comes from
   grains   petroleum   turpentine   seeds

4. Most exports go from
   Boston   San Francisco   New Orleans   New York

5. The number of pounds in a ton is
   1000   2000   3000   4000

6. Napoleon was defeated at
   Leipzig   Paris   Verdun   Waterloo

7. Emeralds are usually
   blue   green   red   yellow

8. The optic nerve is for
   seeing   hearing   tasting   feeling

9. Larceny is a term used in
   medicine   theology   law   pedagogy

10. Sponges come from
    animals   farms   forests   mines

11. Confucius founded the religion of the
    Persians   Italians   Chinese   Indians

12. The larynx is in the
    abdomen   head   throat   shoulder

13. The piccolo is used in
    farming   music   photography   typewriting

14. The kilowatt measures
    rainfall   wind-power   electricity   water-power

15. The guillotine causes
    death   disease   fever   sickness

16. A character in David Copperfield is
    Sinbad   Uriah Heep   Rebecca   Hamlet

17. A windlass is used for
    boring   cutting   lifting   squeezing

18. A great law-giver of the Hebrews was
    Abraham   David   Moses   Saul

19. A six-sided figure is called a
    scholium   parallelogram   hexagon   trapezium

20. A meter is nearest in length to the
    inch   foot   yard   rod

Copyright 1920 by World Book Co. From Paul Davis Chapman, Schools as Sorters, *New York University Press, 1988.*

Superintendent's Statement on Reforming the High Schools

I've inherited a 19th-century school district in a 20th-century city. It's time for some changes. The following proposals are based on reforms that are sweeping the nation, reforms developed by the finest universities.

Up until now we've run pretty much on the "common school" system. We've assumed that all students are the same, that all should be trained to be President of the United States. Well, my friends, not all our students are going to be President. In 1890, when fewer than 10 percent of 14- to 17-year-olds were in high school, this probably made sense. But by 1920 over a third of all teenagers were in high school, and not all these kids are well-served by such a difficult academic curriculum. Nor is our society as a whole well-served by such a system. As the revered Stanford educator, Lewis Terman, reminds us, we have both "gifted and defective" children in school and they need to be taught differently. It's too bad, but as Ellwood Cubberley, Dean of Education at Stanford points out, in our schools we have "many children of the foreign-born who have no aptitude for book learning, and many children of inferior mental qualities who do not profit by ordinary classroom procedure."

■ Therefore, I propose segregating students into four tracks, each with a different curriculum: Track #1: Feeble-minded; Track #2: Dull; Track #3: Average; and Track #4: Superior. This will allow us to adapt a given course of study to students' individual needs. As suggested by one California school administrator, the lower tracks will naturally train students for "definite hand occupations as opposed to brain occupations."

■ There will be no guesswork in placing students in different tracks. They will be placed scientifically, on the basis of test scores. A system of guidance counseling will assist students in the interpretation of test scores, and to help them plan a personally rewarding and socially useful occupation.

■ Lots of the people entering Central City schools are immigrants. These immigrants are worrisome for a number of reasons. Instead of identifying themselves as Americans, they see themselves as Hungarians or Italians. Some of them identify with the working class against the owners, or even with radicals, people who want to overthrow our form of government. In order to insure that all children become loyal Americans I'm proposing the following: To encourage students to learn about democracy, all schools will have student councils, and every day all students will pledge allegiance to the flag. In all classes we will teach that our system of government is the best in the world. Through clubs, athletics, school assemblies, school newspapers, and the like, we will encourage students to identify not with their social class or radical group, but with their school. We will teach them to be patriotic to their country and patriotic to their school.

School Reform Meeting Questions

Be prepared to explain the following in your presentation at the school reform community meeting.

1. In one or two sentences, describe what you see as the purpose(s) of schooling.

2. Do you support the superintendent's plan for "tracking?" Why or why not? If you don't support the plan, how do you propose to deal with the variety of social backgrounds and skill levels in Central City high schools?

3. Do you support the superintendent's plan for increased testing and guidance counseling? Why or why not?

4. Do you support the superintendent's curricular and extracurricular proposals? Why or why not? Do you have any other suggestions?

Corporate Executive

You are an executive with a large and prosperous corporation. There are a lot of problems in the country, problems that pose serious challenges to public education. In your eyes, the schools have not been meeting these challenges very successfully. For example, before 1900, fewer than one out of every 10 kids between the ages of 14 and 17 was enrolled in high school. This is a real problem because people not in school become juvenile delinquents, turn to crime or worse, join radical groups like the Industrial Workers of the World (IWW). And besides, there simply aren't enough jobs to go around for everyone who wants one.

Also, lots of those entering schools are immigrants. They don't speak much English and haven't learned anything of what it means to be an American. Instead of identifying themselves as Americans, these immigrants see themselves as Hungarians or Italians. Some identify with the working

class against the owners, or even see themselves as radicals. In Lawrence, Mass., in 1912, a massive strike involving 30,000 workers—teenagers, men, women, almost all immigrants—led by IWW radicals, defeated the mill owners. What is this country coming to? You need to make sure that the children of immigrants identify themselves as loyal, responsible Americans—and that they don't identify with one social class against another.

Besides all the immigrants arriving in Central City, there are lots of people leaving the farms to come to the city. These immigrants and farmers aren't used to the factory ways of the city. They aren't used to being prompt, working by the clock, doing repetitive work, obeying orders from a boss, etc.—all skills and attitudes needed to succeed as a factory worker. Their children are not ready to meet the challenges of modern life. You want the schools to turn out good factory work-

ers—but also serve the needs of your children, who are certainly not going to be factory workers.

Up until now, the high schools in Central City have been "common schools" with one curriculum for all students. With few exceptions, everyone took the same subjects in the same classes: boys with girls, bright kids with dull kids. The problem is that in earlier times, very few people went to school, so if you had a high school diploma, it meant something—you could get a good job in the business world. These students tended to be from upper-class or middle-class families. But now, with all these farm kids and immigrants entering the schools, there's no way that all of them are going to get these high-paying jobs. You need to figure out a way for the school system to train the future bankers and the future factory hands in the same classrooms—or at least in the same schools.

Hungarian Immigrant

Let's get one thing straight: You didn't move to the United States to take anybody's job. At the turn of the century conditions were tremendously difficult in Hungary. You owned a little plot of land, but when wealthy farmers began buying machinery to harvest their crops, you simply couldn't compete. You could starve or move. When labor contractors began showing up, they promised good jobs and high wages if you would travel to the United States—a real land of milk and honey. The traveling conditions both in Europe, on the ship coming over, and within the United States were difficult beyond belief. But finally you arrived in Central City, home of Miller and Jones, a giant manufacturer of railroad cars.

Instead of milk and honey you found grease and grime. Even though in Hungary you were a skilled farmer, here you were called "unskilled labor."

Your pay was low, but at least work was steady—for a while. But then you realized that you were guaranteed nothing. Often you'd work only six months out of the year and be laid off the rest of the time. Needless to say, during these periods there were no unemployment benefits. As an unskilled worker you had no security. At times your friends would not be hired back by Miller and Jones; younger, stronger workers would be hired to take their places. With no formal education, no access to additional training, and no big bank account, you have little hope of escaping this life of poverty.

There may be little hope for you, but there is hope for your children. In America, education is free. You've been told that a high school diploma guarantees a young person a decent job. Just because you are an unskilled laborer doesn't mean that your children

will suffer the same fate. They might be teachers, clerks, shopkeepers or even doctors or lawyers. That's why you will sacrifice anything to send your children to school. They will be in the same classes with the sons and daughters of bankers and businessmen, architects and artists. They will read the same books, write the same essays and solve the same equations. In school, rich and poor will mean nothing. Your children are smart. There will be no limit to what they can accomplish. You want them to learn to be Americans, but you are proud of your Hungarian culture and also want them to value that heritage. Your children learn quickly and already speak two languages. You have absolute confidence they will be able to thrive in high school and go on to get good jobs.

Black Activist

You are a black activist in Central City. Over the years you've worked with a number of organizations to promote civil rights and independence for black people. Sometimes you've worked with groups that make alliances with whites, other times you've worked with black-only organizations. You join with whomever you see as capable of effectively fighting racism in Central City and the country as a whole.

For years there weren't many black people in Central City. Most blacks came North during World War I. Conditions were horrible in Mississippi. Your family worked as sharecroppers there, growing cotton and a few vegetables. It seemed like you were always in debt to the white landlord. Everything you had to buy was expensive; but they paid you next to nothing for the crops you raised. Anyone who protested would be beaten or even killed. Blacks were denied the right to vote and the kids went to crummy schools. When people heard there were jobs up north, practically your whole county emptied out overnight.

But conditions in Central City have become increasingly difficult since the war. Perhaps the biggest problem is job discrimination. Employers hire blacks in only the most dangerous, worst-paid and dead-end jobs. Even when you have the skills and education that qualify you for good jobs, the jobs still go to white people. The Ku Klux Klan is a strong force in Central City. They want to make sure that blacks stay poor and powerless and don't get too "uppity" and start demanding good jobs, better housing, and decent schools.

You are especially concerned about the education of black children. While schools are not formally segregated in Central City, you know that black children are discriminated against. One recent study found that 50 percent of black girls in Central City schools were classified as "retarded" and put in "special classes," whereas only 4 percent of native-born whites were classified this way. For this you blame racist administrators and teachers.

Many school officials say that they want to teach children the skills they will need in "real life." They assume blacks will continue to be janitors and maids and so want to teach you to be good—and happy—janitors and maids. But you want your children to get a good academic education so they can become anything they set their minds to. However, some people complain that this kind of education will only make black children resentful. As one judge warned recently, education should not put "fool ideas of rising and equality into [black] folks' heads, and [make] them discontent and unhappy." In your view, in an unjust society, education *should* make young people discontented. It should fill their heads with dreams of equality and give them the tools—reading, writing, knowledge of their history—that will allow them to make their dreams real.

You hope that the more education children have, the unhappier they will be with the racism in Central City and the larger society. A good education should help give children the skills to organize for a better, more just, society. What you want from the superintendent of schools in Central City, and the school system as a whole, is a commitment to fight racism.

PLANTING, BY THOMAS HART BENTON

During World War I, many southern blacks gave up sharecropping and moved north.

IWW Member

You live in Central City, USA, and are a member of the Industrial Workers of the World, a radical labor union. You're concerned about school because you care about children, but also because you see schools as a place where people learn about what is expected of them by society. You see changing the schools as part of a larger movement for changing the whole society.

Much is now different in America. The society is more and more divided between rich factory owners and workers who own nothing but their own ability to labor. As far as you in the IWW are concerned, the problems of working people will only begin to be solved when workers take over all the workplaces and run them together for the benefit of the whole society—not just for the private profit of the owners.

As long as owners run industry for their own profit, there will be continual conflict between them and the workers they control. You believe that all wealth is produced by the workers, so all wealth should be controlled by the workers—what do owners produce?

Thus, the goal of the IWW is not only for higher wages or shorter hours, but to change the whole society. Workplaces and all of society should be run by the people who produce, the people who do the work. And schools should help people learn the skills to run the whole society.

In the IWW you don't believe in the idea of "follow the leader." Your goal is for every worker in the country to be a "leader." Recently, you read a speech by Eugene Debs, an IWW founder. Debs summed up the IWW belief:

The average working [person] imagines that he must have a leader to look to; a guide to follow, right or wrong. … You have depended too much on that leader and not enough on yourself. I don't want you to follow me. I want you to cultivate self-reliance. If I have the slightest capacity for leadership I can only give evidence of it by "leading" you to rely on yourselves.

That's what democracy is all about as far as you're concerned: everyone a leader, a thinker, a participant—regardless of race, sex or class background. And that's what schools should promote for all the students, not just the ones from rich families. Schools should model a truly democratic, classless society.

Middle-Class Person

You consider yourself "middle-class"—maybe upper-middle-class. You manage a small variety "five and dime" store; your father was a clerk for a large machine shop in town. The changes going on in Central City make you nervous—not so much for yourself, but for your children.

When you were young, the common wisdom was that if you went to high school and you graduated, you were guaranteed a good, solid middle-class or business job. You might become a clerk or a factory superintendent, or go on to college to become a lawyer or a doctor. The ticket was high school graduation, and for the most part only the upper and middle classes went to high school. But now everything is changing. In the last twenty years or so the population of Central City has tripled. Quite a number of people are coming into town off the farms, but most of the newcomers are immigrants from overseas. These people, many of whom can't even speak English, think that in America the streets are lined with gold. Problem is, the immigrants think that the way to get some of that good American gold is to send their kids to high school.

Why is this a problem? Because there aren't enough good jobs to go around. A university did a survey recently. They asked high school kids what they wanted to be when they grew up. Just over 90 percent wanted to be some kind of professional person, clerk or business person; only 4 percent wanted to work in a factory. But in the real world, only about 18 percent of the jobs are those kind of decent middle-class jobs. Over 60 percent are factory jobs or farmwork of some kind. You hate to think of yourself as selfish, but these statistics mean that there are going to be lots of people competing for the jobs that should belong to your children.

You know that in a fair competition your child would succeed. But what is happening now is that all these immigrant kids and farm kids who can barely read or write are crowding into the same classes. Soon, a high school diploma won't be worth anything. You want your child to read classic literature, take mathematics, write essays and research papers, learn the history of this great country and master the workings of our form of government. But all these slow learners are going to hold everyone back. And they are also disruptive, many of them juvenile delinquents.

The world is a different place. Today, good jobs require more education. You might even have to send your children to college. But what if they've had an inferior high school education because of all these rowdy newcomers?

'Salt of the Earth' Grounds Students in Hope

By S. J. Childs

How do I teach Global Studies without depressing students with all those stories about injustice? How do I investigate the effects of colonialism and globalization but not perpetuate a view of victimization? How do I help students think critically about the suffering in the world without making it one long sad story?

Over the years I included in my curriculum examples of resistance, set up simulations and activities where students challenged the system or put themselves in the role of change makers. Still, I was sending too many students into the world as cynical young adults when what I wanted was to empower students to become active citizens—thinking critically about society, identifying its problems and working toward solutions. I wanted to start this school year with one hopeful story we could return to repeatedly. I found it in *Salt of the Earth*, a compelling and dramatic film that demonstrates alliances, solidarity, and resistance.

Salt of the Earth was made in 1953 about a coal mining strike in New Mexico. It deals with the struggle for worker equality as well as the fight for racial and gender equity. Many of the actual mine workers and families played parts in the film. Because of its pro-labor sentiments, the U.S. government saw the film as Communist propaganda and blacklisted it. The lead actress in the film, Rosaura Revueltas, was even deported to Mexico before the film was finished. This red-baiting campaign is documented in the Feminist Press book on the film.

Collective Triumph

The film shows the collective triumph of a town over the mine owners. The heroine is Esperanza, the wife of one of the miners. She and the other women in town not only give men their support, they provide them with leadership and sacrifice—inserting themselves into a union discussion, taking over the picket line when the men cannot, and going to jail. This film celebrates alliances—between the women and the mineworkers, the Anglo and the Mexican workers.

I first planned to show this video within the opening week of the course in 2001, but Sept. 11 and "Operation Enduring Freedom" took over the country and my curriculum. Yet the discussion of the blacklisting of *Salt of the Earth* fit perfectly with a look at the

U.S.A. Patriot Act's expansion of police powers and Press Secretary Ari Fleisher's warning to "watch what you say." We examined who might be swept up in the government's broad definition of "terrorist" (see "Whose Terrorism?" in the Rethinking Schools publication, *Whose Wars? Teaching About the Iraq War and the War on Terrorism*) and identified the similarities between the broad use of the term terrorist and the earlier use of the word communist to mean someone who is against U.S. policies.

Resistance—how people make change and challenge injustice—became the course's central theme. Through their analysis of *Salt of the Earth*, students engaged in a close-up examination of how change happens and what is needed to create social movements.

Although *Salt of the Earth* is a black-and-white film, students quickly became engaged with the story and the characters. The students watched as Esperanza (whose name means Hope) overcame her role as frustrated and isolated housewife to join other women on the picket line when their mining husbands could no longer do so. They clapped when Esperanza gave her husband a quick lesson in gender politics when he moans about taking care of the kids. He tells her, "If you think I'm gonna play nursemaid from now on, you're crazy. I've had these kids all day." She shouts back, "I've had them their whole lives!" Students cheered as the jailed women refuse to be cowed by the police, and when the whole town comes to their aid as they are evicted from their company-owned housing.

Acts of Resistance

During the film, I asked kids to list the acts of resistance they saw (see box). I wanted them to be able to identify how often the characters worked for change and how even the littlest acts can add up to great change. Their list included Esperanza standing on the picket line when her husband Ramón told her not to, Ramón telling the company man he wanted his workers to be safe, women asking to vote at the union meeting, Ramón refusing to strike a police officer after being hit, the townspeople returning the furniture to a house after an eviction, the women demanding food in jail, the son skipping school to stay with the picketers and forming a kid brigade. Students noticed that what most of the characters were doing was standing up for what they thought was right and speaking out. "They are fighters and do what they believe is right," wrote Matt.

I wanted students to see themselves in these fighters, to recognize the strength they have to "do what they believe is right." I wanted them to recognize that change-makers aren't always impressive heroic figures, but ordinary people like themselves, doing small things for a bigger cause. I asked them to explain what they had in common with any of the characters.

Some were unable to see any similarities, even as they articulated them. Rithy, a student leader, said, "I don't see that they have anything in common with me, except some leadership skills and a will to change things." Others found a lot to relate to in the film. "I am half Mexican, and sadly some still look down upon us, and believe we are all 'dirty,'" wrote Nerissa, "Esperanza was 100 percent right and so was everyone else. They fought for a better life and to show that Mexicans are just as equal as

everyone else and will go to any lengths for their cause. I would do the same."

Eric, a gay activist who started our Gay-Straight Alliance at Franklin, wrote, "As a homosexual, I feel as though my rights aren't acknowledged. I feel a connection with Esperanza's fuel and fire and her desire to organize and win. Her fight for equality is worthy. I am working for the same thing."

Catey, who identifies herself as a conservative Christian, could see a common bond between herself and the miners' wives. "I am like the group of women that wanted to participate in the strike. I have a hard time sitting back and letting others control things. I like to be involved in organizing, planning, and executing."

Responding to Film

I also asked students to respond to dialogue from the film. Many students reacted to a scene where Esperanza

gives her defeated husband a talking to after he puts her down. "Why must you say to me, 'Stay in your place'? Do you feel better having someone lower than you? . . . I don't want anything lower than I am. I am low enough already. I want to rise. And push everything up with me as I go." Students appreciated Esperanza's hopefulness and her inclusivity. "She doesn't want others to suffer as she has," Eric wrote: "She cares about other people in spite of the hard times she has gone through."

The history of the film is as compelling as its story, because the making of the film itself stands as an example of resistance. Excerpts from the book *Salt of the Earth* could be a valuable supplement to showing the film. The book includes interviews and stories about the making of the film. That the government viewed the making of the movie as dangerous both amused and alarmed my students, who saw possible

---

Worksheet Questions on 'Salt of the Earth'

Salt of the Earth was made in 1953 about a mining strike in New Mexico. It deals with the struggle for worker equality and for racial and gender equity. The film was made during the McCarthy era, and it was blacklisted for containing "Communist propaganda." Please view the film carefully, taking notes, so that you can answer the following questions thoroughly.

1. List the various alliances you see throughout the film. When did people cross out of their comfort zones or groups to help others and when did they act in solidarity?

2. List the various instances of resistance during the film. When do you see people working for change, challenging authority or the status quo?

3. What are the necessary elements for successful resistance?

4. What do you have in common with any of the characters or any of the groups in the film?

5. Discuss one quote from the film.

6. This film, according to the U.S. government, contained dangerous propaganda. What ideas in this film were considered dangerous and to whom?

7. Tell a story, in as much detail as you can, that shows what you mean when you say "we." In other words, tell about a time when you acted as an ally for someone or in solidarity with someone, or when someone acted in solidarity with or as an ally for you. Use the elements of narrative—dialogue, blocking, character development, setting description, etc. Show, don't tell.

parallels in today's political climate.

Anna noted the importance (and the danger) of casting actual mine workers and their families in key roles in the film. "Using real people in the film showed us who these 'enemies of the state' really were and that they were willing to stand up to anyone to get this film made. These ordinary people, these struggling people were making a difference."

In our brainstorm after the film, students identified several key elements of resistance:

- Time and patience.
- Determination and a willingness to struggle.
- Common beliefs and clear goals.
- Equity—a chance for all voices to be heard.
- A plan—arrived at together divided into baby steps with lots of alternatives.
- Organization—divided responsibility, small groups.
- Courage—taking risks in spite of fear.
- Caution—using good judgment.
- Alliances—connection to larger causes/connection to other groups.

I wrote this list on big poster paper and taped it on the wall, where it stayed the entire year. We often referred back to it and added on. For example, after we watched a documentary film on the black union struggle in apartheid South Africa, I asked students to discuss why union members were willing to take serious risks for this cause and what other elements of resistance they would add to our list. They added:

- Leadership.
- Education about and for the cause.
- Music and song.
- Faith/inspiration/religion.
- Use of the media—incidents that catch media attention.

Just recently we discussed what the Native population of the Northwest Territories could do as their culture is threatened by "Western media influence" and Canada's desire for oil. Catey gestured to the list and said, "What about alliances? The Canadian government isn't going to back down easily. These folks need help. Aren't there other groups who share the same goals?" We then discussed what kinds of groups might be interested in working with the Inuit and Dene.

Being able to tie all our studies back to the theme of resistance helps us shift our focus from oppression and despair to organizing, determination, planning, solidarity, and hope. After viewing the film *Trinkets and Beads* about the fight of the Huaorani Indians in eastern Ecuador against oil companies' drilling in the Amazon rainforest, I asked students whether they saw any similarities between this story and *Salt of the Earth*. Elizabeth said the Huaorani marching through the streets of Quito reminded her of the women taking over the picket line in *Salt of the Earth*. "You could tell that the people watching them thought they shouldn't be there. But I was so glad to see it. They were doing exactly what needed to be done." Jared said that Moi, a Huaorani leader, reminded him of Esperanza. "Moi is tough. He is fighting back when it seems hopeless. But he knows he has to win."

What's So Dangerous?

Before Sept. 11, I had not thought to emphasize the issue of what was so dangerous about *Salt of the Earth* and to whom. But I added this question in order to help students connect the film with current issues. They did much more than that. Students recognized that Esperanza and the women were challenging a gender hierarchy, while Mexicans and Anglos working together confronted expectations of racial division that benefited mine owners who depended on a divide-and-conquer strategy to maintain their power. And, they knew that striking workers chal-

lenged corporate power.

But the students also surprised me with their awareness of more subtle issues. In class discussion, one student said, "The film celebrates people working together and caring for one another in a way that makes it safer to take risks. Working miners from other communities supported the non-working strikers. It showed to what lengths people go to help one another and that they share a common cause. Our society doesn't want to celebrate this kind of caring. It likes to foster competition." In class, Catey put it bluntly, "The very idea of resistance itself is what was so dangerous." In writing she went further. "If a group of people got together and organized themselves, then they can change things. That concept was dangerous to the United States." Her sentiments echo those of Juan Chacon, who played Ramón in the film, one of the actual mine workers and the union leader of Local 890. He says, "This picture isn't against. It's for! It shows what we can do when we organize and we and Anglo workers organize together. The companies around here have always been afraid of Anglo-Mexican unity. [They try to] separate us from our brothers."

More than I could have hoped, using *Salt of the Earth* and coming back to it all year has shifted the dialogue in our class and the focus for my students. This is not to say that sadness and frustration doesn't overtake us as we study the events of the day and the patterns of globalization, but now students have ideas and a vision to fight back with. ∎

S. J. Childs teaches at Franklin High School in Portland, Ore.

Salt of the Earth *and* Trinkets and Beads *are available from www.teachingforchange. org. The book* Salt of the Earth *is available from Feminist Press, Old Westbury, NY: 1978.* Rethinking Globalization *and* Whose Wars? *are available from Rethinking Schools, www.rethinkingschools.org.*

The Funeral of Martin Luther King, Jr.

By Nikki Giovanni

His headstone said
FREE AT LAST, FREE AT LAST
But death is a slave's freedom
We seek the freedom of free men
And the construction of a world
Where Martin Luther King could have lived and
preached non-violence

ATLANTA
4-9-'68

Since the 1960s, Nikki Giovanni, a poet, essayist, and children's book author, has been active in expressing the need for black awareness and unity. (See p. 212 for lesson ideas.)

SUSAN LINA RUGGLES

PART FOUR

RETHINKING OUR ASSUMPTIONS

Schools are often exhorted to be neutral and objective in their inter-actions with children. Yet schools have never been value-free. Politics, culture, and ideology shape all aspects of school life—from teachers' favoritism toward some students to unexamined premises guiding curriculum.

The writers in this chapter invite teachers to reflect on how they classify children, understand the sources of student failure, view history, and think about race, gender, language, sexual orientation, and class.

My Dirty Little Secret
Why I don't grade papers

By Linda Christensen

I have a secret: I don't grade student papers. Now, don't get me wrong. That doesn't mean that I toss them in the fire, "accidentally" lose them, turn them over to student teachers, stamp them with a six-trait writing analysis and plug in numbers, or push them through some kind of computerized grade machine.

I discovered early on that if I wanted to produce writers, I needed to let go of grades.

Creating Meaningful "Work"

Our grading should match our pedagogy. In my classroom I attempt to prefigure aspects of the kind of society I want my students to live in: a society where the work is meaningful and intrinsically rewarding, where people grapple with big ideas that they care about in an environment where they can talk, read, write, and think without worrying about failure or ridicule.

Students need to feel that their work is important, relevant, and meaningful. If not, why should they spend time working on it? I was reminded of this recently when I demonstrated a narrative lesson in a classroom at Madison High School in Portland, Ore. Madison's student body comes from diverse cultural, racial, linguistic, and economic backgrounds. Students had just read *Breaking Through*, a short memoir by Francisco Jiménez about growing up in a migrant family and trying to fit in as a teenager (Houghton Mifflin, 2001). The students and I examined a point in

the memoir where Jiménez describes going to graduation wearing a white t-shirt because his family couldn't afford to buy him the required white shirt. We also read Gary Soto's story "The Jacket," as well as a number of stories written by my former students.

We talked about buying clothes to fit in, desiring clothes we can't afford, receiving clothes that we don't want from people we love. The topic fits my criteria. It's about big ideas: poverty and acceptance. Students struggle with finding a place to belong, but they also want to avoid being a target of other students' ridicule for wearing the "wrong" clothes or shoes. Many are desperate to fit in—even when "fitting in" means joining a group that rejects the standard teen scene of tight low-riding jeans and shrink-wrap tops.

As we started the writing, I told the students, "Find your passion. Write your way into a story that you want to tell." Damon didn't write about clothes. He wrote about getting a gift he didn't want from his foster parents. He wrote about living in foster homes, about learning how to lie about gifts he didn't want. He also wrote a list of questions about his next home and his next school—he was headed into his 12th home the week after I gave the assignment. He wondered if his new "family" would like him. He wondered if he would make friends at his new school. Fitting in meant a lot more to Damon than wearing the right clothes.

Because the assignment was open enough for Damon to write about what was important to him and what was on his mind, he did. Because I want

Damon to keep writing, I didn't put a grade on it. Instead we had a conversation at the end of the period where I talked to him about what I loved about the piece, and I told him the truth: Many adults and students need to read his piece. I gave him a few suggestions for revision.

He's experimenting with making his story into a narrative essay, tied together with vignettes about the skills he's learned in foster homes. He sent me the next draft via email from the library near his new "home." Damon's not writing for a grade. He doesn't even attend Madison anymore. He's writing because this is a topic he cares about. He's writing because someone is listening to him, and he hopes that through his writing, more people will understand what it's like to live in a foster home.

And before you say, "I can't talk with 150 students after class," I understand. I can't either. I talk with them when we work on revisions in the computer lab, during breaks, during lunch, and after school. When Jefferson, where I spent my teaching career, had tutor time during the school day, I made appointments with students. I also structure revision time during class, so that I can work with students while they are revising. Most often, I start conversations in the margins of their papers—making comments, noting what I love, asking questions when I'm confused, and sometimes making suggestions or reminding them of another student's piece or class talk.

I see responding to student papers as part of the teaching process rather than the evaluation process. Instead of taking my time writing comments on first drafts, for example, students read their papers out loud, and their classmates give them feedback. (I call it a read-around because my students sit in a circle, and we read around the circle. (See p. 213 for details.) At the begin-

ning of the year, the feedback is always positive. Later in the year, we add suggestions for strengthening pieces. We start with what we love about the piece, what's working—a great opening, the use of humor, the rhythm in a certain

read-arounds in class. Not only does the author get to hear comments about his/her work, but the rest of the class gets a chance to hear some pretty amazing stuff. Like when we heard Nicole's home language paper,

> Because the assignment was open enough for Damon to write about what was important to him and what was on his mind, he did.

line, a flashback that builds the reader's understanding of character. I point out techniques the writers are using intuitively, so that fellow students can pick up the strategies and use them in their writing.

But the read-around is also a place for me to informally assess common problems in class papers—lack of evidence, sloppy transitions, weak introductions—as well as individual problems. The read-around, which provides a real audience for writing, allows me to teach, assess, and move students to the next draft.

Students in every class I've taught have made it clear that the read-around was the best part of my teaching. Adam wrote:

> There is so much to learn about good writing. I know that a lot of what shaped my writing was not the diagramming sentences or finding the subject and verb that we learned in grade school, but the desire to learn more about what I'm hearing around me. Just hearing the work of good writers makes an incredible difference. When I find something I really like, I ask myself, "What was it about that piece that made me get all goose-bumpy?" That's why I think it is really important to have those

I don't think there was anyone who wasn't touched by it. Everyone had felt, at some point, like that and her paper was able to capture those feelings and describe them perfectly. At the same time, everyone thought, "How can I write like that?" We all learned from the paper. Now, this is only one example, but almost every day we share, something like this happens.

Another response strategy I use is a variation on the small response group. Instead of reading papers out loud, pairs of students exchange their pieces and write letters to each other based on the criteria of the paper. In the letters—which typically run two pages—students point out what's working, where they had questions, and which criteria were present or missing. They also give suggestions for revision. Students benefit from reading each other's papers by noticing how someone else approached a similar topic and by reading with an editor's eye: What's working? What's missing? What would help this paper? This is a skill they can transfer back to their own work.

Grades as Wages
In too many classrooms, grades are the "wages" students earn for their labor.

Teachers assign work, students create products, and grades exchange hands. There are problems with this scenario. Students who enter class with skills—especially reading and writing skills—in order to raise their grades. Numbers and grades "assess" or judge the paper, rather than provide feedback about how to improve it. Too many of my students had learned to negotiate the five-paragraph essay), because scripts are easier to teach and easier to grade. Unfortunately, they fail to engage students in real writing. Real writing is messy. And students often don't "get" how to write narratives or essays the first time we teach them. They need lots of practice without judgments; they need to be told what they are doing right, so they can repeat it; they need to examine how to move to the next draft.

I see responding to student papers as part of the teaching process rather than the evaluation process.

are rewarded with higher grades. They already know how to write the paper; they just need to figure out what the teacher wants in it. Essentially, they take what the teacher talks about in class and reproduce it in a paper. Students who lack these basic skills are at a disadvantage. Unless there has been an explicit teaching of how to write the papers, they may not know how to produce the products the teacher expects. As a result, they receive lower grades.

Instead of rewarding or punishing students with grades, I believe that we need to "live out our ideals" as Myles Horton exhorts us, by creating situations where students, like Damon, learn to care about the work they produce. Of course, this means creating meaningful and important work that students want to do and creating communities where good work can happen. It also means explicitly teaching students how to write essays, articles, stories, poems, and memoirs and finding real audiences to read that work.

Revision: It's Never 'Done'

Numbers on a six-trait analysis or grades for content and mechanics on the top of the papers don't teach students how to write, nor do they push them to their next drafts. These methods either assume that students are "done" or that they will care enough to go back and attempt to fix their drafts

difficulties of writing by turning in hurried drafts pulled together without much thought. They received their C's or D's, and they were "done" with their writing. The grades let them escape learning how to write.

When Keith Caldwell from the National Writing Project visited the Oregon Writing Project in 1980, he used a great analogy. He said, "As soon as you put a grade on a piece of writing it's done. Don't grade it and you signal that it can still be revised, still worked on." He compared writing to baking pastries. Grades, according to Caldwell, are the frosting. They signal that the donut or the sugar cookie is heading for the showcase. It's done.

Because I want my students to view their writing as a process, I refuse to let them be "done." If students turn in drafts that represent their best work at that point in time, they receive full credit for the writing. Students who don't have a draft receive no credit. When students turn in rushed drafts that clearly aren't their best efforts, I return them and ask them to redo the papers. Students regularly write and rewrite papers they care about a number of times. I remember Anne Lennon, a senior, lamenting in her end-of-the-quarter portfolio: "Seven drafts on this essay and I'm still not done!"

Too often, writing—and thinking—in school becomes scripted (hence the

But What About Report Cards?

Because I work in public schools that still churn out report cards, I must give students grades at the end of each quarter and semester. And I do—based on the total points earned for each grading period. The difference is that I don't put grades on individual papers. They receive all of the credit possible or they redo the papers. For example, a first draft of an essay is typically 150 points; a revision is 300 points. But they only receive the points—all of the points—if they write a paper that meets the criteria. (See box, next page.)

I'm sure there are folks who will shake their heads at the lack of rigor or standards in my system, but I believe my system is rigorous and that I hold students to meaningful standards. They don't pass my class if they can't write an essay or narrative—even if they complete all of the class work. I will work with them until they can write, but I will not accept work that doesn't meet the exit criteria.

The Ideal World Faces Reality

Here's the rub in this idyllic world: I don't always select topics that students find meaningful, and there are academic formats—literary essays, for example—that students would rather pull their teeth out than complete. But I feel compelled to teach them to write in these formats.

I struggle to create assignments that make academic formats compelling. One year, my seniors at Jefferson read *Yellow Raft on Blue Water* by Michael Dorris. The novel is told in the voices of three Native-American women. It starts in the present day and moves backwards as the women unfold their perspectives on events that shaped them. In my class, students wrote about key moments from their lives. Then they invited their parents or other important people to write about the same moments from their points of view. If students couldn't get a parent or friend to write, they wrote about the events themselves, but from another person's point of view. It was a powerful assignment, and students shared incidents of abuse, alcoholism, and drug addiction, as well as other problems. It was hard to turn from this emotionally charged work to writing essays, but it was necessary because I wanted my students to also know how to navigate academic writing.

Instead of asking them to write traditional literary essays, I invited students to include their lives in the essays, to bring in their stories in the same way they had during class discussions. Dina wrote:

I was raised in a home of five children, six including myself. My father was an alcoholic and a drug addict. My mother was on her way to the same behavior. She hid my father's problem for many years until our home was falling apart. My father was a ladies' man, sharing himself with others while my mother said nothing, pretending everything was all right. He would come home drunk, and they would fight and he would move out for periods of time, and return after awhile. My mother continued to take him back and try to keep the marriage and family as one. Regardless of the hurt she felt

Christensen's Grading Policy

Grades: Your grades will be based a number of criteria:

Basic Concepts of Class: In order to pass this class, you must demonstrate that you have learned the major concepts of the course. These will change from quarter to quarter, but sample outcomes might include writing an essay that demonstrates your understanding of historical or literary material or using historical facts to critique a document.

Completion of Daily Work: Daily work is the place we practice the skills needed for learning long-term skills. On a basketball court, team members might learn passing skills. In here, you will learn how to write at the college level by completing shorter writing assignments first or by completing a reading journal in preparation for writing an essay about a novel.

Class Participation: This class demands that you not only complete the work, but also contribute to class discussions. You contribute by listening while others speak, giving positive feedback, speaking on topic, learning how to take turns talking, taking notes during discussion that will help you write later, disagreeing with ideas rather than people. You also contribute by respecting other members of the class. No one should feel vulnerable in this room. We learn best in an atmosphere of tolerance where people can take risks. So expect positive, rather than negative, critique from your classmates and me.

Homework: Homework is an extension of the work in class. Often, it will be relevant only in the context of our class work. For example, if we are studying welfare reform or the politics of language and you don't do the reading, you will not be able to participate or understand the class discussion related to the reading. Similarly, we will write essays, narratives, or poetry that parallel our reading assignments. If you do not do your homework, you will miss the connection.

Difficulty: There will be times when emergencies come up or when you do not understand the homework. In the event this happens, call me at home and I will either grant you more time or explain the work more thoroughly. You may also set up appointments to work with me after school or during lunch.

Extensions: Because I expect quality work, from time to time I will return your essays, narratives, and poetry so you can take more time to polish or rework them. I don't expect you all to be Alice Walkers, but I do expect that you will take time to learn how to write—which means learning how to rewrite. I will teach you, but in order to learn, you must practice.

inside, she wouldn't let it slow her down. At least, I never saw that it did. Co-dependent is what I call her behavior today.

Reading *Yellow Raft on Blue Water* by Michael Dorris I found that he dealt with the topics of dysfunctional families and co-dependent issues. The character Christine reminded me of my mother.

Dina learned to write a literary essay, but one that had personal meaning for her.

Dina went on to include specifics from the novel to develop her essay, comparing her mother and Christine from the novel. She learned to write a literary essay, but one that had personal meaning for her.

Student Reaction

Nicole's reaction to my grading philosophy cemented my belief that I was doing the right thing. Nicole enrolled in one of my classes every year beginning with her sophomore year. The first year, Nicole was frozen by her fear of making a mistake. She attended daily, she responded to other students' papers, but she resisted writing—and this was in Writing for Publication, where writing was essential. In the opening days of her junior year, when a rather smug student made a negative remark about a classmate's paper during a read-around, I didn't have to say a word. Nicole jumped in and talked about the importance of finding what works in a paper. She set the tone for the year—and she finally wrote.

In a mid-year class evaluation of my senior course, Contemporary Literature and Society, Nicole raised her hand. "I like that you don't grade our papers. I went through Sabin Elementary and Beaumont Middle Schools with Mira. Every time the teacher would hand back our papers, Mira's would have an A and mine would have a C. It made me feel like I wasn't as smart as Mira. Now when I look over at Mira's paper, I see that we both have comments from you written all over them. It's a conversation, not a competition."

Mira, the valedictorian, also liked comments instead of grades. "What tells me more about my writing? A grade or the comments and questions you write in the margins?" In fact, Mira looked for colleges that wrote narrative evaluations of their students rather than grading them. (Now, she teaches writing at the college level and writes magnificent poetry.)

Peter, a skeptic in the no-grade process, entered my junior class with strong writing skills. By the end of his second year with me, he wrote in his class evaluation:

> The way you have us make comments (what did you like about the piece of writing) has helped me deal with people. My skin is thick enough to take a lot of abuse just because I've always had a fairly high opinion of some of the things I can do. I didn't realize a lot of other people don't have that advantage. After a while I found out positive criticism helped me more than negative too.

I keep William Stafford's poem "At This Point on the Page" over my desk because it reminds me of the fear I still feel when I turn a piece of writing over to someone to read: Will you like it? Did I do a good job? And what I mean is: Do you like me? Am I OK?

At This Point on the Page
Frightened at the slant of the writing,
  I looked up
at the student who shared it with
  me—
such pain was in the crossing of each t,
and a heart that skipped—lurched
  —in the loop of the y.
Sorrowing for the huddled lines my
  eyes had seen—
The terror of the o's and a's, and those
  draggled g's,
I looked up at her face,
not wanting to read farther, at least
  by prose:
the hand shook that wrote that far on
  the page,
and what weight formed each word,
  God knows.

When I start a new class with students, I need to remind myself to begin with praise, to find what's working, to find the beauty before I find fault. To remember that when I teach writing, I'm teaching the writer, not the piece. Will my words keep them writing or send them scurrying for cover?∎

Linda Christensen (LChrist@aol.com) is director of the Oregon Writing Project at Lewis and Clark College and is an editor of Rethinking Schools *magazine.*

Expectations and 'At-Risk' Children

One teacher's perspective

By L. C. Clark

My principal and I have a fine working relationship. He has come to understand that I do not "do" Halloween (even as a child I never liked the holiday), and I never nag him about scheduling difficulties before 8:30 a.m. We share a common philosophy of education and know precisely why we come to work each morning—the kids! Generally, we are civil and never have "words" in the presence of others unless we are in the midst of a staff meeting where all those assembled have "lost it," know they have "lost it," and have every intention of forgetting what was said (or shouted) upon entering the local watering hole.

Yes, Mr. Smythe and I are doing quite well except for one thing. In my opinion, he does not hold the same expectations for my minority children, many of whom come from lower socioeconomic backgrounds than most of the majority children. These children are often referred to as children "at-risk."

Before I continue, please understand that I do not believe this man is bigoted or lacking in respect for these children. On the contrary, I feel that his expectations come out of deep concern and caring for them. It is just that I see him as being so sensitive to the many difficulties and disasters which often occur in the children's home environments that he cannot accept the notion that even in the midst of crisis they have a responsibility to get an education, and we have a responsibility to expect them to go about acquiring one.

KATHERINE SLEETER

Though we do share a common philosophy of education, our particular methods of implementing our shared beliefs are quite different. I am of the opinion that his methodology, which focuses on assisting children in building self-esteem exclusively through the affective domain, manifests itself in lower expectations of the children. These lower expectations negatively influence the children's ability to grow intellec-tually and socially. In other words, he focuses on the idea that by being tolerant and understanding of their difficulties in the school setting, and not pushing too often or too hard, we can help them to develop higher self-esteem. I, on the other hand, assert that if children are firmly and continually encouraged to function in school by developing appropriate school behaviors to facilitate their learning, their self-esteem will rise because they will see themselves as learners, capable of functioning fully in an academic setting.

Jamie's Story

I can illustrate our dilemma by describing an incident which transpired several months into the last school year.

Jamie, one of my 17 low-achieving math students, came running into class shortly after the class began. Jamie told me he had been in the administrative assistant's office trying to get out of losing his lunch recess for "roofing" a ball. I reminded him that math class began at 9:10 sharp, and it was to his benefit to be on time so as not to feel lost or confused during the class discussion.

I continued the lesson and watched as Jamie retrieved his book and a piece of paper. As various children came up to the chalkboard to solve problems, I noticed that Jamie was not writing. I walked over to him and asked if he had a pencil or needed a new one. He did not have a pencil, so I sent him over to a cabinet to get one.

Twenty-five minutes into the period, students were instructed to have a partner look over their homework before handing it in and going on to their next assignment. Jamie did not move. I went over to him and asked if there was a problem. He informed me that he had not done his homework. (Out of seven assignments due that week Jamie handed in two. Those two papers were completed because I sat with him during his study break as he worked independently.) I told Jamie to

see me before reporting to his lunch recess with the administrative assistant. Then, I instructed him to go to one of the math stations to get a class assignment completed.

After school I related Jamie's behavior and performance to Mr. Smythe, hoping to get some feedback on how to get Jamie back on track in math. I reminded him that while Jamie had demonstrated good understanding of some number concepts and had done well with his basic facts (addition, subtraction, and multiplication through the sixes table), his overall rating was far below average and his progress was erratic.

Mr. Smythe stood in silence for a moment and then proceeded to tell me that it was possible that Jamie had

---

Teachers and Cultural Styles

By Asa G. Hilliard III

I remain unconvinced that the explanation for the low performance of culturally different "minority" group students will be found by pursuing questions of cognitive or learning styles. I believe that the children, no matter what their style, are failing primarily because of systematic inequities in the delivery of whatever pedagogical approach the teachers claim to master—not because students cannot learn from teachers whose styles do not match their own.

There is a protocol of interactive behaviors of teachers who, for whatever reasons, have low expectations for students. Research in this area shows that teachers tend to:

■ Demand less from low-expectation students ("lows") than from high-expectation students ("highs").
■ Wait less time for lows to answer questions.
■ Give lows the answer or call on

someone else rather than try to improve the lows' response through repeating the question, providing clues, or asking a new question.
■ Provide lows with inappropriate reinforcement by rewarding inappropriate behaviors or incorrect answers.
■ Criticize lows more often than highs for failure.
■ Fail to give feedback to lows' public responses.
■ Pay less attention to lows and interact with them less frequently.
■ Call on lows less often than highs to respond to questions.
■ Seat lows farther away from the teacher than highs.
■ Use more rapid pacing and less extended explanations or repetition of definitions and examples with highs than with lows.
■ Accept more low-quality or more incorrect responses from low-expectation students.

■ Interact with lows more privately than publicly.
■ In administering or grading tests or assignments, give highs but not lows the benefit of the doubt in borderline cases.
■ Give briefer and less informative feedback to the questions of lows than to those of highs.
■ Use less intrusive instruction with highs than with lows, so that they have more opportunity to practice independently.
■ When time is limited, use less effective and more time-consuming instructional methods with lows than with highs.■

Asa G. Hilliard III is Professor of Urban Education at Georgia State University. He is co-author of Saving the African American Child.

The above is an excerpt reprinted with permission of the National Education Association.

had difficulty in class because of an incident which had occurred in his home last evening that required police involvement. I acknowledged his comment and waited for his input regarding alternatives for assisting Jamie with his learning. Neither of us spoke, and it dawned on me that what he had said about the previous evening was his response to my (and Jamie's) dilemma. It was somewhat unnerving, but I decided that the time had come for the issue of expectations to be addressed. My question was: "How many times are we going to use the problems that happen at home to excuse ourselves from requiring Jamie to function as a learner in an academic setting?"

'At Risk' of Not Being Taught

The "Jamie" story, one of many, has serious implications for teachers, administrators, and, most especially, students who are considered to be "at-risk." I have observed that oversensitivity which manifests itself in repeated acceptance of children's problems while not addressing solutions involving academic concerns is inappropriate for several reasons.

First, it presumes that the problem is temporary. This can lull teachers and administrators into thinking that everything will be all right tomorrow (next week, next year). Some children are in dysfunctional families and it is highly unlikely that the conditions precipitating their difficulties will be relieved during their school years. However, this does not mean that parents are not to be notified or looked to for assistance when children do not behave appropriately.

For instance, in developing a plan to get Jamie to be more responsible about being prepared and on time for class, I contacted his grandmother. I explained Jamie's problem and how it was hurting him academically, then solicited her ideas for what I could do to change his

behavior. She told me that Jamie liked to watch television after dinner, and she would not allow him to watch TV if he did not "act right" in school. After sharing other possibilities, we agreed that whenever Jamie acted irresponsibly he would: (1) call home at the end of the school day to tell his grandmother of the accumulated time wasted due to being tardy or unprepared and (2) lose 30 minutes or more of viewing time depending on the accumulated time and frequency of offenses. By the end of the third marking period (early April), Jamie was occasionally late and unprepared, but he had come to understand that he had to take responsibility for his behavior and the consequences of his actions.

The second reason not addressing solutions is inappropriate is that not working on a solution with a child takes away his or her opportunity to develop positive ways to cope within the school, as well as outside of its walls, when problems arise. Case in point, Jamie often missed out on participating in extracurricular events, such as T-ball and softball, because he would fail to take the flier home or forget to return the permission slip on time.

One day some other children were getting ready to go to an after-school practice when Jamie became angry and started yelling. He confronted one of the boys, called him "stupid" and the softball team "dumb." I moved Jamie away from the boy, then asked him if he had received the same T-ball form at the same time as the other children. When he said he had, I told him to think about why he was not on the team. Jamie left to go home.

The following morning I asked Jamie if he now knew why he was not on the team. He was silent for awhile and then admitted that he had forgotten to return the slip. I asked if he knew what he would do next time. He replied, "Put it (the slip) in my pocket

and bring it back the next day." I suggested he apologize to the other boy. Jamie knew what his responsibility was and how to carry it out.

By adhering to a relativistic philosophy, educators in effect lock those considered to be "disadvantaged" or "at-risk" into the very situations from which education should free them. Intended acts of compassion result in outcomes which promote subtle racism. While I hold the position that expectations must reflect a belief in a child's ability to meet the established standards of an academic community, I am not advocating such a rigid adherence to any standard that the humanity of a child be sacrificed. Rather, I am insisting that compassion be tempered with reason, so that a child deemed "at-risk" be allowed to fully develop and experience his or her power—intellectually, socially, and emotionally.

The issue of expectations which arose in my relationship with my principal has not been resolved. It is extremely difficult to bring the word "racism" into a discussion without creating either discomfort (which makes the dialogue hesitant and shallow) or dissension (which threatens to cut off dialogue completely). But, realizing that holding lower expectations for "at-risk" youngsters (even out of compassion) threatens their intellectual and social/emotional growth commands that the courage to acknowledge the real problem be found.

A relationship, whether personal or professional, reflects the degree of trust and respect between the individuals involved. I believe that between my principal and myself there exists a level of trust and respect that will advance the dialogue which needs to begin and hold the relationship intact even as we may stand against one another. ■

L. C. Clark is an elementary school teacher in New York state.

Teaching Standard English: Whose Standard?

by Linda Christensen

When I was in 9th grade Mrs. Delaney, my English teacher, wanted to demonstrate the correct and incorrect ways to pronounce the English language. She asked Helen Draper, whose father owned several clothing stores in town, to stand and say "lawyer." Then she asked me, whose father owned a bar, to stand and say "lawyer." Everyone burst into laughter at my pronunciation.

What did Mrs. Delaney accomplish? Did she make me pronounce lawyer correctly? No. I say attorney. I never say lawyer. In fact, I've found substitutes for every word my tongue can't get around and for all the rules I can't remember.

For years I've played word cop on myself. I stop what I'm saying to think, "Objective or subjective case? Do I need I or me here? Hmmm. There's a lay coming up. What word can I substitute for it? Recline?"

And I've studied this stuff. After all, I've been an English teacher for over 30 years. I've gone through all of the Warriner's workbook exercises. I even found a lie/lay computer program and kept it in my head until I needed it in speech and became confused again.

Thanks to Mrs. Delaney, I learned early on that in our society language classifies me. Generosity, warmth, kindness, intelligence, good humor aren't enough—we need to speak correctly to make it. Mrs. Delaney taught me that the "melting pot" was an illusion. The real version of the melting pot is

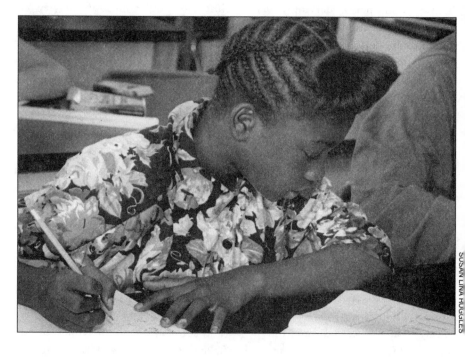

that people of diverse backgrounds are mixed together and when they come out they're supposed to look like Vanna White and sound like Dan Rather. The only diversity we celebrate is tacos and chop suey at the mall.

Unlearning "Inferiority"

It wasn't until a few years ago that I realized grammar was an indication of class and cultural background in the United States and that there is a bias against people who do not use language "correctly." Even the terminology "standard" and "nonstandard" reflects that one is less than the other. English teachers are urged to "correct" students who speak or write in their home language. A friend of mine, whose ancestors came over on the Mayflower, never

studied any of the grammar texts I keep by my side, but she can spot all of my errors because she grew up in a home where Standard English was spoken.

And I didn't, so I've trained myself to play language cop. The problem is that every time I pause, I stop the momentum of my thinking. I'm no longer pursuing content, no longer engaged in trying to persuade or entertain or clarify. Instead I'm pulling Warriner's or Mrs. Delaney out of my head and trying to figure out how to say something.

"Ah, but this is good," you might say. "You have the rules and Mrs. Delaney to go back to. This is what our students need."

But it doesn't happen that way. I try to remember the rule or the catchy phrase that is supposed to etch the rule in my mind forever, like, "people never get laid," but I'm still not sure if I use it correctly. These side trips cost a lot of velocity in my logic.

Over the years my English teachers pointed out all of my errors—the usage errors I inherited from my mother's Bandon, Oreg., dialect, the spelling errors I overlooked, the fancy words I used incorrectly. They did this in good faith, in the same way, years later, I "correct" my students' "errors" because I want them to know the rules. They are keys to a secret and wealthier society and I want them to be prepared to enter, just as my teachers wanted to help me.

And we should help kids. It would be misleading to suggest that people in our society will value my thoughts or my students' thoughts as readily in our home languages as in the "cash language," as Jesse Jackson calls it. Students need to know where to find help, and they need to understand what changes might be necessary, but they need to learn in a context that doesn't say, "The way you said this is wrong."

When Fear Interferes

English teachers must know when to correct and how to correct—and I use that word uneasily. Take Fred, for example. Fred entered my freshman class unwilling to write. Every day during writing time I'd find Fred doodling pictures of Playboy bunnies. When I sat down and asked him why he didn't write, he said he couldn't.

I explained to him that in this class his writing couldn't be wrong because we were just practicing our writing until we found a piece we wanted to polish, in the same way that he practiced football every day after school, but only played games on Fridays. His resistance lasted for a couple of weeks. Around him other students struggled with their writing, shared it with the class on occasion and heard positive comments. Certainly the writing of his fellow students was not intimidating.

On October 1, after reading the story "Raymond's Run" in Toni Cade Bambara's book *Gorilla, My Love* (Random House, 1972), about trusting people in our lives, Fred wrote for the first time: "I remember my next door neighbor trusted me with some money that she owed my grandmother. She owed my grandmother about 25 dollars." Fred didn't make a lot of errors. In this first piece of writing it looked like he had basic punctuation figured out—except for the odd capitals in the middle of the sentence. He didn't misspell any words. And he didn't make any usage errors. Based on this sample, he appeared to be a competent writer.

However, the biggest problem with Fred's writing was that he didn't make mistakes. This piece demonstrates his discomfort with writing. He wasn't taking any risks. Just as I avoid lawyer and lay, he wrote to avoid errors instead of writing to communicate or think on paper.

When more attention is paid to the way something is written or said than to what is said, students' words and thoughts become devalued. Students learn to be silent, to give as few words as possible for teacher criticism.

Valuing What We Know

Students must be taught to hold their own voices sacred, to ignore the teachers who have made them feel that what they've said is wrong or bad or stupid. Students must be taught how to listen to the knowledge they've stored up, but which they are seldom asked to relate.

Too often students feel alienated in schools. Knowledge is foreign. It's about other people in other times. At a conference I attended, a young woman whose mother was Puerto Rican and whose father was Haitian said, "I went through school wondering if anyone like me had ever done anything worth-

Language Prison

By Linda Christensen

All day words
run past my tongue

words tumble and fall
and you catch
the wrong ones
and count them back to me

All day I watch
my tongue

for words
that slip
down the slope of my
neighborhood

words that separate
me from you

words that you catch
and hold against me

All day I watch
for words misshapen
or bent
around my too thick tongue

run-down at the heel words
thin soled words

words that slip
from my tongue

words that tell of mops
and beer
and bent backs

words that shape my world
against a different map
than yours

All day I watch my tongue
for words

while or important. We kept reading and hearing about all of these famous people. I remember thinking, 'Don't we have anyone?' I walked out of the school that day feeling tiny, invisible, unimportant."

As teachers, we have daily opportunities to affirm that our students' lives and language are unique and important. We do that in the selections of literature we read, in the history we choose to teach, and we do it by giving legitimacy to our students' lives as a content worthy of study.

One way to encourage the reluctant writers who have been silenced—and the not-so-reluctant writers who have found a safe but sterile voice—is to ask them to recount their experiences. I sometimes recruit former students to share their writing and their wisdom as a way of underscoring the importance of the voices and stories of teenagers. Rochelle Easton, a student in my senior writing class, brought in a few of her stories and poems to read to my freshmen. Rochelle, like Zora Neale Hurston, blends her home language with Standard English in most pieces. She read the following piece to open a discussion about how kids are sometimes treated as servants in their homes, but also to demonstrate the necessity of using the language she hears in her family to develop characters:

> "I'm tired of washing dishes. Seems like every time our family gets together, they just got to eat and bring their millions of kids over to our house. And then we got to wash the dishes."
>
> I listened sympathetically as my little sister mumbled these words.
>
> "And how come we can't have ribs like the grownups? After all, ain't we grown?"
>
> "Lord," I prayed, "seal her lips while the blood is still running warm in her veins."
>
> Her bottom lip protruded farther and farther as she dipped each plate in the soapy water, then rinsed each side with cold water (about a two second process) until she felt the majority of suds were off.
>
> "One minute we lazy women that can't keep the living room half clean. The next minute we just kids and gotta eat some funky chicken while they eat ribs."
>
> … Suddenly it was quiet. All except my little sister who was still talking. I strained to hear a laugh or joke from the adults in the living room, a hint that all were well, full and ready to go home. Everyone was still sitting in their same spots, not making a move to leave.
>
> "You ought to be thankful you got a choice."
>
> Uh-oh. Now she got Aunt Macy started. …

After reading her work, Rochelle talked about listening to her family and friends tell their stories. She urged the freshmen to relate the tales of their own lives—the times they were caught doing something forbidden, the times they got stuck with the dishes, the funny/sad events that made their freshman year memorable. When Rochelle left, students wrote more easily. Some. Some were afraid of the stories because as Rance said, "It takes heart to tell the truth about your life."

But eventually they write. They write stories. They write poems. They write letters. They write essays. They learn how to switch in and out of the language of the powerful as Rochelle does so effortlessly in her "tired of chicken" piece.

Sharing Lessons

And after we write, we listen to each other's stories in our read-around circle where everyone has the opportunity to share, to be heard, to learn that knowledge can be gained by examining our lives. In the circle, we discover that many young women encounter sexual harassment, we learn that store clerks follow black students, especially males, more frequently than they follow white students, we find that many of our parents drink or use drugs, we learn that many of us are kept awake by the crack houses in our neighborhoods.

Before we share, students often understand these incidents individually. They feel there's something wrong with them. If they were smarter, prettier, stronger, these things wouldn't have happened to them. When they hear other students' stories, they begin to realize that many of their problems aren't caused by a character defect. For example, in Literature and U.S. History, a young man shared a passionate story about life with his mother, who is a lesbian. He loved her, but felt embarrassed to bring his friends home. He was afraid his peers would think he was gay or reject him if they knew about his mother.

After he read, the class was silent. Some students cried. One young woman told him that her father was gay and she'd experienced similar difficulties, but hadn't had the courage to tell people about it. She thanked him. Another student confided that his uncle had died from AIDS the year before. What had been a secret shame became an opportunity for students to discuss sexual diversity more openly. Students who were rigidly opposed to the idea of homosexuality gained insights into their own homophobia—especially when presented with the personal revelations from their classmates. Those with homosexual relatives found new allies with whom they could continue their discussion and find support.

Sharing also provides a "collective

text" for us to examine the social roots of problems more closely: Where do men and women develop the ideas that women are sexual objects? Where do they learn that it's OK for men to follow women or make suggestive remarks? Where is it written that it's the woman's fault if a man leers at her? How did these roles develop? Who gains from them? Who loses? How could we make it different? Our lives become a window to examine society.

Learning the 'Standard' Without Humiliation

But the lessons can't stop there. Fred can write better now. He and his classmates can feel comfortable and safe sharing their lives or discussing literature and the world. They can even understand that they need to ask "Who benefits?" to get a better perspective on a problem. But still when they leave my class or this school, some people will judge them by how their subjects and verbs line up.

So I teach Fred the rules. It's the language of power in this country, and I would be cheating him if I pretended otherwise. I teach him this more effectively than Mrs. Delaney taught me because I don't humiliate him or put down his language. I'm also more effective because I don't rely on textbook drills; I use the text of Fred's writing. But I also teach Fred what Mrs. Delaney left out.

I teach Fred that language, like tracking, functions as part of a gatekeeping system in our country. Who gets managerial jobs, who works at banks and who works at fast food restaurants, who gets into what college and who gets into college at all, are decisions linked to the ability to use Standard English. So how do we teach kids to write with honesty and passion about their world and get them to study the rules of the cash language? We go back to our study of society. We ask: Who made the rules that

govern how we speak and write? Did Ninh's family and Fred's family and LaShonda's family all sit down together and decide on these rules? Who already talks like this and writes like this? Who has to learn how to change the way they

of language errors, fail teacher entrance exams, they will internalize the blame; they will believe they did not succeed because they are inferior instead of questioning the standard of measurement and those making the standards.

Students must be taught to hold their own voices sacred, to ignore the teachers who have made them feel wrong or bad or stupid.

talk and write? Why?

We make up our own tests that speakers of Standard English would find difficult. We read articles, stories, poems written in Standard English and those written in home language. We listen to videotapes of people speaking. Most kids like the sound of their home language better. They like the energy, the poetry, and the rhythm of the language. We determine when and why people shift. We talk about why it might be necessary to learn Standard English.

Asking my students to memorize the rules without asking who makes the rules, who enforces the rules, who benefits from the rules, who loses from the rules, who uses the rules to keep some in and keep others out, legitimates a social system that devalues my students' knowledge and language. Teaching the rules without reflection also underscores that it's OK for others—"authorities"—to dictate something as fundamental and as personal as the way they speak. Further, the study of Standard English without critique encourages students to believe that if they fail, it is because they are not smart enough or didn't work hard enough. They learn to blame themselves. If they get poor SAT scores, low grades on term papers or essays because

We must teach students how to match subjects and verbs, how to pronounce lawyer, because they are the ones without power and, for the moment, have to use the language of the powerful to be heard. But, in addition, we need to equip them to question an educational system that devalues their life and their knowledge. If we don't, we condition them to a pedagogy of consumption where they will consume the knowledge, priorities, and products that have been decided and manufactured without them in mind.

It took me years to undo what Mrs. Delaney did to me. Years to discover that what I said was more important than how I said it. Years to understand that my words, my family's words, weren't wrong, weren't bad—they were just the words of the working class. For too long, I felt inferior when I spoke. I knew the voice of my childhood crept out, and I confused that with ignorance. It wasn't. I just didn't belong to the group who made the rules. I was an outsider, a foreigner in their world. My students won't be. ∎

Linda Christensen (LChrist@aol.com) is director of the Oregon Writing Project at Lewis and Clark College and is an editor of Rethinking Schools *magazine.*

Seeing Color

By Lisa Delpit

As a new teacher, I was delivering my first reading lesson to 1st-grade students in inner-city Philadelphia. I had practically memorized the publisher-provided lesson dialogue while practicing in front of a mirror the night before.

"Good morning, boys and girls. Today we're going to read a story about where we live, in the city." A small brown hand was raised. "Yes, Marti." Marti had been a kindergartner in the informal classroom where I completed student teaching.

"Teacher, how come you talkin' like a white person? You talkin' just like my momma talk when she get on the phone!"

Needless to say, the practiced lesson was put aside as we relaxed into my more typical informal and culturally familiar interaction patterns. And I was once again struck by the brilliant perception of 6-year-olds.

This and other vignettes of my teaching career surfaced as I reread Vivian Gussin Paley's fascinating *White Teacher*. There was no stopping the flood of scenes of children, parents, and teachers, for Paley's writing is so vivid, so classroom-centered, so immediate that anyone who has ever taught—or ever thought about teaching—cannot help being drawn into the daily dramas she describes perfectly. *White Teacher*, originally published in 1979, was reissued in 1990, probably because Paley was awarded a prestigious MacArthur Foundation fellowship in 1989. She was the first classroom teacher so honored.

The book details Paley's development as she struggled to learn to teach diverse—particularly African-American—children in her kindergarten classrooms. Her first teaching jobs were in the segregated schools of the South, where she became the school radical by telling everyone that she wanted an integrated class, that society forced her to teach only white children. When she moved back North, she found herself teaching white children in a white suburb. She had an occasional black student—one the child of the live-in maid of a prominent family, two others when the school board attempted some minor integration. And her encounters with these children caused Paley concern. One avoided looking at her and only responded to her questions with "Yes'm." Another, Fred, joined an aggressive group of six white kids. When the teachers came into Paley's room under various pretenses to, as Paley says, "check out the two black children," they all singled out Fred. "You've got your hands full with him." "Shouldn't he be in a special class?"

RODRIGUEZ

Color Blindness

At the first faculty meeting Paley raised the issue that even though all the children in Fred's small group behaved as he did, teachers singled out Fred because of his color. After vigorous discussion, the faculty reached a consensus: "More than ever we must take care to ignore color. We must only look at behavior, and since a black child will be more prominent in a white classroom, we must bend over backward to see no color, hear no color, speak no color." Paley found herself confused by such directives when children themselves raised issues of color. In one instance a little white child told a little black girl that she looked like chocolate pudding. Was that an insult? Should Paley reprimand the white child? She found herself trapped not only by the school's position but by her own liberal upbringing: "We showed respect by completely ignoring black people as black people. Color blindness was the essence of the creed."

Insight came when Paley moved to a Midwestern city and took a job at an integrated private school. Although most of the faculty and professional staff were white, about a third of the students were children of color. Early on she had a meeting with a black parent. "Mrs. Hawkins told me that in her children's previous school the teacher had said, 'There is no color difference in my classroom. All my children look alike to me.' 'What rot,' said Mrs. Hawkins. 'My children are black. They know they're black, and we want it recognized. It's a comfortable natural difference. At least it could be so, if you teachers learned to value differences more. What you value, you talk about.'"

Thus began the journey toward acknowledging and valuing differences. When Michelle, black and vivacious, pointed to a picture in a book and said she wished she looked like the pink-cheeked blond girl on the page, Paley recalls, "I could have easily ignored this. Maybe Juli Ann, white and plain, wished she looked like the girl in the book too ... But Michelle had a special, obvious reason. I knew I must say something. 'Michelle, I know how you feel. When I was little I also would have liked to look like this little girl. She doesn't look like anyone in my family, so I couldn't have looked like her. Sometimes, I wish I had smooth brown

skin like yours. Then I could always be dark and pretty.' Michelle looked down at her skin. So did everyone else. I don't know what she was thinking. But I knew the feelings I had expressed were true, though I did not know it until I spoke."

> To say you don't see color is to say you don't see children.

In Paley's chronicle of her development of learning from and with her students over five years, she encounters Steven's angry, "DON'T TALK TO ME. I don't have to listen to no white lady. … Don't nobody white look at me. Don't talk to me. You stink. Fuckers!" Kenny didn't want to take off his jacket because the teacher might not like what his T-shirt said: "SUPERNIGGER, guardian of the oppressed." Clare, from a West Indian family, was in such unfamiliar cultural territory that she was almost diagnosed as retarded. Another Kenny, whose physical prowess and bravado were amazing as long as he was outside tumbling with his brothers, was so timid during school activities that he became speechless if required to perform some small task in front of the whole class.

It is important that this book has been reissued. Never has there been so much talk about "restructuring" schools. While legislators, governors, and various "experts" debate the virtues of "site-based management," "merit pay," "choice," or "accountability schemes," there is little talk about the kind of "restructuring" that must happen before we can make any headway with education: the restructuring of

interpersonal relationships. While the number of children of color in our public schools is rapidly rising, the number of teachers of color continues to decline. More than ever, white teachers will be teaching African-American children.

As a teacher-educator, I have worked with white students who will be tomorrow's teachers, and I have many African-American friends who have done the same. The attitude that Paley brought to her first black students—that to acknowledge their color would be to insult them—is prevalent among our young white people about to join the teaching profession. One of my teacher-education colleagues told me that Paley's book was the only book she had found that helped her students understand that to say you don't see color is to say you don't see children. Her students were then able to understand that people could be proud of their color and their differences and that the teacher could help this process.

Qualities of a Good Teacher

Paley exhibits other behavior and attitudes that I try to instill in future teachers. First and foremost, she is an observer of children. When something goes wrong with a child, she does not assume that the cause necessarily lies within the child. She looks to her own teaching and to her own lack of knowledge. She realizes that she probably misses much of the intelligence of the children who are from another culture. She points out that when a child who shares her own Jewish background makes comments about meat and dairy dishes, she receives instant messages about his or her intelligence. But when several black children tell her that "black people don't eat pig. Only white people eat pig," she is honest enough to say, "I think I am missing part of the picture presented by many black children by not being familiar with the context within which certain simple statements are made."

She also seeks to learn from adults who look like the children she teaches. Many white teachers, with the best of intentions, believe that they know what is best for all children. And because they view themselves as liberals, they believe that their behavior is above reproach. In Paley's words, "My luggage had 'liberal' ostentatiously plastered all over it, and I thought it unnecessary to see what was locked inside." Believing in their "rightness," some liberal white teachers do not seek the opinions of parents or teachers of color, and they even subtly discredit those opinions if offered. Paley, on the other hand, often sought the insights of the parents of her black students, and she worked with them to find solutions to problems. When teachers are teaching children who are different from themselves, they must call upon parents in a collaborative fashion if they are to learn who their students really are.

Paley also learned from an African-American woman who worked with her as a student teacher one year. Janet was an older woman and an exceptional teacher with lots of experience teaching in preschool. Paley watched how she handled situations and asked questions about her own performance. That Paley was different from most teachers can be verified by Janet's reaction to the rest of the staff, with whom she was withdrawn and silent. When Paley asked her about it, Janet said she didn't feel comfortable with most white teachers because "they either avoid talking about race like it was a plague, or else they look at me only when black kids are discussed as if the ghetto is the only thing I know anything about." White teachers can utilize culturally diverse colleagues as learning resources only if they respect them and their opinions—not a typical scenario in today's schools.

Paley's book and her approach to children have many strengths, and I could not hope for a more sensitive white teacher of African-American children. Yet I worry. Paley asks, "How much does it matter if a child cannot identify ethnically or racially with a teacher? Does it matter at all? If the teacher accepts him and likes him as he really is, isn't that enough?" I suspect she and I might differ.

Remaining Questions

I wonder whether so many of the African-American children in her classes would have expressed a desire to be white if their teacher had been black. I feel for Ayana when she and Rena were helping Paley put away blocks and Rena said, "White people tell lies." I surmise from other conversations in the book that several of Paley's black students have been exposed to the philosophies of the Nation of Islam and carried some of those discussions from home into the classroom. "That's right, they do tell lies," Ayana agreed. Paley asked, "Do all white people tell lies?" Paley continues: "Ayana read my face. 'Uh … no. Not all white people.' She looked guiltily at Rena." Clearly Ayana must have been expending energy in this classroom determining what she could and could not say to this white teacher whom she loved and trusted. And this is an instance that Paley was aware of. In how may other situations in this class did Ayana and other black children have to spend time and energy working out the complexities of what was appropriate for a non-black audience?

By contrast, I recall the easiness with which Marti, in my opening vignette, could bring up race with me and the ease with which I could slip into our comfortable way of interacting. I also recall my understanding, appreciation, and suppressed laughter—and my white co-teacher's shock and hurt until we discussed the incident—when Doris, in perfect imitation of older black women, put her hands on her hips as my co-teacher was leading her to the "time-out" chair: Doris said, "You better take your hands off my clothes. People's mamas have to pay for their clothes!"

My own daughter is not yet 2 years old, but of course I have begun to think about what kind of school environment I want for her. After spending hours searching for black-oriented books and taking a brown felt-tip pen to white toy figures, I do not want her to come home, like many of my friends' children who have attended predominantly white preschools and kindergartens, and say that she's ugly because she's brown or that she wants long blond hair and blue eyes. I don't want her to spend much of her thinking power trying to figure out what she should or shouldn't say to a white teacher. In other words, when she is 5 years old, I want her to be nourished and nurtured as she would be at home. I don't want her to feel alien or different. I want her to believe that she and people who look like her are gorgeous, smart, and in charge of things. I strongly want her to be in an African-American environment. There will be time later to learn about differences, to learn to struggle in a sometimes hostile environment. But when she's 5, I don't want her too far from home.

Paley praises the integrated kindergarten environment. But she does not have to worry about being a minority of color. In fact, she declined an offer to teach in an inner-city school because she didn't think she could handle being in the minority again, as she felt she had been in the South. Should we inflict such difficult status on our 5-year-olds? ∎

Lisa D. Delpit is an Eminent Scholar and Executive Director of the Center for Urban Education and Innovation at Florida International University in Miami.

"Seeing Color" originally appeared in the Hungry Mind Review.

When Small Is Beautiful
An interview with Héctor Calderón

Héctor Calderón is principal at El Puente Academy for Peace and Justice in Brooklyn, N.Y. El Puente, which means "the bridge" in Spanish, bridges the arts, health, environment, and education. The school shares a mission with the community organization that created it: to nurture leadership for peace and justice. It was one of 40 schools founded in a five-year period by grants from the New Visions Foundation. Located in the Williamsburg neighborhood, the academy serves 160 students, 80 percent of whom are Latino. Fifty-nine percent live below the poverty line, and 90 percent are eligible for free and reduced-price school lunches. As of 2001, 80 percent of students graduated in four years.

Calderón spoke with Catherine Capellaro, former managing editor of Rethinking Schools *magazine, in 2005.*

How did El Puente Academy for Peace and Justice come to be?

El Puente as a leadership center has been around since 1982. But in 1993 we had the unique opportunity to envision what a school could look like. We had been successful in developing training for young people to become leaders in peace and justice. The heart of our mission is to inspire and nurture leadership. Kids did activities here: dancing, mural painting, or doing community health and environment internships. We engaged young people in a dialogue about this kind of life, this way of being. We were coming from the perspective of potential, rather than deficit. In most organizations, young people have to

JOE MATUNIS

have a problem: They're drug addicts, or pregnant teens, or they have to identify themselves as something of a problem to get help. We wanted to shift that perspective and wanted to say, "OK, let's talk about your issues from the perspective of where you want to go, from the perspective of your potential."

There's an old saying that goes, "It takes a village to raise a child." We said, if it takes a village to raise a child, why not help raise the village? That was the mission that Luis Garden Acosta along with Frances Lucerna, two of the co-founders of El Puente, the organization, decided to embark upon. We took a lot of the ideas we had developed in the leadership center (the after-school program) to the academy. We tried to create a seamless program that would start at 8:00 in the morning and end at 8:00 at night.

How does the school develop leaders for peace and justice?

There's a four-year vision. When

we create our curriculum, the fundamental question that we try to answer is "Who am I?" So all curricula in the 9th grade has that as a central theme. In global studies, in English, in math, in science, they all are trying to figure out who they are. For example, if I'm a history teacher, then you understand yourself historically, culturally. In English, we look at literature that deals with questions of identity. We read a lot of books, from *Down These Mean Streets* by Piri Thomas, to *Bodega Dreams*, to *Drown* by Juno Diaz, coming-of-age stories that young people can identify with because the experiences resemble their own. There is study in science of self, which is biology, where they discover themselves as biological beings. They study life from conception to development and life around them. In math, you're also writing your personal narratives and experiences with mathematics.

This must take an enormous amount of coordination among teachers. How do you pull it all together?

There were three things that we realized early on, three conceptual frameworks or tenets that we abide by. One was that disciplines came out of the needs and experiences of people. Whether you're teaching math, science, history, language—all of them were created because there were real community needs. We say that if disciplines came out of the needs and experiences of people, why are we separating community or community organizing from school?

The second tenet is that knowledge in its natural state is holistic. In most

Student mural painters from El Puente.

schools, you learn math here, you learn English here, you learn history here. It loses the synergy between the disciplines. How do they speak to each other? That translates into questions from young people, like, "Why are we doing this?" "How is this connected to what I'm learning in history?" So kids might be doing essays in English, for example, and we give them an essay in history and they're like, "Whoa, why are we doing this here?" That's because there's a loss of those connections. There are larger connections at the conceptual level, like how the theme of identity goes through all the subject areas. Young people begin to see how each of the disciplines speak to it.

The last tenet is [Paulo Freire's] idea of education for liberation. By liberation we mean the struggle to become fully human. We say that because at some level we are born fully human, but because of dehumanizing conditions—particularly for young people of color—they experience a lack of affordable housing, lack of health care, lack of access to good education, to things we need to help us develop

in a way that allows us to become fully human. That struggle is a struggle for liberation. And I think schools have a profound obligation and duty to really allow young people to become fully developed and nurtured, to become the best they can be.

What does that look like in practice?

One example is the sugar project, which began in 1996 and 1997. We were looking at trying to create an integrated arts project. It's a way of really infusing the arts throughout the curriculum and at the same time letting the disciplines speak to community issues, particularly because of the history of Williamsburg, where Domino Sugar is four or five blocks away from the school. At one point Domino Sugar distributed 50 percent of the United States' sugar. It was refined right at this plant. Many of the parents of the young people who came here worked at some point or another at Domino Sugar. We wanted to take the issue of sugar and look at it as a collaboration between community artists, organizers, academy facilita-

tors, as a way of integrating language arts, history, government, visual arts, dance, and music. We looked at the history of sugar and how it came from Europe and the history of slavery—to really create something rich and profound as a subject of study.

We looked at the implications of sugar. If I was a chemistry teacher, I was looking at the composition of sugar and the chemical structures that make up sugar. History teachers looked at the history of slavery in the sugar plantations in the Caribbean and throughout the South. The health class looked at the effects of sugar, particularly in the crisis of obesity. The economics teacher was looking at the labor of sugar: the Domino sugar factory and their use of labor in this country, the wages that people get paid, and who got to work there. Students did a lot of oral history projects with former Domino workers.

All these ideas and projects culminated in an outdoor performance at our community garden where we recreated a lot of these things, the history of sugar, the effects of sugar. It became a carnival-like procession complete with stilt-walkers, performed through the streets of the community. The whole community came out and really just embraced the project. It was a great way of bridging the community and the work that we were doing. All the integrated arts projects have that as a final component.

What is the current theme at El Puente Academy?

This year the project is health. As part of that we're looking at Radiac Research Corporation. Radiac is a low-level nuclear waste disposal plant, the only one in New York State—a block away from the school. If anything were ever to happen in that place, it would release a toxic cloud that would engulf all of Williamsburg and parts of lower

Manhattan. We want to stop the permit this year for Radiac operating the plant on the waterfront.

Williamsburg reads like a "Who's Who of Environmental Hazards." We have the Williamsburg Bridge, we have the Brooklyn-Queens Expressway, where cars are constantly emitting carbon monoxide into the air. We also have a nuclear plant right here. Every year, one project we do is to measure the level of particulates, and students look at the health effects of these particulates.

We also have one of the biggest underground oil spills, bigger than the Exxon Valdez. It's still spilling; they can't stop it; it's underground and it's been ongoing. We are part of what they call "the lead belt" and the "the asthma belt."

Asthma is a huge issue in this community. Through the Community Health and Environment Group, which is an organizing arm of El Puente, our students are doing surveys of the level of asthma in this community. We count within a 10-block radius and identify many families as having asthma. As part of the work, we try to provide extra services to those families. Biology takes on another dimension for our students when they're studying the respiratory system and they are looking at asthma and how it affects that population.

One of the things that the health coordinator at El Puente did was help students look at the Dominican and Puerto Rican populations that live primarily in the south side of Williamsburg. We found out that there is a higher incidence of asthma in Puerto Ricans. Then we tried to find out why that was. We looked at natural remedies that Dominicans use that may not be as prevalent in the Puerto Rican population. We had a whole presentation of this and it was really fascinating. That report was pub-

Student mural painters from El Puente.

JOE MATUNIS

lished in a health journal. It was really the first time that a community-based organization's work was actually published in a medical journal. This is what we mean by community knowledge, really engaging in this kind of work that we feel is important.

How are themes developed, proposed, or selected?

Usually we bring together a lot of people, a team of stakeholders who are thinking about different things. … And then we pick a theme based on our conversation. This year [we discussed] three questions: What do you think is the greatest issue affecting our communities? Which issue are you personally invested in? What is the issue you feel you have the greatest capacity to influence?

For example, the issue I felt was facing our community is gentrification. Personally, I was invested in the issue of police brutality. And, lastly, I think the greatest place where the public can influence and really change things is the environment. I think there were enough of those common

answers around, and that's how we chose the idea of the health/environment theme.

Once the theme is chosen, a group of facilitators/artists begins to brainstorm different angles and takes on the issue. Classes are developed. We have what we call educational options. A lot of those classes directly speak to the integrated arts project. The design team really is the glue that keeps all the different things together. They decide what the culminating piece will look like and, ultimately, they will keep the curriculum tight and together so that everybody is on board with the work that we're trying to do.

How does the size of El Puente contribute to being able to implement curriculum like you're describing?

Size is definitely a key. On one level, it's great that I can go to any of my students. I know their names, who they are, where they live, the families they come from. I know something about what they're personally invested in. If you're putting a curriculum forward that deals with community, one of the key factors for any organizer is to know your community. What are they invested in? What are their self-interests? Being small allows us to really create the kind of close-knit communities that we have. It allows us to really serve the interests of our young people.

> The sugar project is a way of really infusing the arts throughout the curriculum and at the same time letting the disciplines speak to community issues.

If we were larger, we could do this kind of work, but it would clearly be more difficult to be as attuned as we are to our young people. Size really matters—and it matters because I can go to staff and coordinate in ways that if I had a larger staff would be much harder. We also have a whole complementary group of people that are honorary staff people who are part of the community-based organization. They also integrate with us in the work that we do.

How tied to the standards and Regents exams does El Puente have to be?

The work that we do is very rigorous and it hits a lot of the standards that are put out there for subject areas. For example, in an economics class, students are looking at lending practices of banks in our neighborhood. They talk about redlining. That project became a part of creating a report in which we disaggregated data by race, class, gender, and geography and looked at the disparity in lending practices. They took that to the city council. I think all of that requires

rigorous learning. We give Regents, but for me, it's not the only gauge. We also do portfolio assessments in which we tie those assessments closer to the curriculum that we're teaching. So students have to take all the Regents that they would have to take at any other school. They also have to pass at a level of competence in each of six portfolios.

How do you define "rigor"?

If you can really find answers to fundamental problems that are plaguing the community, that is rigorous. It takes a lot of work, a lot of effort. People understand that the work we are doing is explicitly tied to bettering the community.

What does a school for social justice mean to you? Why do you think this orientation is important?

Schools were meant to address a need within the community, a need to educate people. Why would we want to educate our young people? Clearly, every generation must build on the next generation. With us it's about educating young people who don't understand the fundamental responsibility to the world and the environment in which they live.

Whether we're using the arts to get there or you're using the sciences to get there, we all as citizens of the world have a responsibility to make the world we live in much better. The Native Americans talk about building

for seven generations. I think, in many ways, schools have really become about educating the self, devoid of community.

A lot of schools think they've done their mission if they educate kids who go to Harvard and become great at whatever they do. We want our kids to go to the best schools. We want them to have access to a great education. But we also ask the fundamental question: For the sake of what? For the sake of what are we educating our young people? It has to do with this sacred covenant that we have with the world around us. We have a moral and civil obligation to really make the world a better place. To me, the idea of social justice is not some pie-in-the-sky thing: It begins with our students. It begins in daily acts, in understanding the connection between what they learn in school and the community they live in. It begins in practical applications of their knowledge to better the world they live in. ∎

I Won't Learn from You!

Confronting student resistance

By Herbert Kohl

Years ago, one of my 5th-grade students told me that his grandfather Wilfredo wouldn't learn to speak English. He said that no matter how hard you tried to teach him, he ignored whatever words you tried to teach and forced you to speak to him in Spanish. When I got to know his grandfather I asked, in Spanish, whether I could teach him English and he told me unambiguously that he did not want to learn. He was frightened, he said, that his grandchildren would never learn Spanish if he gave in like the rest of the adults and spoke English with the children. Then, he said, they would not know who they were. At the end of our conversation he repeated adamantly that nothing could make him learn to speak English, that families and cultures could not survive if the children lost their parents' language, and, finally, that learning what others wanted you to learn can sometimes destroy you.

I discussed Wilfredo's reflections with several friends, and they interpreted his remarks as a cover-up of either his own fear of trying to learn English or his failure to do so. These explanations, however, show a lack of respect for Wilfredo's ability to judge what is appropriate learning for himself and his grandchildren. By attributing failure to Wilfredo and refusing to acknowledge the loss his family would experience through not knowing Spanish, they turned a cultural problem into a personal psychological problem:

CLEO PHOTOGRAPHY

They turned willed refusal to learn into failure to learn.

I have encountered willed not-learning throughout my 40 years of teaching, and believe that such not-learning is often and disastrously mistaken for failure to learn or the inability to learn.

Learning how to not-learn is an intellectual and social challenge; sometimes you have to work very hard at it. It consists of an active, often inge-

nious, willful rejection of even the most compassionate and well-designed teaching. Not-learning tends to take place when someone has to deal with unavoidable challenges to her or his personal and family loyalties, integrity, and identity. In such situations, there are forced choices and no apparent middle ground. To agree to learn from a stranger who does not respect your integrity causes a major loss of self.

The only alternative is to not-learn and reject their world.

The Lessons of San Antonio

I remember visiting some teacher friends in San Antonio many years ago. I was there trying to help in their struggles to eliminate anti-Latino racism in the public schools in the barrios. There were very few Latino teachers and no Latino administrators in barrio schools in the parts of San Antonio where my friends worked. Many of the administrators were Anglo, retired military personnel from the San Antonio air force base who had hostile, imperialist attitudes towards the children they taught and the communities they served.

In one junior high I was invited to observe a history class by a teacher who admitted that he needed help with this particular group of students, all of whom were Latino. The teacher gave me a copy of his textbook, and I sat in the back of the room and followed the lesson for the day, which was entitled, "The first people to settle Texas." The teacher asked for someone to volunteer to read and no one responded. Most of the students were slumped down in their desks and none of them looked directly at the teacher. Some gazed off into space, others exchanged glimpses and grimaces. The teacher didn't ask for attention and started to read the text himself. It went something like, "The first people to settle Texas arrived from New England and the South in ..." Two boys in the back put their hands in their eyes; there were a few giggles and some murmuring. One hand shot up and that student blurted out, "What are we, animals or something?" The teacher's response was, "What does that have to do with the text?" Then he decided to abandon the lesson, introduced me as a visiting teacher who would substitute for the rest of the period and left the room.

I don't know if he planned to do that all along and set me up to fail with the students just as he did, or if his anger at being observed overcame him and he decided to dump the whole thing on me. Whatever the motivation, he left the room, and I was there with the students. I went up front and reread the sentence from the book and asked the class to raise their hands if they believed what I had just read. A few of them became alert, though they looked at me suspiciously as I continued, "This is lies, nonsense. In fact, I think the textbook is racist and an insult to everyone in this room." Everyone woke up and the same student who had asked the teacher about animal life turned to me and asked, "You mean that?" I said I did, and then he interrupted and said, "Well, there's more than that book that's racist around here."

I said that it was obvious that the textbook was racist, it was there for everyone to read, but wondered how they detected racism in their teachers. The class launched into a serious and sophisticated discussion of the way in which racism manifests itself in their everyday lives at school. And they described the stance they took in order to resist that racism and yet not be thrown out of school. It amounted to nothing less than full-blown and cooperative not-learning. They accepted the failing grades it produced in exchange for the passive defense of their personal and cultural integrity. This was a class of school failures, and perhaps, I believed then and still believe, the repository for the positive leadership and intelligence of their generation.

Not-Learning Is Not Failure

Until we learn to distinguish not-learning from failure and respect the truth behind this massive rejection of schooling by students from poor and oppressed communities, it will not be possible to solve the major problems of education in the United States today.

Risk-taking is at the heart of teaching well. That means that teachers will have to not-learn the ways of loyalty to the system and to speak out for, as the traditional African-American song goes, the concept that everyone has a right to the tree of life. We must give up looking at resistant students as failures and turn a critical eye towards this wealthy society and the schools that it supports.

No amount of educational research, no development of techniques or materials, no special programs or compensatory services, no restructuring or retraining of teachers will make any fundamental difference until we concede that for many students, the only sane alternative to not-learning is the acknowledgment and direct confrontation of oppression—social, sexual, and economic—both in school and in society. Education built on accepting that hard truth about our society can break through not-learning and lead students and teachers together, not to the solution of problems but to direct intelligent engagement in the struggles that might lead to solutions. ■

Herbert Kohl is author of 36 Children. *This essay is dedicated to the memory of Betty Rawls and the struggle for justice. Excerpted from the book* I Won't Learn from You and Other Thoughts on Creative Maladjustment *(The New Press, 1994.)*

Food Is Not for Play

By Jean Hannon

Not everyone's mealtimes look like mine.

There will not necessarily be enough food tomorrow.

Food is not for play.

These are the lessons I learned from Ana, and this is how she taught me:

Five-year-old Ana entered our classroom and went immediately to the large container of plastic snow play toys. She retrieved the dish-like items (recycled yogurt and applesauce containers) and meticulously placed them all in a neat row. Then Ana moved down the line of dishes carrying a much larger container and a makeshift ladle. She painstakingly scooped something invisible (to me) into each smaller container.

I understood that Ana was playing her version of "house"; she was dramatizing mealtime at the orphanage in northern China where she had spent most of her young life. Ana had moved to her new home and new family only three weeks before joining our classroom.

Harrison, a classmate, quickly learned that the simplest and most effective way to terrorize Ana was to make lunging gestures toward her open lunch box. Harrison never actually took any of Ana's carefully packaged and abundant lunchbox contents. But he intimidated Ana with the idea that he could take her food. Ana would cry, Ana's new friends would scold Harrison, and he would smirk. As I soothed Ana, I would talk to Harrison and encourage him to consider Ana's perspective.

Not all of the learning centers in our kindergarten classroom were available

KATHERINE STREETER

to the children every day. Some I kept for "special." It was a Friday in February and the children stood around one particular center in acute anticipation. As I removed the cover from the sensory table, Ana shrank back in horror. I had presented the class with a play area filled with rice. In it was enough to feed how many for how long? And I was encouraging the students to stick their hands into that food, to measure, to manipulate, to play! The look on Ana's face at the moment I lifted that cover and she first understood what I was suggesting has not left me in the intervening 10 years.

That experience helped me to conclude that using food for art or play is misguided.

Young children mostly believe their teachers. They believe that their teachers know a great deal and are generally truthful. Young children repeat their teachers' platitudes and embrace their classroom gestures. When young children play school they model their dramatic behavior after that of their teachers, and their imitative play is often embarrassingly accurate.

I have come to realize just how confusing my use of food for play and art was, not only for Ana, but for all my young students. While we collected cans of food "for the hungry," I also facilitated a lesson where students glued beans to cardboard to outline the letters of their names. I nagged the children to eat their lunches and not throw away food, but followed it by encouraging them in tactile exploration at the rice table. Perhaps because they wanted to continue feeling safe and cared for by a competent and thoughtful adult, the children did not question my particular brand of hypocrisy. Still, how could they not have been confused by the discrepancy between what I said about the value of food and the other lessons I provided?

Several things were inherent in my lessons: a disconnect between consumers, food, food workers, and ultimately the earth itself, a finite resource. Inherent also was the message of "them" and "us." "We" have enough and we can therefore waste. "They" do not have enough and must rely on the more fortunate and/or capable "us."

I believe guilt is a useless emotion unless it leads to change. Ana's lessons forced me to reevaluate and change my teaching practice: In our classroom food is no longer part of our art or play. ∎

Jean Hannon currently teaches 2nd grade at Badger Road Elementary School near Fairbanks, Alaska. Ana was in Hannon's kindergarten class at Badger Elementary.

The Politics of Children's Literature
What's wrong with the Rosa Parks myth

By Herbert Kohl

Issues of racism and direct confrontation between African-American and European-American people in the United States are usually considered too sensitive to be dealt with directly in the elementary school classroom. When African Americans and European Americans are involved in confrontation in children's texts, the situation is routinely described as a problem between individuals that can be worked out on a personal basis. In the few cases where racism is addressed as a social problem, there has to be a happy ending.

This is most readily apparent in the biographical treatment of Rosa Parks, one of the two names that most children associate with the Civil Rights Movement, the other being Martin Luther King, Jr.

The image of "Rosa Parks the Tired" exists on the level of a national cultural icon. Dozens of children's books and textbooks present the same version of what might be called "Rosa Parks and the Montgomery Bus Boycott." This version can be synthesized as follows:

In 1955, Rosa Parks was arrested in Montgomery for refusing to give up her seat on a bus to a white person.

Rosa Parks was a poor seamstress. She lived in Montgomery, Ala., during the 1950s. In those days there was still segregation in parts of the United States. That meant that African Americans and European Americans were not allowed to use the same public facilities such as restaurants or swimming pools. It also meant that whenever the city buses were crowded, African Americans had to give up seats in front to European Americans and move to the back of the bus.

One day on her way home from work Rosa was tired and sat down in the front of the bus. As the bus got crowded she was asked to give up her seat to a European-American man, and she refused. The bus driver told her she had to go to the back of the bus, and she still refused to move. It was a hot day, she was tired and angry, and she became very stubborn.

The driver called a policeman, who arrested Rosa.

When other African Americans in Montgomery heard this, they became angry too, so they decided to refuse to ride the buses until everyone was allowed to ride together. They boycotted the buses.

The boycott, which was led by Martin Luther King, Jr., succeeded. Now African Americans and European Americans can ride the buses together in Montgomery.

Rosa Parks was a very brave person.

This story seems innocent enough. Rosa Parks is treated with respect, and the African-American community is given credit for running the boycott and winning the struggle. On closer examination, however, this version reveals some distressing characteristics that serve to turn a carefully planned movement for social change into a spontaneous outburst based upon frustration and anger.

The following annotations on the previous summary suggest that we need a new story, one not only more in line with the truth but one that shows the organizational skills and determination of the African-American community in Montgomery and the role of the bus boycott in the larger struggle to desegregate Montgomery and the South.

Correcting the Myth

1. Rosa Parks was a poor, tired seamstress. She lived in Montgomery, Ala., during the 1950s.

Rosa Parks was one of the first women in Montgomery to join the National Association for the Advancement of Colored People and was its secretary for years. At the NAACP she worked with chapter president E.D. Nixon, who was also vice president of the Brotherhood of Sleeping Car Porters. Parks learned about union struggles from him. She also worked with the youth division of the NAACP, and she took a youth NAACP group to visit the Freedom Train when it came to Montgomery in 1954. The train, which carried the originals of the U.S. Constitution and the Declaration of Independence, was traveling around the United States promoting the virtues of democracy. Since its visit was a federal project, access to the exhibits could not be segregated. Parks took advantage of that fact to visit the

train. There, she and the members of the youth group mingled freely with European Americans who were also looking at the documents. This overt act of crossing the boundaries of segregation did not endear Parks to the Montgom-

> ## The image of 'Rosa Parks the Tired' exists on the level of a national cultural icon.

ery political and social establishment.

Parks' work as a seamstress in a large department store was secondary to her community work. In addition, as she says in an interview in *My Soul Is Rested*, she had almost a life history of "being rebellious against being mistreated because of my color." She was well known to African-American leaders in Montgomery for her opposition to segregation, her leadership abilities, and her moral strength. Since the 1954 *Brown v. Board of Education* decision, she had been working to desegregate the Montgomery schools. She had also attended an interracial meeting at the Highlander Folk School in Tennessee a few months before the boycott. Highlander was known throughout the South as a radical education center that was overtly planning for the total desegregation of the South. At that meeting, which dealt with plans for school desegregation, Parks indicated that she intended to participate in other attempts to break down the barriers of segregation. To call Rosa Parks a poor tired seamstress and not talk about her role as a community leader is to turn an organized struggle for freedom into a personal act of frustration. It is a thorough misrepresentation of the Civil Rights Movement in Montgomery and an insult to Parks as well.

2. In those days there was still segregation in parts of the United States. That meant that African Americans and European Americans were not allowed to use the same public facilities.

The existence of legalized segregation in the South during the 1950s is integral to the story of the Montgomery bus boycott, yet it is an embarrassment to many school people and difficult to explain to children without accounting for the moral corruption of the majority of the European-American community in the South.

Locating segregation in the past is a way of avoiding dealing with its current manifestations and implying that racism is no longer a major problem.

Describing segregation passively ("There was still segregation" instead of "European Americans segregated facilities so that African Americans couldn't use them") also ignores the issue of legalized segregation, even though Parks was arrested for a violation of the Alabama law that required segregation in public facilities. It doesn't talk overtly about racism. And it refers to "parts" of the United States, softening the tone and muddying the reference to the South.

I've raised the question of how to expose children to the reality of segregation and racism to a number of educators, both African-American and European-American. Most of the European-American and a few of the African-American educators felt that young children do not need to be exposed to the violent history of segregation. They worried about the effects such exposure would have on race relations in their classrooms and especially about provoking rage on the part of African-American students. The other educators felt that, given the resurgence of overt racism in the United States, allowing rage and anger to come out was the only way African-

American and European-American children could work toward a common life. They felt that conflict was a positive thing that could be healing when confronted directly and that avoiding the horrors of racism was just another way of perpetuating them. I agree with this second group.

3. Whenever the city buses were crowded, African Americans had to give up seats in front to European Americans and move to the back of the bus.

Actually, African Americans were never allowed to sit in the front of the bus in the South in those days. The front seats were reserved for European Americans. Between five and ten rows back, the "colored" section began. When the front filled up, African Americans seated in the "colored" section had to give up their seats and move toward the back of the bus. Thus, for example, an elderly African American would have to give up his or her seat to a European-American teenager at the peril of being arrested.

4. One day on her way home from work Rosa was tired and sat down in the front of the bus.

Parks did not sit in the front of the bus. She sat in the front row of the "colored" section. When the bus got crowded she refused to give up her seat in the "colored" section to a European American. It is important to point this out as it indicates quite clearly that it was not her intent, initially, to break the segregation laws.

At this point the story lapses into the familiar and refers to Rosa Parks as "Rosa." The question of whether to use the first name for historical characters in a factual story is complicated. One argument is that young children will more readily identify with characters presented in a personalized and familiar way. However, given that it was a sanctioned social practice in the South during the time of the story for Euro-

pean Americans to call African-American adults by their first names as a way of reinforcing the African Americans' inferior status (African Americans could never call European Americans by their first names without breaking the social code of segregation), it seems unwise to use that practice in the story.

In addition, it's reasonable to assume that Parks was not any more tired on that one day than on other days. She worked at an exhausting full-time job and was also active full time in the community. To emphasize her being tired is another way of saying that her defiance was an accidental result of her fatigue and consequent short temper. Rage, however, is not a one-day thing, and Parks acted with full knowledge of what she was doing.

5. As the bus got crowded she was asked to give up her seat to a European-American man, and she refused. The bus driver told her she had to go to the back of the bus, and she still refused to move. It was a hot day, she was tired and angry, and she became very stubborn. The driver called a policeman who arrested Rosa.

This is the way that Parks, in her book *My Soul Is Rested*, described her experiences with buses:

I had problems with bus drivers over the years because I didn't see fit to pay my money into the front and then go to the back. Sometimes bus drivers wouldn't permit me to get on the bus, and I had been evicted from the bus. But, as I say, there had been incidents over the years. One of the things that made this [incident] ... get so much publicity was the fact that the police were called in and I was placed under arrest. See, if I had just been evicted from the bus and he hadn't placed me under arrest or had any charges brought against me, it probably could have been just another incident.

In the book *Voices of Freedom* by Henry Hampton and Steve Fayer, Parks describes that day in the following way:

On Dec. 1, 1955, I had finished my day's work as a tailor's assistant in the Montgomery Fair Department Store and I was on my way home. There was one vacant seat on the Cleveland Avenue bus, which I took, alongside a man and two women across the aisle. There were still a few vacant seats in the white section in the front, of course. We went to the next stop without being disturbed. On the third, the front seats were occupied and this one man, a white man, was standing. The driver asked us to stand up and let him have those seats, and when none of us moved at his first words, he said, "You all make it light on yourselves and let me have those seats." And the man who was sitting next to the window stood up, and I made room for him to pass by me. The two women across the aisle stood up and moved out.

When the driver saw me still sitting, he asked if I was going to stand up and I said, "No, I'm not."

And he said, "Well, if you don't stand up, I'm going to call the police and have you arrested."

I said, "You may do that."

He did get off the bus, and I still stayed where I was. Two policemen came on the bus. One of the policemen asked me if the bus driver had asked me to stand and I said yes.

He said, "Why don't you stand up?"

And I asked him, "Why do you push us around?"

He said, "I do not know, but the law is the law and you're under arrest."

Mere anger and stubbornness could not account for the clear resolve with which Parks acted. She knew what she was doing, understood the consequences, and was prepared to confront segregation head-on at whatever sacrifice she had to make.

6. When other African Americans in Montgomery heard this, they became angry too, so they decided to refuse to ride the buses until everyone was allowed to ride together. They boycotted the buses.

The connection between Parks' arrest and the boycott is a mystery in most accounts of what happened in Montgomery. Community support for the boycott is portrayed as being instantaneous and miraculously effective the very day after Parks was arrested. Things don't happen that way, and it is an insult to the intelligence and courage of the African-American community in Montgomery to turn their planned resistance to segregation into a spontaneous emotional response. The actual situation was more interesting and complex. Not only had Parks defied the bus segregation laws in the past, according to E.D. Nixon, in the three months preceding her arrest at least three other African-American people had been arrested in Montgomery for refusing to give up their bus seats to European-American people. In each case, Nixon and other people in leadership positions in the African-American community in Montgomery investigated the background of the person arrested. They were looking for someone who had the respect of the community and the strength to deal with the racist police force as well as all of the publicity that would result from being at the center of a court challenge.

This leads to the most important point left out in popularized accounts of the Montgomery bus boycott. Community leaders had long considered a boycott as a tactic to achieve racial justice. Of particular importance in this discussion was an African-American women's organization in Montgomery called the Women's Political Council (WPC). It was headed by Jo Ann Gibson Robinson, a professor of English at Alabama State University in Montgomery, an African-American university. In 1949, Gibson was put off a bus in Montgomery for refusing to move to the back of an almost empty bus. She and other women resolved to do something about bus segregation.

The boycott was an event waiting to take place, and that is why it could be mobilized over a single weekend. Parks' arrest brought it about because she was part of the African-American leadership in Montgomery and was trusted not to cave in under the pressure everyone knew she would be exposed to, not the least of which would be threats to her life.

This story of collective decision-making, willed risk, and coordinated action is more dramatic than the story of an angry individual who sparked a demonstration; it is one that has more to teach children who themselves may one day have to organize and act collectively against oppressive forces.

7. The boycott, which was led by Martin Luther King, Jr., succeeded. Now African Americans and European Americans can ride the buses together in Montgomery. Rosa Parks was a very brave person.

The boycott was planned by the WPC, E. D. Nixon and others in Montgomery. Martin Luther King, Jr. was a new member of the community. He had just taken over the Dexter Avenue Baptist Church, and when Nixon told him that Parks' arrest was just what everybody was waiting for to kick off a bus boycott and assault the institution of segregation, King was at first reluctant. However, the community people chose him to lead, and he accepted their call. The boycott lasted 381 inconvenient days, something not usually mentioned in children's books. It did succeed and was one of the events that sparked the entire Civil Rights Movement. People who had been planning an overt attack on segregation for years took that victory as a sign that the time was ripe even though the people involved in the Montgomery boycott did not themselves anticipate such a result.

Concluding Thoughts

What remains then, is to retitle the story. The revised version is still about Rosa Parks, but it is also about the African-American people of Montgomery, Ala. It takes the usual, individualized version of the Rosa Parks tale and puts it in the context of a coherent, community-based social struggle. This does not diminish Parks in any way. It places her, however, in the midst of a consciously planned movement for social change, and reminds me of the freedom song "We Shall Not Be Moved," for it was precisely Parks' and the community's refusal to be moved that made the boycott possible.

When the story of the Montgomery bus boycott is told merely as a tale of a single heroic person, it leaves children hanging. Not everyone is a hero or heroine. Of course, the idea that only special people can create change is useful if you want to prevent mass movements and keep change from happening. Not every child can be a Rosa Parks, but everyone can imagine herself or himself as a participant in the boycott. As a tale of a social movement and a community effort to overthrow injustice, the Rosa Parks story opens the possibility of every child identifying herself or himself as an activist, as someone who can help make justice happen. ∎

Herbert Kohl is an educator and author of numerous books. He writes the "Good Stuff" column for Rethinking Schools *magazine.*

In Memory of Crossing the Columbia

By Elizabeth Woody

for Charlotte Edwards Pitt and Charlotte Agnes Pitt

My board and my blanket were Navajo,

but my bed is inside the River.

In the beads of remembrance,

I am her body in my father's hands.

She gave me her eyes

and the warmth of basalt.

The vertebrae of her back,

my breastplate, the sturdy

belly of mountainside.

"Pahtu," he whispered in her language.

She is the mountain of change.

She is the mountain of women

who have lain as volcanoes

before men.

Red, as the women much loved,

she twisted like silvery chinook

beyond his reach.

Dancing the Woman-Salmon dance,

there is not much time to waste.

Elizabeth Woody (Warm Springs Wasco/Navajo) is author of *Seven Hands, Seven Hearts: Prose and Poetry* and *Luminaries of the Humble*. (For lesson ideas, see p. 212.)

Heather's Moms Got Married

Creating a gay- and lesbian-friendly classroom

By Mary Cowhey

ABE HERZOG-ARBEITMAN, 2ND GRADE, NORTHAMPTON, MASS.

When it comes to issues of family diversity, teacher self-censorship remains the status quo in many schools. Often this is based on the fear of raising potentially controversial topics. When schools do get involved in promoting gay-straight alliances and so forth, it is usually at the secondary level. Most people still get queasy talking about gay and lesbian issues at middle or—heaven forbid—elementary levels.

I teach at an elementary school in Northampton, Mass., where many of my students are raised by lesbian parents. My education in teaching family diversity and learning from my families began on the first day of my career, before I even set foot in my classroom. Visiting the home of one student, I was greeted by a parent wearing a button that read, "We're here. We're gay. And we're on the PTA." She and her partner began talking about being foster parents for the state Department of Social Services and being adoptive parents. I asked if they would be willing to advise me on good books and teaching ideas.

Based on my experiences over the course of eight years of teaching, here are some of my recommendations for teachers in elementary schools:

Do not presume that students live in traditional families with both married heterosexual birth parents. Name a wide variety of configurations possible in the diversity of human families. Part of that naming process includes using books and resources that portray family diversity, including the video, *That's a Family*. [See p. 174 for more resources.] Invite students to respond to the question, "Who is in your family?" Allow students to share and display their family stories and pictures.

Explore and challenge gender stereotypes with your students. Use children's books such as *Amazing Grace, William's Doll, Oliver Button Is a Sissy, China's Bravest Girl: the Legend of Hua Mu Lan, Riding Freedom,* and *Beautiful Warrior* as springboards for discussions. Activities can include students brainstorming lists of stereotypical behavior for boys and girls, then making captioned drawings of boys and girls engaging in nonstereotypical behaviors. These can be made into a class book or hallway display, "Boys Can/Girls Can." Once students learn to question gender stereotypes, they can recognize and reflect on stereotypical characters and behaviors in other books and media. They can extend their understandings of stereotypes to recognize and challenge other forms of bias.

Teach a lesson on teasing and name-calling. Children's literature, such as *Oliver Button Is a Sissy* or *The Hundred Dresses* can be an excellent point of departure for discussion and activities. These can help establish a baseline of classroom expectations that we are all respected members of this classroom community and that no put-downs will be tolerated.

Answer students' questions about gay and lesbian issues in a straightforward, educational manner. Do not ignore or quash their curiosity. Remember that the two main points of reference are respecting differences and equality for all people. Elementary children are not asking about sexuality. When they ask what "gay" means, it's sufficient to say, "Gay is when a woman loves a woman or a man loves a man in a romantic way."

Replace the phrase "moms and dads" with "parents and guardians" in your classroom and in your school. Do this in informal conversation, classroom teaching, and official school documents such as registration forms and emergency cards. Not only is this phrase more inclusive for students with gay or lesbian parents, but also for those being raised by foster parents, grandparents, aunts, and others. It accepts and affirms all of the families in your school.

Consider showing a video like *Oliver Button Is a Star* as part of a professional development workshop for faculty and staff. *Oliver Button Is a Star* is a documentary that weaves a reading and musical production of *Oliver Button Is a Sissy* with interviews with adults like

---

Resources on Family Diversity

All Families Are Different
Nonfiction
By Sol Gordon
Prometheus Books, 2000, 50 pp.
Written by a clinical psychologist, this illustrated book for readers 7 and older defines families in multiple ways, considering economic and racial factors as well as including same-sex, divorced, and foster parents.

All Families Are Special
Fiction
By Norma Simon
Albert Whitman and Company, 2003, 32 pp.
A teacher tells her students she is going to be a grandmother, initiating a conversation about family diversity in which students share how their home lives are similar or different. Colorful illustrations complement an appropriately sensitive book for young readers.

Families All Matter Book Project
Curriculum
aMaze, P.O. Box 17417, Minneapolis, MN 55417
612-824-8090
info@amazeworks.org
This literature-based elementary school curriculum includes annotated lists of children's books, creative activities, and a teachers' guide. Many aspects of family diversity are covered.

That's a Family: A Film for Kids About Family Diversity
Nonfiction, VHS
Women's Education Media, 2180 Bryant St., Ste. 203, San Francisco, CA 94110
415-641-4616
womedia.org
Children's voices are central to this gentle approach to talking about and developing respect for family diversity.

---

arctic explorer Ann Bancroft, author/illustrator Tomie dePaola, and dancer Bill T. Jones, who recall their childhood experiences. It includes scenes (some from my classroom) where 1st and 2nd graders do activities about name-calling and challenging gender stereotypes. *That's a Family* and *It's Elementary* are good choices too.

In the event that you encounter an intolerant colleague, administrator, or parent, keep the following points in mind:

■ The diversity of families in our school is more beautiful and complex than any one of us could presume to know. Whether we have any self-identified ("out") gay- or lesbian-parented families in our school community or not, it is safer to assume that they are here than not.

■ An estimated one in 10 students may grow up to be gay or lesbian adults.

■ All of our students deserve a safe and supportive school experience.

■ Gays and lesbians are entitled to the same rights as others. We are talking about equal rights, not special rights.

■ We are not talking about "sexuality" when we discuss gay and lesbian issues any more than we are discussing sexuality when we read Cinderella or any other story with all heterosexual characters. ■

Mary Cowhey teaches 2nd grade at Jackson Street School in Northampton, Mass. She is author of Black Ants and Buddhists.

Thoughts on Teaching Native American Literature

By Joseph Bruchac

My own first experiences in teaching American Indian literature came after three years in West Africa. I returned to the United States in 1969 and found myself at Skidmore College near my home town of Greenfield Center, N.Y., an instructor with little chance of tenure who had been given a job because there was a last-minute opening at the school.

That was OK with me. My main objective had been to come home to my Abenaki grandfather in whose house I'd been raised. He lived only three miles east from the college, an easy ride on a bicycle through the hills and backroads at the edge of the Kaydeross Range. As I rode from the dawn towards the west, I passed fields which had been filled with Mohawk corn, and within my line of sight to the north were the mountains and the old, still hidden burial places of some of my own ancestors. The road passed a stone's throw from samp mortars worn deep into bedrock where corn and acorns had been ground into flour for thousands of years. Just south of that road were streams where my grandfather and I caught trout and said words of thanks to the fish spirits.

Somehow, being home made it easier to be a "low man on the academic totem pole"—one of *their* favorite images, no irony intended—teaching freshman composition and little else. It was in 1970 that the first Native American literature course was taught at Skidmore, during their one-month winter term. I wasn't allowed to teach it, though by then I was being allowed to teach a single course in black literature. "Topics in American Indian Literature" was taught by a senior faculty member who used a lot of work from anthropologists and a little contemporary Indian writing. He used Kroeber's *The Inland Whale*, some creation stories, threw in a few poems by poets who were Indian. He tried his best and he consulted with me—with apologies.

"You ought to be teaching this, Joseph, but you know how it is."

"Totem pole?" I said.

He nodded, without irony. "You understand."

Along the way he set up a reading. One of those who spoke was Harry W. Paige, whose book, *Songs of the Teton Sioux*, had been his Ph.D. thesis at the State University of New York at Albany for his doctorate in English—the first doctorate in English from SUNY/ Albany. Harry's book wasn't bad, and it was a result of a lot of time spent among the Teton Sioux. He gave his talk, followed by Duane McGinnis (not yet Niatum) and myself. Duane, a Klallam poet and editor, had been invited to campus to talk to that special one-time-only Native American literature course and I was, after all, of Indian descent and had published a few things here and there. In the audience that night was William Fenton, whose lifetime of study of the Iroquois was evidenced by many books and articles and the emeritus chair of anthropology at the same SUNY/Albany that gave Paige his degree.

In fact, I'm pretty sure Bill Fenton was there for Paige—not for Duane and myself. After the readings and talk, the question and answer session got around to such things as vocables in traditional songs—"nonsense words," as Fenton put it—and storytelling traditions. "There are," Fenton said, "no more traditional Iroquois storytellers. I knew the last one and he died some years ago." There was some disagreement that night, and I leave it to your imagination as to which two people were the most vocal in their disagreeing.

Imagine we only knew Shakespeare's work through a racist missionary with a tin ear who transcribed one play from a verbal recounting by an octogenarian who never liked the theater much.

My Own Directions

I begin at Skidmore and with those details because I feel it sets the scene for my own directions as a writer of Native American literature and a teacher of the literature of Native Americans. Those details also lend themselves well to some points I'd like to make about teaching Native American literature. First, however, another story.

Not long ago, I was invited to do a storytelling program at a college in Vermont. While there, I had dinner with several people who have been teaching Native American literature in college. Our conversation was an illuminating one for me, because it pointed out how widespread the teaching of Native American literature is becoming and just how needed are some directions in HOW and WHAT to teach in such courses. One of the people said that he was having a hard time finding texts. Another said that he was using Frederick Turner's 1973 volume *The Portable Native American Reader* and beginning with Creation myths, but that he had some misgivings about the accuracy of the translations, though he didn't know enough to know for sure how good they were. The third teacher of Native American literature mentioned taking a course in how to teach Native American literature from a certain professor. Someone else at the table knew that

professor and mentioned that when she taught Native American literature as a visiting professor at their school, the few Native American students on campus had signed up for the course but all dropped it because they found something objectionable about it. No one knew what.

A Lot of Listening

I do a lot of listening in such conversations. Partly because I was raised to listen and partly because when academic conversations start, it isn't that easy to break into them. Even when people ask you a direct question, they often try to answer it themselves before you can open your mouth. So I waited. These people I was having dinner with were good folks and their interest and their concerns were very real. *When you're ready to listen*, I thought. *When it is quiet enough*. And when it was quiet enough, I began to say a few words about how I have approached the teaching of Native American literature. And unless you've lost patience by now with my slow developing style, you're about to read some of those words.

When we speak about Native American literature today, it is, in many ways, like speaking of African literature. More accurately, it is how speaking about African literature would be if we were living in an Africa which had lost 90 percent of its population in the last 500 years and was being run as a single united continent by European colonials. As is the case with Africa,

when we speak of "Native American literature," of "American Indian literature" or (as they say in Canada) "Native literature," we are speaking of many literatures, especially when we refer to that work which comes from what might loosely be called (though there were, in fact, a number of writing and mnemonic recording systems in North America) "Oral Tradition." Just as Zulu oral poetry from southern Africa is very different from the traditions of the griots of Mali in the northwest of Africa, the Haudenosaunee (as the "Iroquois" call themselves) epic of the founding of their Great League of Peace is not at all like the deer songs of the Yaqui.

When you approach the totality of "Native American literature," you are confronted by an incredibly vast body of work. It comes out of, in just the area now called the continental United States, more than 400 different languages and distinct cultures. It is thousands of years old. Yet, without any special preparation, without any real grounding in the cultures which produced those many literatures, without any familiarity with the languages from which they were translated (seldom by native speakers and all too often translated in very slipshod and inappropriate ways), teachers on the university and even high school level are expected to teach this "Native American literature." Not only that, most of those teachers have never visited a Native American community or spoken with a single Native American. It is, to say the least, daunting. To put it another way, as one of my friends and teachers, a Pueblo elder known to the world as "Swift Eagle," said, "It's dumb!"

The first full-fledged Native American literature course I taught was in a maximum security prison. I was, by then, no longer in Skidmore's English Department. My terminal contract had been terminated. Other job opportunities in other parts of America had been possible, but I wasn't about to leave my native soil again. Eventually, I'd been rehired by Skidmore's external degree program to develop and direct a college program at Great Meadow Correctional Facility. I stayed with that job for eight years. In addition to being an administrator, I taught a course now and then. African Literature, Black Literature, and finally, in 1975, Introduction to Native American Literature.

If I'd had my druthers, I would have begun any Native American literature course not in the classroom, but in the woods. (That would have been *just fine* insofar as the men in my class at Great Meadow went. They understood what I meant, but that got almost as big a laugh from them as the proposed course in Astronomy at the prison that was nixed by the Deputy Superintendent in charge of security when the professor said that field trips outside at night would be necessary). It was important, I told that class, to have a sense of the American earth, of the land and the people as one.

I divided the syllabus into four directions and focused on the literary traditions of one particular Native nation from each corner of the continent. To the east, we looked at the People of the Long House, the Haudenosaunee. We began with poems written in English by Maurice Kenny and Peter Blue Cloud before turning to the epic story of the Founding of the Great League, listening to recordings of Mohawk social dance songs as we did so. To the south, we began with poems of Leslie Silko and Simon Ortiz and we read Silko's *Ceremony* and Momaday's *House Made of Dawn* in the context of the healing traditions of Navajo and Pueblo cultures. To the north, we looked at James Welch's novel *Winter in the Blood*. To the west, we focussed on translations of Lakota and Cheyenne traditional songs while we read Lance Henson's poetry. Again, as with the Iroquois material, we listened to the music of the people, including not just grass dance songs, but also Floyd Westerman singing "Custer Died for Your Sins." We looked at maps of America (and allowing any maps into the prison was a major struggle), and we talked about history, from east to west, from north to south. It was one of the best classes I'd ever taught, and I still have some of the papers written by those men.

Four Simple Directions

Although there have been other courses in Native American literature that I have taught since then—in seminar courses for senior citizens, at Hamilton College and at the State University of New York at Albany—and a great deal of new Native American work and work about Native American literature has come into print, I have not really changed my approach to teaching Native American literature. There are four simple directions that I follow (in addition to those cardinal ones) and I would suggest them as applicable for others who wish to teach Native American literature.

1. Clearly define what you mean by "Native American literature." Remember the breadth and diversity of what we call "American Indian." Remember that we are referring, in fact, to many nations within this nation; to many literatures, literatures which each come from a national identity and a strong sense of place. You might make a good case that contemporary Native American writing in English is one continuous literary body, but when you look at the influence of the old traditions and then look at those traditions themselves, you recognize that you're seeing just the tip of the iceberg.

To my mind, it is best to teach introductory courses focusing on the work written in English, to think of these courses as only the beginning and to hope for both the knowledgeable instructors and the opportunity for schools to offer more advanced studies—a course in Haudenosaunee Literature 301 or Momaday 405—just as we offer introductory courses in British literature and then give our advanced students a chance to study the Victorians or Shakespeare.

'Native American literature,' is a vast body of work coming out of hundreds of languages and cultures.

2. Teach the work in context. The Native American view of life as reflected in literature (whether in English or originally in an earlier native language) is holistic. Remember that if you are teaching Native American literature well, you are not just teaching literature, you are also teaching culture. To understand the work—or to begin to understand it—it must be seen as it was *used*. The word is regarded as alive, not just syllables and symbols. An understanding, for example, of the traditional Navajo Night Chant is impossible without knowing the place of the Night Chant in the practices of healing, without recognizing that it is only one part of an event which involves the participation of dozens or even hundreds of individuals, that it is meant to be sung in a certain place at a certain time, and that the making of a sand painting depicting a particular event in Navajo mythology is intimately connected to it. Similarly, it is difficult to teach a modern work such as Silko's

Ceremony without some awareness of the place and purpose of similar healing and storytelling traditions among the Pueblo people.

3. Pay attention to continuance. Be aware of the strong connections in all Native American writing between what the western world calls "past" and "present." I am not just talking about the awareness of literary tradition—though that works at least in part as an analogy—but of something more than that. Many of the native languages deal with "time" in a very different way than does English. Similarly, the time sense of many contemporary Native American novels can seem strange, circuitous, even circular. Continuance is an important word for me in dealing with Native American writing. I stress this continuance by constantly linking contemporary Native writers to their roots, to their people and their places, their traditions.

4. Be wary of work in translation. My own approach is, for introductory courses at least, to place the strongest emphasis on contemporary work written in English and to use a few *carefully* selected translations from the old traditions in direct relation to those newer writings. A great many stories, songs, ceremonies, and the like which can be found in books are flawed in many ways. In some cases, the translations are bowdlerized or inaccurate. Imagine what it would be like if Shakespeare's plays had been written in Lakota and we only knew his work in English through a single translation of *Othello* done by an 18th-century puritanical and racist Baptist missionary with a tin ear who transcribed the play from a verbal recounting of it by a slightly senile octogenarian who never liked the theater that much. From my own knowledge of certain Native American languages and some of the translations that have been foisted off as legitimate,

I can assure you that I am not exaggerating the injustices that have been done. In some cases, in fact, rather than translations, the so-called myths and legends that we find in any number of places are sometimes made up from the whole cloth—oft involving a tragic love between a boy from one tribe and a girl from another and either a lover's leap or a canoe going over whatever high waterfall is handy to the translator's fevered imagination.

Another point about work in translation to keep in mind is that some things which have been recorded or translated have been recorded or translated without the permission of the native people who own that work. Much of Native America's traditional culture is *living* in the strongest sense of that word. Revealing that culture to the uninitiated is sacrilegious. A good teacher of Native American literature needs to know enough to be able to know which works need to be shown special respect. I cannot emphasize that word *respect* strongly enough. In some cases it may even mean NOT discussing something. That is a hard direction for people with the western mindset to follow, that western mindset which says "Tell it all, show it all, explain it all." I feel that those with that mindset would be better off avoiding the teaching of Native American literature.

Sense of Sound

When using Native American literature in translation, it is safest to use work which has been translated by Native scholars themselves. Alfonso Ortiz and J. N. B. Hewitt are two examples. There are also a number of ethnologists whose reputations and whose relations with the people whose work they translated are quite reputable. Dennis Tedlock and Frances Densmore represent some of the best in contemporary and early 20th-century work. I also like to have access to both the English translation

and the original language. Then, even a nonnative speaker can have some sense of the sound and rhythms as they were meant to be. But, again, show respect. Walk slowly. *Listen* to Native people.

Native American literature, as we now have the chance to offer it, is more than just an extra area, more than just a little diversity for the curriculum. It is the literature of a continent (of two continents, in fact, but I'll confine myself to the area north of Mexico for now), and it is a literature continually growing, being created and rediscovered. It is said that when Columbus touched onto the island of Hispaniola he didn't know where he really was. He didn't have, you might say, a good sense of direction. I certainly hope that future teachers of Native American literature will at least avoid that mistake of a European coming into contact with something new. I hope they will see where they are, see which way is south, which way is west, which way is north, and which way to look if they want to see the light of dawn. ■

Joseph Bruchac is a poet, storyteller, teacher, author, and co-editor of Keepers of the Earth: Native American Stories and Environmental Activities for Children.

The above article originally appeared in SAIL, Studies in American Indian Literature. *Reprinted with permission of the author.*

Why Students Should Study History

An interview with Howard Zinn

The following is condensed from an interview with Howard Zinn, author of A People's History of the United States, The Politics of History, Declarations of Independence *and other works. Zinn has taught history and political science at Spelman College in Atlanta and at Boston University. He was interviewed by Barbara Miner of* Rethinking Schools.

Why should students study history?

I started studying history with one view in mind: to look for answers to the issues and problems I saw in the world about me. By the time I went to college I had worked in a shipyard, had been in the Air Force, had been in a war. I came to history asking questions about war and peace, about wealth and poverty, about racial division.

Sure, there's a certain interest in inspecting the past and it can be fun, sort of like a detective story. I can make an argument for knowledge for its own sake as something that can add to your life. But while that's good, it is small in relation to the very large objective of trying to understand and do something about the issues that face us in the world today.

Students should be encouraged to go into history in order to come out of it, and should be discouraged from going into history and getting lost in it, as some historians do.

What do you see as some of the major problems in how U.S. history has been taught in this country?

One major problem has been the intense focus on U.S. history in isolation from the world. This is a problem that all nations have, their nationalistic

JOSEPH BLOUGH

focus on their own history, and it goes to absurd lengths. Some states in this country even require a yearlong course in the history of that state.

But even if you are willing to see the United States in relation to world history, you face the problem that we have not looked at the world in an equitable way. We have concentrated on the Western world, in fact on Western Europe. I remember coming into my first class in Spelman College in Atlanta in 1956 and finding that there was no required course in black history, or Asian or African history, but there was a required course in the history of England. And there on the board was this chart of the Tudors and the Stuarts, the dynasties of England.

For the United States, emphasis has been particularly glaring in terms of Latin America, which is that part of

the world closest to us and with which we've had the most to do economically and politically.

Another glaring problem has been the emphasis in teaching American history through the eyes of the important and powerful people, through the presidents, the Congress, the Supreme Court, the generals, the industrialists. History textbooks don't say, "We are going to tell the story of the Mexican War from the standpoint of the generals," but when they tell us it was a great military victory, that's exactly what they are doing.

Taking that as an example, if one were to have a more inclusive view of the war with Mexico, what would be some of the themes and perspectives one would include?

The Mexican War is an example of how one event raises so many issues. You'd have to see the war first of all as more than a military action. So often the history of war is dominated by the story of battles, and this is a way of diverting attention from the political factors behind a war. It's possible to concentrate upon the battles of the Mexican War and just to talk about the triumphant march into Mexico City, and not talk about the relationship of the Mexican War to slavery and to the acquisition of territories which might possibly be slave territories.

Another thing that is neglected in the Mexican War is the viewpoint of the ordinary soldiers. The soldiers who had volunteered for the Mexican War—you didn't need a draft because so many people in the working classes were so destitute that they would join the military on the promise of a little bit of pay and mustering out money and a little bit of prestige—the volunteers went into it not really knowing the bloodshed it would involve. And then so many of them deserted. For example, seven regiments of General Winfield Scott deserted on the road to Mexico City.

You should tell the story of the Massachusetts volunteers who went into the Mexican War. Half of them died, and the half who returned were invited to a homecoming party and when a commanding officer got up to address the gathering, they booed him off the platform.

I think it's a good idea also to do something which isn't done anywhere so far as I know in histories in any country, and that is: tell the story of the war from the standpoint of the other side, of "the enemy." To tell the story of the Mexican War from the standpoint of the Mexicans means to ask: How did they feel about having 40 percent of their territory taken away from them as a result of the war? How did they view the incident that President Polk used as a reason for the beginning of the war? Did it look real or manufactured to them?

You'd also have to talk about the people in the United States who protested against the war. That would be the time to bring up Henry Thoreau and his essay, "Civil Disobedience."

You'd have to look at Congress and how it behaved. You'd have to look at Abraham Lincoln, who was in the House of Representatives during the Mexican War. You'd learn a lot about politicians and politics because you'd see that Abraham Lincoln on the one hand spoke up against the war, but on the other hand voted to give money to finance the war. This is so important because this is something that is repeated again and again in American history: the feeble opposition in Congress to presidential wars, and then the voting of funds for whatever war the President has initiated.

[For a student activity on the Mexican War, see p. 116.]

How do you prevent history lessons from becoming a recitation of dates and battles and congresspersons and presidents?

You can take any incident in American history and enrich it and find parallels with today. One important thing is not to concentrate on chronological order, but to go back and forth and find similarities and analogies.

You should ask students if anything in a particular historical event reminds them of something they read in the newspapers or see on television about the world today. When you press students to make connections, to abstract from the uniqueness of a particular historical event and find something it has in common with another event—then history becomes alive, not just past but present.

And, of course, you must raise the controversial questions and ask students, "Was it right for us to take Mexican territory? Should we be proud of that, should we celebrate that?" History teachers often think they must avoid judgments of right and wrong because, after all, those are matters of subjective opinions, those are issues on which students will disagree and teachers will disagree.

But it's the areas of disagreement that are the most important. Questions of right and wrong and justice are exactly the questions that should be raised all the time. When students are asked, "Is this right, is this wrong?" then it becomes interesting, then they can have a debate—especially if they learn that there's no simple, absolute, agreed-upon, universal answer. It's not like giving them multiple choice questions where they are right or wrong. I think that's a tremendous advance in their understanding of what education is.

Teachers must also address the problem that people have been mis-educated to become dependent on government, to think that their supreme act as citizens is to go to the polls and vote every two years or four years. That's where the history of social movements comes in. Teachers should dwell on Shay's Rebellion, on colonial rebellions, on the abolitionist movement, on the populist movement, on the labor movement, and so on, and make sure these social movements don't get lost in the overall story of presidents and Congresses and Supreme Courts. Emphasizing social and protest movements in the making of history gives students a feeling that they as citizens are the most important actors in history.

Students, for example, should learn that during the Depression there were strikes and demonstrations all over the country. And it was that turmoil and protest that created the atmosphere in which Roosevelt and Congress passed Social Security and unemployment insurance and housing subsidies and so on.

How can teachers foster critical think-

> Questions of right and wrong and justice are exactly the questions that should be raised all the time.

ing so that students don't merely memorize a new, albeit more progressive, set of facts?

Substituting one indoctrination for another is a danger and it's very hard to deal with. After all, the teacher, no matter how hard she or he tries, is the dominant figure in the classroom and has the power of authority and of grades. It's easy for the teacher to fall into the trap of bullying students into accepting one set of facts or ideas. It takes hard work and delicate dealings with students to overcome that.

The way I've tried to deal with that problem is to make it clear to the students that when we study history we are dealing with controversial issues with no one, absolute, god-like answer. And that I, as a teacher, have my opinion and they can have their opinions, and that I, as a teacher, will try to present as much information as I can but that I may leave out information. I try to make them understand that while there are experts on facts, on little things, on the big issues, on the controversies and the issues of right and wrong and justice, there are no experts, and their opinion is as good as mine.

But how do you then foster a sense of justice and avoid the trap of relativity that, "Well, some people say this and some people say that"?

I find such relativity especially true on the college level, where there's a great tendency to indecisiveness. People are unwilling to take a stand on a moral issue because, well, there's this side and there's that side.

I deal with this by example. I never simply present both sides and leave it at that. I take a stand. If I'm dealing with Columbus, I say, look, there are these people who say that we shouldn't judge Columbus by the standards of the 20th century. But my view is that basic moral standards are not different for the 20th century or the 15th century.

Birmingham, Ala., 1963: African Americans attacked with fire hoses during an anti-segregation demonstration. The force of the water from these hoses often was powerful enough to rip bark from trees.

I don't simply lay history out on a platter and say, "I don't care what you choose, they're both valid." I let them know, "No, I care what you choose; I don't think they're both valid. But you don't have to agree with me." I want them to know that if people don't take a stand the world will remain unchanged, and who wants that?

Are there specific ways that teachers can foster an anti-racist perspective?

To a great extent, this moral objective is not considered in teaching history. I think people have to be given the facts of slavery, the facts of racial segregation, the facts of government complicity in racial segregation, the facts of the fight for equality. But that is not enough.

I think students need to be aroused emotionally on the issue of equality. They have to try to feel what it was like, to be a slave, to be jammed into slave ships, to be separated from your family. Novels, poems, autobiographies, memoirs, the reminiscences of ex-slaves, the letters that slaves wrote, the writings of

Frederick Douglass—I think they have to be introduced as much as possible. Students should learn the words of people themselves, to feel their anger, their indignation.

In general, I don't think there has been enough use of literature in history. People should read Richard Wright's *Black Boy*; they should read the poems of Countee Cullen; they should read the novels of Alice Walker, the poems of Langston Hughes, Lorraine Hansbury's *A Raisin in the Sun*. These writings have an emotional impact that can't be found in an ordinary recitation of history.

It is especially important that students learn about the relationship of the United States government to slavery and race.

It's very easy to fall into the view that slavery and racial segregation were a Southern problem. The federal government is very often exempted from responsibility for the problem, and is presented as a benign force helping black people on the road to equality. In our time, students are taught how

Eisenhower sent his troops to Little Rock, Ark., and Kennedy sent troops to Oxford, Miss., and Congress passed civil rights laws.

Yet the federal government is very often an obstacle to resolving those problems of race, and when it enters it comes in late in the picture. Abraham Lincoln was not the initiator of the movement against slavery but a follower of a movement that had developed for 30 years by the time he became president in 1861; it was the antislavery movement that was the major force creating the atmosphere in which

History Book Resources

Apteker, Herbert (editor) (1990). **A Documentary History of the Negro People of the United States, Vols. 1–4**. Citadel Press. An extremely valuable, I am tempted to say indispensable, collection, not at all dry, as are some documentaries.

Brown, Dee (editor) (1971). **Bury My Heart at Wounded Knee**. Holt, Rinehart & Winston. A moving collection of statements and recollections by American Indians which gives you their point of view in a vivid, passionate way.

Carroll, James (2006). **House of War**. Houghton Mifflin. Gives us not just a history of the Pentagon, but a sweeping and critical history of U.S. foreign policy throughout the Cold War. Carroll, once a priest, now a novelist and columnist for the *Boston Globe*, has done prodigious research and writes brilliantly about the militarization of the nation after World War II.

Chomsky, Noam (1992). **Year 501.** South End Press. Here, the nation's most distinguished intellectual rebel gives us huge amounts of information about American foreign policy, and puts it into historical perspective, going back to the Columbus era.

Drinnon, Richard (1990). **Facing West**. Schocken. A brilliantly written account of imperial expansion by the United States, not just on the American continent against the Indians, but overseas in the Philippines and in Vietnam.

Foner, Eric (1988). **Reconstruction: America's Unfinished Revolution**. Harper & Row. A rich, vivid, epic-like narrative of those extraordinary years 1863 to 1877, by one of the leading "new historians."

Hampton, Henry, and Steve Fayer, with Sarah Flynn (editor) (1990). **Voices of Freedom.** Bantam. An oral history of the black movement for civil rights, from the 1950s to the 1980s, much of its material coming out of the research done for the TV documentary *Eyes on the Prize.*

Hofstadter, Richard (1974). **The American Political Tradition.** Vintage. A classic of American history, beautifully written, an iconoclastic view of American political leaders, including Jefferson, Jackson, Lincoln, Wilson, and the two Roosevelts, suggesting more consensus than difference at the top of the political hierarchy.

Hope Franklin, John (1974). **From Slavery to Freedom**. Knopf. The classic overview of Afro-American history by the nation's leading black historian.

Lerner, Gerda (editor) (1977). **Black Women in White America: A Documentary History.** Random House. A rare glimpse into the lives, the minds, the spirits of that doubly oppressed group, ranging from slavery to our time. A wonderful sourcebook.

Lynd, Staughton (editor) (1966). **Nonviolence in America.** Bobbs-Merrill. A valuable examination of the ideas, in their own words, of early Quaker dissidents, abolitionists, anarchists, progressives, conscientious objectors, trade unionists, civil rights workers, and pacifists, from the colonial period to the 1960s.

Martínez, Elizabeth (editor) (1991). **500 años del pueblo chicano: 500 Years of Chicano History.** Southwest Organizing Project. Marvelous photos but also an exciting bilingual text loaded with valuable history.

Takaki, Ronald (1993). **A Different Mirror.** Little, Brown & Company. A splendid, comprehensive look at the role ethnic minorities have played in American history. Eloquent, powerful, meticulously researched.

Takaki, Ronald (1989). **Strangers from a Distant Shore.** Penguin. Gives us what has been glaringly missing from our traditional histories, the story of Asian Americans, from the early years of the republic through the dramatic, tragic experiences of Chinese and Japanese immigrants to the arrival of refugees from Southeast Asia.

Williams, David (2005). **A People's History of the Civil War.** New Press. Departs radically from the traditional histories of the Civil War, which center on great battles or on Lincoln and the generals. Williams, a scholar from the deep South, tells us the untold stories of the class conflict inside both South and North during the war. It is a refreshing and provocative approach.

Yellen, Samuel (1974). **American Labor Struggles.** Pathfinder. This brings to life the great labor conflicts of American history, from the railroad strikes of 1877 to the San Francisco general strike of 1934.

Young, Marilyn (1991). *The Vietnam Wars, 1945-1990.* Harper Collins. A superb history of U.S. involvement in Vietnam.

—Howard Zinn

Editors' note: Don't forget Zinn's A People's History of the United States (1981, Harper and Row) and Voices of a People's History of the United States (with Anthony Arnove, 2004, Seven Stories), which uses speeches, letters, poems, and more to bring "people's history" to life.

emancipation took place following the Civil War. And it was the president and Congress and the Supreme Court that ignored the 13th, 14th, and 15th Amendments after they were passed. In the 1960s it wasn't Johnson and Kennedy who were the leaders and initiators of the movement for race equality, but it was black people.

In addition to focusing on social movements and having a more consciously anti-racist perspective, what are some other thematic ways in which the teaching of history must change?

I think the issue of class and class conflict needs to be addressed more honestly because it is ignored in traditional nationalist history. This is true not just of the United States but of other countries. Nationhood is a cover for extreme conflicts among classes in society, in our country, from its founding, from the making of the Constitution. Too often, there's a tendency to overlook these conflicts, and concentrate on the creation of a national identity.

How does a teacher deal with the intersection of race, class, and gender in terms of U.S. history, in particular that the white working class has often been complicit, consciously or unconsciously, in some very unforgivable actions?

The complicity of poor white people in racism, the complicity of males in sexism, is a very important issue. It seems to me that complicity can't be understood without showing the intense hardships that poor white people faced in this country, making it easier for them to look for scapegoats for their condition. You have to recognize the problems of white working people in order to understand why they turn racist, because they aren't born racist.

When discussing the Civil War, teachers should point out that only a small percentage of the white population of the South owned slaves. The rest of the white population was poor and they were driven to support slavery and to be racist by the messages of those who controlled society—that they would be better off if the Negroes were put in a lower position, and that those calling for black equality were threatening the lives of these ordinary white people.

Feminists march on August 26, 1970, the 50th anniversary of women's suffrage, in a nationwide "strike for equality" called by the National Organization for Women.

Picket sign from a protest in 1941 during a time of heightened labor unrest, when Walt Disney fired union organizers on his art staff.

In the history of labor struggles, you should show how blacks and whites were used against one another, how white workers would go out on strike and then black people, desperate themselves for jobs, would be brought in to replace the white workers, how all-white craft unions excluded black workers, and how all this creates murderously intense racial antagonisms. So the class and race issues are very much intertwined, as is the gender issue.

One of the ways of giving some satisfaction to men who are themselves exploited is to make them masters in their own household. So they may be humiliated on the job, but they come back home and humiliate their wives and their children. There's a wonderful short story by a black woman writer, Ann Petry, "Like a Winding Sheet" that should be required reading in school. It's about a black man who is humiliated on the job and comes home and, on the flimsiest of reasons, beats his wife. The story is told in such a way as to make you really understand the pent-up anger that explodes inside a family as a result of what happens out in the world. In all these instances of racial and sexual mistreatment, it is important for students to understand that the roots of such hostility are social, environmental, situational, and are not an inevitability of human nature. It is also important to show how these antagonisms so divide people from one another as to make it difficult for them to solve their common problems in united action.

How can you teach white students to take an anti-racist perspective that isn't based merely on guilt over the things that white people have done to people of color?

If such a perspective is based only on guilt, it doesn't have a secure foundation. It has to be based on empathy and on self-interest, on an understanding that the divisions between black and white have not just resulted in the exploitation of black people, even though they've been the greatest victims, but have prevented whites and blacks from getting together to bring about the social change that would benefit them all. Showing the self-interest is also important in order to avoid the patronizing view of feeling sorry for someone, of giving somebody equality because you feel guilty about what has been done to them.

At the same time, to approach the issue merely on the basis of self-interest would be wrong, because people should learn to empathize with other people even where there is no visible, immediate self-interest.

In response to concerns about multiculturalism, there's more lip service to include events and perspectives affecting women and people of color. But often it's presented as more facts and people to learn, without any fundamental change in perspective. What would be the approach of a truly anti-racist, multicultural perspective in U.S. history?

I've noticed this problem in some of the new textbooks, which obviously are trying to respond to the need for a multicultural approach. What I find is a bland eclecticism where everything has equal weight. You add more facts, you add more continents, you add more cultures, you add more people. But then it becomes a confusing melange in which you've added a lot of different elements but without any real emphasis on what had previously been omitted. You're left with a kind of unemotional, cold combination salad.

You need the equivalent of affirmative action in education. What affirmative action does is to say, look, things have been slanted one way for a long time. We're going to pay special attention to this person or to this group of people because they have been left out for so long.

People ask me why in my book, *A People's History of the United States*, I did not simply take the things that I put in and add them to the orthodox approaches so, as they put it, the book would be better balanced. But there's a way in which this so-called balance leaves people nowhere, with no moral sensibility, no firm convictions, no outrage, no indignation, no energy to go anywhere.

I think it is important to pay special attention to the history of black people, of Indians, of women, in a way that highlights not only the facts but the emotional intensity of such issues.

Is it possible for history to be objective?

Objectivity is neither possible nor desirable.

It's not possible because all history is subjective, all history represents a point of view. History is always a selection from an infinite number of facts and everybody makes the selection differently, based on their values and what they think is important. Since it's not possible to be objective, you should be honest about that.

Objectivity is not desirable because if we want to have an effect on the world, we need to emphasize those things which will make students more active citizens and more moral people.

How can a progressive teacher promote a radical perspective within a bureaucratic, conservative institution? Teachers sometimes either push

the limits so far that they alienate their colleagues or get fired, or they're so afraid that they tone down what they really think. How can a teacher resolve this dilemma?

The problem certainly exists on the college and university level—people want to get tenure, they want to keep teaching, they want to get promoted, they want to get salary raises, and so there are all these economic punishments if they do something that looks outlandish and radical and different. But I've always believed that the main problem with college and university teachers has been self-censorship. I suspect that the same thing is true in the high schools, although you have to be more sympathetic with high school teachers because they operate in a much more repressive atmosphere. I've seen again and again where college and university teachers don't really have a problem in, for instance, using my *People's History* in their classrooms, but high school teachers always have a problem. They can't get it officially adopted, they have to get permission, they have to photocopy parts of it themselves in order to pass it out to the students, they have to worry about parents complaining, about what the head of the department or the principal or the school superintendent will say.

But I still believe, based on a lot of contact with high school teachers over the past few years, that while there's a danger of becoming overly assertive and insensitive to how others might view you, the most common behavior is timidity. Teachers withdraw and use the real fact of outside control as an excuse for teaching in the orthodox way.

Teachers need to take risks. The problem is how to minimize those risks. One important way is to make sure that you present material in class making it clear that it is subjective, that it is controversial, that you are not lay-

ing down the law for students. Another important thing is to be extremely tolerant of students who disagree with your views, or students who express racist or sexist ideas. I don't mean tolerant in the sense of not challenging such ideas, but tolerant in the sense of treating them as human beings. It's important to develop a reputation that you don't give kids poor grades on the basis of their disagreements with you. You need to create an atmosphere of freedom in the classroom.

It's also important to talk with other teachers to gain support and encouragement, to organize. Where there are teachers unions, those are logical places for teachers to support and defend one another. Where there are not teacher unions, teachers should always think how they can organize and create a collective strength.

Teachers don't always know where to get those other perspectives. Do you have any tips?

The orthodox perspective is easy to get. But once teachers begin to look for other perspectives, once they start out on that road, they will quickly be led from one thing to another to another.

So it's not as daunting as people might think?

No. It's all there. It's in the library. ∎

To the Young Who Want to Die

By Gwendolyn Brooks

Sit down. Inhale. Exhale.
The gun will wait. The lake will wait.
The tall gall in the small seductive vial
will wait will wait:
will wait a week: will wait through April.
You do not have to die this certain day.
Death will abide, will pamper your postponement.
I assure you death will wait. Death has
a lot of time. Death can
attend to you tomorrow. Or next week. Death is
just down the street; is most obliging neighbor;
can meet you any moment.

You need not die today.
Stay here—through pout or pain or peskiness.
Stay here. See what the news is going to be tomorrow.

Graves grow no green that you can use.
Remember, green's your color. You are Spring.

Gwendolyn Brooks was the first African American to win the Pulitzer Prize for poetry, in 1950. One of the foremost African-American poets in the nation's history, she died in 2000. (See p. 212 for lesson ideas.)

Students from the organization Sistas and Brothas in the Bronx speak to the media about overcrowding at their high school.

PART FIVE

BEYOND THE CLASSROOM

No classroom is an island. Teachers soon become painfully aware of how factors beyond the classroom limit what they can accomplish with their students.

Overcrowded classes, tracking, crumbling social services, social inequality, and the isolation of teachers themselves all undermine effective education.

As the writers in this chapter argue, reform-minded teachers must complement their efforts inside their classrooms with alliances to transform the schools, districts, and communities they work in.

Why We Need to Go Beyond the Classroom

By Stan Karp

School power comes in many pieces.

Most teachers committed to social justice understandably focus on their own classrooms where they have daily opportunities to project a vision of democracy and equality. Whether it's developing curriculum that includes the real lives of our students, encouraging young people to examine issues of race, class, and gender as they build academic competence, or organizing activities that promote cooperative skills and spirit, classroom teachers can often find ways to promote social justice despite the institutional agendas and bureaucratic practices imposed upon us.

But what if we stop at the classroom door? What if critical teachers see their role only in terms of classroom practice? Is our job solely to create "safe spaces" inside an often ineffective and oppressive educational system? Can we sustain ourselves for years as committed professionals by focusing solely on the 30, 60, or 150 students for whom we assume direct responsibility each September? What about the other arenas of educational activity beyond our classrooms: schoolwide change, community and district education politics, teacher unionism, and national education reform? What do these have to do with next week's lesson plans?

One unavoidable answer is that teachers will never really succeed at their jobs until conditions of teaching and learning improve dramatically. We need more resources, better preparation and support, smaller classes, more

Milwaukee teachers and community members demonstrate for public school support.

effective partnerships with the communities we serve, and, especially in poorer areas, a vision of social change that can replace poverty and despair with progress and hope. We need effective responses to violence, racism, drug abuse, family crisis and the many other problems that surface daily in our classrooms. Teachers have to address these problems in the course of their professional lives as surely as our students have to study and do their homework to achieve individual academic goals.

Schools Are Social Battlegrounds

Adding "extracurricular" activism to a classroom teacher's workload may seem overwhelming. But it is a necessity that's been forced upon us. Whether the issue is vouchers, funding, multiculturalism, testing, or tracking, schools have become public battlegrounds for competing social and political agendas. Yet many "reform" proposals would only make matters worse. If education reform is going to make schools more effective, more equitable and more democratic institutions, the voices of grassroots teachers, parents, and students are essential. If we don't help to change our schools from the bottom up, we will have them changed for us from the top down.

Education activism is also crucial to finding the allies we need. It is naive to believe that we can transform our schools and our students' lives by ourselves. While we can admire and strive to emulate teachers who through hard work and commitment manage to perform classroom "magic," the real hope for educational transformation does not lie in the development of isolated "superteachers," but in the reconstruction of school life. We need better, more collaborative relations with our colleagues and the space to nurture those possibilities. We need better, more cooperative relations with parents and communities, particularly where cultural and racial differences exist. And we need more democratic practices in our schools, our unions, and our districts, which can only come with contacts and activism beyond classroom boundaries.

Finally, critical teachers need to move beyond the classroom because to do otherwise would undercut the very efforts we make each day. If we recognize that effective education requires students to bring their real lives into their classrooms and to take what they learn back to their homes and neighborhoods in the form of new understanding and new behavior, how can we not do the same? Critical teaching should not be merely an abstraction or academic formula for classroom "experimentation." It should be a strategy for educational organizing that changes lives, including our own.

Teachers who find these arguments compelling will face tough challenges. As activist educators struggle to figure out "where to put the lever," it is useful to keep in mind the contradictory character of the institutions we seek to change and understand just why successful school reform is so hard.

Consider for example the current wave of reform framed by the No Child Left Behind Act. (See p. 200.) Under NCLB, the federal government is using test scores to identify which schools will face an escalating series of mandatory "reforms" ranging from intervention by outside consultants to wholesale dismissal of school staff to the imposition of private management on public schools.

Yet even according to a study by the conservative Thomas B. Fordham Foundation (an enthusiastic supporter of NCLB) the "reform interventions" mandated by the new law have a "success rate" of well below 50 percent, (even when that success is measured in narrow test score terms.). According to the study, "Several lessons can be drawn from America's previous experience with state and district-level interventions into failing schools:

■ Some turnaround efforts have improved some schools, but success is not the norm.

■ No particular intervention appears more successful than any other.

■ Interventions are uneven in their implementation and always hard to sustain.

■ It is nearly impossible to determine which interventions offer the most bang for the buck because they are attempted in very different situations."

These findings resonate with my own experience as a classroom teacher and school reformer for over 30 years in Paterson, N.J. Having lived through state takeovers, school reconstitutions, site-based management, small school restructuring, state standards and testing (and more testing), and "whole school reform" initiatives of all kinds, it's hard not to conclude that school reform fails more often than it succeeds. While there are many model schools, model classrooms, and model educators from which we can learn a great deal, there are no model districts, no model states, and no model systems that have put in place and sustained the policies and programs needed to deliver quality education and outcomes to all children. Why should this be so?

Ultimately, the reasons have less to do with the flaws of any specific reform strategy or intervention than with the historic reality that schools have always had a dual character.

On the one hand, public schools remain perhaps our most important democratic institution. They are the product of decades of effort to give substance to the nation's promises of equal opportunity, self-improvement and success through hard work and achievement. Schools play a key role in American dreams of class mobility and generational progress, and their success or failure has a daily impact on the lives and prospects of millions of children and families.

At the same time, schools historically have been instruments for reproducing class and race privilege as it exists in the larger society. The low academic performance of schools in poor areas, the inadequate facilities, the endemic underfunding, the persistence of tracking and resegregation, the notorious administrative instability and shallow trendiness of reform efforts, the toleration of failure and disrespect for communities of color, all reflect real relations of inequality and injustice

Schools have never been just about educating children. They are also about constructing social and political power.

that permeate our society. Through ideology, gatekeeping, various forms of stratification, and bureaucratic, often authoritarian, administration, schools function as a large sifting and labeling operation that recreates and justifies existing distributions of wealth and power. In many ways, schools reproduce the very inequality that American mythology professes they are designed to overcome.

inevitably takes place within the context of this dual character of schooling. The choices made push schools in one direction or the other along a continuum from promoting social justice to reinforcing the status quo. Whether any

> There are many educators, parents, and advocates at all levels pushing the system to realize its most ambitious and democratic possibilities.

This dual character of schooling—its democratic promise and its institutional service to a society based on class, race, and gender privilege—invariably generates contradictory impulses when it comes to reform. At every turn, the gap between the promise and practice of schooling creates a tension: Should curriculum reflect a mainstream hegemony or a multicultural pluralism? Should schools endorse traditional values or promote independent, critical thought? Are standards being raised to bar the door to some or assure better outcomes for all? Should parents and classroom teachers have as much to say about reform agendas as governors and corporate executives? Should schools be as concerned with promoting anti-racist attitudes as marketable skills? Will new forms of assessment provide better ways to report and improve student performance or more effective ways to sort and label kids for predetermined slots in society?

To be sure, answers to complicated questions of educational policy cannot be reduced to either/or propositions. But the debate over policy options

particular reform initiative improves or impoverishes life in the classroom often depends on how it fits into this larger context.

This is one reason that reforms cannot be judged by their rhetorical promises or short-term effect on test scores. Instead they must be measured by their real impact on classrooms and their ability to deliver more democratic classroom experiences and more equitable results and outcomes across the system.

Take for example, the current enthusiasm in reform circles for small school experiments. Small schools show promise in large part because they attempt to change the social relations of schooling; done well, they can create a more human scale and more supportive environment for collaborative, personalized interaction among students, teachers, and communities. They can nourish creativity and mutual accountability in powerful ways that large, traditional schools cannot. Small schools can also introduce elements of choice, pluralism, and innovation into historically bureaucratized and stagnant systems.

But like most reforms, small schools can also be developed in problematic ways. They can become specialized magnets that select only the "best" students and most involved parents. They can claim a disproportionate share of

resources for a relatively small slice of the student population. Instead of providing models of systemwide reform, they can be insulated pockets of privilege, resegregation, and tracking. It all depends on which of the system's dual tendencies prevails. This is one reason for keeping a sharp eye on the big picture and asking "who benefits and who does not" whenever a reform proposal is put on the table.

Of course, there are many educators, parents, and advocates at all levels pushing the system to realize its most ambitious and democratic possibilities. These heroic efforts need encouragement in the face of hard choices and daunting problems. But they also need a healthy dose of realism about the nature of the system we're trying to move.

Unfortunate as it may be, schools have never been just about educating children. They are also about constructing social and political power. Real school reform must be about challenging it.

None of this is reason for despair or inaction. But it is cause for some hard thinking when it comes to deciding where to invest one's time and energies. In rethinking education activism along with our teaching, we need to measure our choices against the possibilities each issue offers to move our classrooms and communities closer to more just and more democratic arrangements.

School site councils. Site-based management reforms have faded in recent years as the standards and testing crusade has moved school power away from schools, classrooms, and teachers to state and national bureaucracies. Experience has also yielded some cautionary lessons about whether changes in "governance" necessarily translate into better classrooms and about how much responsibility teachers should assume for managing a system where power remains firmly in the hands of hierarchical bureaucracy.

Still, at its best, site-based reform can open a credible process for replacing hierarchical and bureaucratic forms of school governance with more representative and democratic structures. As educator Deborah Meier has written, "a democratic school culture is the best professional development." Where site councils have real power, parents, teachers, and others in a school community can make significant decisions about resources, curricula, and school policies in ways that can nourish community/school/teacher collaboration. Site councils can become places where members of a school community work to reconcile different perspectives and priorities, and learn to build trust and respect over the long term.

At its worst, however, (and here comes that dual character again) site-based reform can become simply another bureaucratic layer in a system that doesn't work. It can consume valuable time and energy in a seemingly endless cycle of unproductive meetings designed to give a veneer of legitimacy to bureaucratic agendas. Instead of representative bodies, site councils can be empty shells dominated by administrative appointees, or bodies that marginalize parents (or classroom teachers) in ways that promote old antagonisms rather than new alliances. They can also become pawns in a cynical process of imposing austerity, breaking union power, or otherwise administering policies of educational retrenchment rather than reform.

Questions to Consider

Whether or not a particular site-based project is worth a teacher's investment of time and energy probably depends on the answers to a variety of questions: Has the council been created in response to a top-down directive or is it the product of grassroots, union, or community action? Does the site coun-

cil have direct control over resources or policies that can have substantial impact on the school? Is the site council a place where teachers and parents really have a chance to engage in dialog and form alliances? Is the process characterized by an increase in communication, access to information, and debate by key constituencies? Is site-based reform accompanied by a tangible investment in the time and training needed to make it work? Is there buildingwide or districtwide discussion of how such reform will change the roles of all concerned, or is it being grafted onto existing structures?

Even where the answers to such questions are mixed, asking them will help measure the potential of a given site-based project and prepare teachers for critical participation in the process.

Teacher Unions

Teacher unions offer another mix of opportunities and obstacles for teachers looking to effect change. Like public schools themselves, teacher unions are both deeply flawed institutions, and, at the same time, indispensable to hopes for educational democracy and justice.

Labor unions in general, and teacher unions in particular, have won historic rights and better conditions for those they represent. In most school systems, unions serve as some check on the arbitrary power of the politicized bureaucracies that manage school districts. More significantly, they are an important reservoir of collective strength and resources for reform that need to be protected from a variety of anti-labor crusades in education today, including privatization, voucher schemes, and legal restrictions on organizing and the right to strike.

Unfortunately in too many cases, teacher unions have become bureaucratic partners in the management of failing school systems. Like other labor organizations, they often suffer from undemocratic and uninspiring internal practices which demobilize and fragment their memberships instead of enlisting them in creative campaigns for better schools. And like most other social institutions, they have been deformed by the persistence of racism and sexism which has at times crippled their ability to respond effectively to complex issues like affirmative action

---

10 Things You Can Do Beyond Your Classroom

1. Serve on a local school council.

2. Become active in your union.

3. Breathe new life into a standing union/school committee (e.g., instruction, community outreach, curriculum).

4. Organize a teachers' study or discussion group.

5. Write an op-ed for the local newspaper about how NCLB is affecting your school and classroom.

6. Help distribute Rethinking Schools.

7. Join a local community organization with an interest in schools (e.g., the NAACP or a local neighborhood coalition).

8. Investigate and publicize tracking policies in your school.

9. Flood your faculty room with provocative materials about critical teaching.

10. Investigate and publicize education funding policies in your state.

For related resources, organizations, and periodicals, see pp. 215-231.

versus seniority rights, the need to close the gap between communities of color and predominantly white professional staffs, and the building of parent-teacher partnerships.

Teacher unions have too often adopted short-sighted, defensive perspectives on key reform issues, sometimes focusing too narrowly on salary

But some of the responsibility for the failures of teacher unions is our own. Too often progressive-minded teachers abstain from union activity, lumping the union with the administration as "them." I know I felt that way myself when I first entered the teaching profession. It was only after having these attitudes challenged by com-

union work leads you to conclude that the space for change in your local is limited, you're likely to have made valuable contacts, and positioned yourself and others for a broader challenge to the union status quo as the education crisis deepens and more unions find business-as-usual strategies unequal to the tasks before them.

Teacher Study and Support Groups

Another major reason for critical teachers to look beyond the classroom is to break out of the confining isolation they often face. Most school cultures are not very supportive of critical thought, change, or even collaboration among staff. Starting a teachers' study group can be a way of finding allies to sustain committed teaching over the long haul. A teacher group might begin as an informal after-school social hour where teachers trade stories, resources, and ideas. To encourage discussion beyond the "gripe session stage" (a chronic tendency that infects many faculty rooms) it's often helpful to pick a specific topic like tracking, assessment, or discipline, read a background article, and then talk about the issue's impact on your own school and classrooms. Once a group establishes some cohesion and continuity, it can address more difficult issues such as multicultural relations among teachers and students, or differing parent-teacher perspectives. It's often useful to invite outside participants for frank conversations about sensitive issues often avoided in typical "inservice" programs.

Discussion or study groups have a variety of attractions for teachers looking to move beyond the classroom. They're flexible, and can set their own agendas and pace without interference. If the interest in one school is insufficient to sustain a group, teachers from several schools can begin coalescing a local network of progressive educators.

A teacher group might begin as an informal after-school social hour where teachers trade stories, resources, and ideas.

and contract concerns at the expense of a broader vision of educational justice and change. As a result they can pit the short-term interests of their members against the long-term interests of schools and the communities they serve. Ultimately this weakens public support for both unions and schools. Whether the issue is identifying and helping ineffective teachers, prioritizing scarce resources, acknowledging community and parent concerns in contract talks, or otherwise facilitating the reform of existing school systems, teacher unions have too often been committed to a narrow defense of existing arrangements. The consequences can be devastating for both school systems and teachers. In Chicago and New York, reforms to increase community and parent power were instituted, to a large extent, against union opposition, weakening the reforms in both cases. Elsewhere unions have stubbornly refused to address the issue of "bad teachers," thereby helping to magnify and sensationalize what in actuality is a marginal issue, while at the same time failing to address the dismal state of teacher preparation and in-school support.

mitted teachers working for reform in both the NEA and the AFT that I reconsidered my assumptions and saw possibilities I had overlooked.

Teacher unions are our organizations or, at any rate, they should be, and while it would be naive to ignore the obstacles that bureaucratized unions can place in the path of rank-and-file activism, it is self-defeating to surrender in advance. Many locals are starved for the participation of committed members. Others may be genuinely committed to the interests of teachers and kids but have no awareness of critical perspectives or alternative teaching strategies. Moreover, it's not necessary to pursue the possibilities of union activism by starting with a frontal attack on the existing leadership. Most teacher unions have a variety of committees and forums that offer possibilities for initiative and debate. A teacher looking for connections with other colleagues and potential allies should definitely consider becoming a building delegate, reviving a dormant instructional committee, organizing a classroom discussion caucus, or proposing a union-sponsored community forum on some hot educational issue. Even if a year or two of

They can draw on a variety of national resources and networks for ideas and support (see Resources, p. 215–231), and can develop into a safe space for critical reflection and mutual support not readily available elsewhere. Eventually, discussion and study can lead to action, public discussion, and local campaigns to improve schools. With public attention increasingly focused on education, a local teacher group has the potential to evolve into an important local, grassroots institution. One person posting a sign on the faculty bulletin board or approaching a few colleagues can initiate a low-risk strategy that can pay big dividends.

Local, State, and National Education Activism

The opportunities discussed above can each provide ways to promote social justice in education, and at the same time sustain individual teachers in their daily efforts in the classroom. But there are many key educational issues that will be determined, not primarily inside local schools and classrooms, but in the larger context of community, state, and national politics. These include voucher plans, which threaten to divert public funds to private schools, and privatization schemes, which propose divesting in the very concept of public education and turning over schools to private managers. It also includes legal battles now underway in dozens of states over school funding inequities which reproduce society's racial and class divisions, create a patchwork of rich schools and poor schools, and breed crippling inequality. It also increasingly includes the imposition of state and national testing standards which bureaucratically drive school curricula and limit teacher autonomy in the classroom, often in ways that hinder effective instructional practices. Teachers need to be informed about these issues and, where possible, help to resolve them in positive ways.

In the final analysis, however, what's important is not that classroom teachers assume an impossible burden of individual responsibility for solving all the social and educational problems that affect their classrooms. What matters is that they see and, as much as possible, understand the connections between those classrooms and the society around them, and realize that efforts to apply critical teaching are tied to broader efforts to promote democracy and equality in society. If teachers can find ways to link the two, they will strengthen both. ∎

Stan Karp (stan.karp@gmail.com) taught English and journalism for 30 years in Paterson, N.J. He is currently director of the Secondary Reform Project at the Education Law Center in Newark, N.J., and an editor of Rethinking Schools *magazine.*

Teacher Activist Groups

The number of social justice teacher support and activist groups is growing all the time. Below are some local groups that have their own websites; some also maintain listservs.

Education Not Incarceration (ENI)
Oakland, Calif.
www.ednotinc.org

Literacy for Social Justice Teacher Research Group (LSJTRG)
St. Louis, Mo.
www.artsci.wustl.edu/~mrmosley/lsjtrg/about.htm

New York Collective of Radical Educators (NYCoRE)
New York
www.nycore.org

Portland Area Rethinking Schools (PARS)
Portland, Ore.
www.portlandrethinkingschools.org

Teachers for Social Justice (T4SJ)
San Fransisco area
www.t4sj.org

Teachers for Social Justice (TSJ)
Chicago
www.teachersforjustice.org

Teachers Unite
New York City
www.teachersunite.net

Rebellion Against the North Side

By Naomi Shihab Nye

There will be no monograms on our skulls.
You who are training your daughters to check for the words
"Calvin Klein" before they look to see if there are pockets
are giving them no hands to put in those pockets.

You are giving them eyes that will find nothing solid in stones.
No comfort in rough land, nameless sheep trails.
No answers from things which do not speak.

Since when do children sketch dreams with price tags attached?
Don't tell me they were born this way.
We were all born like empty fields.
What we are now shows what has been planted.

Will you remind them there were people
who hemmed their days with thick-spun wool
and wore them till they fell apart?

Think of darkness hugging the houses,
caring nothing for the material of our pajamas.
Think of the delicate mesh of neckbones
when you clasp the golden chains.
These words the world rains back and forth
are temporary as clouds.
Clouds? Tell your children to look up.
The sky is the only store worth shopping in
for anything as long as a life.

Naomi Shihab Nye is an acclaimed poet, essayist, and teacher. She is author and/or editor of more than 20 books. (See p. 212 for lesson ideas.)

Teachers Teaching Teachers

By Linda Christensen

"Teachers teaching teachers is like the blind leading the blind," a literacy "expert" told Portland Public Schools (PPS) administrators in the fall of 2005, while discussing my three-year writing proposal for elementary schools. My plan included classroom teachers sharing strategies and lessons to improve writing in grades 3 through 5. Instead, elementary teachers got yet another outside expert with a program and a large price tag.

During my seven years as a curriculum specialist designing professional development in Portland Public Schools, I wanted teachers to see themselves as curriculum producers, as creative intellectuals rather than technicians serving out daily portions of someone else's packaged or downloaded materials. I attempted to create spaces where teachers could work together to develop their own curriculum and discuss education issues.

School districts write mission statements about creating citizens of the world, but more and more, they want teachers to become robotic hands who deliver education programs designed and shipped from sites outside of our classrooms.

If we want an educated citizenry, we need teachers who know how to think about their students' needs and write their own curriculum in collaboration with others.

In recent years, the No Child Left Behind (NCLB) legislation has pushed administrators to grab quick solutions to get a fast "bump" in their test scores. Instead of taking the time to build teacher capacity by improv-

DAVID McLIMANS

ing instruction or creating schools as learning communities where teachers have opportunities to have honest discussions about classroom practice, share successful lessons and strategies, or examine student work together, more and more administrators opt for what I call "boxed" professional development—from fill-in-the-blank writing curricula to "stick-the-kid-on-the-computer" reading and math programs.

When high school language arts teachers in Portland were asked by the Professional Development Committee

—a group founded by the school district and the Portland Association of Teachers—which professional development programs had the greatest impact on their students' learning, they overwhelmingly named the Portland Writing Project, the Summer Literacy Curriculum Camp, and the Professional Development Days—which were all led by classroom teachers.

Teachers stated that these three programs were practical and related specifically to their content. The programs gave them models of new strategies and curricula, hands-on practice, and time for collaboration and implementation. Teachers also said they appreciated the support of ongoing professional development, instead of the one-shot variety. What struck me in reading the surveys and talking with teachers was that the top-down approach of telling teachers what to do without engaging

plan for implementation, the leaders of these inoculation sessions expect teachers to take the theory back and apply it in their classrooms. This is like taking students to the Louvre, showing them great art, and expecting them to reproduce it without giving them any lessons on drawing and painting.

Daughter, Monica Sone's autobiography, which takes place during the Japanese-American internment. The participants, co-directors, and I developed role plays and writing assignments using the book, primary source documents, children's books, or other parallel texts on the topic. While the co-directors and I provide the framework for the summer institute, each teacher develops and teaches a writing lesson that contributes to the unit. For example, Alexis Aquino-Mackles, a 1st-grade teacher, read a section of *Nisei Daughter* that described how Sone's family burned "everything Japanese: Japanese dolls, music, swords, Japanese poetry." Then she read a section from *Farewell to Manzanar* where a Japanese-American mother breaks her family's heirloom dishes one at a time rather than sell them to the vultures who lurked in Japanese-American neighborhoods during the evictions and bought families' valuables at ridiculously low prices prior to the internment. She gave each member of our class a broken piece of pottery and had us write an interior monologue from the character's point of view about that moment.

> Teachers learn the strategies by doing the strategies, not by having someone talk about 'participatory, engaging, hands-on curriculum.'

them in active learning is as ineffective in professional development as it is in the classroom.

In the same way that some teachers insult students by assuming that they have no knowledge, history, culture, or language, some schools and school districts insult teachers by assuming that they come to professional development without any prior knowledge or expertise. For example, last year a literacy "expert" came to town with her bag of tricks. She landed at a school that had a literacy team representing teachers across the disciplines. Instead of finding out what they knew, she proceeded to teach them about "think alouds," graphic organizers, textbook previewing, and reading strategies they'd already been implementing in their classrooms.

Another common professional development pitfall is the series of overheads, which is currently being replaced by the dancing PowerPoint presentation, with too-simple bulleted points about complex issues like inclusion of special education students or English Language Learners in mainstream classrooms, as if naming a problem constituted addressing it. Without any modeling, discussion, or time to

Portland Writing Project

The Portland Writing Project (PWP), a collaboration between Portland Public Schools and the Oregon Writing Project at Lewis & Clark College, is one of the almost-200 sites of the National Writing Project (NWP). The Portland Writing Project models the pedagogy it hopes teachers will take back to their classrooms, but it also encourages teachers to constantly reflect on their classroom practice and revise their teaching based on their observations. Like the NWP, the PWP doesn't preach one way to teach writing; it teaches the writing process. But in Portland, we also help teachers learn to develop their own curriculum.

Every summer for most of the past 20 years, 25 K–12 Portland Public Schools teachers have gathered to share writing strategies and lessons with each other during an intensive (9 a.m. to 4 p.m.) four-week class; they receive 10.5 university credits for participating. At our site, my co-director and I choose a multicultural novel that situates our teaching in a period of U.S. history, so that teachers can learn to integrate history, reading, novel study, writing, and students' lives into their lessons.

For a number of years we read *Nisei*

Tanya McCoy, a high school science teacher, asked each of us to bring a baggie full of soil from our garden. After conducting experiments on the soil and discussing how different the soil would be in the mostly desert-like settings of the internment camps, we wrote about our experiments.

Our intention is not for teachers to grab this particular unit and obediently follow the lessons; instead we aim to equip teachers to think in interdisciplinary terms and see themselves as curriculum developers, not consumers of other people's curriculum. The work around *Nisei Daughter* is an important example, but only because it provides a model for how teachers of any grade level or content area might approach developing units of study. I intentionally model curriculum that struggles with racism and inequality of all kinds, that encourages teachers to think about engaging students in why there is inequality and oppression, and that looks for places of solidarity, hope, and alternatives.

All the teachers in the PWP also participate in reading groups, writing response groups, role plays, and simulations. They write every assignment. They learn the strategies by doing the strategies, not by having someone talk about "participatory, engaging, hands-on curriculum." They know revision strategies because they use them as they write and revise their own narratives, essays, and poetry. They can teach students methods for opening narratives or strategies for knocking their classmates' socks off with their dialogue because they learn how to write like writers during the institute. Teachers also reflect after each activity on how they will use or adapt the strategies in their classrooms. They meet in grade-level groups throughout the four weeks to plan for the following year. It is their activity, their plans, and their growth that provides the content and the goal of this kind of professional development.

The intent of the PWP is not to "fix" broken teachers; it provides a rich environment for teachers to practice literacy, to have hard conversations about thorny issues that surface in their classroom practice. This is the kind of dialogue that simply can't happen in top-down trainings or when teachers are handed a packaged curriculum created at Princeton.

Of course, not all teachers who attend the summer institute bring stellar practice. Some are victims of bad writing instruction themselves; others have internalized the need to look outside of their classroom for answers, to find an expert or guru to follow instead of becoming their own experts. During the four weeks, the co-directors and I work with participants to tease out what they do know and what they can share. We try to validate and expand their knowledge—in the same way we respond to students in our classrooms.

> We aim to equip teachers to think in interdisciplinary terms and see themselves as curriculum developers.

PWP teachers continue to meet monthly during the year following the summer institute. (Some teachers have continued to come to these meetings for a number of years, and almost 100 teachers gather for our yearly writing retreat in February.) They discuss the implementation of strategies in their classroom. They bring in student work to examine, successful lessons to share, and problems to ponder and solve.

Because many teachers have not experienced a classroom that engages their hearts and minds while also teaching them to read and write critically, it is essential that professional development do more than describe good classroom practice. We can't just hand teachers a program to implement. Teachers need to participate in this kind of pedagogy as a student experiences it in order to understand why this kind of instruction is necessary. For example, Ellie Hakala, language arts teacher, said at one PWP meeting, "I never realized how important students' sharing their work was until I went through the Writing Project. When I wrote a great piece, I wanted everyone to hear it, not just my small group. I wanted to hear what others had written. Now my students want to share all the time as well."

Summer Curriculum Camps

In collaboration with a group of language arts teachers representing each of our high schools, I designed the Curriculum Camp specifically to give teachers time to create curriculum and to bring a more diverse, multicultural, contemporary reading list into our high school language arts classrooms. Instead of just buying the books and putting them in bookrooms across the city, I wrote a grant to pay teachers to come together and write curriculum guides to help teach the novels. Of course, it would have been cheaper and faster to buy prepackaged curriculum for teachers to open each fall and follow the directions. But our group wanted to hone teachers' capacities to create curriculum from the ground up, so we chose to take the time and spend the money to share and build teacher knowledge. Because the novels, like the ones we chose for the Portland Writing Project, included sensitive cultural, racial, and gender issues as well as historic events that not all teachers were familiar with, we knew it was important to spend time researching background knowledge and talking about how to teach the novels. We wanted to expand the repertoire of instructional strategies that teachers use, but we also wanted to link those strategies to deeper, more challenging content.

Our intent was to integrate the canon, but also to share the expertise of our skilled teachers as we wove reading and writing strategies into these study guides. (Many of these teachers participated in the Portland Writing Project sometime during the past 20 years.) Many of us needed to learn how to teach reading and writing skills more effectively. Using the PWP model of teachers teaching teachers, we took turns teaching workshops that shared effective strategies while we built our units.

We received a grant from the privately funded Portland Public School Foundation for $40,000—enough to purchase sets of books for every high school and to pay two teachers from each school their hourly wage for 30 hours of work. Other teachers volunteered to come for credit. They were hungry for a community where they could learn and share with each other. At the end of the first summer one teacher wrote, "I have learned that we are our best resources."

Six years later, we continue to meet for a week each summer, scrounging money from various grants or the district's coffers. In fact, more than 90 percent of PPS high school language arts teachers, as well as a number of ESL, special education, and social studies teachers, attended at least one summer camp by the time I retired from PPS in 2006.

We spend part of each morning discussing provocative readings and topics or attending reading or writing workshops that participants asked us to provide. We talk about the tough issues: How to differentiate our curriculum with an increasingly diverse student body, how to work with students who don't speak or write Standard English, how to teach students to design their own essay topics. Then teachers move into work groups to develop curriculum on new novels, nonfiction texts, or hot topics. For example, teachers have created curriculum on *Persepolis, Kite Runner, Fences, Thousand Pieces of Gold,* as well as *Fast Food Nation, Nickel and Dimed,* and *Smoke Signals.*

The curriculum camp provides another lesson for professional development: New teachers need time to grow their practice with skilled professionals. During the Summer Curriculum Camp first-year teachers and veteran teachers a year or two from retirement work side-by-side developing curriculum and learning new skills. As one first-year teacher wrote, "Being new to teaching, the greatest thing

> Teachers engaged in conversations about racism in their city and learned how to teach about it at the same time.

about the Literacy Project has been ... learning tons about everything, soaking up as much as I can. Up to this point, I really had a limited collection of strategies to use."

During the first summer of the literacy camp, I told my colleagues that I was less interested in the curriculum guides we produced than the process of teachers working together and learning from each other. Mistake. The guides are also important. They are the written legacy of our summer work. But the guides also indicate our curricular weaknesses and blind spots. Some are brilliant. Others limp along with too many Internet downloads and not enough inspired teaching. Some miss the point. After each summer, I reviewed the guides to see what lessons we learned and what we missed as we create our work for the following summer.

If we purchased guides for the books or distributed anthologies with questions and writings mapped out for the teachers, we would miss these opportunities to learn together to build curriculum for the students who populate our schools. While published guides may be slicker in presentation than ours, they lack the creative struggle of teachers making decisions about the best way to introduce the book, the best way to teach how to read this particular text.

Professional Development Days

How do teachers get better at their craft? How do we create "lifelong learners" in the teaching profession? If we don't reach beyond our classrooms to learn new strategies or engage in debates with our colleagues, we can grow rigid and narrow. No matter how long we've been teaching or how good we are, we can always benefit from gathering with colleagues and sharing new curriculum ideas and strategies, talking about new issues that have surfaced, or discussing old issues that we still need to tackle.

As teachers, professional development needs to provide us with time-outs from our work, so we can step back and ask the questions about our daily practice that needle us. We need time to think, discuss, debate, find new strategies and resources for our classrooms and ourselves. Too often professional development is provided in tiny morsels from 3:30 to 5:30 after we have taught all day—or squeezed into an hour one morning a month. Fortunately, the Portland Association of Teachers and Portland Public Schools hammered out an agreement to provide five paid professional development days for teachers each year. Originally, the days were set aside to give teachers time to become familiar with the state standards, work samples, and scoring rubrics. For a number of years these days were divided between school-based professional development and district professional development.

During the seven years I worked as the high school language arts curriculum specialist, I met regularly with the high school literacy leaders, a group composed of one language arts liaison from every comprehensive and alternative high school. Together, we decided to commit our professional development days to disseminating the curriculum guides developed during the summer, sharing strategies, discussing the impact of district or state initiatives on our classrooms (like high school reform), or bringing in occasional speakers to address hot issues, like untracking.

A few years ago we started developing interdisciplinary workshops with social studies, ESL, and special education teachers. These days broke us out of our classrooms and content areas to share our practice, but also helped us disseminate the curriculum we developed each summer. During this time, we engaged as intellectuals with other teachers in meaningful discussions about our content—and the world. Instead of sitting in rows, listening to some "expert" tell us about effective classroom practice, we experienced it with our colleagues.

For example, on a recent professional development day, Carmel Ross and Lisa Walker, two of the teachers who developed curriculum for the novel *Bronx Masquerade*, shared one of the strategies from their summer work. They led participants on a treasure hunt, a prereading activity that develops background knowledge prior to entering a unit of study. Their interactive workshop taught about the main characters of the Harlem Renaissance and demonstrated how to get "TAG, ELL, SPED, and Johnny out of their seats and into your curriculum."

In another workshop, Hyung Nam, a social studies teacher, led language arts, social studies, and ESL colleagues in a lesson on "Institutional Racism and Segregation in the Post-Civil Rights Era and in Portland." His lesson centered on two central questions: How do segregation and racial disparities persist after the Civil Rights Era? How does Portland's history with segregation and environmental racism compare to the national history? Hyung's lessons explored the multiple causes of racial segregation and environmental racism while helping students understand how institutional racism is perpetuated today. His workshop included a mock trial and examination of local history with ongoing segregation and racism. Teachers not only learned new pedagogy, they walked away with information, including handouts and historical documents on the structural features of racism to use with their students. They experienced learning by participating in the trial, not by reading about it. They engaged in conversations about racism in their city and learned how to teach about it at the same time.

Teachers who present—and over the years we have worked to enlist as many teachers as presenters as possible—learn twice as much. They not only engage as participants in the workshops throughout the day, they also gain clarity about their own practice by sharing it with other teachers. In presenting to their colleagues, they teach their lessons, but they also teach the underlying assumptions about good pedagogy and content knowledge that animate their work.

Teacher-centered professional development doesn't happen unless district—and school—administrators and curriculum leaders have intimate knowledge of teachers' practice. Just putting teacher X in front of the faculty will not lead to the kind of professional development I am advocating. Curriculum leaders must take the effort

> Teacher-centered professional development doesn't happen unless district—and school—administrators and curriculum leaders have intimate knowledge of teachers' practice.

to listen to teachers' conversations when they talk about their classrooms and their students, they must observe teachers at work with students and colleagues, and they must look for exemplary practice and curricular expertise. Ultimately, they must have a vision of professional development that puts classroom teachers at the center. ■

Linda Christensen (LChrist@aol.com) is director of the Oregon Writing Project at Lewis and Clark College and is an editor of Rethinking Schools *magazine.*

Equity Claims for NCLB Don't Pass the Test

By Stan Karp

Ever since the "No Child Left Behind" legislation* was passed in 2001, supporters have made a series of claims about how the law will help kids, parents, and schools, especially in poor communities. The real impact that NCLB is having on schools and classrooms is considerably different from these claims:

Claim: Annual standardized testing is the key to bringing school improvement and accountability to all schools. "For too long," says the Department of Education, "America's education system has not been accountable for results and too many children have been locked in underachieving schools and left behind. ... Testing will raise expectations for all students and ensure that no child slips through the cracks."

Reality: The huge increase in federally mandated testing will hurt school performance, not improve it. Over the past two decades, most states and local districts already have dramatically increased the use of standardized tests without solving the problems of poor schools. NCLB requires states to develop literally millions of new tests at a cost of more than $7 billion. With states spending only about $20 per student developing these tests, many are unreliable and inappropriately used. As one researcher noted, "There is more public oversight of the pet industry and the food we feed our dogs than there is for the quality of tests we make our kids take."

STUART GOLDENBERG

Many studies show that standardized testing does not lead to lasting increases in student achievement. Researchers at Arizona State University completed the largest study ever done on the issue. They concluded that "high-stakes" testing "that decides whether students graduate, teachers win bonuses and schools are shuttered, an approach already in place in more than half the nation, does little to improve achievement and may actually worsen academic performance and dropout rates."

When schools become obsessed with test scores, they narrow the focus of what teachers do in classrooms and limit their ability to serve the broader needs of children and their communities. Overreliance on testing diverts attention and resources from more promising school improvement strategies like smaller class size, creative curriculum reform, and collaborative professional development. High-stakes tests push struggling students out of school, and encourage schools to adopt inappropriate practices for younger children in an effort to "get them ready for the tests." Overuse of testing can also encourage cheating scandals and makes schools and students vulnerable to inaccurate and, at times, corrupt practices by commercial testing firms.

Claim: The new law will use test scores to hold schools accountable for serving all students. For the first time, the spotlight will be put on achievement gaps that schools have traditionally covered up, and schools will be forced to address inequalities in student achievement that they have failed to deal with in the past.

Reality: The comparative reporting of student scores by subgroups does put a useful and important spotlight on achievement gaps. But NCLB uses these gaps to label schools as "failures," without providing the resources or support needed to eliminate them. The law includes an unrealistic and underfunded federal mandate that by 2014, 100 percent of all students, including special education students and English language learners, must be proficient on state tests. Schools that don't meet increasingly unreachable test score targets face an escalating series of sanctions that have no record of success as school improvement strategies, but do promote privatization and "market reform" of public education, for example by moving resources away from the neediest schools to pay private, for-profit companies to provide "supplemental tutoring." Instead of an appropriate educational strategy, these policies leave schools and children behind as the federal government retreats from the nation's historic commitment to improving universal public schooling for all kids.

Inequality in test scores is one indicator of school performance. But test scores also reflect other inequalities in resources and opportunities that exist in the larger society and in schools themselves. The federal government has not made wiping out inequality a high priority when it comes to tax policy, unemployment policy, minimum wage policies, health or child welfare policies. The Bush administration tried to cut food stamp programs, temporary assistance for needy families, child nutrition, foster care, child support enforcement, health insurance programs for children, and childcare grants to states. Why are standardized test scores in public schools the only area of public policy in which the administration has mandated 100% equality among all population groups? Can you imagine the federal government saying all crime must be eliminated in 12 years or we'll privatize the police? All citizens must be healthy in 12 years or we will shut down the healthcare system?

Some politicians seem to be trying to turn the problems of poor schools into a campaign to destroy public education. We need to ask when the same politicians who oppose civil rights, affirmative action, more spending for social programs, and universal health care suddenly became champions of poor black and brown children and their families.

Claim: The new law mandates that students historically exempt from the testing pool, such as special education students and English language learners, must now take tests and have their scores counted. These groups also must achieve "100 percent proficiency" within 12 years. This will force schools to improve student achievement for groups of students who have previously been left behind.

Reality: The inclusion of special education and Limited English Proficient students in the testing calculations makes it harder for schools to reach the unreasonable "adequate yearly progress" targets, but it does nothing to improve educational services to these children. The law's punitive preoccupation with high-stakes testing is narrowing the focus of curricula and impoverishing educational experiences for all children. It is also forcing students to take inappropriate and unhelpful mandated assessments, like tests in languages they don't understand.

If the federal government wanted to help special needs students, it would fully fund the Individuals with Disabilities Education Act (IDEA), as called for repeatedly by education advocates. (The federal government currently provides less than half the funding authorized by the IDEA.) It would also support effective bilingual education programs for English language learners and encourage assessment practices that promote content learning and language acquisition simultaneously. Instead, the new regulations greatly restrict the use of effective bilingual education programs and promote a kind of "English only" intolerance.

Claim: The new federal law gives parents in failing schools more choices.

Reality: The law theoretically gives parents the right to take students out of struggling schools and to leave those schools behind. But it does not guaran-

> ## When schools become obsessed with test scores, they limit their ability to serve the broader needs of children and their communities.

tee them any new places to go. In districts where some schools are labeled "failing" and some are not, the new law may force increased class sizes by transferring students without creating new capacity. NCLB does not invest in building new schools in failing districts. It does not make rich districts open their doors to students from poor districts. NCLB's transfer policies don't give poor parents any more control over school bureaucracies than food stamps give them over the supermarkets. They are a "supply-side" fraud that seems designed to manufacture a demand for vouchers and ultimately to transfer funds and students to profit-making private school corporations.

NCLB also obligates schools that don't make "adequate yearly progress" for three years to provide "supplemental tutoring" services. The majority of approved providers for these services are private companies that do not have to meet the same "highly qualified" standards as public school teachers. They stand to profit from largely unregulated and unmonitored access to potentially $2 billion in public funds each year. Some districts have had to eliminate their own tutoring programs in order to pay for more expensive private programs that serve fewer kids. For example, to comply with NCLB, Southtown, Ill., eliminated a tutoring program that served 250 students with certified teachers in small classes of 10 and replaced it with a more expensive program that pays Sylvan Learning Center to serve 50 to 60 students.

Claim: NCLB gives poor schools more resources to improve.

Reality: NCLB dramatically increases mandates for school and student performance, but it has been funded at tens of billions of dollars below originally promised levels (and over 10 times less than the federal government spent on the war in Iraq through 2006).

A study of 20 states of the school services, remedial programs, and other expenditures needed to reach NCLB mandates found that it would take about a 30 percent annual increase in current school spending for states to come close to meeting the law's own narrow test-score goals. That's about $130 billion a year, or about 10 times current funding for Title I programs. The estimated costs of just developing and administering the additional tests that NCLB requires may be more than twice what the law provides.

NCLB does provide for a special school improvement fund, but the President has never requested, and Congress has never authorized, any money for it. Instead, NCLB "school improvement funds" are taken by diverting funds from Title I—the single largest federal education program, originally designed to support schools with high concentrations of poor students—to state education departments to develop plans to implement NCLB sanctions. The result is what the Center for Education Policy recently called "a shell game, in which states take funds away from districts with the greatest concentrations of low-income children and give them to other districts" to finance the imposition of NCLB penalties.

Claim: The law puts real pressure on districts to change bureaucratic business-as-usual, which is why it is generating so much heat.

Reality: NCLB is increasing educational bureaucracy instead of reducing it. It moves educational decision making away from classrooms, schools, and local communities, where it belongs, and puts it in the hands of state and national politicians and bureaucrats. The law promotes one-size-fits-all "solutions" to complicated problems of educational and social inequality and substitutes standards and tests for the

more difficult and more costly reforms that real school improvement requires.

Some advocates for children and schools, desperate for signs of hope amidst the wasteland of social and economic policies emanating from Washington, have struggled mightily to find positives in NCLB. They point to the pressure on schools to account for all students, the promise of better choices for parents in the poorest communities, the emphasis on improving teacher qualifications. But years of inconsistent and underfinanced implementation have kept none of these promises. Reasonable people may continue to differ on various aspects of NCLB, but the core of the law has been laid inescapably bare: tests, more tests, and punitive sanctions that create a misleading impression of systematic failure and that hurt public education far more than they help those who have been poorly served by it.

NCLB needs to be transformed from a test, punish, and privatize law into a real school improvement law. The obsessive reliance on standardized testing, the punitive sanctions, the chaotic transfer plans, the gross underfunding, and the educational malpractice that the law imposes on special education and bilingual students all need major revision. Only if and when that happens can "no child left behind" become a legitimate rallying cry for schools and their advocates. ∎

*For more on the impact of NCLB and proposals to change the law, visit www.rethinkingschools.org and www.fairtest.org.

Stan Karp (stan.karp@gmail.com) taught English and journalism for 30 years in Paterson, N.J. He is currently director of the Secondary Reform Project at the Education Law Center in Newark, N.J., and an editor of Rethinking Schools magazine.

Why Standardized Tests Are Bad

By Terry Meier

No phenomenon poses a greater threat to educational equity, and ultimately to the quality of education in this country, than the escalating use of standardized achievement tests.

Fueled by public concern that schools are less rigorous than they used to be, standardized tests are increasingly prescribed as the "get tough" medicine needed to return excellence to our classrooms. Across the country, standardized tests are now routinely used to determine how and when students advance, from 1st grade through graduate school.

Standardized tests, which are notorious for their discriminatory effect on students of color, clearly threaten whatever small measures of educational equity have been won in recent decades. What is less obvious is that standardized tests threaten the educational experience of all children.

Because standardized tests are a constant reality in students' lives, it is essential that parents understand the biases and limitations of such tests. Yet, as in so many other educational areas, parents are often excluded from the debate because they are deemed unable to understand the issue's complexity.

Tests are called "standardized" when the same test is given under similar conditions to large groups of students, whether districtwide, statewide, or nationwide. Most standardized tests ask multiple-choice questions and are corrected by a computer which recognizes only one "right" answer.

Decades of research have documented the biases in standardized

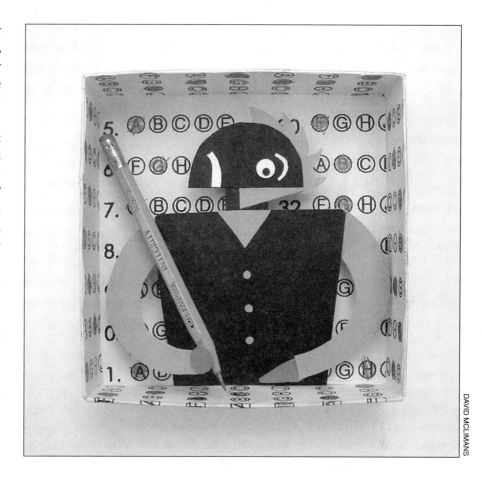

DAVID MCLIMANS

tests, with students of color bearing the brunt of that discrimination. Across age groups, standardized tests discriminate against low-income students and students of color. While girls tend to do better on standardized tests at an early age, by high school and college their scores are on average below those of males, according to FairTest, a national group based in Cambridge, Mass., that lobbies against the growing use of standardized tests.

Advocates of testing argue that standardized achievement tests do not create inequities within schools, they merely reflect preexisting inequities.

According to this argument, children of color and low-income students tend to perform less well on standardized tests because they receive an inferior education.

Two false assumptions support this view. One is that standardized tests are a valid measure of excellence. The second is that standardized tests can be used to improve education, especially for low-income students and students of color.

Standardized achievement tests tend to focus on mechanical, lower-order skills and to reward students' rapid recognition of factual information. For example, standardized reading tests for young children stress phonics and the recognition of individual words. Research on learning to read, however, has shown the importance of integrating oral language, writing, reading, and spelling in a meaningful context that emphasizes children understanding what they read, not merely sounding out words. Similarly, research on teaching math stresses the importance of young children learning concepts through firsthand experience, while achievement tests for young children define math as knowing one's numbers.

Thus teachers face the dilemma of providing instruction that they know fosters a student's understanding, versus drilling students in isolated skills and facts that will help them do well on standardized tests.

It's not that students don't need to work on isolated skills sometimes, especially when they're first learning to read and write. But such work is only a means to the larger end of applying those skills in a meaningful context. Removed from context as they are on standardized tests, such skills are meaningless. Held up as a measure of achievement, they become mistaken for what is most important instead of what is ultimately trivial.

There is little, if any, connection between quality instruction and standardized test performance. Consider, for example, a successful high school English class in which students learn to write thoughtful, original essays in clear, concise language about topics they genuinely care about and that draw on their experiences. Assume that the teacher taught students to edit their work so that grammatical errors were rare.

Yet what does the American College Testing (ACT) Program test? Whether a student knows if the word "pioneered" is preferable to "started up by," or if "prove to be" is preferable to "come to be," or if "reach my destination" is pref-erable to "get there."

The point is that the choice is stylistic, dependent upon what one is trying to say and to whom. Removed from real life, the choice is meaningless. It reveals nothing about a student's competence in reading and writing.

Consider another example, from a standardized reading achievement test where the child was asked to determine the "right" answer in the following selection:

Father said: Once there was a land where boys and girls never grew up. They were always growing. What was Father telling?

The truth   A lie   A story

Any of these could be the "right" answer. If the father were speaking metaphorically, referring to mental and not physical growth, he could be telling the truth. It could also be a lie, for in black speech the word "lie" can also mean a joke or a story. And, of course, its initial "once" signals the conventions of fiction/fairy tales. (Hoover, Politzer, and Taylor, 1987, p. 91)

Standardized tests also ignore the skills and abilities needed to function in a complex, pluralistic society—such as the ability to work collectively in various social and cultural contexts, to adjust to change, to understand the perspectives of others, to persevere, to motivate, to solve problems in a real-life context, to lead, to value moral integrity and social commitment. As Harvard psychologist Howard Gardner points out, "there are hundreds and hundreds of ways to succeed, and many different abilities that will help you get there."

It is tragic that at the time when many developmental psychologists stress a broad and complex conception of intelligence and ability, and when one needs multiple talents to function effectively in the world, we have come to define excellence in our schools within the narrow parameters of what

can be measured by standardized tests.

Clearly, standardized tests neither measure excellence nor foster it in our schools. So why the emphasis on such tests?

The fundamental reason is that the tests provide a seemingly objective basis upon which to allocate limited educational resources—to decide who gets into the best classes, high schools, or colleges. To that end, test items are deliberately selected so as to maximize differences between high and low scorers. By design, only some people will do well on the tests.

There can be little doubt that if a large percentage of white middle-class students performed poorly on standardized tests, the test results would be viewed as invalid and discriminatory. There is no similar concern for students of color, despite some 25 years of extensive documentation of cultural bias in standardized testing.

Those who argue that it is possible to make standardized tests less discriminatory by removing their cultural bias seriously underestimate the enormity of their task. What is a "culture-fair" test in a multicultural society? And who could design such a test? The truth is that any knowledge worth having is inextricably linked to culture and to context—and thus can't be reduced to measurement on a standardized test.

In the final analysis, the most fundamental question to be answered about standardized testing is not why students of color tend to perform less well than white students, or even what can be done about it. Rather, the fundamental question is what is wrong with a society which allocates its educational resources on the basis of tests which not only fail to measure excellence, but which discriminate against the vast majority of its minority population? ∎

Terry Meier is an associate professor in the Wheelock College Graduate School in Boston.

Lineage

By Margaret Walker

My grandmothers were strong.
They followed plows and bent to toil.
They moved through fields sowing seed.
They touched the earth and grain grew.
They were full of sturdiness and singing.
My grandmothers were strong.

My grandmothers are full of memories
Smelling of soap and onions and wet clay
With veins rolling roughly over quick hands
They have many clean words to say.
My grandmothers were strong.
Why am I not as they?

Margaret Walker was one of the youngest African-American poets to publish a full volume of poetry. She won the Yale Younger Poet award in 1942 for her book *For My People*, her master's thesis at the University of Iowa. (See p. 212 for lesson ideas.)

Students Mobilize for Immigrant Rights

By Ryan Knudson and Al Levie

Viviana, who had lived in the United States for only two years, walked nervously to the speaker's podium at a press conference on the steps of her high school. Although she was remarkably confident in her ability to communicate with friends and classmates in English, she hesitated to deliver a speech in English to several hundred people. As the crowd of parents, students, community members, clergy, politicians, and press listened, she began to speak.

"My name is Viviana Pastrana," she began. "I am a sophomore and I am an immigrant with papers, with permission to live here. I am a member of a group called Students United for Immigrant Rights because I want to support immigrants and struggle with them, especially with undocumented immigrant students."

She continued, telling the story of a friend, an undocumented immigrant who has been in the United States most of her life, and who will not be able to afford a university education in Wisconsin simply because of her immigration status.

Viviana is a student at William Horlick High School in Racine, Wis., where we both teach. Al is a history and sociology teacher at Horlick, and Ryan teaches English as a second language to mainly Mexican immigrant students. Horlick has a diverse student body. About 18 percent of the students are Latino, 24 percent African-American, 2 percent Asian, and 56 percent European-American. More than 20 per-

Carla Rotger (left) and Juan Marquez lead a march of 1,500 students and community members calling for a referendum on school spending.

cent of the students qualify for free or reduced lunch. The Racine community as a whole has similar demographics.

Over the past two school years, students have created change within their school and their community through their work in a student organization called Students United for Immigrant Rights that addresses social issues that closely affect them and their friends and families. Giving students opportunities to organize and become active around the issue of immigrant rights has helped change the culture of our school and created and strengthened bonds among students, families, the school, and the community. It has also helped students from marginal-

ized groups become actively engaged, academically successful, and to rise to positions of leadership in the school and the community.

The Group's Origins

Students United for Immigrant Rights evolved out of a lesson that Al presented to students in his Latino-American History class. The class initially attracted mainly second- and third-generation Chicano students, along with a handful of immigrant students. Students viewed the PBS video series *Matters of Race* (available at www.pbs.org/mattersofrace). One segment was about a dramatic increase in numbers of Mexican immigrant workers moving to a small town in the southern United States. The students were appalled at the depictions of open racism on the part of white townspeople in the film. This led to a class discussion on the struggles that immigrants face both in the South and around Racine. At the students' urging, Al took a personal day the very next day to participate in a rally with several students. At the rally, Al met people from Voces de la Frontera (Voices of the Border), an immigrant workers' group from Milwaukee; this connection would prove mutually beneficial.

The event drew coverage in the *Racine Journal-Times*, which printed anti-immigrant letters. Richard Peterson's letter read, "Hello, what don't you understand? You are here illegally, why should you get any justice?" This letter set up a classroom discussion/response activity where students wrote individual and group rebuttals. The *Journal-Times* printed all of the students' letters on its op-ed page. Readers took the students' letters seriously, and weighed in both positively and negatively in response. In effect, Latino-American History students became the catalyst for a community discussion on immigrant rights that was carried out on the op-ed page of the *Journal-Times*.

Soon thereafter, Christine Neumann-Ortiz, the director of Voces de la Frontera, contacted Al to tell him that state Rep. Pedro Colón of Milwaukee had introduced a bill in the Wisconsin Assembly that would allow undocumented immigrant students to attend state institutions of higher education at resident tuition rates. Al invited two representatives of Voces de la Frontera to speak to the Latino-American History class about the issue and the legislation. Ryan brought his English as a second language (ESL) students to the talk, and again, students wanted to take action. They arranged a field trip to Madison for a legislative committee

hearing on the bill (AB 95). Students prepared testimony to deliver on behalf of undocumented immigrant students.

At the hearing, an undocumented immigrant student named Marylu Garcia made a strong argument in favor of the bill. "Some people say that immigrants should not receive any governmental help because they don't pay their taxes, and that they are taking away from the United States illegally," she said. "The reality is that immigrants do pay their taxes. But they are not able to collect them. So how can they be stealing money, when they are actually giving it away? Immigrants take the worst, low-paying jobs that no citizens want. And you call that fair? When immigrants are actually being exploited?" As the local press picked up on the issue, the students became known as strong proponents of the bill, which never made it out of committee.

Shortly thereafter, with financial assistance from Voces de la Frontera, Al, his wife Jennifer, Voces de la Frontera leader and longstanding community activist Maria Morales, and seven of the most active students traveled to Washington, D.C. The Center for Community Change organized three days of activities centering on the DREAM Act and Student Adjustment Act. These federal acts would offer undocumented students a pathway to citizenship, in-state tuition for college, and opportunities to apply for federal financial aid. Students trained in lobbying techniques and spent a day lobbying elected representatives.

They participated in a mock gradu-

ation ceremony at the U.S. Capitol and marched to the Department of Education to deliver letters highlighting the fact that thousands of dreams were being denied because of lack of access to higher education. The *Washington Post* interviewed Xavier Marquez and Marylu Garcia and featured Xavier's picture on the front page the follow-

> This work has helped change the culture of our school and strengthened bonds among students, families, and the community.

ing day. The assistance of community groups made it possible to choose students based on academic achievement in their Latino-American History class, their past participation in immigrant rights activities, and their future commitment to working for immigrant rights.

Marylu Garcia shared her testimony at the DREAM Act rally.

Afterward, students who participated in the trip to Washington organized a Cinco de Mayo celebration at Horlick High School. The event was partly a fundraiser to pay for the Washington trip, partly a celebration of Latino heritage, and partly an opportunity for students to report to the community what they had been doing. The theme of the event was "Latino-American History Students Making History." Local Latino leaders spoke, community members prepared a Mexican meal, and students spoke and created displays about all of the events they had participated in. Hundreds of Latino students, family members, community members, and school officials came together for the first time for a school event.

The publicity about the Washington trip and the Cinco de Mayo celebration triggered anti-immigrant comments from a community member at a Racine Board of Education meeting. The speaker also called for Al's dismissal, saying that he was teaching children to "raise hell." Upset about the field trips to Madison and Washington, Renee Bradley, a community member, asked, "What, I ask you, does this have to do with Latin American history? Absolutely nothing. This has to do with an immigration issue. And because Mr. Levie feels too passionately about it, he is using and abusing his position as a teacher to advance his political views. ... This is unacceptable. He is taking these children out of school to learn how to rally for immigrant rights? That's not appropriate." She added that, "Of course, [the students] are going to feel passionate about [immigrant rights]. Half of them are illegally in the country." (Actually, all but two were U.S. citizens, so passion for the issue didn't necessarily correlate to immigrant status.)

Al gave the students who partici-

Students hold a protest and mock graduation ceremony.

dents explained what they had learned as a result of the trip. The students' and parents' approach was a marked contrast to the shrill testimony of the anti-immigrant speaker, and the issue of Al's dismissal died at that meeting.

At a debriefing meeting to discuss

Voces de la Frontera. Being connected to Voces gave Students United financial resources and staff support on immigrant issues. It also became a conduit to the community outside of school. The club began meeting informally to plan the next event, a Mexican Independence Day celebration in September. By the following school year, we had established a monthly meeting schedule. At our first meeting in September, we held elections for officers. Between two and four students competed for each position. Our executive board is made up of a president, vice president, secretary, treasurer, and two immigrant student liaisons. The immigrant student liaison positions exist to encourage greater participation by immigrant students and to ensure that two immigrant students will sit on the board. Between 20 and 40 members attend the monthly after-school meetings, which are chaired by the president or vice president. Discussions focus on anything from ideas for political action to plans for a student barbecue. As the club has grown and received local attention, other teachers have begun

Vivian worked as hard—and with as much pride—to support immigrants' rights as she would have on any term paper or presentation.

pated in the Washington trip a copy of the meeting transcript and asked them to show their parents. Maria Morales, the president of the Racine chapter of Voces de la Frontera, called a meeting with the parents where they decided to go to the next school board meeting to let the board know they appreciated the school board's giving their children the opportunity to participate in the trip. Kids and parents thanked the board for allowing them to participate, and stu-

the Cinco de Mayo event, students agreed they wanted to continue working on immigration issues even after the Latino-American History class ended. Ryan suggested forming an official school club. Several students arranged a meeting with the school's directing principal, Nola Starling-Ratliff, who gave permission. The students asked us to become club advisors, and Students United for Immigrant Rights became the student affiliate of

asking about forming chapters in their schools.

Since its inception, Students United for Immigrant Rights has been active. Students wore graduation caps and gowns to demonstrate for granting of in-state tuition for undocumented students and traveled twice to Milwaukee for visits by President Bush and the Republican Congressman F. James Sensenbrenner. When Mark Belling, a conservative Milwaukee talk radio personality, referred to Mexican Americans as "wetbacks" on the air, Luisa Morales, the communications director of Students United, wrote a position paper that was published as a guest editorial in the *Racine Journal-Times*. Luisa also delivered the students' position in a speech before Milwaukee Area Technical College officials asking them to pull more than $57,000 in advertising from Belling's radio station. Recently students held a mock graduation rally and press conference at our high school, participated in a rally at Casa de la Esperanza in Waukesha, and traveled to Madison to lobby lawmakers to keep pro-immigrant education provisions in the state budget. At the invitation of State Representative Pedro Colón, Al and Xavier Marquez traveled to Madison to deliver testimony about the same provisions. All of these events featured state and local lawmakers delivering statements in support of extending educational opportunities to undocumented immigrant students. At two events, immigrant students delivered heartfelt speeches in favor of in-state tuition, and opposing the REAL ID act, a measure that would deny drivers' licenses to undocumented immigrants.

The Changing Culture

Since beginning to organize students around the issue of immigrant rights, we have noticed changes in the interpersonal dynamics between immigrant and Chicano students. Before students began getting involved, there was mutual distrust and misunderstanding between immigrant students and Chicano students (those whose parents or grandparents were Mexican immigrants, but who themselves were born in the United States). Immigrant students saw Chicano students as sometimes being ashamed of their heritage because they often spoke little or no Spanish, and often seemed more American than Latino. The Chicano students often avoided helping or even talking to immigrant students. Many immigrant students refused to take bilingual English classes because many Chicano students took them. According to Marylu Garcia, "The Chicanos were not going to talk to the Mexicans unless the Mexicans went to them first. Both groups have a lot of pride, and neither group wants to give it up." Physical altercations in the hallways and the cafeteria were not uncommon. As teachers who were trying to unite and organize students, this realization troubled us.

When the Chicano students in Al's Latino-American History class began taking action, Ryan began encouraging his immigrant students to get involved. Soon a handful of members of both groups began reaching out to the other group, making a point to involve each other in discussions, saying hello in the hallways. Maria Vital, an immigrant student, credits Estela Cabrera, a Chicana student, with helping to break down barriers: "Estela is one of the girls who can speak English with Chicanos and Spanish with immigrants. She talked to everybody and introduced immigrants to Chicanos."

Estela began hanging out in Ryan's ESL classroom between classes, chatting in Spanish with immigrant students. Marylu gives credit to Xavier Marquez, saying that members of both

> State and local lawmakers delivered statements in support of extending educational opportunities to undocumented immigrant students.

groups feel that they are better than members of the other group and that they have to be like Xavier—"willing to talk to everybody." Not surprisingly, Estela, Xavier, and other students who reached out were eventually elected to leadership positions, treasurer and president, respectively, and are now working together to promote the club to both Chicanos and immigrants. This is not to say that the rift has been totally healed, because it hasn't. But where a year ago there was no collaboration at all, we are now seeing friendships form.

For immigrant students, action on immigrant issues has obvious and immediate importance. It is also important to the families of the Chicano students, who have either faced the same struggles, or know people who have. The leadership of Students United places a large importance on continuing to unite the club's members. Xavier says, "All Latinos face racism, both U.S. citizens and immigrants. When we unite we can finally make things better for ourselves, our community, and our country." Maria Vital says, "We have come together because we need to do things united."

The relationship between the school

and Latino students is also beginning to change. Horlick directing principal Starling-Ratliff says, "We have seen a dramatic reduction in the Latino suspension rate. [The students' activism] has broken down divisions among students and elevated the level of thinking. They talk and act on issues that are real to themselves and their communities."

Students United for Immigrant Rights leaders are now in hot demand, being actively recruited for leadership positions in other groups. Xavier has become a leader in student government, and took a very visible role in a fight to pass a school referendum. History teacher Jacqueline Loiacono saw Xavier in the hallway one day and invited him into her class to talk about harnessing anger to bring about positive change. She says, "He was in the hallway for a different reason, but he jumped right in. He was a life example of the community organizing that we had been discussing. The kids were just staring at him in awe. One student even wrote about him in her final exam, he made such an impression."

Student leaders are being recognized for their newfound skills and their mature attitudes and interpersonal communication skills, all of which they attribute to their involvement in Students United for Immigrant Rights. As Latino students have seen their peers in positions of leadership, they seem be taking more pride in their school, and realizing that being involved in school while trying to create change in society is actually a good thing. Viviana says,

> ### As Latino students have seen their peers in positions of leadership, they seem be taking more pride in their school.

"Supporting the rights of immigrant students has made students want to come to school more."

When Viviana developed the speech she later delivered to Wisconsin legislators, members of advocacy groups, and the general public, she worked as hard—and with as much pride—as she would have on any term paper or presentation. Her family drove 40 miles in the snow to hear her speak. She has earned the respect of her immigrant peers, Chicano students, and other students and staff, who previously knew her only as a student with limited English proficiency, struggling to succeed in school.

It seems to us that by helping students understand the struggles they face, and by teaching them to organize around those issues, we have earned the respect and trust of our students. As a result, many students have responded by improving their attendance, and increasing their dedication to academic success. As Marylu said, "Being involved in the club has helped me see that my weaknesses weren't as weak as I thought. The club helped me learn about my ability to make my voice heard." Marylu often comes to class with new information on immigration issues and asks if she can write about it, initiative that she rarely displayed before joining the club.

One of our most important goals in helping to organize Students United for Immigrant Rights was to involve Latino families in the school. The lack of involvement in school by Latino families was something that concerned teachers and administrators alike. Because we invite families to all Students United events, parents are beginning to get more involved and seem to feel more comfortable in a school setting. They also are encouraging their children to put more of a priority on education. Families seem excited about the possibilities that active involvement gives their children.

A shift was apparent when Al's job was on the line and many parents showed up at the Board of Education meeting to support him. It is now common for parents, even those who speak no English, to show up at Students United meetings. Some parents are as dedicated as their children, participating in every activity that Students United offers and volunteering to do more. One parent shows up at events that her children don't even attend.

Students United for Immigrant Rights continues to grow. We have started a chapter at Park High School in Racine. A few teachers from other districts have contacted us asking how they can set up similar organizations. Several events have increased the group's exposure, and the club attracts more students from more diverse backgrounds. At a recent cookout, it was encouraging to see so many students from different ethnic backgrounds coming for hotdogs and hamburgers, playing volleyball, and throwing water balloons. And, as a clipboard circulated, many students signed up to spend the first few weeks of summer break planning and taking action with Students United for Immigrant Rights. ∎

Ryan Knudson and Al Levie teach at William Horlick High School in Racine, Wis. For more information, visit www. immigrantrights.net.

PART SIX

RESOURCES

We can thoroughly "rethink our classrooms," but if we lack resources, we'll be less effective in turning our ideas into reality. In this chapter we offer lists of quality materials helpful to any teacher interested in promoting social justice. Do not be misled when we indicate that certain materials are oriented to age groups other than those you work with. High school students can benefit greatly from looking at books intended for younger children, while teachers can adapt more sophisticated materials for use with children in the lower grades.

We also include a teaching guide that offers ideas on how to use the poems throughout this book.

Poetry Teaching Guide

By Linda Christensen

Poetry is by turns playful, respectful, angry, and political. Because poetry is so closely related to music, it provides students an easy slide into writing. Advice? Leave the critic at the door until students feel connected and comfortable. After each assignment, ask students to circle up their desks and read-around their poems. (Sometimes cookies and milk make these special occasions—even in a high school classroom.)

Family Poems

Lineage, p. 205; Father Was a Musician, p. 83; Forgiving My Father, p. 35.

Family poems are a way for students to bring their homes and their lives into the classroom. They also provide an opportunity for students to praise a loved one—a mother, father, brother, aunt, grandparent, or someone who has played that role in their lives. Parent relationships are rarely easy, so allowing students a range of choices is helpful. Sometimes students have angry feelings that need to be expressed as well. "Forgiving My Father" might not praise a family member, but it is a legitimate expression of anger. Beginning poets often write "ghost poems"— vague poems full of abstractions about their love for their mother, friend, or pet. This poetry assignment forces them to become concrete by describing details from photographs, clothing their ghosts.

1. A few days before this activity tell students that they will be writing about a person in their family. (Be sensitive to the fact that some students may not have a traditional two-parent family.

Talk about how families might have different formations.) Encourage students to bring some pictures from home. The pictures should include family members they might want to write about. Some students will forget the pictures, but they can still write using the questions below as prompts.

2. As a warm-up, ask students to share their pictures in pairs or in small groups, depending on the size and comfort level of the class. This sharing will happen anyway; initiate it before the activity so it won't interrupt while students are writing.

3. Have students read the three poetry selections out loud. Sometimes it helps if you read the poetry first. Read with passion, then ask a student to read it again. Ask students, "What do we learn about this person? What lines show us what the person is like?" If students don't mention it themselves, I point out

how Walker indicates the kind of work her grandmothers did, the details about their hands, "smelling of soap and wet clay." Try to get them to note that she uses the sense of smell as well as the sense of sight. Watson uses sound. You might point out her use of language— "halting only to mend a chord or two." We don't literally mend music, but her words allow us to see her father going back over a musical passage.

4. Encourage students to remember details about their person. Ask: What do you remember them doing? Gardening? Cooking? Painting? Polishing the car? Fishing? Was there a certain dress, hat, shirt, style of pants that makes you remember them? Did they have any habits? Did they play with their glasses, smoke a pipe, burn the biscuits? Did they repeat sayings?

5. When their "pump is primed," turn off the lights in the classroom or find

some kind of signal to break from brainstorming to writing. It helps if you write too.

Praise Poems

My Hair Is Long, p. 18; what the mirror said, p. 76.

Many poets find it necessary to praise themselves because the standards of beauty in the dominant culture are European-American or set by the fashion industry. For example, Lucille Clifton and Maya Angelou praise big women—going against the norm of beauty that holds thinness as the standard. Writing praise poems gives students a positive way to look at themselves, but these poems also speak against the negative portrayals too often associated with their neighborhood, race, gender, nationality, size, school. Follow the guidelines for the parent poem, but ask students to write praise poems about themselves.

1. Ask students to think of something about themselves, their school, community, or culture that deserves praise, but may not receive it. Ask a few students to share ideas so they can help shake loose ideas for classmates.

2. Read "My Hair Is Long" out loud and have students look at the poet's list of comparisons. Ask what comparisons they would use to describe their hair, lips, eyes, hands. They might have their own pictures to look at while writing. (Poems and photos make a wonderful bulletin board.)

3. Older students like the sassy tone of Clifton's poem. They could look in mirrors and begin their poems, "what the mirror says." Sometimes students feel awkward praising themselves, but may find one attribute to praise.

Ballad/Story Poems

To the Young Who Want to Die, p. 186.

This is an angry poem. It shouts; there are no pretty pansies waiting to be picked here. This poem breaks students' stereotypes that poetry has to be

---

How to Do Read-Arounds

In *Rethinking Our Classrooms* we've talked a lot about students sharing their lives, but they need a safe space to start. The read-around is the classroom equivalent to quilt making or barn raising. It is the public space—the *zocolo* or town square—of my room. During our read-around, we socialize together and create community, but we also teach and learn from each other.

We always sit in a circle for the read-around, so every student is visible. At the beginning of the year, I ask students to write a compliment for each reader. I make it clear that no one is allowed to make critical comments about a paper. We focus on the positive—on what works. As each person reads, classmates take notes and give positive feedback to the writer. Sometimes, we formally hand out the notes to each writer. We also applaud each writer for having the courage to read in front of the class.

I require that all students read some assignments like the poem "Where I'm From" (see the Rethinking Schools book *Reading, Writing, and Rising Up*). I also offer to read pieces anonymously for shy or reluctant students. Some students are eager; their hands are always in the air. Other students are too cool; this is why I give them points for sharing. They can maintain their smooth façade, and act like they are just reading for the extra credit. Sometimes students want to share, but they need to be coaxed.

I ask students to respond to the content of the piece—what they like about the arguments, the ideas. They respond to its style. I ask them to be specific. What line, what phrase did they like? Did they like the imagery, the repetition? Instead of working on a deficit model—what's wrong with this piece—we work on a positive model: What's right? What can we learn from it?

During the read-around, students provide each other accessible models of writing. I encourage them to listen for what "works" in their peers' pieces, to take notes on what they like, and then to use those techniques in their own writing. During the read-around I point out particular writing strategies. I might note how Aaron used a list in his poem or how Brandon opened his essay with an anecdotal introduction.

I might ask Alisha to re-read a section of her essay so that we can notice her transitions. I do this consistently in each read-around to bring students' attention to the writers' tools.

Before we begin the read-around, I point out particular ways they can respond:

■ **Respond to the writer's style of writing.** What do you like about how the piece was written? Do you like the rhyme? The repeating lines? The humor? (Later, these points can change, particularly if you are focusing on a specific skill—like introductions, transitions, evidence, and imagery.)

■ **Respond to the writer's content.** What did the writer say that you liked? Did you like the way Ayanna used a story about her mother to point out how gender roles have changed?

■ **Respond by sharing a memory that surfaced for you.** Did you have a similar experience? Did this remind you of something from your life?

■ **As the writer reads, write down lines, ideas, words or phrases that you like. Remember: You must compliment the writer.**

about "lovely" things.

1. Ask students to read the poem out loud. This makes for dramatic reading. You might give it to students to read in advance so they can practice. This poem is even better if students can memorize and act it out.

2. After the poem is read, ask for reactions. What's going on in the poem? Ask someone to summarize the "story" of the poem. You might even ask how this poem differs from "typical" poems.

3. Ask students to make two columns on their paper. (It helps to model this on the board or overhead.) At the top of one column write: People Who Make Me Angry; at the top of the other write: Things That Make Me Angry. You might write down a few items under each category to get them started.

4. Ask them to circle one or two of the topics. Some students may be able to write their poems at this point. Others might need to get more details. Have them write it first as a letter. They can put the name of the person at the beginning, "Dear Aunt Macy" or "Dear Joe Camel" or "Dear Budget Cutters," then write why they are angry. Encourage them to tell the story. "I am angry because ..."

5. Encourage or demonstrate how to cut a paragraph down to a poem by lining it out and picking out their best lines or details for the poem. Sometimes it helps to work with a partner.

Ancestor/Heritage Poems

To My People with Retinitis Pigmentosa, p. 51; In Memory of Crossing the Columbia, p. 172; Lineage, p. 205.
Students belong to many intersecting communities: family, school, region, race, nationality, sports, and as Jim Jackson demonstrates, even the community of people who share a disease. This poetry lesson invites students to talk about their particular history. It's especially powerful during a unit on families or autobiography.

1. Begin by asking students to describe all of the communities they belong to. Then ask them to list those communities. Model this on the board with your own diverse memberships. Students might share their lists as a way of expanding ideas.

2. Ask for volunteers to read the poetry aloud. Read the poems through at least twice.

3. After reading each poem, talk about it. What community did this writer describe? Do they have a sense of why heritage is important to the poet? Note the strong imagery in Elizabeth Woody's description of her heritage. She recalls the location as well as her ties to her Navajo ancestors.

4. Ask students to choose one of the communities they noted and list some ideas about it. Some students who belong to more than one racial group may choose to write about that. Robert Smith, a senior at Jefferson High School, wrote: "What are you if you're not black and you're not white?/ I am both, so how could I choose just one?/... I am not a blank space between black and white .../I am a black man who has never touched the sands of Africa./I am a European looking for riches./ I am a slave stripped away from his home .../I am the red faces who walked the Trail of Tears./ I am my mother's father whose face is covered by a white hood./ I am the German soldier who spilled my Jewish blood./ I am the South African Republic that beat my black grandmother. ..."

Dialogue Poems

Honeybees, p. 55; Two Women, p. 128.
Dialogue poems are effective to use where controversy or different opinions might arise: a plantation owner and an enslaved person, Hiroshima bomb victim and an Enola Gay pilot.

But the poem can also point out similarities between people who might not appear to have much in common on the surface: for example, a Salvadoran immigrant and an African American whose family migrated from the South. The dialogue poem also works with literature. While studying *Grapes of Wrath*, for example, students could write a dialogue between the machines pushing over homes and the families forced off their lands.

1. Before class starts, choose two students to prepare a dramatic reading. Assign one student the bold-faced part, the other student the regular typeface.

2. Read the poem as a dialogue. To convey the power of the poem, the student readers can stand in opposite corners of the room and, in full voice, recite the lines back and forth.

3. Distribute copies of the poem to the entire class. If you are using "Two Women," provide students some background information about Chile to explain the references in the poem.

4. Elicit response to the poem. Discuss what makes it so powerful. Point out the subtle differences in lines—how even the addition of one or two words underscores the deep inequality of the two women's lives: "We had to eat rice"—"We had rice."

5. As a group, brainstorm possible topics for a unit you are currently studying. Think about what the different pairs might say. Model the first few lines of a dialogue poem by eliciting lines from the students on a common topic. In partners or alone, write dialogue poems based on the content studied in class. ■

Videos

Unless otherwise noted, these films are available in video stores (though sometimes it requires a bit of hunting) and are appropriate for students in high school and, in many cases, middle school. Many are available from Teaching for Change, www.teaching forchange.org.

Battle of Algiers (121 min.)

This is a troubling film that describes the Algerian struggle against French colonialism. Made just a few years after independence, the film features many of the actual participants of the war and only one professional actor, in the role of a French military official in Algiers. Although it would be a mistake to view the film as a celebration of terrorism, the film certainly demands that the audience consider the causes of terrorism. *Battle of Algiers* has now been released as a box-set of DVDs that includes several helpful background

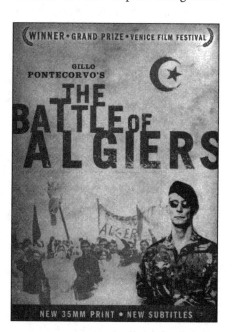

documentaries on the making of the film, its social context, and the impact the film had after its release.

Breaker Morant (approx. 115 min.)

A feature film about the Australian role in the Boer War in South Africa. However, the issues it raises allow us to use it during a unit on Vietnam. Three Australians are tried for war crimes against white Afrikaner civilians. The film poses questions about the culpability of individuals caught in an evil enterprise of "empire building."

Hearts and Minds (112 min.)

This powerful Academy Award–winning documentary about the war in Vietnam is a metaphorical collage of interviews, battle footage, and daily life. Students need a good deal of background about the war prior to viewing, but if they're prepared, it can be an extraordinarily rich resource. Some of the scenes and individuals are unforgettable, as our students, years later, testify. Note: A scene in a Saigon brothel is sexually explicit. The filmmakers included it in part to explore the war's effect on Vietnamese women, as well as U.S. soldiers' attitudes towards these women.

Eyes on the Prize—Fighting Back: 1957–1962 and
Eyes on the Prize—A Nation of Law? 1968–1971
(60 min. each)

The entire PBS *Eyes on the Prize* series on the history of the Civil Rights Movement is worthwhile. These two episodes are especially dramatic ones. The first recounts the struggle to desegregate Central High School in Little Rock,

Breaker Morant.

Ark., and the University of Mississippi. The second covers the police murder of Chicago Black Panther leader Fred Hampton and the Attica Prison uprising in New York state. *Fighting Back* is a compelling mixture of documentary footage and candid interviews with participants. Our students are particularly moved by the stories of the youngsters who volunteered to integrate Central High and are amazed and outraged at the vicious resistance they encountered.

In 1969, FBI chief J. Edgar Hoover labeled the Black Panther Party the number-one threat to the internal security of the United States. The FBI called the Panthers' free breakfast for children program a "nefarious activity." *A Nation of Law?* is a troubling video about established authority's concept of "order" and the measures it will take to preserve that order.

Modern Times.

The Killing Floor (118 min.)

Two African-American men migrate from the country to Chicago during World War I and work in a packing house. They respond differently to the challenges presented. The film deals forthrightly and effectively with racism in the workplace and the union and ends with the 1919 riots and their aftermath.

Matewan (100 min.)

John Sayles's feature film about a strike in a mining town in Appalachia. Mine owners bring in black workers in an attempt to break the strike. Can Italian immigrants, white Appalachians, and African Americans work together? Should they even bother to try? An engaging and well-crafted film. (The short essay "Why Matewan?" from John Sayles's book *Thinking in Pictures: The Making of the Movie Matewan* can also be used in class.)

Modern Times (85 min.)

We use only the first 20 minutes of this Chaplin classic in a unit on the history of work and workers. It's a wonderful resource to discuss the psychological effects of assembly line work. In one hilarious scene, Chaplin as the Little Tramp is assaulted by an automatic

Video Teaching Strategies

By Bill Bigelow and Linda Christensen

In Portland, Ore., we have a network of informal video lending libraries. Teachers call each other to locate videos and DVDs that can offer our classes an added dimension of humanity and immediacy—"What do you have on South Africa/the women's movement/Vietnam?" It's not unusual to discover a wonderful resource, totally new to us, that has been in someone's curriculum for years.

Different videos lend themselves to different teaching strategies. We've found announcing the assignment before viewing helps keep students focused and better prepares them for post-viewing discussion. Here are a few of the activities we've initiated using some of the "videos with a conscience" listed here.

Interior Monologue

With students, we brainstorm the dilemmas or choices faced by various characters in a movie: Frank, in *The Killing Floor*, when he decides to cross the picket line set up by white union members; Danny, in *Matewan*, when company thugs threaten to kill him if he reveals their plans; Breaker Morant, when he is convicted of war

crimes; Molly, in *A World Apart*, when her mother is "detained" by South African police; etc. Students then write a character's interior monologue—that individual's thoughts and feelings during a particular event. Afterwards, in a circle, we encourage students to read their pieces and suggest that they take notes on a particular question. For example, with *A World Apart*, students can reflect on how people in South Africa maintained their hope in the face of such enormous injustice. The question or questions posed allow students to draw additional insights from the group portrait of the collected interior monologues. See p. 126 for more on interior monologues.

Poetry

Instead of, or in addition to, interior monologues, students can be encouraged to write poems. Our student Mira wrote, "Poetry made history come to life. When we wrote after [the film on the Vietnam war] *Hearts and Minds*, I was there. I was a soldier. I identified with what was going on. I felt their feelings. I got more involved. This wasn't just history. This was life. Poetry helped me examine

why the war happened because I got inside the people who witnessed it." In *Hearts and Minds*, we asked students to note powerful images or quotes from the people interviewed. Afterwards, students shared a number of these and we distributed a sheet of film quotes that we'd collected. We then offered a series of poems to suggest different structures students might borrow. Several of these were from Yusef Komunyakaa's *Dien Cai Dau*, and Vietnamese poems from the anthology *Of Quiet Courage*.

We followed the read-around of students' pieces with a discussion of the issues raised. The result was a much higher degree of student empathy than had we simply discussed the film without writing, or assigned the writing without giving students a chance to hear each other's pieces.

Critique

With films like *The Santa Fe Trail* or cartoons like *Peter Pan*, *Beauty and the Beast*, or *The Little Mermaid*, we distribute "critical viewing" questions for students to think about. For example:

1. Who makes decisions?

eating machine being tested by the company in an attempt to make the workday more efficient. This excerpt is also useful to prompt students to reflect on how the structure of the workplace affects workers' relationships with each other.

Remember My Lai (60 min.)

This is an extraordinary documentary about the My Lai massacre that first aired as a PBS "Frontline." This is much more complex and morally riveting than a simple retelling of what happened. Interviewed are participants, both U.S. and Vietnamese. Sig-

nificantly, and rarely mentioned, some Americans disobeyed orders that day. Who they were and what they did is included here. (Check libraries—not available from PBS.)

Salt of the Earth (94 min.)

Made in 1953, and set in "Zinctown, New Mexico," *Salt of the Earth* uses a combination of actors and nonprofessional community people to tell its story. And a great story it is. Sparked by a mine accident, the workers, mostly Mexican Americans, go on strike. Safety is the issue, but is inextricably linked with racial discrimination as Anglo

miners work in pairs, while Mexican Americans are forced to work alone.

But this is especially a feminist story, as women insist that their issues for indoor plumbing and hot water in the company-owned housing also be included as a demand of the all-male union. This struggle comes to a head as Esperanza, wife of one of the strike activists, confronts her husband, Ramon, about his failure to treat her as an equal: "Have you learned nothing from this strike? Why are you afraid to have me at your side? … Do you feel better having someone lower than you? Whose neck shall I stand on to make

---

2. Who follows orders?

3. Who speaks?

4. Who is silent?

5. What causes conflict and how is it solved?

6. What role does money and/or material possessions play in the story/history?

7. What roles are women, men, people of color, the differently abled, working-class people, and the poor given?

8. Why do you think the video contains the biases that it does? Who benefits and who suffers from the images and values promoted in this video?

The last question is a difficult one, but it's important that as we teach students critical skills, we encourage them to think about the deeper "why?" questions, encourage them to push beyond simply describing what may be wrong with a given piece of media. In this instance, raising the question is more important than arriving at the "correct" answer. After viewing, we may discuss the film based on these questions or we might encourage them to write from their observations. Using their notes, drawing on experiences in their own lives, and incorporating insights from readings, students can write critical essays. Another possibility is to allow students to reconstruct a

given story from a more equitable, more multicultural standpoint.

Trial

A number of the films included here deal with violations of human rights, discrimination, and bigotry: homophobia and anti-gay violence in *The Times of Harvey Milk*; the unprovoked murder of Black Panthers Fred Hampton and Mark Clark in *Eyes on the Prize*; the imprisonment and abuse of political prisoners by British authorities in northern Ireland; and the massacre of civilians in *Remember My Lai*. Determining "guilt" can encourage students to reflect on complex ethical, political, and historical questions. For example, in *Remember My Lai*, we divide the class into five groups representing Lt. Calley, U.S. soldiers who carried out Calley's orders to shoot civilians, Lt. Calley's superior officers, the Vietnamese National Liberation Front, and the "system," as represented by U.S. corporate and government leaders. They all stand accused of the murder of innocent civilians at My Lai, and each group gets an indictment listing charges against them. The teacher plays the prosecutor. Each "defendant" is prosecuted and argues against the charges, at times pointing an accusing finger at one or more of the other groups. Stepping out of their

roles, students assign amounts of guilt or innocence to each group. Who's responsible? The ones who pulled the triggers? The ones who gave the orders? The ones who sent them there in the first place?

Tea Party

Some films require more concentration or background than others, and a "tea party" activity can work well as a pre-viewing activity. For example, the film *Battle of Algiers*, about Algerian resistance to French colonialism, is in black and white, is subtitled and actually begins at the end of the story before it circles back. As an introduction to the individuals and issues students will encounter in the film, we distribute short roles of some of the characters—e.g., Ali la Pointe, the criminal-turned-revolutionary who attacks French authorities in Algiers; and Col. Phillipe Mathieu, the French commander who designs the ruthless counterinsurgency campaign against the Algerian nationalists. In role, students encounter some of the key individuals they will meet in the film and get a preview of the film's drama and difficult moral issues. For more on the use of tea parties, see the Rethinking Schools books *Reading, Writing and Rising Up* (p. 115), *Rethinking Our Classrooms, Vol. 2* (p. 37); and *The Line Between Us* (p. 43).

me feel superior? … I want to rise and push everything up as I go."

Salt of the Earth celebrates the possibility of people being able to create a very different, very much better society through solidarity and collective action. When we first showed the film a number of years ago, we worried that students would be put-off by a black-and-white film that had quite a bit of amateurish acting and melodramatic music. We were wrong. What the film lacks in polish, it more than makes up for in substance. And most students recognize that. [See S. J. Childs's article on the use of this film with her students, p. 141.]

Santa Fe Trail (approx. 100 min.)

Starring Errol Flynn, Ronald Reagan, and Olivia de Haviland, this 1940 film slanders the Abolition movement and John Brown. Errol Flynn, as the future Confederate general Jeb Stuart, is the good guy who throughout the film maintains that the South will solve its problems if only left alone to work them out. We use the film during a unit on U.S. slavery and slave resistance to encourage students to critique the ways the media can manipulate history.

Some Mother's Son (112 min.)

From start to finish, students are riveted by this poignant dramatization of the hunger strikes initiated by imprisoned Irish Republican Army members in 1981. Based on true events, it explores the struggle in Northern Ireland from the standpoint of two mothers of IRA prisoners, each of whom responds very differently to her son's political involvement and incarceration. Although this film was unfairly slapped with an R rating for some harsh language and violence, this should not deter teachers who want to expose students to the complexities of the Irish "Troubles."

Thousand Pieces of Gold (105 min.)

This feature film is a generally decent adaptation of Ruthann Lum McCunn's novel about Lalu Nathoy, a Chinese-American pioneer woman. Set in the 1870s on the West Coast, *Thousand Pieces of Gold* subtly compares Lalu's situation and the legal status of Chinese Americans with the enslavement of African Americans. We combine the video with the novel, some pieces from *The Big Aiiieeee!, The Forbidden Stitch,* and *Making Waves: An Anthology of Writings by and About Asian American Women.*

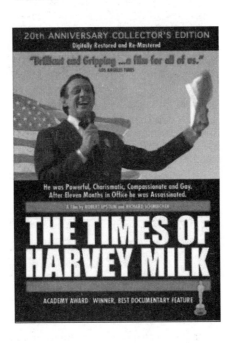

The Times of Harvey Milk (90 min.)

A sad but inspirational look at the life and death of San Francisco Supervisor Harvey Milk and at the gay rights movement. Milk was the first openly gay elected official in the United States. This is a good film to begin to chip away at students' homophobia. It's personal, funny, sad, and infuriating.

Union Maids (55 min.) and Seeing Red (100 min.)

Two documentaries, both nominated for Academy Awards, from filmmakers Jim Klein and Julia Reichert. With interviews, music, and archival footage, *Union Maids* tells the story of three women who helped build industrial unions in the 1930s and 1940s. The three are great storytellers. It's lively history, a must-use. With more characters, but with the same humor and drama, *Seeing Red* chronicles the rise and fall of the U.S. Communist Party. It's hard to imagine teaching about the McCarthy period without using this film.

A World Apart (114 min.)

A feature film based on the life of white South African Ruth First—a member of the then-outlawed African National Congress. It's especially effective with students in high school and middle school because the events are seen largely through the eyes of First's daughter, who appears to be about twelve. Some background is necessary, but the film effectively explores the terrain of government repression, the risks of political activism, and the toll on the life of one family. So many of the commercial films on South Africa have white protagonists—*A Dry White Season* and *Cry Freedom,* for example—but given that limitation, we think this may be the best of them.

In addition to the videos listed above, children's cartoon stories—such as *Peter Pan, The Little Mermaid, Beauty and the Beast, Popeye,* and *Snow White*—are useful in prompting students of all ages to think about social messages imparted in different media. Because no student feels that a cartoon is over his or her head, it's a student-friendly medium that helps kids develop critical thinking skills. Some of the older cartoons are even more helpful in this respect, as they do not have the multicultural veneer of some of the more recent Hollywood cartoon releases. See "Critique," above.

—Bill Bigelow and Linda Christensen

Books for Young People

Contributors to Rethinking Our Classrooms *recommended these books for addressing social justice themes with students.*

Early Childhood

Recommended by Ann Pelo, an early childhood educator at Hilltop Early Childhood Center in Seattle:

Swimmy, by Leo Lionni. New York: Knopf Children's Paperbacks, 1963. Swimmy is a fish, left alone, sad, and afraid after his companions are eaten by a much larger fish. After a lonely stretch of time, he comes across a school of fish just like his own. They're not swimming, though, but hiding behind rocks and weeds, afraid of being eaten. Swimmy organizes the fish, teaching them to swim together in the shape of a giant fish. Together they travel the ocean, unafraid of the bigger fish because of their collective power. This simple story is a jumping-off point for conversations with very young children about the power of organizing as a community, strategizing together to overcome challenges, and pooling effort and resources.

The Streets Are Free / La calle es libre, by Kurusa, illustrated by Monika Doppert. Toronto: Annick, 1985. Children in a crowded barrio in Caracas, Venezuela have no place to play tag, soccer, baseball, or leapfrog. They try to play in the streets, but are scolded by adults aware of the danger. "The streets are free!" the children protest. Their collective anger and determination lead them to city hall, where they ask that an

abandoned lot be converted to a park and playground. The children's bold act rallies their community. Eventually, the city bureaucrats concede and the empty lot is given to them, and everyone works together to create the park. This book is based on the true story of the San Jose de la Urbina in Caracas. When I read it with young children, we talk about the importance of naming injustice collectively and working with a community to create change. Children are dazzled by this story of the power of children, often exclaiming, "This really happened, right?"

Sí, Se Puede! / Yes, We Can! Janitors Strike in L.A., by Diana Cohn, illustrated by Francisco Delgado. El Paso, Texas: Cinco Puntos Press, 2002. Carlitos's mother is a janitor in Los Angeles who becomes active in the Justice for Janitors campaign. When the campaign organizes a strike, the mother becomes a community leader. At school, Carlitos discovers that some of the other children's parents are also on strike. He suggests to his teacher that they make a trip to the picket line. When the day

of their trip arrives, Carlitos is proud to join the strikers, holding his sign, "I love my Mama. She is a janitor." His mother continues to work with Justice for Janitors after her own strike is settled. This story makes visible both the people who clean offices and hotels and the movement for justice for janitors and other low-income workers. It introduces young children to these people and opens questions for them to consider: Who cleans our building? Are they treated fairly? Why don't we ever see them? Can we meet them? It also sparks conversations about the power of collective political action and organized campaigns. It includes an essay by Luis J. Rodriguez.

Freedom Summer, by Deborah Wiles. New York: Atheneum Books, 2001. This potent story of the friendship between an African-American boy and a white boy unfolds in the deep South as civil rights legislation is enacted. Joe and John Henry are eager to swim together in the town pool now that desegregation laws have been passed. The boys are stunned when they arrive at the pool to see it being filled in with cement. This moment is a turning point for both boys, and arm-in-arm they take a bold step into anti-racist activism. When I read this with preschoolers, we tell the story sometimes from Joe's perspective and sometimes from John Henry's perspective, to give the kids opportunities to experience the injustice of racism and the power of activism from the vantage points of white people and African Americans.

Recommended by Katie Kissinger, an early childhood consultant in Boring, Oreg.:

Skin Again, by bell hooks, illustrated by Chris Raschka. New York: Hyperion / Jump at the Sun, 2004. This is a picture book with limited words and a powerful message, which makes it usable with very young children all the way through adults. It is my favorite book to read as a closing to my workshops about having important and more comfortable conversations with children about skin color differences. bell hooks's primary message in *Skin Again* is that we all have different colors of skin that we can feel great about, but "skin is only a covering, it cannot tell our story." The book is another wonderful gift from the woman who has written so much about liberatory education and teaching for freedom with adults.

(Editors' note: Don't forget Kissinger's excellent bilingual book, All the Colors We Are: The Story of How We Get Our Skin Color, *Redleaf Press, 1994.)*

Elementary School

Recommended by Mary Cowhey, who teaches 2nd grade at Jackson Street School in Northampton, Mass.:

I Will Be Your Friend: Songs and Activities for Young Peacemakers, book and CD. Montgomery, Ala.: Teaching Tolerance, 2003. This book and CD contain 23 activities and 26 great songs, including "1492," "Paz y Libertad," "What Can One Little Person Do?" and "Freedom, Oh Freedom." Although I can't carry a tune (the CD bails me out), I recognize the power of singing songs about friendship, peace, freedom and the struggle for justice both in the streets and in the classroom. I go back to this resource again and again all year. It is available for free from www. teachingtolerance.org.

Peace Begins with You, by K. Scholes. San Francisco: Sierra Club Books, 1990. This is a gentle, soft-spoken, but powerful book about peace that I use with my 1st- and 2nd-graders. It addresses the reality of human conflict, from the personal level of family and friends to the global level. It talks honestly about the need to negotiate and compromise and shows that solutions are not easy to reach or perfect but are a better choice than violence.

Hey, Little Ant!, by Phillip and Hannah Hoose. Berkeley, Calif.: Tricycle Press, 1998. This humorously illustrated story, written in verse, depicts a debate between a boy who is about to squish an ant on the sidewalk and an ant, who thinks he shouldn't do it. The two parts can be sung as a song or done as a great choral reading. I use this story with 1st- and 2nd-graders as well as adults, as a springboard for philosophical discussions about the nature of power.

Recommended by Rachel Cloues, who teaches 4th grade at Sanchez Elementary School in San Francisco:

The Librarian of Basra: A True Story from Iraq, by Jeanette Winter. San Diego, Calif.: Harcourt, 2004. This beautiful, illustrated story of a dedicated librarian in war-torn Iraq speaks to me and my students of the devastating effects of war and the power of

hope and community. It is an incredibly accessible story with which to prompt discussions of war and peace, education, and democracy. I like to share it with my class before we visit a public or school library because it reminds us all of how lucky we are to have access to books and education.

A Day's Work, by Eve Bunting, illustrated by Ronald Himler. New York: Houghton Mifflin / Clarion, 1994. A teacher concerned with social justice can never go wrong with a book by Eve Bunting! This one is a heart-rending story of Francisco, who lives in California, and his recently arrived (and presumably undocumented) grandfather, who speaks only Spanish. Bunting gracefully addresses the difficulty of being a day worker, including such issues as fair pay, honesty, pride, and respect. As the interpreter, Francisco lies to their employer about his grandfather's gardening experience in order to get them hired. They mistakenly pull up plants instead of weeds and must make amends in order to earn their pay. This is a sophisticated story with many angles and perspectives to explore with children at almost any grade level. My 4th-grade students, mostly immigrants themselves, sympathize with Francisco's hard job as an interpreter for adults.

The People Shall Continue, by Simon Ortiz, illustrated by Sharol Graves. San Francisco: Children's Book Press, 1988. An honest overview of Native American history told in a rhythmic style suggesting the oral traditions of the people whose story it is. Beginning with a combination of creation myths and presenting a Native perspective of historical events in the United States up to the present day, *The People Shall Continue* is an excellent read-aloud for classes learning about U.S. history, Native America, and different tribes. In my classes, students have discussed and dramatized various parts of the story. I like to read this book as an introduction and conclusion to units about Native America.

The Sneetches and Other Stories, by Dr. Seuss. New York: Random House, 1961. A classic and perhaps overlooked story for teaching about racism, discrimination, and/or peer pressure. The playful Sneetches finally learn that whether or not they have "stars upon thars," they all share the same beach and must get along with one another. I like to emphasize Sylvester McMonkey McBean's role as a businessman capitalizing on the Sneetches' low self-image and connect the story to units on advertising and economics.

This short story never fails to generate discussion about treating people fairly no matter what they look like.

Recommended by Kelley Dawson Salas, who teaches 4th grade at La Escuela Fratney in Milwaukee, Wis., and is an editor of Rethinking Schools *magazine:*

América Is Her Name / La llaman América, by Luis Rodríguez, illustrated by Carlos Vázquez. Willimantic, Conn.: Curbstone Press, 1998. América is a girl from Oaxaca, Mexico, who has moved to Chicago and is floundering in school. She hears her teacher tell another teacher she's "illegal" and gets the idea that she doesn't belong in the United States. After a guest poet visits América's class, she begins to find her voice by writing about her experiences back home, but her father ridicules her work, telling her it's no use since she'll spend her life cleaning, working, and raising kids. América continues to write anyway, and eventually achieves academic success and a sense of belonging. I find this story useful for helping students question stereotypes of immigrants and encouraging children to think broadly about their possibilities in life.

My Name Is Jorge on Both Sides of the River, by Jane Medina, illustrated by Fabricio Vanden Broeck. Honesdale, Pa.: Boyds Mills Press, 1999. This bilingual poetry book shares common themes in immigrant children's lives through the experiences of the narrator, Jorge. Jorge makes friends with English- and Spanish-speaking kids at his new school, tries new foods offered to him by his Anglo peers, and feels proud when he recites poetry to his class. He also wonders why his grades are worse in the United States than in Mexico, feels insulted when a classmate calls his English-as-a-second-language class "Mexican dummy time," and leaves the public library without a library card after the librarian insults his mom for being illiterate. A moving, engaging, and funny book that helps students explore the joys and difficulties in the lives of immigrant children.

Friends from the Other Side / Amigos del otro lado, by Gloria Anzaldúa, illustrated by Consuelo Méndez. San Francisco: Children's Book Press, 1993. In this bilingual book, a Mexican-American girl named Prietita befriends a recent Mexican immigrant named Joaquín. She stands up to her cousin and his friends when they tell Joaquín, "Go back where you came from." When the Border Patrol comes looking for "illegals," she hides Joaquín and his mom so they won't be caught. I use this book to help students learn about xenophobia and how to be an ally.

Recommended by Bob Peterson, who teaches 5th grade at La Escuela Fratney in Milwaukee, Wis., and is an editor of Rethinking Schools *magazine:*

The Captive, by Joyce Hansen. New York: Scholastic, 1994. Inspired by the true story *The Life of Olaudah Equiano or Gustavus Vass, the African*, this book is written from the perspective of a young African who is kidnapped and

brought to New England and struggles to return to his homeland. I use this in literature circles every year with my 5th-graders, who find it fast-paced and riveting. The story is rich in historical detail. The first several chapters are set in Africa and help pierce stereotypes of what Africa was like in the 17th and 18th centuries. A secondary character, a white indentured servant, allows for comparisons between the oppression of enslaved Africans and poor whites. For an extension activity, I use Virginia Hamilton's retelling of Equiano's story in *The People Could Fly* and Tom Feeling's amazing drawings in *The Middle Passage*. *The Capitve* is also great to use a whole-class read-aloud.

Dragon's Gate, by Laurence Yep. New York: Harper Collins, 1993. I use this book in literature circles when my 5th-grade class studies immigration and/or post–Civil War American history. The main character is a Chinese youth who comes to America in search of the "golden mountain," only to be thrown into the intolerable working conditions of building the transcontinental railroad. Issues of racism, working-class solidarity, unions, and courage are all bound up in a beautifully written novel that my students love. The richness of the story offers many extension ideas. One that has been particularly effective for me is to have the students assume they are the main character and write back to their mother (who stayed in China) about life in the new America. This is part of Yep's *Golden Mountain Chronicles*; the other one I'd highly recommend is *The Traitor*, which takes place in Wyoming in 1885 and tells the story of the conflict between white and Chinese miners.

The Fragile Flag, by Jane Langton. New York: Harper and Row, 1984. Often, the children in my 5th-grade classroom want to do something about the injustices that come to light when we discuss a current event issue or other subject. *The Fragile Flag* is a modern-day fantasy in which a group of children lead a massive march on the White House to stop the new "Peace Missile." It's a great chapter book to read as a read-aloud or in literature circles. For extension activities, I have students discuss the book in the context of past and present peace movements, the military budget, and the role of children in past social movements—using video *The Children's March* (available from Teaching Tolerance), which highlights the children's role in the 1963 Birmingham civil rights struggle.

Richard Wright and the Library Card, by William Miller, illustrated by Gregory Christie. New York: Lee & Low Books, 1997. A wonderfully illustrated book that describes the great African-American author Richard Wright's attempt to get access to all-white libraries. I use this book as a read-aloud at the beginning of the school year to spark a discussion of the importance of reading and how social movements and struggles have been necessary to secure the right to access libraries

and schools. I also tell the story of the struggle of women to get an education, using the example of Elizabeth Blackwell, who had to fight her way into medical school in the mid-1840s. This book is also a good way to introduce Wright's works to older students.

High School

Recommended by Linda Christensen, who teaches 11th and 12th grades at Grant High School in Portland, Oregon, and is an editor of Rethinking Schools *magazine:*

Hope Was Here, by Jane Bauer. New York: Penguin / Puffin, 2002. I look for books that honor blue-collar work. *Hope Was There*, an adolescent novel by Joan Bauer, not only respects waitresses, it also demonstrates how high school students can become political activists. Hope, the main character in Bauer's novel, raises waitressing to both a religion and an art. She understands how to connect with people through service. She doesn't dismiss the importance of her work or underestimate the humanity of her customers. But Bauer's novel is about more than waitressing. It's also about a high school girl whose mother and father abandoned her and about young people who work to elect a short-order cook as mayor of Mulhoney, Wis. I could see using this novel with 5th-grade through high school students as a precursor to a unit on working for change in a school or a community. This book is hopeful. In an age of despair, we need to give students models for how to make change.

Kindred, by Octavia Butler. Boston: Beacon Press, 1979. I have used *Kindred* in a variety of ways over the years in American Literature—both as a stand-alone text and as part of a slavery/resistance literature circle. Butler, an award-winning novelist, uses elements of science fiction to transport

Dana, an African-American woman who lives in California in 1976, to save her white ancestor. Butler examines how slavery destroys both blacks and whites, but through her storytelling she also examines literacy, gender roles, power and resistance. My 11th- and 12th-grade students find the work compelling to read; however, the novel contains vivid depictions of violence, racism, and racial epithets.

Spoken Soul, by John Rickford and Russell Rickford. New York: John Wiley & Sons, 2000. Although *Spoken Soul* tells the story of African-American Vernacular English (Ebonics), it reads like a novel. I use chapters of the book during my unit on the politics of language, but I also use it when I teach *Their Eyes Were Watching God* and *Fences*.

Thousand Pieces of Gold, by Ruthann Lum McCunn. Boston: Beacon, 2004. This historical novel tells the story of Lalu/Polly—a Chinese woman who is sold/stolen into slavery. I like the way McCunn marries history and fiction, teaching students about Chinese exclusion laws and Chinese immigration into the Northwest during the late

1800s. The strength of this book is its thematic development of social justice issues including gender equality and slavery. This book can be used with grades 10, 11, and 12.

Warriors Don't Cry, by Melba Patillo Beals. New York: Simon & Schuster, 1995. In this autobiography, Melba Patillo Beals, one of the Little Rock students who integrated Central High School in 1957, recounts her struggle to overcome segregation and institutionalized racism. Blending adult commentary with teenage experience, this book hooks students into one of the most compelling civil rights battles in our nation's history. The text reads easily, but does not spare the details of the physical and psychological abuse suffered. I love teaching this book. I use it in high school, but it could be used in middle school as well. One caution is that racial epithets are used in the text.

Various Ages

Recommended by Leonore Gordon, a social worker who works with children in New York City:

Rising Voices: Writings of Young Native Americans, edited by Arlene Hirschfelder and Beverly R. Singer. New York: Atheneum Books, 1992. This gem of a book contains poetry written by young American Indian poets ranging from early elementary school through high school. Through the the candid, poignant voices of the poets in *Rising Voices*, a landscape emerges of racism, past and present, towards the Native peoples; thus, many of the poems became a spur to class discussion about chunks of American history not taught often enough. I have used this book countless times to teach low-income, mostly black and Hispanic 5th- and 6th-graders in Brooklyn, N.Y. The poems offer a powerful glimpse into their authors' lives, and the read-

ings are short enough to leave time for discussion about the issues raised. My students have exchanged letters, poems, books, and even food with these poets, whose environments range from the red soil of New Mexico to the lakes of northern Minnesota. My students' poems about their surroundings stood in stark contrast to the poems written by their pen-pals about watching eagles fly across open fields.

Funny Boy, by Shyam Selvadurai. New York: Harcourt, 1997. This book is a "double-feature": As a history lesson, it tracks the emergence and explosion of tensions within Sri Lanka through the eyes of a young boy. As a "coming-out story," it depicts his shift from childhood games to early-adolescent awareness of his attraction to other boys. This tender, sensitive view of the world of a Sri Lankan boy who prefers play-acting weddings to playing baseball reveals how a civil war affects young people who are already busy enough trying to get through childhood and adolescence. It also teaches about the terrible consequences visited upon

families during civil war. Sound familiar? Sudan? Romeo and Juliet? Darfur? Iraq? We'd better get to work helping our students communicate across cultures as early as possible! This novel opens a doorway to dialogue about differences of all kinds with our middle school and high school charges.

She Would Not Be Moved: How We Tell the Story of Rosa Parks and the Montgomery Bus Boycott, by Herbert Kohl. New York: The New Press, 2005. Essential reading, especially for elementary school teachers who year after year pass on to their impressionable students an image of Rosa Parks as a weary older black woman who just decides she finally has to sit down, and then, presto!, the birth of a civil rights movement. Kohl blows this all into the sky as he tells the real story of Rosa Parks and the organized planning of a whole community that preceded the actual day of Parks's refusal to get up from a seat intended for a white person. The best part? We gain even more admiration for the late, great, indomitable Mrs. Parks.

Curricula and Teaching Resources

All of the following resources are available from Teaching for Change, www.teachingforchange.org, 800-763-9131. All starred resources are also available from Rethinking Schools, www.rethinkingschools.org, 800-669-4192.

Affirming Diversity: The Sociopolitical Context of Multicultural Education, Second Edition, Sonia Nieto. White Plains, N.Y.: Longman, 1996. Of the scores of books on multicultural education, Nieto's is one worth reading. The central message of this 422-page book is that multicultural education is essential to promote the academic achievement of students of color; it is a message that comes through powerfully in her clear explanations of related issues of bilingual education and critical pedagogy and her numerous case studies that give voice to students of different backgrounds.

Anti-Bias Curriculum: Tools for Empowering Young Children, Louise Derman-Sparks and the A.B.C. Task Force. Washington, D.C.: National Association for the Education of Young Children, 1989. Perhaps the best book for the early child/primary level on how to teach about all forms of bias and what to do about it.

Beyond Heroes and Holidays: A Practical Guide to K-12 Anti-Racist, Multicultural Education and Staff Development, New Edition, edited by Enid Lee, Deborah Menkart, and Margo Okazawa-Rey. Washington, D.C.: Teaching for Change, 2006. A remarkable collection of lesson plans and staff development activities as well as critical examinations of key equity issues such as bilingual education and tracking. Contains an extensive resource guide of teaching and learning resources and many helpful websites.

BRIDGE, Building a Race and Immigration Dialogue in the Global Economy, edited by Eunice Hyunhye Cho, Francisco Argüelles Paz y Puente, Miriam Ching Yoon Louie, and Sasha

Khokha. Oakland, CA: National Network for Immigrant and Refugee Rights, 2004. Although aimed at educators working with adults, rather than at classroom teachers, this is an imaginative and critical resource for teaching about immigration. One of the guide's strengths is to ground immigration in the context of race and globalization. The book also has a substantial and helpful section on immigration throughout U.S. history.

Caribbean Connections series, edited by Catherine Sunshine. Washington, D.C.: Teaching for Change/EPICA, 1991 (volumes published by various publishers). Stories, interviews, songs, drama, and oral histories, accompanied by lesson plans for secondary language arts and social studies. Separate volumes on: Puerto Rico, Jamaica, the Dominican Republic, Regional Overview, and Moving North.

Colonialism in the Americas: A Critical Look (1991) and **Colonialism in Asia: A Critical Look** (1993), Susan Gage. Victoria, BC: VIDEA. Sophisticated descriptions of colonialism in an easy-to-read, comic book format. Through dialogue and cartoons, each booklet traces the development of colonialism and its legacy. Teaching ideas are included in each volume.

Education Is Politics: Critical Teaching Across Differences, K-12, edited by Ira Shor and Caroline Pari. New York: Boynton/Cook, 1999. In memory of Paulo Freire, the essays in this collection describe critical practices by teachers committed to transformation in and beyond the classroom. They show culturally diverse educators constructively taking sides and refusing to fit students or themselves quietly into the status quo.

Failing Our Kids: Why the Testing Craze Won't Fix Our Schools, edited by Kathy Swope and Barbara Miner. Milwaukee: Rethinking Schools, 2000. More than 50 articles provide a compelling critique of standardized tests and also outline alternative ways to assess how well children are learning. The long arm of standardized testing reaches into every nook and cranny of education. Yet relying on standardized tests distorts student learning, exacerbates inequities for low-income students and students of color, and undermines true accountability.

The Field Guide to the Global Economy, Second Edition, Sarah Anderson and John Cavanagh with Thea Lee. New York: The New Press, 2005, second edition. Illustrated with charts, graphs, and political cartoons, this accessible and engaging guide reveals the harmful effects of corporate-driven globalization. It explains current trends in the global economy, the driving forces behind globalization, and the organizations and individuals working to reverse these destructive forces.

Freedom's Unfinished Revolution: An Inquiry into the Civil War and Reconstruction, The American Social History Project. New York: The New Press, 1996. Lively prose, primary documents, illustrations, and photographs bring this key period of U.S. history to life and invite students to study Reconstruction in depth. This 302-page book includes exercises and discussion questions. By the authors of *Who Built America?*

Keepers of the Earth: Native American Stories and Environmental Activities for Children, Michael J. Caduto and Joseph Bruchac. Golden, CO: Fulcrum Inc., 1988. Features a collection of North American Indian stories and related hands-on activities designed to inspire children. An interdisciplinary approach to teaching about the earth and Native-American cultures.

Lesbian, Gay, Bisexual, and Transgender Rights: A Human Rights Perspective, David M. Donahue. Minneapolis: Human Rights Resource Center, University of Minnesota, 2000. This curriculum encourages thoughtful examination and responsible action about sexual identity issues within the context of human rights. Helps learners see their responsibility to take action to promote and protect the human rights of all.

Lies My Teacher Told Me: Everything Your American History Textbook Got Wrong, James W. Loewen. New York: New Press, 1994. Loewen's book is an entertaining and eye-opening demything of key aspects of American history. It's both an effective critique of some of the most widely used history texts and an alternative history.

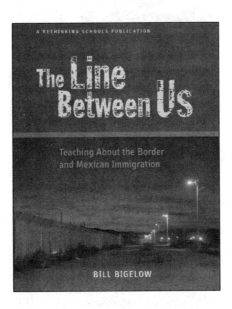

*****The Line Between Us: Teaching About the Border and Mexican Immigration,** Bill Bigelow. Milwaukee: Rethinking Schools, 2006. This is the best resource for teaching about the roots of Mexican migration to the United States and the human and ecological consequences of "free trade" in Mexico. The book includes a narrative of how Bigelow's students respond to learning about these issues as well as full lesson plans for role plays, simulations, short stories, poetry, and background readings.

Making the Peace: A Violence Prevention Curriculum, Paul Kivel and Allen Creighton. Alameda, CA: Hunter House, 1997. A comprehensive teaching handbook with all the information needed to implement a 15-session core curriculum. It offers step-by-step instructions for sessions, anticipates difficult issues that may arise, and suggests ideas for follow-up both within the classroom and within the school or youth program.

*****The New Teacher Book: Finding Purpose, Balance, and Hope During Your First Years in the Classroom,** Kelley Dawson Salas, Rita Tenorio, Stephanie Walters, and Dale Weiss, editors. Milwaukee: Rethinking Schools, 2004. The first few years of many teachers' careers are fraught with uncertainty, anxiety, and frustration. This book offers new teachers encouragement and lots of practical advice in getting off to a good start in their careers, dealing with students and pedagogy, and connecting their classroom work to the world beyond school. It's a guidebook on how to live one's ideals when the schools and school systems we work in don't always support those ideals.

*****Open Minds to Equality: A Sourcebook of Learning Activities to Affirm Diversity and Promote Equity,** Third Edition, Nancy Schniedewind and Ellen Davidson. Milwaukee: Rethinking Schools, 2006. This resource both inspires teachers to teach for justice and provides classroom-ready ideas that work. The lessons integrate various curricular areas and are presented in a sequential fashion. Includes an excellent resource bibliography. Also by Schniedewind and Davidson is *Cooperative Learning, Cooperative Lives: A Sourcebook for Learning Activities for Building a Peaceful World*, W.C. Brown Company, 1987.

Peters Projection World Map, New York: Friendship Press. This is a map, not a book, but it comes with a teaching guide. It presents all countries according to their true size. Traditional Mercator projection maps distort sizes, making Europe appear much larger than it actually is. *A New View of the World* by Ward Kaiser is a handbook on the Peters map.

A People's History of the United States: 1492–Present, Howard Zinn. New York: HarperCollins, 1995 (revised). The best single-volume history of the United States. No teacher should be without a copy. Some sections are readable by high school students.

*The Power in Our Hands: A Curriculum on the History of Work and Workers in the United States, Bill Bigelow and Norm Diamond. New York: Monthly Review Press, 1988. Role plays and writing activities help students explore issues about work and social change. An essential curriculum for history and economics teachers or for school-to-work programs.

Putting the Movement Back into Civil Rights Teaching, edited by Deborah Menkart, Alana D. Murray, and Jenice L. View. Washington, DC: Teaching for Change and Poverty & Race Research Action Council (PRRAC), 2004. This comprehensive volume offers lesson plans and articles to help K–12 teachers focus on the activist dimension of the Civil Rights Movement—too often taught as the creation of Great Leaders. This collection focuses our curricular attention on the grassroots nature of the Civil Rights struggles.

*Reading, Writing, and Rising Up: Teaching About Social Justice and the Power of the Written Word, Linda Christensen. Milwaukee: Rethinking Schools, 2000. In this practical, inspirational book, Christensen draws on her long career as a high school teacher to describe her vision of teaching reading, writing, and language courses that are rooted in an unwavering focus on social justice. Includes essays, lesson plans, and a remarkable collection of student writing.

Readings for Diversity and Social Justice: An Anthology on Racism, Antisemitism, Sexism, Heterosexism, Ableism & Classism, edited by Maurianne Adams, et al. London: Routledge, 2000. An invaluable anthology of over ninety readings by some of the fore-

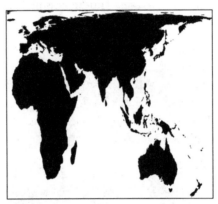

Portion of Peters Projection Map.

most scholars in the fields of education and social justice, including Gloria Anzaldúa, Patricia Hill Collins, bell hooks, Michael Omi, Ronald Takaki, Beverly Daniel Tatum, Cornel West, and Iris Marion Young. Covers the scope of social oppressions, emphasizing interactions among racism, sexism, classism, anti-Semitism, heterosexism, and ableism.

Resistance in Paradise: Rethinking 100 Years of U.S. Involvement in the Caribbean and the Pacific, edited by Deborah Wei and Rachael Kamel. Philadelphia: American Friends Service Committee, 1998. In 1898, the United States annexed the Pacific Islands of Guam, Hawai'i, and Samoa, as well as Cuba, Puerto Rico, and the Philippines. This major event in U.S. history is barely mentioned in school textbooks. *Resistance in Paradise* fills the gap with over 50 lesson plans, role plays, and readings for grades 9–12. Includes illustrations, cartoons, maps, and photographs.

*Rethinking Columbus, Second Edition, edited by Bill Bigelow and Bob Peterson. Milwaukee: Rethinking Schools, 1998. This widely acclaimed book asks educators to think about the racial and cultural biases in traditional tales of "discovery" and provides numerous teaching ideas that encourage students to think critically about these myths. An essential volume for teacher education. Greatly expanded from the first edition, which sold almost a quarter of a million copies. A *Rethinking Columbus* slide show is available from www.teachingforchange.org.

*Rethinking Globalization: Teaching for Justice in an Unjust World, edited by Bill Bigelow and Bob Peterson. Milwaukee: Rethinking Schools, 2002. The book includes chapters on the colonial roots of global inequality, the global economy, sweatshops, child labor, global food issues, the environment, and teaching for hope. This is the only teaching resource that approaches globalization with depth and breadth. Includes role plays, interviews, poetry, stories, background readings, cartoons, audiovisual resources, and extensive teaching ideas.

*Rethinking Mathematics: Teaching Social Justice by the Numbers, edited by Eric Gutstein and Bob Peterson. Milwaukee: Rethinking Schools, 2005. This unique collection of more than 30 articles shows teachers how to weave social justice principles throughout the math curriculum, and how to integrate social justice math into other curricular areas as well. The book offers teaching ideas, lesson plans, and reflections by practicing classroom teachers and distinguished mathematics educators.

*Rethinking Our Classrooms: Teaching for Equity and Justice, Volume 1, Second Edition, edited by Wayne Au,

Bill Bigelow, and Stan Karp. Milwaukee: Rethinking Schools, 2007. This collection includes creative teaching ideas, classroom narratives, and hands-on examples of ways teachers can promote values of community, justice, and equality—and build academic skills.

*Rethinking Our Classrooms: Teaching for Equity and Justice, Volume 2, edited by Stan Karp, Brenda Harvey, Larry Miller and Bill Bigelow. Milwaukee: Rethinking Schools, 2001. Supplements and extends many of the themes in the first volume of *Rethinking Our Classrooms*. Practical from-the-classroom stories from teachers about how they attempt to teach for social justice.

Scarves of Many Colors: Muslim Women and the Veil. Audiotape by Joan Bohorfoush and Diana Dickerson. Curriculum by Bill Bigelow, Sandra Childs, Norm Diamond, Diana Dickerson, and Jan Haaken. Washington, DC: Teaching for Change, 2000. This award-winning audiotape and curriculum engage students in thinking critically about stereotypes of "covered" Islamic women. The audiotape introduces a range of U.S. and Middle Eastern women who tell stories and offer insight. The curriculum offers four classroom-tested lessons, including a role play/tribunal on "Women and the Veil," with accompanying student handouts. A lively addition to any Global Studies, psychology, sociology, women's studies, world history, or teacher education curriculum.

Teaching About Asian Pacific Americans: Effective Activities, Strategies, and Assignments for Classrooms and Communities, edited by Edith Wen-Chu Chen and Glenn Omatsu. Lanham, MD: Rowman and Littlefield, 2006. This collection of imaginative, participatory classroom lesson plans and background information provides an overview of the hidden history and

contemporary issues facing Asian-Pacific Americans and Pacific Islanders. It fills a void in textbooks and traditional curricula, which generally ignore the diversity and depth of the Asian-American experience.

Teaching for Diversity and Social Justice: A Sourcebook, edited by Maurianne Adams, Lee Anne Bell, and Pat Griffin. New York: Routledge, 1997. A compilation of course syllabi, lessons, and resources for college courses and staff development on issues of racism, sexism, classism, anti-Semitism, heterosexism, and ableism.

Teaching Economics as if People Mattered: A High School Curriculum Guide to the New Economy, Tamara Sober Giecek. Boston: United for a Fair Economy, 2000. Field-tested by high school teachers, this innovative economics curriculum looks at the human implications of economic policies. These 21 lesson plans are designed to stimulate dialogue and encourage active student participation in the high school or college classroom.

That's Not Fair: A Teacher's Guide to Activism with Young Children, Ann Pelo and Fran Davidson. St. Paul, MN: Redleaf Press, 2000. Children have a natural sense of what's fair and what's not. This book helps teachers learn to use this characteristic to develop children's belief that they can change the world for the better. Includes real-life stories of activist children, combined with teachers' experiences and reflections. Original songs for children and a resource list for both adults and children.

*Transforming Teacher Unions: Fighting for Better Schools and Social Justice, edited by Bob Peterson and Michael Charney. Milwaukee: Rethinking Schools, 1999. A vital tool for anyone working in or with teacher unions today. The 25 articles look at exemplary

practices of teacher unions from the local to national level, and present new visions for the 21st century. Addresses the history of teacher unionism and connects issues of teacher unions, classroom reform, local communities, and social justice.

Voices of a People's History of the United States, edited by Anthony Arnove and Howard Zinn. New York: Seven Stories Press, 2004. This book offers source documents that amplify the themes in Howard Zinn's classic, *A People's History of the United States,* including diary excerpts, speeches, poems, original news articles, and more. Each chapter "shadows" the original book, providing lots of classroom-friendly material.

Who Are the Arabs: The Arab World in the Classroom, Steve Tamari. Washington, DC: Center for Contemporary Arab Studies, Georgetown University, 1999. History, poetry, photographs, maps, short stories, and articles by and about the Arab-speaking world. This 12-page booklet is available free if requested along with an order for other titles from Teaching for Change.

*Whose Wars? Teaching About the Iraq War and the War on Terrorism, Rethinking Schools editors. Milwaukee: Rethinking Schools, 2006. This is the best collection available on how to teach about the war. It includes classroom-tested resources for social studies, language arts and math classes: interactive lessons about U.S. involvement in Iraq and the history of the Iraq war, explorations of how language is used and abused by policymakers, ways to help students think critically about military recruitment, and creative ideas for using videos about the war. The collection incorporates poetry, imaginative writing, math activities, discussion, and critical reading strategies.

Periodicals

Adbusters: www.adbusters.org; 1243 West 7th Ave., Vancouver, BC V6H 1B7; 800-663-1243. Canadian journal that promotes critical thinking about consumer culture. See Organizations.

ColorLines Magazine: www.colorlines.com; 900 Alice Street Suite 400, Oakland, CA 94605; 510-653-3415. Published six times a year. Award-winning magazine covering race, culture, and community organizing, focusing on issues affecting communities of color.

Dollars and Sense: www.dollarsandsense.org; 29 Winter Street, Boston, MA 02108; 617-447-2177. Easy-to-understand articles on the economy from a critical perspective. Indispensable for economics teachers.

The Ecologist: www.theecologist.org; PO Box 326, Sittingbourne, Kent ME9 8FA, UK. Challenges basic assumptions about "development," "progress," and "growth," helping students and teachers consider the environmental consequences of globalization.

FairTest Examiner: See Organizations: National Center for Fair & Open Testing.

Green Teacher: www.greenteacher.org; 95 Robert St., Toronto, Ontario, M5S 2K5; 416-960-1244. Emphasizes hands-on education on environmental issues.

In These Times: www.inthesetimes.com; 2040 N. Milwaukee Ave., Chicago, IL 60647; 773-772-0100. Monthly news magazine that promotes an anti-corporate perspective on national and international issues.

Labor Notes: www.labornotes.org; 7435 Michigan Ave., Detroit, MI 48210; 313-842-6262. Excellent monthly newsletter dealing with ongoing union and rank-and-file activities.

Middle East Report: www.merip.org; 1500 Massachusetts Ave. NW, Suite 119, Washington, DC 20005; 202-223-3677. Astute analyses of events in the Middle East since 1971.

Monthly Review: www.monthlyreview.org; 146 W. 29th St. #6W, New York, NY 10001; 212-691-2555. Thoughtful socialist monthly providing Marxist analyses of global issues. Important publisher of progressive books.

The Nation: www.thenation.com; 33 Irving Place, New York, NY 10003; 212-209-5400. Weekly. Valuable articles on world and national events from a progressive perspective.

New Internationalist: www.newint.org; PO Box 1063, Niagara Falls, NY 14304; 905-946-0407. Colorful monthly magazine on global inequality. Reproducible for students. Themes include child labor, global warming, the AIDS crisis, etc.

New Youth Connections: www.youthcomm.org; 224 W. 29th St., New York, NY 10001; 212-279-0708. Monthly newspaper written by high school students. Also publishes *Foster Care Youth United*.

NACLA Report: www.nacla.org; North American Congress on Latin America, 38 Greene Street 4th Floor, New York, NY 10113; 646-613-1440. 6 issues a year. Detailed analyses on Latin American and Caribbean issues.

Our Schools/Our Selves: www.policyalternatives.ca; Canadian Centre for Policy Alternatives, 410-75 Albert St., Ottawa, ON, Canada, K1P 5E7; 613-563-1341. Covers schools and global economic trends, environmental activism, feminism, commercialism, labor, the arts, and more.

The Progressive: www.progressive.org; 409 East Main Street, Madison, WI 53703; 608-257-4626. *The Progressive* is an eclectic social justice monthly magazine. It features columns by Howard Zinn and Barbara Ehrenreich, and analytical articles, interviews, reviews, and reports on activism.

Radical Teacher: www.radicalteacher.org; PO Box 382616, Cambridge, MA 02238. Offers many valuable articles and teaching ideas from a critical standpoint.

Rethinking Schools: www.rethinkingschools.org; 1001 E. Keefe Ave., Milwaukee, WI 53212; 800-669-4192; fax: 414-964-7220. Quarterly magazine focusing on social justice and equity. Covers policy issues like No Child Left Behind, charter schools, school funding, and teacher unionism as well as on exemplary K-12 teaching. (See also Curricula and Teaching Resources.)

Teaching Tolerance: www.teachingtolerance.org; 400 Washington Ave., Montgomery, AL 36104; 334-956-8200. Mailed twice a year to teachers at no charge, provides accessible articles and a valuable resource section. Published by Southern Poverty Law Center. Offers free teaching materials on the Civil Rights Movement and other peace and social justice subjects.

Z Magazine: www.zmag.org. 11 issues a year. Covers current events from a critical perspective. Valuable column on the politics of the media. See also Organizations.

Organizations

See also Teacher Activist Groups, p. 193.

Adbusters Media Foundation: www. adbusters.org; 1243 West 7th Ave., Vancouver, BC, V6H 1B7, Canada; 604-736-9401. Adbusters describes itself as "a global network of artists, activists, writers, pranksters, students, educators and entrepreneurs who want to advance the new social activist movement of the information age." Adbusters publishes a magazine of the same name, sponsors Buy Nothing Day and TV Turnoff Week, produces clever "uncommercials" and seeks to agitate so that folks "get mad about corporate disinformation, injustices in the global economy, and any industry that pollutes our physical or mental commons."

American Federation of Teachers: www.aft.org; 555 New Jersey Avenue, NW, Washington, DC 20001; 202-879-4400. Resources and information from one of the national teachers unions.

The Applied Research Center: www. arc.org; 900 Alice St. Suite 400, Oakland, CA 94607; 510-653-3415. ARC is an important public policy, educational and research institute whose work emphasizes issues of race and social change. Publishes the acclaimed *ColorLines Magazine*—see the listing under Periodicals.

Center for Community Change: www. communitychange.org; 1536 U Street NW, Washington, DC 20009; 202-339-9300, toll-free: 877-777-1536. Center for Community Change brings attention to national issues of poverty and offers organizing expertise to address issues ranging from public housing to immigration to public schools. Its Education Team supports grassroots organizing for public school reform and publishes valuable reports and the "Education Organizing" newsletter.

Children's Defense Fund: www. childrensdefense.org; 25 E Street NW, Washington, DC 20001; 202-628-8787. This website offers a great deal of information about the CDF and its positions on critical issues affecting children, especially minorities and the disabled. Also includes position papers and background materials on many topics, and a host of links to other resources on the web.

Corporate Watch: www.corpwatch.org; 1611 Telegraph Ave. #702, Oakland, CA 94612; 510-271-8080. A must-visit site for activists who want to keep tabs on the behavior of corporations. Lots of timely news and impressive archives of corporate misdeeds.

Economic Policy Institute: www. epinet.org; 1333 H Street NW, Suite 300, East Tower, Washington, DC 20005; 202-775-8810. The mission of the Economic Policy Institute is to provide high-quality research and education in order to promote a prosperous, fair, and sustainable economy. The Institute stresses real-world analysis and a concern for the living standards of working people.

ESR Metro (Educators for Social Responsibility, Metropolitan Area): www.esrmetro.org; 475 Riverside Dr. Room 550, New York, NY 10115; 212-870-3318. For years, ESR Metro has been an outstanding resource for workshops and teaching materials about peace, justice, and conflict resolution.

Facing History and Ourselves: www. facing.org; 16 Hurd Road, Brookline, MA 02445; 617-232-1595. An education project that targets hatred, prejudice, racism, and indifference by focusing on teaching students about the Holocaust. Resources, workshops, and newsletter.

Fairness & Accuracy In Reporting: www.fair.org; 112 W. 27th Street, New York, NY 10001; 212-633-6700. FAIR is a national media watch group that has been offering well-documented criticism of media bias and censorship since 1986. FAIR publishes the indispensable *Extra!*, an award-winning magazine of media criticism, and regular updates, available via their listserv. FAIR also produces a weekly radio program, CounterSpin. An excellent source to get students thinking critically about media coverage of world events.

Food First/Institute for Food and Development Policy: www.foodfirst. org; 398 60th Street, Oakland, CA 94618; 510-654-4400. Since its founding in 1975, Food First has published some of the most useful books on food and hunger issues. Through their publications and activism they continue to offer leadership to the struggle for reforming the global food system from the bottom up. Their catalog is online at their website.

Gay, Lesbian, Straight Educators Network (GLSEN): www.glsen.org; 90 Broad St. 2nd Floor, New York, New York 10004; 212-727-0135. GLSEN is the leading national organization fighting to end antigay bias in K-12 schools. The organization offers many useful resources. The GLSEN-initiated student organizing project provides support to young people as they "form and lead gay-straight alliances—helping them to change their own school environments from the inside out."

Global Exchange: www.global exchange.org; 2017 Mission Street #303, San Francisco, California 94110; 415- 255-7296. Global Exchange is a human rights organization dedicated to promoting environmental, political, and social justice around the world. In the late '90s it was perhaps the most important organization drawing attention to Nike's sweatshop abuses. Their expansive website is a valuable student resource for learning about any important global issue.

Media Education Foundation: www.mediaed.org; 6 Masonic St., Northampton, MA 01060; 413-584-8500. The Media Education Foundation is a nonprofit educational organization devoted to media research and production of resources to aid educators and others in fostering analytical media literacy. They have produced some extraordinary, classroom-friendly videos on critical issues.

National Association for the Education of Young Children: www.naeyc.org; 1313 L Street NW, Suite 500, Washington, DC 20005; 800-424-2460. Publishes Young Children and other useful materials.

National Association for Multicultural Education: www.nameorg.org; 5272 River Road Suite 430, Bethesda, MD 20816; 310-951-0022. NAME provides resources and support that help educators promote "a philosophy of inclusion that embraces the basic tenets of cultural pluralism," and "promoting cultural and ethnic diversity as a national strength."

National Center for Fair & Open Testing (FairTest): www.fairtest.org; 342 Broadway, Cambridge, MA 02139; 617-864-4810. The major clearinghouse for information and activism on countering testing injustice and staying abreast of No Child Left Behind developments. See especially *FairTest Examiner*, a quarterly newsletter on assessment issues.

National Clearinghouse for English Language Acquisition and Language Instructional Educational Programs: www.ncela.gwu.edu; 2121 K Street NW, Suite 260, Washington, DC 20037; 800-321-6223. News, discussion groups, and resources for educators working with linguistically and culturally diverse students.

National Education Association: www.nea.org; 1201 16th St. NW, Washington, DC 20036; 202-833-4000. The nation's largest teachers union.

National TV-Turnoff Week: www. tvturnoff.org; TV-Turnoff Network, 1200 29th Street NW Lower Level 1, Washington, DC 20007; 202-333-9220. The annual No-TV observation occurs every April. The website offers fact sheets, quotes, and additional research on the impact of television.

National Women's History Project: www.nwhp.org; 3343 Industrial Drive Suite 4, Santa Rosa, CA 95403; 707-636-2888. The project has a variety of K-12 curriculum materials, and also holds workshops and training seminars.

New Mexico Media Literacy Project: www.nmmlp.org; 6400 Wyoming Blvd. NE, Albuquerque, NM 87109; 505-828-3129. Excellent materials on critical media literacy teaching.

Public Education Network (PEN): www.publiceducation.org; 601 Thirteenth Street NW, Suite 710 South, Washington, DC 20005-3808; 202-628-7460. PEN is a national association of local education funds (LEFs) and individuals working to advance public school reform in low-income communities. PEN seeks to build public demand and mobilize resources for quality public education for all children. PEN's weekly emailed "Newsblast" is a widely used resource and is free upon request.

Rainforest Action Network: www. ran.org; 221 Pine Street, Suite 500, San Francisco, CA 94104; 415-398-4404. RAN works to protect the earth's rainforests and support the rights of their inhabitants through education, grassroots organizing, and nonviolent direct action. Theirs is a must-visit comprehensive website that includes a wealth of information, including ideas for activities and activism with students, classroom-friendly factsheets, and links to indigenous rainforest groups.

Resource Center of the Americas: www.americas.org; 3019 Minnehaha Ave., Minneapolis, MN 55406; 612-276-0788. The Resource Center provides information and develops programs that demonstrate connections between people of Latin America, the Caribbean, and the United States. Over the years they have published a great deal of curriculum in this area. Their website includes an online catalog of these and other classroom materials, along with resources on critical issues about the Americas.

Sexuality Information and Education Council of the United States (SIECUS): www.siecus.org; SIECUS NY Office, 130 West 42nd Street, Suite 350, New York, NY 10036-7802; 212-819-9770. SIECUS has been a voice for sexuality education, sexual health, and sexual rights for over 40 years. SIECUS advocates for the right of all people to accurate information, comprehensive education about sexuality, and sexual health services and works to create a world that ensures social justice and sexual rights. Excellent source of research and educational materials, including K–12 curricula.

Teaching for Change: www. teachingforchange.org; PO Box 73038, Washington, DC 20056-3038; 800-763-9131. Publisher of excellent multicultural, social justice teaching materials, such as the widely used collection, *Beyond Heroes and Holidays.* The Teaching for Change catalog is the best U.S. resource for social justice teacher materials.

United for a Fair Economy: www. ufenet.org; 29 Winter Street, Boston, MA 02108; 617-423-2148. UFE provides numerous resources to organizations and individuals working to address the widening income and asset gap in the United States and around the world. They publish useful training and curriculum materials, and their website features an economics library, research library, and fact sheets.

ZNet/Z Magazine: www.zmag.org; 18 Millfield St., Woods Hole, MA 02543; 508-548-9063. Z Net is one of the most amazing websites we know of. Forums, commentaries from around the world, song lyrics for 530 songs-with-a-conscience, courses, analyses on global issues of all kinds. Many precollege students might find some of the writing a bit hard-going, but there is an awful lot here. *Z Magazine* is available the old-fashioned way—see Periodicals.

Poetry Credits

"Lions," by Langston Hughes. *The Sweet and Sour Animal Book*, Oxford University Press, New York, 1994. Reprinted by permission of Harold Ober Associates Incorporated.

"Ode to My Socks," by Pablo Neruda. Reprinted by permission of University of California Press. *Selected Odes of Pablo Neruda*, trans./ed. Margaret Saye Peden. Copyright © 1990 Regents of the University of California, Fundación Pablo Neruda.

"My Hair Is Long," by Loyen Redhawk Gali. Reprinted by permission of the author.

"Honeybees," by Paul Fleischman. *Joyful Noise: Poems for Two Voices*, HarperCollins, New York, 1988. Reprinted by permission of HarperCollins Children's Books.

"what the mirror said," by Lucille Clifton. *two-headed woman.* Copyright © 1980 University of Massachusetts Press. Reprinted by permission of Curtis Brown, Ltd.

"Father Was a Musician," by Dyan Watson, student at Jefferson High School. From *Rites of Passage, Jefferson High School Literary Magazine*, Portland, Ore., 1990-1991. Reprinted by permission of the author.

"Forgiving My Father," by Justin Morris. From *Rites of Passage, Jefferson High School Literary Magazine*, Portland, Ore., 1994-95. Reprinted by permission of the author.

"Rayford's Song," by Lawson Inada. *Legends from Camp*, Coffee House Press, Minneapolis, 1992. Reprinted by permission of the author.

"Rebellion Against the North Side," by Naomi Shahib Nye. *Hugging the Jukebox*, Breitenbush, Portland, 1984. Reprinted by permission of the author.

"The Funeral of Martin Luther King, Jr.," by Nikki Giovanni. *Black Feeling, Black Talk, Black Judgement* (1971). Copyright © 1968, 1970 by Nikki Giovanni. Reprinted by permission of HarperCollins Publishers. William Morrow.

"At This Point on the Page," by William Stafford. *The Way It Is: New & Selected Poems*, Graywolf, St. Paul, Minn., 1998. Reprinted by permission of Kim Stafford.

"In Memory of Crossing the Columbia," by Elizabeth Woody. *Seven Hands, Seven Hearts: Prose and Poetry.* Eighth Mountain Press, Portland, Oreg., 1994. Reprinted by permission of the author.

"To the Young Who Want to Die," by Gwendolyn Brooks. *The Near Johannesburg Boy*. Third World Press, Chicago, 1987. Reprinted with permission.

"Lineage," by Margaret Walker. *This Is My Century: New and Collected Poems*, Copyright © 1989 by Margaret Walker. Reprinted by permission of the University of Georgia Press, Athens, Georgia. ∎

Index

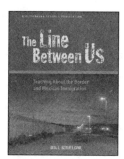

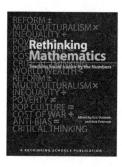

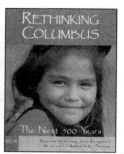
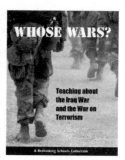
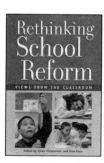

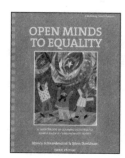

RETHINKING SCHOOLS

FOUR EASY WAYS TO ORDER

❶ **CALL TOLL-FREE:** 1-800-669-4192 8am-9pm (ET) M-F
❷ **SECURE ONLINE ORDERING:** www.rethinkingschools.org
❸ **FAX ORDER FORM TO:** 802-864-7626
❹ **MAIL ORDER FORM TO:** Rethinking Schools, P.O. Box 2222, Williston, VT 05495

MASTERCARD, VISA AND PURCHASE ORDERS ACCEPTED

Name _____

Organization _____

Address _____

City/State/Zip _____

Phone _____

E-mail _____

METHOD OF PAYMENT

☐ Check or money order made payable to Rethinking Schools
☐ Purchase order   ☐ MasterCard   ☐ Visa

Credit Card No._____

Exp. Date _____

Authorized Signature _____

QUANTITY	TITLE/ITEM	UNIT PRICE	TOTAL

MAIL TO: Rethinking Schools, P.O. Box 2222, Williston, VT 05495
FAX TO: 802-864-7626
CALL 1-800-669-4192 FOR A FREE CATALOG OF ALL OUR MATERIALS

* U.S. shipping and handling costs are 15% of the total (minimum charge of $4.00). Canadian shipping and handling costs are 25% of the total (minimum charge of $5.00). Subscriptions already include shipping costs. Payment in U.S. dollars.

Subtotal $_____
Shipping $_____
Donation $_____
TOTAL $_____

2BROCV1

If you liked *Rethinking Our Classrooms, Volume 1*, then *Rethinking Schools* magazine is for you!

Take advantage of this special discount coupon to receive the country's leading magazine for school reform.

INTRODUCTORY OFFER!
Subscribe today and save!

☐ **$22** Two-year subscription (*Save $17.60 off the cover price!*)
☐ **$14** One-year subscription (*Save $5.80 off the cover price!*)

☐ Please send me a free catalog of all your materials
☐ Bill me
☐ Enclosed is my check payable to Rethinking Schools

Name _____

Organization _____

Address _____

City/State/Zip _____

Phone _____

E-mail _____

"Rethinking Schools is a teacher's close friend — insightful, intelligent, and compassionate. I have read, used, and loved this publication for over a decade. I'm a better teacher because of it."

—MICHELE FORMAN, 2001 National Teacher of the Year

RETHINKING SCHOOLS

P.O. Box 2222, Williston, VT 05495 • toll-free: 800-669-4192 • fax: 802-864-7626

2BROCV1

NO POSTAGE
NECESSARY
IF MAILED
IN THE
UNITED STATES

BUSINESS REPLY MAIL
FIRST-CLASS MAIL   PERMIT NO.2222   WILLISTON VT

POSTAGE WILL BE PAID BY ADDRESSEE

RETHINKING SCHOOLS
PO BOX 2222
WILLISTON VT 05495-9940